Women, Androgynes, and Other Mythical Beasts

Wendy Doniger O'Flaherty

Women, Androgynes, and Other Mythical Beasts

The University of Chicago Press
Chicago and London

for
DAVID SHULMAN
and
DAVID KNIPE

The University of Chicago Press, Chicago 60637
The University of Chicago Press, Ltd., London

Paperback edition 1982
Printed in the United States of America

89 88 87 86 85 84 83 3 4 5 6

Library of Congress Cataloging in Publication Data
O'Flaherty, Wendy Doniger.
Women, androgynes, and other mythical beasts.
Bibliography: p. 345.
Includes index.
1. Mythology, Hindu. 2. Sex. 3. Animals, Mythical. 4. Androgyny (Psychology) I. Title.
BL2001.2.036 294.5'2'1 79-16128
ISBN 0-226-61849-8 (cloth)
0-226-61850-1 (paper)

Contents

Preface

In 1977–78 I presented a series of papers at various academic gatherings and taught a course at the Graduate Theological Union in Berkeley, California, on androgynes and theriomorphic women in myths. By the time I had presented the last paper, a disquieting sense of *déja vu* made me realize that I had turned all of the meetings, ostensibly devoted to widely disparate subjects, into forums for the development of a single theme: the use of sexual metaphors and animal symbols to express religious concepts of the relationships between men and women, gods and goddesses, and humans and deities. It was but the work of a single summer to revise the papers in order to make explicit this implicit thread. The result is an integrated development of closely interrelated themes, though it is a literary love child rather than the product of planned scholarly parenthood.

The informality of most of the meetings for which the original papers were prepared—the feeling that one was among friends and the knowledge that the ideas were to be presented orally—inspired a lightness of approach. One result of these relaxed conditions is a higher incidence of what I regard as humor and others may regard as flippancy. I hope this will not be misconstrued as evidence that I am laughing at the myths; I certainly am not. I have always regarded the Purāṇic stories about the Hindu gods as the very best stories in the world, rich in human wisdom and metaphysical truth. But this particular selection of topics revolves around sex as depicted in mythology, and I am surely not alone in finding sex more often than not very funny or in finding mythology—particularly Indian mythology—often intentionally hilarious. It seems to me therefore entirely appropriate to write about these subjects in high spirits, without denigrating them or making serious themes appear funny by viewing them from a conceptual framework sharply removed from their own; these myths *are* funny. Moreover, as the Hindus are well aware, there is much truth in humor; the world was created out of god's laughter and is merely an illusion wrought by his joyous playfulness (*līlā* in Sanskrit, *tiruviḷaiyāṭal* in Tamil). Chekhov could laugh at his characters because he loved them so, and I write about Hindu myths in the hope of sharing with a wider audience my love for their characters and their authors.

The elation with which I wrote most of this book made me feel, at the time, that the material was consistently fascinating. On rereading it now, I am downcast to find that certain sections of it bore me. Some of this may be attributed to the inevitable postpartum depression or to my own oversaturation with the material; but I think that some passages really *are* dull. I am, nevertheless, loath to omit them altogether, since they contribute essential elements to a general argument that is, I think, in need of all the help it can get. But those readers who are convinced of its rightness by the time they have neared the end of chapter 4 might be warned that they are in for a bit of heavy going in some of the theoretical typologies of consorts at the end of that chapter, in the analysis of the Vedic ritual and the summaries of Irish, Welsh, and Greek variants of the myth in chapter 6, and in the historical analysis of the shifting positions of cow and bull, stallion and mare, in chapter 8. Readers in search of an ultimate conclusion will be disappointed in the abrupt ending of the final chapter, but the essential conclusions are scattered throughout the book, particularly at the ends of chapters 2, 4, 7, and 8.

I would like to apologize to feminist readers for my use of old-fashioned sexist pronouns. We all have our priorities, and in my personal hierarchy politics is easily outranked by aesthetics, despite my growing sympathy with much of the feminist movement. I should also perhaps apologize, on behalf of my texts, for the fact that, although this is a study of myths about images of women, it is based on texts composed by men. This is a simple, unavoidable condition imposed on any student of Hindu mythology; if women composed their own mythologies (about themselves or about men), we do not have them. A partial corrective (or a further obfuscation) may be seen in my own biases: this is a woman's view of a group of men's views about women.

For me, the very best part of a book is the chance to thank the numerous friends, colleagues, and students (not mutually exclusive categories) who have contributed to it. They have responded to the stories, contributed treasures from their own fields, given me bibliographies, and attempted (usually in vain) to protect me from my own natural excesses. Many of their names occur again and again in the footnotes; some have had such a pervasive influence on me that no mere footnote could begin to convey my debt to them. In particular, I want to thank the two to whom the book is dedicated—two friends who have taught me much that is reflected on every page in it, as in the book of my life.

Santa Monica and Chicago
March, 1979

Acknowledgments

Some of the material on which this book is based was presented at academic meetings; some fragments of it have been or will be printed in journals and books. I would like to thank the participants in the meetings for their spirited and imaginative responses, which resulted in numerous improvements in the book, and to thank the publishers of the journals for permission to reprint.

Chapter 2 is based on a paper that was first presented at the SSCR–ACLS Joint Committee on South Asia seminar at the University of Chicago on May 3, 1977, where McKim Marriott, Ralph Nicholas, E. Valentine Daniel, Veena Das, Gloria Rehaja, Paul Friedrich, Milton Singer, and Lee Schlesinger participated. Revised, it was then presented at the symposium on Sexuality and Religion sponsored by the Conference on Religion in South Asia at Wilson College, Chambersburg, Pennsylvania, on May 12–14, 1978, where Richard L. Brubaker was the respondent. An early version of chapter 3 was presented at the annual meeting of the Association of Asian Studies in Chicago on March 30, 1978, where Edward C. Dimock, Peter Claus, and A. K. Ramanujan participated; I am also indebted to my son, Michael Lester O'Flaherty, for information about Billy Batson. Parts of chapter 4 were presented at the Conference on Rādhā and the Divine Consort at the Center for the Study of World Religions, Harvard University, June 17, 1978, where Richard L. Brubaker was the respondent; the section on Pārvatī is to be published in the proceedings of that conference. I am also indebted to William K. Mahony, David Shulman, and A. K. Ramanujan for their tactful but incisive comments on a very rough first draft. Other aspects of the myths treated in chapter 5, "Death as a Dancer in Hindu Mythology," are presented in my contribution to *Sanskrit and Indian Studies: Festschrift in*

Honor of Daniel H. H. Ingalls, edited by Masatoshi Nagatomi et al. (Dordrecht: D. Reidel, 1979).

Chapter 6 is based on a paper presented at the December 29–31, 1977, meeting of the American Academy of Religion in San Francisco, for a panel with Bruce Lincoln, Jaan Puhvel, and David M. Knipe. It never could have been written except with more than a little help from my friends, for only the Indian section is truly "all my own work." For the rest, I had great assistance: Jaan Puhvel and Bruce Lincoln supplied an excellent bibliography at the very start and detailed, tactful criticisms and suggestions for reorganization at the end, as well as offprints of their own articles, full of relevant data and inspiring models; they were also gracious in their despair at my inability to cope with vowel shifts and similar arcana. Dan Melia put me on to the Irish materials; Jock Anderson, Walter Burkert, Hans Dieter Betz, and David Grene supplied much of the Greek material; Alan Dundes made useful suggestions and lent me his own copies of Ernest Jones and Stith Thompson; Jack Stanley shared his ideas on power/pollution and the *Bacchae*. Most of all, I must thank David Knipe for inviting me to do the paper in the first place for the panel that he organized and for giving me the courage to venture out of my safe Indological nest into the exciting jungle of Indo-European studies. (Some of this chapter will be reprinted in the *Festschrift* for V. N. Toporov, edited by Dmitri Segal in Jerusalem).

Parts of chapter 7 were published in an article entitled, "The Submarine Mare in the Mythology of Śiva," in the *Journal of the Royal Asiatic Society* 1971: 9–27. Chapter 8 contains materials that were originally published in an article entitled "The Hindu Symbolism of Cows, Bulls, Stallions, and Mares," in *Art and Archaeology Research Papers* (London) no. 8 (December, 1975): 1–7. Transformed into an illustrated slide lecture, it was delivered as a public lecture sponsored by the Committee on Arts and Lectures, University of California, on November 10, 1975; as the basis of the Evans-Wentz lectures, "Images of Woman in South Asia," that I delivered with Nancy Falk at Stanford University on January 12–13, 1978; and as a lecture in the South Asia Seminar on "Animal and Man in South Asia" for the South Asia Regional Studies program of the University of Pennsylvania on April 27, 1978. Parts of it, augmented with materials from chapters 2, 4, 6, and 7 in this book, were presented in the lecture series "Women in Patriarchal Religions" at the University of Wisconsin at Milwaukee on September 20, 1978, and then furnished the substance of my inaugural lecture at the Divinity School of the University of Chicago on November 6, 1978, the text of which was published in *History of Religions* 19 (1979): 1–25.

An outline of chapter 9 was presented at the symposium on Sexuality and Religion sponsored by the Conference on Religion in South Asia at Wilson College, Chambersburg, Pennsylvania, May 12–14, 1978, in which Rita Gross, Richard L. Brubaker, and Gananath Obeyesekere made particularly useful suggestions. Parts of this chapter, together with parts of chapters 4 and 5, formed the substance of the Arthur O. Clark Lectures that I delivered at Pomona College, Claremont, California, February 28–March 1, 1979.

Finally, I wish to thank two people whose support and assistance were crucial to the final stages of preparation of the manuscript. Brian K. Smith helped me to prepare the index, and Martha Morrow cheerfully typed and retyped the bibliography as I kept adding to it.

Abbreviations

AB	Aitareya Brāhmaṇa
AP	Agni Purāṇa
AŚS	Āpastamba Śrauta Sūtra
AV	Atharva Veda
BAU	Bṛhadāraṇyaka Upaniṣad
BDP	Bṛhaddharma Purāṇa
Bh G	Bhagavad Gītā
Bh P	Bhāgavata Purāṇa
Bhav P	Bhaviṣya Purāṇa
Bh S	Bharadvāja Sūtras
BP	Brahma Purāṇa
Br P	Brahmāṇḍa Purāṇa
BŚS	Baudhāyana Śrauta Sūtra
BVP	Brahmavaivarta Purāṇa
Caraka	Carakasaṃhitā
ChU	Chāndogya Upaniṣad
DBP	Devībhāgavata Purāṇa
DP	Devī Purāṇa
DŚS	Drāhyāyana Śrauta Sūtra
GB	Gopatha Brāhmaṇa
GG	Gītagovinda
GP	Garuḍa Purāṇa
H	Harivaṃśa
JB	Jaiminīya Brāhmaṇa
JUB	Jaiminīya Upaniṣad Brāhmaṇa
Kālikā P	Kālikā Purāṇa
Kalki P	Kalki Purāṇa
Kaṭha U	Kaṭha Upaniṣad

KP	Kūrma Purāṇa
KS	Kāṭhaka Saṃhitā
KSS	Kathāsaritsāgara
KŚS	Kātyāyana Śrauta Sūtra
KU	Kaṭha Upaniṣad
LP	Liṅga Purāṇa
Manu	Mānavadharmaśāstra
Matsya P	Matsya Purāṇa
MBh	Mahābhārata, Critical Edition (Poona)
MBh 1862	Mahābhārata with the commentary of Nīlakaṇṭha
MBP	Mahābhāgavata Purāṇa
MP	Mārkaṇḍeya Purāṇa
MS	Maitrāyaṇī Saṃhitā
MU	Maitri Upaniṣad
PP	Padma Purāṇa
R	Rāmāyaṇa
RCM	Rāmacaritamānasa
RV	Ṛg Veda
Sāmba P	Sāmba Purāṇa
Saura P	Saura Purāṇa
ŚB	Śatapatha Brāhmaṇa
SDS	Sarvadarśanasaṃgraha
Sk P	Skanda Purāṇa
SP	Śiva Purāṇa
SRK	Subhāsitaratnakoṣa (Ingalls' translations)
Suśruta	Suśruta saṃhitā
TA	Taittirīya Āraṇyaka
TB	Tāṇḍya Mahābrāhmaṇa (Pañcaviṃśa)
TS	Taittirīya Saṃhitā
U	Upaniṣad
Vāyu P	Vāyu Purāṇa
Vām P	Vāmana Purāṇa
Var P	Varāha Purāṇa
VDP	Viṣṇudharmottara Purāṇa
VDŚ	Vaśiṣṭhadharmaśāstra
Viṣṇu P	Viṣṇu Purāṇa
VS	Vajasaneyi Saṃhitā

I Introduction

1 Introduction: The Myth of Method in Mythology

A. The Myth

It is fashionable nowadays in writing about mythology to place great emphasis on methodology, often almost to the exclusion of content. A book that applies Claude Lévi-Strauss's technique to Australian mythology is looked to for proof or disproof of the structuralist's formulations rather than for new insights into Australian mythology. It matters little what material you choose to use, or what conclusions you draw from it, as long as you go about it in the right way or, at any rate, in some consistent and replicable way.

I do not want to talk about method right now; I want to get on with the job of interpreting the myths in this book and leave the abstract speculations for another time and place. My assumptions will become evident as the work unfolds, as will my definitions and goals. But since so many of my students—and critics—seem curious to know how I myself go about doing what I do and how, if at all, I can justify it, a brief introduction seems called for, if only to state that I do what I do on purpose, not out of carelessness or naiveté, though I would rather do it than talk about it.

To begin with, it is probably wise to distinguish between methodology in the sense of a method of discovery (how one goes about it) and methodology in the sense of a method of validation (how one justifies what one has done). Most of my remarks will pertain to the former, though clearly the two senses will overlap from time to time; what one sets out to do depends upon what one regards as worth doing, and how one goes about it is determined at least in part by what one is looking for.

There are so many methodologies in the air these days, each of them a jealous god claiming sole right to the scholar's allegiance. But since myths are about so many things—about life and art and the universe and the imagination—almost *everything* in the realms of the natural sciences, humanities, and social sciences is relevant to the study of myths. A myth is like a palimpsest on which generation after generation has engraved its own layer of messages, and we must decipher each layer with a different code book. The different aspects of myths pose different problems, requiring different methods of approach. To be "rigorous" under these circumstances is to ignore the complexity of the subject.

Many mythologists have found it useful to develop a full repertoire of techniques of analysis, an approach often referred to as pluralism. Pejoratively, it is often called eclecticism; one is warned against allowing pluralism to become "eclectic, and therefore despicable" (Kirk 1974, p. 40). The case against pluralism seems to rest on the fear that it will be mechanical ("Keep on trying any old theory until you find one that works"), arrogant ("One of them is *bound* to work"), or superficial ("A little of this, a little of that"). But this need not be so; for it can be argued that one needs to employ more judgment in applying various theories than in applying one, since constant reevaluation is necessary if one is constantly making choices; and perhaps the eclectic approach is less arrogant than the one-track mind that assumes that *it* will always work. Moreover, there is no reason for the eclectic to be a dilettante; breadth need not imply lack of depth. The positive aspect of eclecticism "implies no more than considering all possible approaches to a problem and then selecting those that seem most promising. These are merged with other attitudes and observations into a fresh view, one that does not utterly discount all previous insights. In the bad sense the selection of previous views is a more or less mechanical affair, and the conclusion an unwieldy concoction of discordant bits and pieces" (ibid.). This method, like any other, must be applied with care and self-awareness.

The mythologist committed to the open-ended eclectic approach may be criticized for demonstrating "the disconcerting ability to believe in all kinds of contradictory theories of symbols derived from philosophical hermeneutics on the one hand and the utilitarian theory of symbols and psychoanalysis on the other" (V. Das 1976, p. 577; but cf. Hiltebeitel 1979). It may be disconcerting to some, but it is not difficult to achieve with determination; as the White Queen said to Alice, in response to Alice's complaint that one cannot believe impossible things, "I daresay you haven't had much practice. . . . When I was your age I always did it for half an hour a day. Why, sometimes I've believed as many as six impossible things before breakfast."[1] It takes far less practice to believe in the simultaneous existence of several perhaps contradictory messages in a single myth.

Moreover, this conflict dissolves when one ceases to strive for an overall theory that reconciles or eliminates antagonisms. If one assumes that extant theories are only partially successful, that they capture some but not all of the truth about the data or even all of the truth about only some of the data, then one need not claim to be believing impossible things.[2] Anyone attempting to fathom a profound myth should be encouraged to make use of as many sources of understanding as possible; this is the best way to avoid being brainwashed by any one of them. F. Scott Fitzgerald once received a letter from his daughter, then aspiring to be a writer, in which she said that she was afraid to read any contemporary fiction at all, lest it influence her own emerging style; Scott replied that she must read it *all*, and only then would she be free from any particular influence. If Freud is beginning to make too much sense to you, read Jung; if Lord Raglan has you convinced, read Mary Douglas.

B. The Toolbox of Pluralism

When one is confronting a body of raw material (and this is the first step in any original analysis), it is good to have tucked away somewhere in one's mind all the patterns that other scholars have seen in other materials, all the ways in which they have tried to solve analogous problems. In this way one develops a vocabulary in which to recognize and express the patterns that appear in the new corpus and to formulate new patterns as the need arises. The material itself will usually suggest what is the most appropriate pattern to look for at each point. Often the explicit content of a myth will give a broad hint as to how it might be interpreted: if it is about castration, try Freud; if it is about heresy, try theology. In the first analysis, it pays to be literal-minded; after that (and particularly if the head-on approach fails to bear fruit), one can indulge in the search for more arcane meanings. As we shall see, such meanings are usually there, and one learns to suspect their presence by becoming familiar with the systems of clues that various forms of analysis have built up and by noting these things: certain configurations of the text, such as lack of apparent meaning on the overt level; problems of interpretation in the native tradition; and multiple variations, at certain crucial points in the myth, among the different recensions.

This is the toolbox approach to the study of myth: carry about with you as wide a range of tools as possible, and reach for the right one at the right time. In response to a brief sketch of this approach (O'Flaherty

1976, pp. 9–10), Sheryl Daniel developed a paper entitled "The Tool-Box Approach of the Tamil to the Issues of Karma, Moral Responsibility, and Human Destiny." Her conclusion was that the Tamils themselves maintained several contradictory theories, from among which they chose the appropriate one for dealing with each problem as it arose (S. Daniel 1977). Nor is this technique limited to South India. Mohan Singh Kanota, a Rajput from Jaipur, once remarked that he made use of four medical practitioners in his neighborhood, one practicing Āyurvedic medicine, one homeopathic, one allopathic (i.e., Western), and one Unnani (Muslim). When asked how he chose which one to go to at any particular time, he answered, "It depends on what my illness is." When asked how he knew what his illness was, he replied, "Of course, *we* know what is wrong."[3] Problem-solving techniques that are logically incompatible may be used in tandem as long as one is willing to make one's own diagnosis, to take the responsibility for choosing the "right one," on each separate occasion, rather than choosing a single one, once and for all, as a matter of principle.

Carstairs noted a similar medical eclecticism twenty years ago, directly linked with an eclectic attitude to mythology:

> In the village, no statement, and no narrative, was ever felt to be entirely right or wrong, and so none was discarded. Contradictory, incompatible explanations were allowed to co-exist, as in the case of illnesses, which might be attributed to three different sorts of agency, and treated in three ways at once (Carstairs 1958, p. 91).

Carstairs points out that Hindus not only were not bothered by this pluralism but *were* bothered by any attempt to eliminate alternative views: "For them, it was no less provocative of anxiety to be asked to choose between two incompatible alternatives than it is for us to tolerate our own inconsistency" (ibid., p. 53). Yet he notes in passing that we, too, are in certain circumstances inclined to recognize contradictory aspects of human experience, and the examples that he cites are again directly relevant to the analysis of mythology: the Freudian concept of ambivalence and the Jungian concept of the interplay of opposite tendencies in the personality (ibid.).

There is an old pedigree for Indian eclecticism. The Vedic Indians worshiped several different gods as *the* supreme god, one at a time; this serial monogamy in theism inspired Max Müller to coin the term "Henotheism" (or "Kathenotheism"), "one god at a time." And, in the realm of metaphysics, it was an Indian Buddhist, Nāgārjuna, who epitomized eclecticism with his statement that at least one great mystic event could be viewed in four mutually contradictory ways:

after his final cessation
the Blessed One isnt is
(isnt isnt) isnt is & isnt
isnt isnt is & isnt
(Beyer 1974, p. 214)[4]

Indians carry off this sort of thing better than we do, but we do it too. The Hindu acceptance of contradiction may be facilitated by the fact that Hinduism is orthoprax rather than orthodox: if one behaves correctly, it does not matter what one believes.

The evidence that the Hindus use toolbox approaches themselves—and that they use them in the construction of their mythologies—raises several interesting possibilities of validation. Does the fact that the Hindus behave in this way validate the toolbox method as applied to Hindus? Does it validate it for cultures in which the informants do *not* themselves use it? Does it invalidate it for such people? Or does it make no difference at all? One may feel oneself to be on firmer ground knowing that one is doing something at least similar to what one's informants habitually do, but this is not essential, and one need not accept the corollary that one is on shaky ground if the informant does not endorse the methodology or that, on the other hand, a method that mirrors a native technique is justified if it is otherwise unheuristic. Moreover, in a broader sense, *all* mythologies reflect an eclectic method of construction; for Claude Lévi-Strauss (1966, pp. 16–22) has demonstrated that myth-makers, like *bricoleurs*, piece their cosmologies together with the cultural scraps that are at hand, and Edmund Leach (1970, p. 59) maintains that in combining various versions of a myth the structuralist is merely piecing back together what the culture as a whole has fragmented from an originally multivalent message (O'Flaherty 1973, pp. 12–18).

C. What People Think and What People Think They Think: Explicit and Implicit Levels

These considerations are part of the broader question of levels of analysis. Is one interested in the literal meaning of statements, in commentaries and in the texts themselves, or is one interested in analyzing these statements for submerged meanings? The first enterprise reveals what people think they think—indigenous concepts, dogmas, official creeds, traditional explicit belief systems, the view from inside; and these are essential to any understanding of a myth. This approach has gained many followers in recent years, who aspire to present the myth from the viewpoint of the devotee and insist that the meaning of the myth must be the meaning given it by the native informant.

This is a laudable enterprise, but there are problems in it. In the first place, for the ancient period, the devotees are simply not there to be questioned or observed. And, in the absence of glosses, mythologists are often prone to take the myth too literally, to assume that the author of the text was far more naive than we are, that the ancient Greeks and Hindus (for all their sophistication) didn't really know where babies come from and thought that people could fly if they strapped wings onto their shoulders. On the other hand, if elaborate glosses are in fact available, to take them as the sole measure of the myth may be to substitute the world view of a pedant for the world view of a poet—views that may be totally at odds with each other, even though both come from the same culture. Hindus are particularly prone to ruin their myths when glossing them in order to grind dogmatic axes; just as youth is said to be wasted on children, myths are often wasted on the scholars of their own cultures, whose testimony may be biased, ignorant, or self-deceiving.

To compensate for these inadequacies, the student of myth may be well advised to have recourse to another level of meaning that may be blocked and unconscious in the informant. Literary criticism, as well as psychoanalysis, has shown the value of looking for things the author may not have been conscious of; here one is operating on the implicit level, the structural level, the view from outside. How is this level to be found? Here is where one reaches for the toolbox. Nathan Leites, writing about the operational code of the Politburo (Leites 1951), deduced a theory of rules of behavior derived from external observations, arguing along lines that might be stated thus: "I see that X does Y under conditions A, B, and C; therefore he must be operating under a theory involving A, B, and C." It is possible to extract an "operational code" from a myth, a code whose pattern may be suggested by similar patterns elucidated in the fields of psychology, philosophy, and even the natural sciences. Although this pattern is not derived from indigenous views of the material, it is not imposed inappropriately if it arises from the data, is applied only when and if it fits, and is abandoned when it becomes inadequate. We *can* see patterns that are obscured by the mythmakers' views of themselves.

I have tried to make use of both views in analyzing Hindu myths. Richard Gombrich has demonstrated the value of juxtaposing precept and practice so that they are mutually illuminating (R. Gombrich 1971); Ernst Gombrich supplies a visual image that suggests how one can employ both views at once: "Rubin's Vase" at one moment appears to be a black vase on a white ground; but, if one looks again, it appears to be two white profiles facing each other across a negative black space (E. Gombrich 1973, p. 239). It is easy to see one or the other but difficult to see both at once; the pattern emerges according to what else you put into the picture: add eyes, and it is a face; add flowers, and it is a vase. Add native glosses to a myth, and it reveals a certain shape; frame it with psychological theory or structural expectations, and it reveals a different shape. Thus the devotee's viewpoint and that of the mythologist are both valid, and it is not necessary to decide which of the two is more valid. To strike a balance, I have tried to keep them both in sight while working through the corpus of myths treated in this book.

D. The Pitfalls of Reductionism

It is always tempting to follow to the end of the line any approach that yields good results, but this process inadvertently shuts out other possible insights. A dangerous reductionism results from hanging on to a single tool so tightly that you cannot pick up another even when the original tool has ceased to do the job, like the monkey with his fist stubbornly closed around a fruit in a trap whose door is too small to allow him to draw out the fruit, or the man in the Buddhist parable who fell into a river in flood, was saved by a raft that he found, and for the rest of his life carried it around on his back, on dry land.[5] Theoretical structures help us when we are in a particular kind of trouble with a text (usually flooded by a chaos of material); they should be abandoned when the text makes its meaning clear in its own terms or when a different kind of trouble arises, calling for a different tool.

There is another kind of reductionism characteristic of a different brand of single-mindedness, the kind that wants *one* answer, that rejects the pluralistic approach. Indeed, if a suitably narrow problem is defined, there may be a single answer; but in more complex areas of mythology, any general statement will be either incorrect or uselessly vague and banal. If you ate a dinner of oysters, curry, and chocolate mousse and someone said, "Describe the taste in one word," what could you say? Myths, too, have many tastes, and you need many words to talk about them, many theories through which to savor them. Mircea Eliade is fond of citing a particular passage from William James:

> A Beethoven string quartet is truly, as someone has said, a scraping of horses' tails on cats' bowels, and may be exhaustively described in such terms; but the application of this description in no way precludes the simultaneous applicability of an entirely different description (James 1943, "The Sentiment of Rationality," p. 76).

In order to see the shape of a myth, one has to shine light on it from as many different sides as possible in order to illuminate its many various surfaces; in this way one establishes what philosophers of science term the "robustness" of the objective structure by showing that it is visible from a number of perspectives.[6] Or, to vary the metaphor, it is necessary to view the myth from several different angles in order to find out where it is, just as, by photographing a star from different angles, it is possible to use the parallax of vision to watch it move against its background and hence to judge its distance from us.

When the two reductionist tendencies reinforce each other, when a single theory is used to extract a single meaning from a broad corpus of myths, the result is a thread of truth that may be illuminating when woven into a wider fabric of understanding but is pitifully thin on its own. As long as you know that you are telling only one part of the story, it is worth telling; no one can tell it all, and it is probably the counsel of discretion to tell one part well (reductionism in scope) rather than to tell all of it badly (reductionism in method). But we tend to get caught up in our own models and to believe that what we have decided to focus on really *is* basic or central, and this can be misleading. Any analysis will reduce the myth in some way, and one must be content to minimize this danger while saying as much as possible that communicates a useful insight into the material. One must not be terrorized by the accusation of reductionism.[7]

One way to minimize the static interference between the myth and the reader is to use one's theories with a very light hand, merely to select the materials. A good myth reveals its meanings without the need for heavy scholastic prodding; the theory is a sauce that should enhance the flavor of the natural ingredients, not overwhelm them. (As the British say of the French, "They have to concoct all those elaborate sauces because they do not have our good Scottish beef." In mythology, if not necessarily in *haute cuisine*, it is best to cook in the English manner.) A master mason will not need to use much cement in making a solid stone wall, provided that he chooses or cuts stones that fit closely. A mythologist who chooses his texts wisely and trims them with purpose need not cement them with an elaborate theory proving what he thinks they all mean; if the wall ends up looking like a wall, the stones belong together; it *is* a wall.

This ultimate judgment is personal, subjective, and aesthetic, but it need not be solipsistic, undisciplined, or random. It is the product of what Whitehead terms "speculative Reason" in contrast with methodological or pragmatic Reason: "The power of going for the penetrating idea, even if it has not yet worked into any methodology, is what constitutes the progressive force of Reason" (A. N. Whitehead 1929, p. 45). The "penetrating idea" cannot be *proved* valid, nor is it the result of a consistent, replicable approach to the problem; it is thus antimethodological in both senses of the word (method of discovery or of validation). It tends to be accepted if it sheds light on texts other than those from which it is derived or shows that what seemed to be irrelevant is in fact relevant, that what seemed to be random is in fact part of a pattern. It tends to be accepted if it proves useful to other scholars in the field or works well with other ideas that have been accepted by one's colleagues. This may seem a shaky base on which to build, but it does not differ in these respects from other, more "scientific" frameworks, such as Newtonian and Einsteinian physics.

If the eclectic approach cannot be strictly validated (or invalidated, as Popper would demand), can it at least be methodically applied? To some extent, I think it can. It is a matter of knowledge, perseverance, and flair. Someone once characterized Mircea Eliade's method (or nonmethod, as some of his critics have claimed) as simply this: he reads an enormous amount, remembers it all, and is very, very bright.[8] This is the model to which we all instinctively aspire, no matter what other methodologies we may hitch our wagon to from time to time. Ultimately, one hopes to be able to see correspondences—between myths, between myth and theory, between myth and life. To do this is, once again, to walk in the footsteps of those who made the myths, to imitate their way of constructing paradigms as we may imitate their eclecticism, *bricolage*, and ambivalence.

For this making of "correlations" or "correspondences" is an ancient and enduring facet of Indian religion:

> By calling attention to this term for visionaries and poets, I refer in particular to the ṛṣis' faculty of "seeing connections," "equivalences," "homologies," and "correspondences" discussed by Jan Gonda. This faculty of "seeing connections" would have involved the epic poets not only with correlations between myth and epic, but also between epic and ritual—especially that of the Brāhmaṇic sacrifice. Thus the "mythic exegesis" must coexist with a "ritual exegesis." . . . In some cases, they seem to have perceived . . . correspondences which were meant to deepen one's awareness of the meanings on both the mythic and the epic planes, and ultimately, perhaps, to afford a glimpse of broader unities (Hiltebeitel 1976, pp. 358–60; cf. Gonda 1963, pp. 68–69).

Seen in this light, the sympathetic interpreter of myths is simply one more in a long line of those who have attempted, with varying degrees of success, to piece together parallel paradoxes in the hope of mutually illuminating and enriching them. Like the ancient poets, we must look to the ritual, to other myths, to our own understanding, and to the insights of others in order to hear as many as possible of a myth's voices.

E. In Defense of Procrustean Selection

In building this book, I have cut my stones with a particular purpose in mind. I find myself in my usual position of devil's advocate; I am purposely setting out to present an aspect of Hindu mythology at direct variance with what is usually said about it, both from the inside (by Hindus) and the outside (by Western scholars). Hierogamies are usually regarded as the union of deities of equal power; I have tried to show how they are unequal. Śiva's dance is said to be creative; I have selected myths in which it is destructive. Androgynes are interpreted as symbols of fusion; I have tried to show how they function as symbols of conflict. Cows are taken as positive symbols of the female; I have tried to show their negative implications. I do not for a moment intend to reduce Hindu mythology to any of these limited concepts; but, taken together, they do, I think, suggest a pattern that is there in the material but is often obscured by the more conventional pattern, which I have assumed rather than delineated in this study.

Most of the topics treated in this volume are developments of themes that cropped up in my earlier works, where it was inappropriate to develop the implications that had begun to intrigue me even then. Chapter 2, the pivotal chapter, is the study of sexual fluids, which makes use of the symbolism of cows and mares, human males and females, and androgynes as they are met in the context of human physiology. Chapters 3 through 5 apply this model to the interactions between male and female, human and divine, and their several combinations: human male and female; divine male and female; human male and divine female; human female and divine male. Chapters 6 through 8 apply the hydraulic model of the flow of sexual powers to cows and mares as symbols of different kinds of goddesses in interaction with human and divine males (bulls and stallions). The final chapter explores the symbolism of androgyny in the light of the tensions and paradoxes revealed by the preceding analyses.

As the book developed, the themes seemed to arise naturally out of one another, and I have tried to let them rebound from one level to another, picking up momentum as they pick up additional layers of meaning. There is a cybernetic relationship between many of the themes, betrayed by the heavy incidence of cross-references; the early chapters are (I hope) self-explanatory and form a basis for the later ones, but the patterns revealed by the later chapters are also relevant to the materials of the earlier ones. Several of the patterns are cyclical; it is perhaps therefore not inappropriate that the book itself has a somewhat cyclical form, returning at the end to pick up some of the themes from the beginning and anticipating at the beginning some of the final conclusions.

It might be fair at this point to open up the particular toolbox that I have used for this book.[9] The first level of analysis is concerned with human sexuality as manifest in the interactions between men and women as well as parents and children; on this level, I have "trimmed" the stones in terms of family relationships, added more pebbles from anthropological field studies, and cemented them (lightly, I hope) with two basic theoretical structures: psychoanalytic hypotheses about infant eroticism and interactions within the nuclear family, and the concept of the transfer of coded substance expounded by McKim Marriott. To bring out the second level—the symbolic and narrative content of the myths—(or to look at the first level in a different way), I have tried to highlight the statement and resolution and restatement of certain paradoxes and contrasting categories by means of a simple form of structuralism. The spadework for both of these enterprises involved basic philology—to define Indian terms—and traditional techniques of Indology—to establish chronology and make use of commentaries. Throughout the book, but especially when dealing with Indo-European (chapter 6), Vedic (chapter 2), Temple (chapter 3), and Tantric ritual (chapter 8), I have acted on the hypothesis that myth and ritual are often essentially interrelated.

I have translated all of the Sanskrit texts myself, often summarizing long myths instead of giving full translations. For the reader's convenience, these passages from the Sanskrit appear as indented paragraphs, but this format does not indicate word-for-word translations, as is the usual convention; nor have I employed ellipsis points to indicate omissions, since these would have occurred so frequently as to render the text unreadable. Long quotations from secondary sources are indicated in the conventional manner, but summaries of long myths available to me only in translation (as in the case of the Irish or Welsh texts) are treated in the same manner as the summarized Sanskrit translations.

To set the Indian mare and the Indian androgyne in a more general context, I have made use of Indo-European materials and comparative studies, though I have not employed classical Indo-Europeanist methodology, with which I am uneasy and which in any case would not have been relevant to much of the available data. The reader may perhaps be occasionally troubled about the way that I have incorporated materials from many historical periods and areas of India without giving these materials the formal structure and individual attention that a historian or anthropologist would regard as essential. I can only say that a historian might indeed be able to show significant variations from one period to another (as I have done in several broad areas, such as in the treatment of Vedic and post-Vedic texts in chapter 2 and the discussion of early and late Indo-European attitudes in chapters 6–8) and an anthropologist could certainly point out important differences between regional attitudes; but I have tried to do something else: to evoke an underlying pattern of intellectual and emotional ways of understanding life, a pattern that persists in India in different forms and perhaps with different meanings, over the centuries and over the miles.

Finally, in order to understand the level of the myth on which the human and the divine interact, I have called upon the theological insights that arise from the unique form of history of religions developed by Mircea Eliade. He himself has pointed out that one must try to develop a morphology or typology before going on to attempt to reconstruct the history of a religious form; Linnaeus had to develop a taxonomy of the species before Darwin could write their history.[10] The primary task that I have addressed in this book is to construct a morphology of patterns emerging from ancient texts and contemporary observations; but such a morphology paves the way for a history of the interlocking motifs, and various historical hypotheses have thrust themselves upon me from time to time, particularly in the last four chapters.

When all is said and done, I have tried to let these eloquent stones speak for themselves—and for me.

II Sexual Fluids

2 Sexual Fluids in Vedic and Post-Vedic India

A. The Vedas

From the time of the Ṛg Veda to the present, Indians have tended to view the processes of sexual intercourse and birth in terms of the interaction of various bodily fluids. Their notions about the precise nature of these fluids and the manner of their interaction have varied from time to time and from text to text, but the underlying model emerges fairly clearly from the corpus as a whole. My discussion will be based primarily upon the Sanskrit texts; there are, however, striking resonances between these texts and many Bengali and Tamil sources, which I will cite in passing. These later examples, though necessarily more miscellaneous, even serendipitous, than those from the Vedic material, indicate the persistence of classical ideas in so-called folk traditions or, as is equally likely, the "folk" source of many so-called classical Indian concepts of the human body and of sexual relationships.

Sexual fluids are almost always linked in some way to the process of eating food and to the classical sacrificial ritual (see chart 1); frequently they are also linked to the fluids of the sky and to those of the sacred animals, the cow and the horse. These links raise from the very start the difficult question of how to interpret metaphor in religious texts. What is *meant* when the text says, "The rain is the urine of the sacrificial horse" (*BAU* 1. 1. 1)? How literally is one to interpret symbolic statements? Although there are certainly important differences between the semantic levels of metaphorical discourse and ordinary discourse, there must be some continuity between them if language is to express religious ideas at all. This is a serious problem that cannot be solved here, but it would be well for the reader to keep it in mind in examining the texts adduced in this chapter. The same symbolic equations will have different meanings

Chart 1. Sexual Fluids

	Cosmic	Body		Ritual
		Sex	Food	
Female	Water, rivers	Menstrual blood (*puṣpa, rajas*) Seed (*rati, rasa*)	Milk (*payas*)	Water, fire
Androgynous	Essence (*rasa*) (in plants, women, men)	Blood (*rakta, śonita*)	Blood, poison	Butter (ghee)
Male	Rain (*vṛṣṭi*), ocean	Semen (*retas, vīrya, bīja*)	Semen	Soma, fire

on different levels; "*x* is *y*" may mean "*x* functions in the same way as *y*," or "*x* and *y* produce the same result," or many other things (cf. the saleswoman's cliché: "Madam, that hat *is* you") (see O'Flaherty 1973, pp. 33–34, and Potter 1978, intro.).

Given this dilemma, I still think that it is possible to ask the texts questions about the symbols used in metaphors involving sexual fluids, as well as about the things symbolized. The key is context. Certain ambiguous terms frequently occur in unambiguous contexts that allow us to assign to them specific symbolic values; thus, when the term *payas* occurs in the sentence "The bull sprinkles his *payas* in the cow," we may confidently say that at least one meaning of *payas* is "semen"; and when we read "*Payas* streams from the udder of the cow," we may say that at least one other meaning of *payas* is "milk." When these terms occur in more ambiguous contexts, we may seek to understand those contexts by going back to our growing storehouse of the symbolic ranges of the words, trying to find the meaning that will allow the new sentence to make the best sense in terms of our tentative knowledge of Vedic ideas about these protean fluids. So, too, statements equating the functions of the phallus and the breast support unambiguous interpretations of ambiguous terms, for the contexts imply that a specifically male fluid is equated with a specifically female fluid. Poetic applications of even basic terms always retain a certain measure of ambiguity.

Almost a century ago, Abel Bergaigne pointed out that one must make a choice between simplifying the Vedic lexicon and thereby having to deal with more complex ideas, or complicating the lexicon in order to simplify Vedic ideas (Bergaigne 1883, pp. 468–74). In the first instance, one would simply translate *payas* (milk), *retas* (semen), and related terms as "fluids in motion" and discuss the various ways that fluids move in the Ṛg Veda; in the second instance, one would say that *payas* has the primary meaning of "milk," the secondary meaning of "expressed fluid," and the tertiary meaning of "semen"; one is then forced to decide whether this third usage literally implies that milk comes forth from the phallus or metaphorically illuminates the similarity between these two functions. Although Bergaigne preferred the first method (and many Vedists today still follow him), my own feeling is that Vedic words are more complex than Vedic contexts and that to use various contexts to illuminate rich terms is ultimately more productive than to seek to compress a rich term into a single neutral word that can be plugged into any context; for this leaves us no tool with which to find our way through the jungle of contexts other than the unequivocal—and self-evident—meaning of the word. In making this choice, I realize that I am placing myself in the camp of the weak linguists (as Samuel Johnson said of one such, "He has too little Latin: he gets the Latin from the meaning, not the meaning from the Latin"), but I find this a familiar and congenial group—and one that has made much sense of the Ṛg Veda.

Blood

Let us now turn to the texts themselves. In the Indian view, the most basic of all body fluids (and sometimes, though not always, the basis of all sexual fluids) is blood, which is essential to both male and female. Blood is seldom mentioned in the Ṛg Veda (a surprising fact for such an earthy and martial document); one late and notoriously problematic hymn asks, "Where is the earth's breath, and blood, and soul?" (*RV* 1. 164. 6c). The commentator, Sāyaṇa, interprets this as a reference to the gross body (of earth and blood) and the subtle body (of breath and the soul), in the context of the theory of the component elements (*dhātus*); despite the probable anachronism of this interpretation, the Vedic text itself is certainly an early and clear reference to blood as the essence of the earthly body. Another late hymn of the Ṛg Veda refers to demons who are smeared with the blood of men, horses, and cattle and who steal away the milk of cows (*RV* 1. 87. 16); the two life-substances, blood and milk, are here paired in the context of death (loss of fluid) and related to the two sacrificial animals in a pattern that will remain significant for centuries of Hindu thought on this subject.

There is in the Ṛg Veda one veiled but highly charged reference to female sexual blood—not menstrual blood but the blood of defloration. The "purple and red stain" becomes a dangerous female spirit walking on feet, a witch who binds the husband and makes his body ugly and sinisterly pale: "it burns, it bites, and it has claws, as dangerous as a poison is to eat" (*RV* 10. 85. 28–30, 34–35). Poison is an important negative female sexual fluid in post-Vedic mythology, as we will see, and menstrual fluid is eaten in Tantric ceremonies. The blood in this Vedic passage is not explicitly said to play a role in procreation, but it is in a wedding hymn, resonant with expressions of fertility.

In the Upaniṣads, blood is explicitly incorporated into the model of the body, both unisexual and differentiated: when water is drunk, it is converted into urine, blood, and breath (*CU* 6. 5. 2); when a person dies and the elements of the body disperse, the blood and semen enter the water (*BAU* 3. 2. 13). A woman may theoretically (though improbably) be included among the persons referred to in these texts; the first one poses no special problem for a woman, and the second may imply either that a man's blood and semen enter the water or that a woman's blood and (its equivalent) a man's semen enter the water. But since the word *puruṣa* is used to designate the person in this second sentence, it is almost certainly a man.

Semen

Semen, the essence of the male, is often mentioned in the Vedas, usually in ritual metaphors. *Retas*, the most important word for semen, has as its primary meaning "the outpouring of semen," "the flowing of semen" (Grassmann 1955, p. 1181); in this sense it has the primary connotation of a process rather than a substance, though it is freely applied to many substances, including the embryo engendered by the seed (*RV* 1. 164. 36) (an ambiguity which is also reflected in an equally ambiguous term for the female organ of procreation, *garbha*, meaning womb or embryo). Gods are invoked to impel the seed of a man to procure a human birth (*RV* 10. 184), but semen (*retas*) has a secondary, metaphorical use as applied to the fructifying rain from heaven, the "seed of the clouds" (*RV* 9. 74. 1; 1. 100. 3). So, too, *vṛṣṭi* (rain) and *vṛṣan* (a powerful, virile, or lustful man, or a bull) are both derived from *vṛṣ* (to rain or pour forth). Seed links heaven and earth: man is engendered by divine seed (*RV* 9. 86. 28). The flames of Agni are kindled by the seeds of heaven, and the Soma oblation into the fire is regarded as a seed (*RV* 1. 71. 8; 5. 17. 3; 4. 73. 7). Closely related to semen is urine: the clouds piss down Soma from the "swollen men" (*RV* 9. 74. 4; cf. Wasson and O'Flaherty 1968, pp. 25–34), and rain is the urine of the sacrificial horse, just as Soma is the stallion's seed (*BAU* 1. 1. 1; *RV* 1. 164. 35–36; *TS* 8. 4. 18).

Female Seed

The Vedas begin to suggest that the woman has seed, just as the man does; significantly, this fluid is called "virile milk" (*vṛṣṇyam payas*, more literally "bull-like" or "seed-like" milk): "The wife embraces her husband. Both of them shed the virile milk. Giving forth, she milks (his) juice [*rasa*]" (*RV* 1. 105. 2bc). The word for juice (*rasa*) is a nonsexual word for fluid in the Ṛg Veda; its primary meaning is "liquid," the fluid of life, the sexual secretion (Filliozat 1949, p. 126), and it comes to designate Soma, the oblation, an essence, or a delicious and life-giving elixir; only once (in the verse just cited) does it represent male (or female) seed. Sāyaṇa's gloss on this verse is illuminating: "The two set the virile milk in motion by rubbing together, one against the other, for the sake of engendering progeny. Taking the juice, the vital seed of the man, making it into the form of an embryo, she is milked—that is, she brings it forth in the form of a son." Where the text seems to say that the woman *gives* (female) seed and takes the milk-seed of the man, Sāyaṇa says that she *takes* seed and is "milked" of a child, a view more in keeping with later Hinduism than with the Vedas, where the concept of "milked seed" (*dugdhaṃ vīryaṃ*) is common (*AV* 14. 2. 14d). The commentator reverses the point of the Vedic myth; though he is, I think, wrong about the Ṛg Veda, he is right about what *he* thinks, which is also of interest to us. The more paradoxical view of the Vedic text, which assigns a positive role to the woman, is replaced in the commentary by the more "acceptable" Hindu view of the woman who takes from her husband and gives to her son. Both views continue to exist side by side in later tradition. Elsewhere, too, the Ṛg Veda implies that both mother earth and father sky have seed (*retas*) (*RV* 1. 159. 2; 1. 160. 3; 6. 70. 1). The Upaniṣads instruct a man who is about to impregnate his wife to say to her, "I am heaven, you are earth; let us embrace and place together the seed to get a male child, a son" (*BAU* 6. 4. 20).

Blood and Milk or Butter

One strange passage in the Brāhmaṇas presents a model of the female hydraulic system that contrasts blood with milk:

> Bhṛgu, the son of Varuṇa, went to the other world, where he saw two women, one beautiful and one hideous; he saw a river of

> blood, guarded by a black naked man with yellow eyes, a club in his hand; and a river of butter, guarded by golden men who drew all desires from it into golden bowls. His father told him that the two women were faith and lack of faith and that the black man was anger (*JB* 1. 44. 12–13. Cf. *SB* 11. 6. 1–7; O'Flaherty 1976, p. 340).

In this text, butter is the positive, golden female substance (found in a golden bowl, a common metaphor for the womb, and yielding all desires, like the wishing-cow), while the river of blood represents the negative, black, deadly aspect of female blood. In later texts, butter becomes ambiguous or even androgynous; for it retains its connection with milk, and hence with the female, but in ritual imagery it is metaphorically linked with semen placed in the womb, the golden seed in the cosmic waters, the (male) libation into the (female) fire (O'Flaherty 1973, motif 10c). The blood in the text may be menstrual but is in any case erotic (guarded by a naked man with a phallic club), in contrast with the fertile lake associated with the golden man (the source of golden seed; see ibid., pp. 107–8)—the cow-lake, later to become the ocean of milk. Thus certain basic oppositions are laid down in this highly charged symbolic Vedic passage:

> blood *versus* butter (semen or milk)
> black *versus* gold
> emotion (desire and anger [black man]) *versus* fertility (golden men)
> eroticism *versus* fertility (male and female)
> female *versus* male
> evil female *versus* good female
> death *versus* life

And, finally, the one explicit interpretation offered by the text, a theological interpretation: faith *versus* lack of faith.

Milk and Semen

Although butter and blood and seed are fluids related to female sexuality in the Ṛg Veda, milk is by far the most important female sexual fluid. The basic noun for this fluid is *payas*, which Grassmann defines clearly:

> n. [from *pī* (to swell or become full)], milk; pl., streams of milk. Very often, especially in connection with *duh* or *pī*, used in a metaphorical sense. This word has absolutely no other meaning in the Ṛg Veda. The apparent meanings, "liquid, water, male semen,

> sacrificial drink," are all derived from its metaphorical application (Grassmann 1955, pp. 773–75).

There can be no doubt, therefore, that the primary meaning of *payas* is the female fluid in the breast or udder (the "swollen" object from which the word derives).

Similarly, the verb *duh*, "to milk," is very often applied to an udder or a cow, but it may not be so closely associated with the female as is *payas* (if one accepts Grassmann's Bergaignian analysis of that term); for three out of four of Grassmann's definitions of *duh* involve its metaphorical application to semen:

> to milk. 1) to milk something out of something, also used metaphorically: to milk semen from the bull, liquid from the plant; 2) to milk something out, for example milk, also used metaphorically: Soma juice, blessings, male semen, etc.; 3) to milk the cow, the udder; 4) to cause to flow forth, very often metaphorically, for example to discharge semen, to let rain fall . . . (ibid., pp. 619–22).

Here again the verb seems primarily related to the cow; though this animal is first explicitly cited in Grassmann's third definition of the verb, and the bull appears in the first definition, the examples listed under that definition frequently have "udder" as the direct object; moreover, the past participle, *dugdha*, is a noun meaning "milk." By a rough word count, *duh* is applied to *ūdhar* (udder), *dhenum* (cow), or other unequivocally female words more than thirty times in the Ṛg Veda,[1] in contrast with the relatively few times it is applied to words for "semen" or "bull"; but this is hardly a matter that can be decided by majority vote, for there are many complicating factors. Many of the male references, for example, are coupled with female ones: milking the cow of milk and the bull of seed (*RV* 1. 160. 3), or the bull of heaven milking the udder of the cow of heaven, while he himself is smeared with butter and milked of his seed (*RV* 4. 3. 10). Here, as in several other Ṛg Veda passages (1. 160. 3, just cited; 4. 1. 19; 9. 19. 5; 9. 54. 1; etc.), the "bright milk" (*śukram payas*) is a term for male semen; in later Sanskrit, *śukram*, alone, commonly denotes male semen. The term *duh* becomes still more complex when it is applied to nonsexual entities (like "blessings") or to ambiguously sexual nouns like Soma or butter (*ghṛtam*). According to Grassmann, therefore, the noun "milk" (*payas*) means only milk but is metaphorically applied to semen. The verb "milk" (*duh*), by contrast, may apply equally well to milk or semen; by the time of the Ṛg Veda, it has become androgynous.

There are, however, many instances in which context enables us to break out of this circle, in which it is perfectly clear that the poet intends to highlight the sexual ambiguity of the verb *duh* and to use it as a specific link between semen and milk. Thus the wife is said to milk seed out of her husband (*RV* 1. 105. 2; 1. 179. 4; 9. 19. 5), and, contrariwise, milk is called "the ancient seed" (*RV* 3. 31. 10). One verse seems to refer to earth as a cow with milk and heaven as a bull with seed but then speaks of "his" semen-milk being milked out (*śukraṃ payo asya dukṣata*)—"his" referring either to heaven or to an androgynous heaven-earth (*RV* 1. 160. 3).

Thus, although the primary sense of *payas* is milk and the primary sense of *retas* is seed, through the concept of their similar function—swelling up, pressing out, and pouring forth—they yield the same set of secondary metaphorical applications: rain, water, Soma, oblation, and child. Here one is faced with Bergaigne's dilemma, heightened when *payas* and *retas* are equated with each other: either the lexicon or the poet makes the equation, and it is difficult to determine at which end of the linguistic/metaphoric spectrum the "is" occurs and how much of an "is" it is; but it is certainly clear that at some point, and in some way, the identification is indeed made.

Milk and Soma

The male substance, semen, is ritually combined with the female creative fluid, milk, not in an explicit description of the birth process (which is never directly discussed in the Ṛg Veda) but in the metaphor of the Soma ritual. For although milk is not strictly procreative, it is in a broader sense creative, particularly in the ritual context. Thus Soma juice is likened to a bull full of seed who mingles with the cows (the milk or water that was mixed with the Soma in the ritual) to ensure fertility (*RV* 9. 70. 7; 9. 79. 9). At this point, the metaphors become apparently paradoxical: Soma is also likened to an udder milked of juices which are like cows (*RV* 3. 48. 3; 4. 23. 1; 7. 101. 1; 8. 9. 19; 9. 68. 1; 9. 69. 1; 9. 107. 5; 9. 79. 9. Cf. O'Flaherty 1976, p. 336, and Wasson 1968, p. 43). In this way, Soma is an androgynous deity, sometimes equated with the source of milk, sometimes with milk, and sometimes regarded as seed, the opposite of milk. Seed is equated not only with milk but with Soma; and this Soma in later ritual is replaced by ghee, butter, which is churned out of milk just as, in the Ṛg Veda, the Soma juices are often said to be churned or milked from the ocean (*RV* 5. 47. 3; 9. 64. 8; 10. 115. 3), that is, from the Soma vats metaphorically regarded as an ocean. We have already seen that butter, as contrasted with blood, can serve as an androgynous symbol of milk or of semen. Butter, semen, and Soma are all *essences*, distilled body fluids. Thus, through Soma imagery, the semen of the bull is said to come forth from the milk of a cow and to turn into milk. Even at this early stage we can see the beginnings of androgyny (and hence the potential for unilateral creation) in the symbolism of the male sexual fluid and in its relationship with the female sexual fluid. Soma also partakes in the androgyny of fire and water (usually male and female, sometimes female and male), for it is the Indo-European "fiery liquid."

Soma is often called *payoduh*, "milked of milk," even when he has the form of a bull; his seed is milk (*RV* 9. 19. 5; 9. 54. 1; 9. 108. 8; cf. *AV* 2. 6. 2. 6. 2). A more explicit androgyny occurs in the figure of the rain god Parjanya, some of whose complexities may be related to the androgynous figure of Heaven/Earth, whose milk-seed we have already noted. One hymn to Parjanya revels in this maze of identities, oppositions, and paradoxes:

> [The poet addresses the rain cloud]: Raise the three voices with light going before them, voices that milk the udder that gives honey. [Sāyaṇa suggests that the three voices of Parjanya are the thunder preceded by lightning and followed by rain. The udder is the cloud that is milked of sweet rain, which Parjanya causes to fall from the clouds; in that sense the voices are milked from him by the hymns of praise.]
>
> Creating the calf who is the embryo of the plants, the bull roared as soon as he was born. [The calf is the fire born of lightning, often called the germ or embryo of plants, as in *RV* 2. 1. 14 and 3. 1. 13.]
>
> The god who causes the plants to increase, and the waters, who rules over the entire world, may he grant us the triple refuge and comfort, the triple light that is of good help to us. [The triple light may be the three energies of the sun at spring, summer, and autumn; or fire, moon, and sun; or fire, wind, and sun.]
>
> Now he becomes sterile [f.], now one who gives birth; he takes whatever body he wishes. The mother receives the milk [*payas*] of the father; with it the father and the son increase and prosper. [Sāyaṇa: He becomes a sterile, milkless cow when he does not give rain; then, like a cow, he brings forth, when he rains waters. The mother earth receives the milk of rainwater from the father, heaven; with it, when it has developed into the oblation, the father —the heavenly world—prospers; and with it, in the form of water, the son—the creatures on earth who breathe—also prospers.] He is the bull who places the seed in all (plants); in him is the vital

> breath of what moves and of what is still. Let this truth protect me for a hundred autumns; protect us always with blessings (*RV* 7. 101. 1, 2, 3, 6; cf. *RV* 10. 115. 1).

Parjanya is male and female, the bull and the cow; his rain is milk, seed, and his offspring, his calf. Thus he can give "milk" (seed) to the mother, even as he can become pregnant though he is sterile. Whatever the ambiguity of *payas*, lexically or metaphorically, it here simultaneously designates milk and semen, two extracts regarded as complementary opposites.

Like Parjanya, Tvaṣṭṛ is sexually complex; he is, to begin with, a god who places seed in women to make them pregnant. "The bright bull of a thousand, rich in milk, bearing all forms in his bellies, . . . he is a male, yet pregnant, big, rich in milk. . . . Father of calves, lord of the inviolable (cattle), his seed is calf, afterbirth, fresh milk, the first milk after birth, curd, ghee" (*AV* 9. 4. 1–6). Again, *payas* and *retas* interact in contrast. In the later Vedas, Prajāpati, like Tvaṣṭṛ, is andrygynous; he is said to rub up milk and butter from himself and thus to propagate (*ŚB* 2. 2. 4. 1–8); Prajāpati, the male creator, has the breasts and womb of a woman; the two breasts of Prajāpati are milked by the priest to obtain whatever he desires, and, after creation takes place, Prajāpati is milked out and empty; Prajāpati becomes pregnant with creatures in his womb (*TB* 13. 11. 18; 9. 6. 7; *JB* 1. 225; *ŚB* 2. 5. 1. 3; *MS* 1. 6. 9). If there remains any question about the specificity of the fluid, *payas* is here clearly defined by its anomalous male container—the breast. An even more specific equation is made with reference to Agni: "Seed is milk; milk is female and seed is male, and so together they give life; the god of fire desired the sacrificial cow; his seed became that milk of hers" (*ŚB* 9. 5. 1. 55–56; cf. 2. 3. 1. 14–15; 2. 5. 1. 16).

The equation of a man's seed with his offspring is continued in the Upaniṣads: Death makes his seed into the year, his child, and bears him for a year (as in female pregnancy); he then attempts to eat the child (the usual inversion of feeding with milk) (*BAU* 1. 2. 4). The commentator, Śaṅkara, explains that Prajāpati, as death, produces seed and places himself in it, so that he becomes born as the year; thus Śaṅkara identifies the father with the child.

Seed as Food

In view of the fact that semen is so often compared with milk and Soma, the two quintessential foods (one human, one divine), it is not surprising that the Vedic materials abound in texts in which semen is regarded as a form of food. Butter and honey, frequent metaphors for Soma, also come to be compared with semen. The ritual ingestion of semen or its metaphorical substitutes is ancient: the Avesta gives evidence that the urine of the cow or bull was used in purificatory rituals, and it has been suggested that the drug properties of the Soma remained potent in the urine of anyone who had drunk it, so that it became the practice to drink such urine (Wasson 1968, pp. 25–34 and 71–76). In the *Mahābhārata*, Indra (who is often depicted as a stallion or bull) is said to urinate Soma as an elixir for the sage Uttaṅka, the same hapless Brahmin who, elsewhere in the epic, is forced to swallow the urine and dung of an enormous bull (*MBh* 14. 54. 12–35; cf. 1. 3. 100–105). Nowhere in the Vedic corpus is a woman said to drink seed itself, though there is one hymn in which the god Indra (shedder of seed, drinker of Soma) falls in love with a girl who presses Soma for him in her mouth (*RV* 8. 91; cf. *Bṛhaddevatā* 6. 99–106).

In the Upaniṣads, the drinking of semen is implicit in the basic description of the birth process, a description that persists through later Indian elaborations: the soul of the man who is to be reborn goes to the moon, pours down onto the earth as rain (the old Vedic metaphor for seed shed by the gods in heaven, here applied to a nontheistic process), goes into plants (of which Soma is the king), is eaten (by a man) and transformed into semen that impregnates a woman. This model undergoes several variations. It usually appears in a pejorative description of the process of transmigration experienced by those who fail to enter the path of the flame that leads to the sun and ultimate release; these inferior creatures enter the moon (explicitly identified with Soma) and become food for the gods; then they rain down, become food for men, are eaten, transformed into semen, and placed in women to become embryos (*ChU* 5. 4–8; 5. 10. 3–6; *BAU* 6. 2. 16). Even here the "deluded" creatures, in the midst of their journey, serve as food for the gods, and in a later text the process of recycling is seen as an element in the preferred path, the ritual path of the flame and the sun: the offering made to the gods by living creatures goes through fire to the sun; from the sun comes rain; from rain, food; and from food, living creatures (*MU* 6. 37; cf. *Manu* 3. 76).

Various fluids can be transmuted alchemically into one another, since they can function in the same way. Soma can be used instead of seed, and seed instead of rain. This is more than mere homeopathic magic, though that element is certainly present: if you put Soma into the fire, rain will come down and male children be engendered. But these texts seem to imply more than that: the Soma placed in the fire is actually made of rain in some essential way and will again be made into rain;

there is process as well as metaphorical description.

In these Upaniṣadic texts, the man drinks the food that is to become semen (as the male priest drinks the Soma); apparently the woman plays no significant role in creating the child; she is merely the receptacle for the final stage. Her sexual fluid (milk) will be used only later, to feed him (as he was "fed" to his father before conception took place). In the impregnation process in the Upaniṣads milk appears only in its role as seed substitute: a woman who wishes to have a son should eat rice (itself a symbol of seed) prepared with milk products (ghee, milk, sour milk) or water (*BAU* 6. 4. 14–16). The more of this milk substance that she eats, the more semen substance is produced in her, and so she will have a male child, grown on seminal milk-based foods. Thus there is still no direct ingestion of seed, but merely ingestion of rain or milk that will become seed.

Androgyny and Unilateral Creation through Milk

From these late Vedic texts it is clear that the image of pressing out milk is used in an extremely loose metaphorical sense to indicate any kind of giving forth, as in the image of shedding seed that "droppeth as the gentle rain from heaven." Thus the Ṛg Veda knows of the "milking" of the (female) earth, whose white udder yields Soma as milk for the gods (*RV* 1. 84. 10–11; 2. 34. 2; 5. 52. 16; 5. 60. 5; 8. 101. 5; 10. 123. 1–5); this myth is later expanded in an episode in which the earth, a cow, is milked of other things as well (*ŚB* 1. 8. 3. 15; *AV* 8. 10. 22–29). The second point is that the interchangeability of these essential creative fluids, semen and milk, leads to apparent instances of unilateral creation by male alone or by female alone: things are born from the seed (or the bull) with no reference to the seed entering a fertile receptacle, and things come forth directly from milk (or the cow) without any apparent fertilizing agent.

In particular, we find the image of the pregnant male, the truly androgynous figure, though it is usually a *male* androgyne (see below, chap. 9). Most ancient Indian androgynes are primarily male—men who can have babies as women do. Prajāpati is basically a well-known male god who is suddenly endowed with a womb and breasts. On the other hand, it does not happen that some woman or goddess suddenly finds herself endowed with a phallus or, to her surprise and ours, becomes able to produce children all by herself. Many of these acts of male unilateral creation take place when the "thigh" of the male is churned (*manth*), a verb also applied to the production of butter from milk or the kindling of fire from the two fire sticks (O'Flaherty 1976, pp. 334–35;

cf. Jung 1967, pp. 145–46). Since seed is equated with milk, and the breast is likened to the phallus, to "milk" a man's thigh of seed is equivalent to milking the woman's breast of milk (and the *Kāmasūtras* liken the action of the *yoni* on the *liṅga* to that of the milkmaid's hand on the cow's udder). "Thigh" may simply be a euphemism for a phallus (as in *RV* 8. 4. 1), but in this context it functions as an androgynous symbol, serving as either breast or phallus—or both at once. The equation of thigh and phallus—and the further equation of seed with fire—is apparent from one ancient text: "On the right thigh of the Udgātṛ priest they churn fire; for from the right side the seed is discharged" (*TB* 12. 10. 12). This beneficial ritual churning is in sharp contrast with the churning of the *left* thigh of the evil Vena, from which barbarian tribes were produced (O'Flaherty 1976, pp. 321–31). Thus sexual "churning" can be applied not only to the male and female, "churning" together, but to the fluid of either the male or the female alone (ibid., pp. 333–34). The two parents share *payas, rasa,* and *retas*—the first primarily female, the last primarily male, and the middle one neutral.

Woman as "Field"

The image of the woman as an insignificant receptacle for the unilaterally effective male fluid persists, not only in these early texts but in later ones as well. The woman is the mere "field" in which the seed is sown, not an active partner in the process. This is merely a restatement, on another level, of the facts that semen is regarded as more powerful than uterine blood (in models that see this substance as the female contribution to the birth process) and that the child resembles the father in all socially significant qualities (Marriott 1976; Inden 1976, p. 95). The "field" metaphor is a natural development from the Vedic premise of unilateral creation (already somewhat androcentric) supported by the Upaniṣadic tendency toward misogyny. The early expressions of this idea are often coupled with aggressive and competitive feelings, not only toward the woman but toward the rival seed-sower. The principal text of the fertility ceremony between the queen and the stallion contains, among several verses of truly ingenious obscenity, a passage that demonstrates this attitude toward the woman:

> When a deer eats the barley, one does not approve of the fact that the animal has been nourished; so when a Śūdra woman has a noble lover, she does not bear fruit for growth. [Commentator: The farmer does not think, "Good, the beast has been nourished," but,

> rather, "My crop has been eaten!" So the husband becomes sad, thinking, "She has gone astray."] (*VS* 23. 30–31).

The use of the metaphor of an eaten crop (the inverse of the sowing of seed) is here easily adapted to express an unfavorable attitude to sexual interaction. In the *Bṛhadāraṇyaka Upaniṣad* the cuckolded husband is encouraged to do more than scold:

> If a man's wife has a lover whom he hates, he should spread out a row of reed arrows, their heads smeared with ghee, and sacrifice them, in inverse order, into a vessel of fire, saying, "You have made a libation in my fire! I take away your breath, your sons, your cattle, your sacrifices and good deeds, your hope and your expectations. You have made a libation in my fire, you [Mr. X]." If a Brahmin who knows this curses a man, that man dies impotent and without merit. Therefore one should not try to get on "joking terms" with the wife of a learned Brahmin (*BAU* 6. 4. 12).

This is an interesting example of transferred merit in a sexual context: the cuckold takes away the sons, cattle, and virility of his wife's lover. (The *Atharva Veda* has spells to destroy a man's virility [6. 138; 7. 9], but not to transfer it to the speaker of the hymn.) The arrows smeared with ghee are patent symbols of the phallus with seed, and their inverse order of sacrifice into the fire inverts their normal power to perform. The sacrifice into the fire is here, as so often in the Upaniṣads (see *BAU* 6. 2. 13; 6. 4. 3), a metaphor for impregnation, seed being equated with butter or Soma. Power is lost through seed (the lover's seed defiling the wife) and reclaimed through seed (the ritual use of butter as seed).

Aggression and Competition in Sexual Creation

Seed is also an instrument of power and conflict in the sexual union between husband and wife. This is clear from a *Bṛhadāraṇyaka Upaniṣad* passage that separates eroticism from fertility: "When one desires a woman but does not wish her to conceive, he should enter her, join his mouth with her mouth, inhale, exhale, and say, 'With power, with semen, I reclaim the semen from you.' Thus she comes to be without seed" (*BAU* 6. 4. 10). Two desiderata are accomplished by this: the first, the obvious one, is that the woman does not get the seed, does not become pregnant; the other, perhaps even more important to the ancient Indian, is that the man *gets the seed back*. This concern is the sole basis of another mantra in this text:

> Whether asleep or awake, if one should spill his semen, he should

> touch it and say, "That semen of mine which has today spilled on the earth, or has flowed to plants or to water, I reclaim that semen. Let virility return to me, and energy and strength. Let the fire be put in its right place, on the fire altar [f.]." Having said this, he should take (the semen) with his thumb and fourth finger and rub it between his breasts or his eyebrows (*BAU* 6. 4. 4–5).

Again we find both the ritual metaphor of fire and the seed placed over the heart or brain—the source of sacred ritual power—reclaimed from profane danger.

This ritual is based on the Vedic belief that the normal flow of procreative semen is from plants and water to the human body (*BAU* 6. 2. 16; *CU* 5. 10. 6). The "lost" semen would have reversed that process, flowing back into plants, in the direction of death—the dark half of the cycle and, more particularly, the direction of the death of someone who has not become enlightened (*BAU* 3. 4. 13). The Ṛg Veda states that the dead body, at the time of cremation, dissolves into plants and water (*RV* 10. 16. 3), an idea that may well be of Indo-European origin (see Lincoln 1968); thus the Upaniṣads regard the loss of the seed as a kind of death. Great danger is therefore implied in the *Bṛhadāraṇyaka* text; a few verses earlier, it is remarked that, if a man has intercourse with a woman without knowing the proper mantra, "Women take his good deeds to themselves" (*BAU* 6. 4. 2–3). These four incidents, joined in a single text, supply the beginning of the idea that power, carried by semen, is lost from one's own body and transferred, through sexual contact, to a rival, one's own wife, or another woman.

What, then, is the picture that emerges from these various Vedic metaphors for sexual interaction? First, one must note the primacy of the Vedic ritual as a model for sexual creation; this is hardly surprising, since these are all ritual texts, the ritual being the primary locus in which all other phenomena are mirrored. Yet to a certain extent this is a chicken-or-egg question, for surely there is a deep, perhaps even subconscious, level on which the rituals are created and accepted because of their resonances with the basic processes of human physiology.

Churning fire, pressing a plant, offering libations into fire, are elementary units of ritual activity that are repeated for simple, practical reasons as well as for their unconscious psychological appeal; they are then described in the poetry in terms of the fairly obvious metaphors of sexual friction, milking the breast, shedding the seed. What happens next is that when an actual birth model is finally constructed, beginning sketchily in the Upaniṣads, the model is an almost literal application of the ritual metaphors. Another, and related, example of this procedure may be seen in the way that the *piṇḍa* oblation to the ancestors was used as a basis for the *piṇḍa* model of the creation of the embryo (O'Flaherty 1980, chap. 1).

A second characteristic of the Vedic world view is implicit in the frequent examples of unilateral or competitive procreation that occur in the texts. There are, of course, many examples of more conventional sexual cooperation as well, which I have not bothered to cite; it is the unexpected metaphor that proves ultimately illuminating for the peculiar Indian viewpoint. The Ṛg Veda has a great deal to say about the ways in which men and women make babies together; what is interesting, however, is that other alternatives are also considered, alternatives that I emphasize, with the understanding that they are supplementary to the many texts dealing with normal procreation. Similarly, it is abundantly clear from the Ṛg Vedic hymns of procreation and the Upaniṣadic descriptions of intercourse that the predictable interdependence of phallus and womb had been noticed in the appropriate human contexts and made use of in ritual contexts; nevertheless, it was the less obvious correspondence between the phallus and the breast that furnished the basis for a theoretical model of fluid interaction.

Side by side with conventional observations on where babies come from, the Vedas suggest that a man can create without a woman, a woman without a man. Semen by itself is fertile; milk by itself is fertile; semen may become milk, and milk may become semen. However, since milk is not literally procreative, there is a tendency to emphasize the male's role in sexual engendering; though semen and milk are equal, semen is "more equal." Thus a man may become an androgyne, but a woman seldom does. This Vedic quasi-equivalence becomes further slanted in the Upaniṣadic period, where a man can create alone but a woman never does; where much is said about seed, but, in contrast with the Vedas, very little about milk; where a man must be careful to guard his seed, to get it back from the woman, to keep her from stealing his merit even as he himself would steal away the merit of her defiling lover. Finally, since both semen and milk (or male semen and female semen) are extracts of blood and function independently, they are competitive and mutually destructive; their interaction is potentially dangerous, like the coming-together of matter and antimatter. Semen and milk do not attract each other, as true opposites would (such as Yin and Yang), but repel each other, since they are so much alike in form (white fluids expressed from a "swollen" protrusion on the body) and in function.

Though goddesses are not important to the Ṛg Veda, women are—

important as things to be possessed, like cattle. Fluids of all kinds are in many ways "female"; they are the materials of regeneration, the moist, Dionysian element, whether they flow in the veins of men or of women. Milk is the primary Vedic procreative symbol, but gods are the primary procreative figures. The semen of the gods is therefore identified with milk, which then becomes a male fluid. The corresponding identification, which credits women with seed, is *far* less common in the Ṛg Veda; yet the fact that this identification occurs at all lays the groundwork for the later development of a more egalitarian view of the relative importance of women in procreation.

B. The Post-Vedic Period

In the one Vedic model developed above, the parallel to a man's seed was a woman's milk; the phallus corresponded to the breast, not to the womb. The late Vedas, on the other hand, suggested another model for the woman, attempting to account for her dual sites of sexuality: blood in a man produced semen, while blood in a woman produced female seed *and* milk. Later still, this model was challenged by another: seed in a man corresponded with menstrual or uterine blood (*rajas* or *puṣpa*) in a woman. In true Indian fashion, the Vedic models were also retained, and a bastard compromise was sometimes attempted: blood in a man produced semen, and blood in a woman produced milk, uterine blood, or female seed. This elaborated complex of dualities made good sense in the now well-developed context of the split image of the woman, simultaneously erotic (the mare, whose power centered upon the vagina) and procreative (the cow, whose power centered upon the breast) (O'Flaherty 1976, pp. 346–48; see below, chaps. 6–8).

Blood and Seed

Although in the medical texts blood is androgynous (in the sense of being bisexual or of being the source of both male and female qualities), it tends to become primarily female in most post-Vedic discussions, perhaps because *all* fluids tend to become regarded as female in contrast with solids (or igneous substances), which are male. Thus blood is said to be given to the child by the mother, bone from the father (*MBh* 12. 293. 16–17). In this way, menstrual blood comes to be regarded as the female counterpart to semen in many texts, in contrast with nonsexual blood, which is deemphasized as a sexual fluid in the woman.

Moreover, blood often appears as a metaphor for male semen or as a seed substitute: Śiva produces a son from the blood of Viṣṇu (*Vām P*

2. 31. 84–87), and blood is the source of a number of demons, most notoriously the offspring of the aptly named Raktabīja ("blood-seed"), from whose every drop of blood shed in battle another demon was born; significantly, these rapidly multiplying creatures are disposed of by being eaten (while Kālī herself sucks out the blood of Raktabīja)—the classical inversion of the act of procreation (*Vām P* 44. 30–38; *KP* 1. 16. 123–240; *MP* 88. 39–61; *Matsya P* 179. 1–86; *PP* 5. 43. 1–95). Demons also arise from each drop of the blood of the demon Andhaka, whereupon Śiva creates goddesses to devour them; when these goddesses prove to be an additional threat, Viṣṇu creates yet another band of goddesses from parts of his body, including his genitals, to eat the first group; and then Viṣṇu reabsorbs (i.e., eats) the whole lot (*Vām P* 43; *VDP* 1. 226. 1–82; O'Flaherty 1973, pp. 281–82; cf. p. 271). This corpus is further linked to the cycle of semen as food by the myth of the demon Ruru, overcome by yet another set of insatiable goddesses, who finally consent to accept as their food the testicles of Śiva (*PP* 5. 26. 91–125; *LP* 1. 106. 1–27; *Matsya P* 252. 5–19). This blood-seed imagery persists in contemporary Indian folklore in the belief that semen rather than blood flows from the wounds of a chaste yogi who restrains his seed, a theme to which we shall return. It is also reflected in the widespread fear that a man who receives a blood transfusion from a female will lose his masculinity (Howard 1977).[2]

Blood appears in a woman most significantly in menstrual or uterine blood, *rajas* or *puṣpa*. The first term is derived from the noun denoting "passion"; the second is the word for "flower." According to the medical textbooks, female (uterine) blood unites with the man's semen in order to produce a child (Eliade 1958, pp. 239–54; Meyer 1930, pp. 359–63; O'Flaherty 1980). A daughter is born, in one myth, when a drop of menstrual blood shed by the sixty-four Yoginīs is fertilized by the shadow of a hawk (Elwin 1949, p. 420; O'Flaherty 1973, p. 137); this abnormal primacy of female blood is clearly inauspicious: the child is not only a girl but an insatiable eater of men. The other tradition, that the woman's seed rather than her uterine blood is her contribution to the birth process, makes for ambiguities in several texts: "From desire the semen is born, and from semen the menstrual blood" (*MBh* 14. 24. 5; Meyer 1930, p. 362). This makes sense only if "semen" here is the woman's semen; yet, to fit it with the later theory of the woman's blood as her contributing element (in contrast with the seed, which would make her a more equal partner), this seed is said to be the source of the blood that makes it logically superfluous (and the fluid, moreover, from which the female seed is usually said to be made). A final, if drastic, solution is achieved in the Tantras by the simple unexplained statement that "the blood in the womb is called seed" (*Saṃvarodaya Tantra* 2. 23), just as *raj* commonly denotes female semen (Stablein 1980).[3]

Female Seed

There remains a basic ambiguity in Sanskrit texts as to whether the creative fluid in the womb is female semen or menstrual blood, and this ambiguity is found in the Tamil sources as well. One hesitates to adduce Tamil material in this context, because, though there are certain striking correspondences, there are also some very basic disparities in the underlying world view. Yet to ignore this material—which has been exposed to the Sanskrit tradition and has influenced it in turn—would be needlessly impoverishing. Let me simply preface the discussion with the caveat that there is a great deal of Tamil data on the birth process that does *not* follow the Sanskrit model. Having said that, let me quote a contemporary study from South India that reveals several of the ambiguities encountered in the Sanskrit texts:

> According to T.'s interpretation of *Tirumantiram*, what appears in the vagina at intercourse is the female seed, the same as the male semen. *Tirumantiram* says, "The whiteness that appears in the vessel of semen, in the same way appears in the yoni." . . . T. calls this whiteness "a kind of water in the form of feeling." . . . The textual commentary calls the female substance *cennīr* ("red water, auspicious water") and *curōṇitam*, which are polite words for blood, especially menstrual blood. But intercourse at the time of menstruation is strongly forbidden—it is believed that by such an act that man will die of convulsions—and T.'s interpretation of the female seed as the lubricating fluid in the vagina seems more apt (Egnor 1978, pp. 62–63).

If one interprets this fluid as menstrual blood, intercourse is forbidden; if one interprets it as semen, female semen, intercourse is mandatory, according to the Hindu doctrine that requires a man to impregnate a woman when she comes into season (*ṛtugamana*) (*MBh* 7. 18. 32; *Manu* 3. 46–48). The native informant cleverly solves this dilemma by offering a third, neutral, mediating definition of the fluid as merely an emotional lubricant (perhaps harking back to *rajas*, "passion," as well as to menstrual blood). So, too, a Sanskrit term for female seed (*rati*) means "sexual pleasure," separating the woman's erotic fluid (in the vagina) from her fertile fluid (in the breast) or her destructive fluid (blood in the veins).

The link between the fluid in the womb and the emotion of the womb ("hysteria") is made explicit in South India, where this feeling is also attributed to the male: "The soul comes and mixes in the color of the two people. Color (*cāyam*), this means the juice/the essence (cāram [Skt. *sāra*]) of the two people. . . . What is color? Feeling. Your feeling, another person's feeling. Male feeling, female feeling. A certain kind of juice which is mixed as a result of both" (Egnor 1978, p. 61).

Yet another term for the female sexual fluid, *rasa*, also denotes "emotion." This cluster of affective overtones can be no accident; the female in her genital site is passionate (greedy, taking), while in her maternal site (the breast) she is merely giving. The confusion between female blood and female semen is further heightened by the connection of both of these terms with the protean *rasa*, which designates both female and male fluid in the Ṛg Veda. Among the Bauls of Bengal, *rasa* refers to male semen;[4] according to the medical textbooks, it is equivalent to female seed: "The embryo is born from *rasa*"; (Caraka 4. 3. 18); "From *rasa* comes the blood of a woman that appears at the time of puberty and is called *rajas*" (Suśruta 1. 14. 2). Here *rasa* functions like the "semen" that is the source of menstrual blood in the text cited above; but *rasa* in the broader sense is the fluid (made from digested food) that is consecutively transmuted into blood, flesh, fat, bone, marrow, and semen, comprising the seven *dhātus* or physiological elements.

The conflict between the views that postulate blood or female semen as the woman's contribution to birth is exacerbated by the explicit hierarchical value placed on these substances: the medical textbooks and folk traditions state that it takes sixty drops of blood to make one drop of semen (or milk) (Obeyesekere 1976, p. 213; Egnor 1978, p. 69). But both men and women are said to possess the seven *dhātus*, which include both blood (male and female) and semen (male and female) but *not* milk (merely female). If the woman's substance remains the undistilled raw substance, blood, produced directly from *rasa* fluid (digested food), in contrast with the semen that is refined out of blood as the ultimate of seven increasingly concentrated essences, her contribution is clearly one-sixtieth that of the man. If, however, she is credited with semen of her own—given equality, though androcentric equality—this hierarchy of fluids is negated on the social level by the fact that the male alone is responsible for the "coded substance" of the child. In mythology the woman achieves this equality by creating through milk, refined, like semen, from the blood and therefore its equivalent; this is the earlier physiological model. Here, as elsewhere, one can see the mind of the author of the medical text working hard to create complex epicycles, as it were—to make some sort of logical order out of the inconsistent mythological models he has inherited and feels called upon to reconcile, though they had existed side by side for centuries in the mythological texts, happily contradictory.

The Ṛg Veda, as we have seen, suggests that a woman has seed; and the classical medical texts insist upon this (e.g. Suśruta 1. 14. 18, 3. 2. 38). This idea persists in later periods throughout India, often precipitating a conflict between the blood-semen model of reproduction and the semen-semen model (for the milk-semen model is largely ignored by the medical texts as a straight procreative explanation, though its symbolic importance is still felt in less direct ways). A confusion similar to that of the *Tirumantiram* appears in Orissa (an area near Calcutta):

> The female sexual fluid . . . in Oriyā is called *raja*. This fluid is not menstrual blood—which in colloquial Oriyā is called by different terms—since the woman should not be menstruating at the time of this ritual. It is a colorless fluid which corresponds to semen in the male and like semen is believed to be secreted by the woman at the time of intercourse. Furthermore, in local theories of conception *raja* plays a role symmetrical to that of semen in the conception of a child (Marglin 1978b, pp. 15–16).

Despite the persistence of the blood-semen model as the primary post-Vedic explanation for conception, the *Kāmasūtra* (2. 1) assumes that women do have seed ("If they had no semen, there would be no embryo") and proceeds to argue about whether or not the semen of the woman falls in the same way as that of the man (the final conclusion is that it does). In contemporary Ceylon, thousands of women have been diagnosed as suffering from lack of (female) semen, and doctors cure them with prescriptions analogous to those given to men similarly diagnosed (Obeyesekere 1976, pp. 207–9).

In the post-Vedic myths, when parthenogenesis among females takes place, the model used is usually not the female substance (milk) but the male substance (semen—for which, as we shall see, other substances are frequently substituted). The goddess Pārvatī produced Skanda from her own spittle, and Gaṇeśa was born from the water in which she washed herself after she had made love with Śiva, water mixed with her own seed (*Caturvargacintāmaṇi* 2. 2. 359; *Vām P* 28. 71–72), or from the rubbings of her body when she anointed herself in the bath (*ŚP* 2. 4. 13. 20). The female seed is thus equated with dirt, an interesting reversal of the widespread motif in which the male creates unilaterally (and anally) from dirt or feces in an awkward attempt to mime female pregnancy (Dundes 1962). In India, if a woman wishes to create offspring unilaterally, she must apparently produce seed substitutes to ensure "true" (i.e., male) pregnancy; what she uses in place of the "pure" male seed is dirt. In imitation of the male, the Goddess creates Kālī from her urine after she has made love with Śiva (*Caturvargacintāmaṇi* 2. 2. 366; cf. O'Flaherty 1973, p. 271). The unilateral nature of Gaṇeśa's creation is made clear in a folk etymology of his name, Vināyaka, said to have been given to him because Pārvatī created him "without a husband" (*vinā nāyakena*) (*Vām P* 28. 71–72). Again, working on the male analogy (or rather the male-female analogy with male predominance), two women may have intercourse together, "acting like virile men," so that their two sets of seed mingle to produce a child—but it is a child who lacks bones, for these are given by the male alone (Suśruta 3. 2. 47).

The persistence of the theory of female semen in the face of another, more pervasive theory of conception (the female-blood-plus-male-semen model, which is, incidentally, far closer to our own, since it relates conception to a monthly cycle of female fertility rather than to an ever-present female fluid) might lead one to surmise that there was a desire for some sort of equality, an equalizing of the flow of fluids in sexual contact. But this is not the case. Instead, the putative aggression of the female toward the male seed is simply transferred, and in Tantric texts, which exalt the female, the male is encouraged to take back from the female not only his seed but hers as well, by the so-called fountain-pen technique (Eliade 1958, pp. 232–33; cf. Snellgrove 1959, pp. 35–36, citing *Hevajra Tantra* 1. 7d). In a Tantric ceremony recorded in Orissa, the female seed is eaten rather than sexually reabsorbed; the woman is to secrete her seed at the time of intercourse, but

> The worshipper . . . must not let his seed fall. The female sexual fluid is collected on a flower or a "*bel*" leaf [and is eventually placed in a conch shell]. . . . The ritual concludes with the main worshipper drinking the rest of the content of the conch shell. . . . Instead of the woman receiving within her the male sexual fluid, the opposite process is followed, and it is the man who ingests the female sexual fluid. It is thus very graphically and specifically the inverse of conjugal intercourse and well merits the appellation of "inverse sexual intercourse" (Marglin 1978b, pp. 15–16; cf. *Tantrāloka* 29. 127–28, cited by Tucci 1968, p. 292, and Eliade 1971, p. 101; see also below, chap. 8, sec. L).

This ritual may be based on a more classical Tantric text, in which the *kuṇḍagolaka*, a mixture of both male and female secretions, is collected in a consecrated vessel and eventually eaten. The female part of this mixture is *śonita*, menstrual blood, which is also consumed in other Tantric rituals. This may be an extension to the secondary model (seed-blood) of the reversal first applied by Tantrism to the primary model (seed-seed); in both cases, the female fluid is consumed in clear contrast to its role in non-Tantric Hindu thought, where the male fluid is consumed and the female fluid is "consuming."

Another Tantric text resolves this conflict in a still bolder way: the *yoni* has semen on the left and menstrual fluid on the right; if the procreative wind moves on the right, the child will be male; if on the left, it will be female (*Saṃvarodaya Tantra* 2. 23). Not only is a woman said to have both seed and menstrual blood, but both are said to be actively procreative and to occupy positions opposed to those of the normal order ([male] seed on the right, [female] blood on the left). Yet the male child is born from the right, the female from the left, in the traditional manner—a statement at odds with the locations of the male and female sexual fluids in the womb and perhaps indicating the subconscious persistence of the more "orthodox" model.

Seed Substitutes: Sweat and Tears

In Hindu mythology the instances of unilateral female creation are by far outnumbered by unilateral male creation. The male seed is fertile in itself, particularly the seed of a great ascetic who has kept it within him for a long time and is therefore "one whose seed is never shed in vain" (*amogharetas*); that is, he engenders a child every time he sheds his seed, no matter where he sheds it. Even an ordinary man's seed is basically the source of life, as is evident from the Upaniṣadic tradition; in Dharmaśāstra, too, the seed remains more important than the womb (*Manu* 9. 35). The seed shed by a powerful male may fall into any of a number of womb substitutes (a pot, the earth, a river, or someone's mouth) and produce an embryo. In addition, other fluids from the body of the male may serve as seed substitutes, particularly sweat and tears (O'Flaherty 1973, pp. 272–73). Śiva begets a demon from a drop of his sweat shed upon the earth; he produces the demon Andhaka from a drop of the "sweat of passion" that falls from his forehead into the fire of his own third eye; and his sweat of anger produces various demons when he destroys the sacrifice of Dakṣa (*MBh* 12. 274. 45; *Matsya P* 252. 5–6; *Vām P* 44. 41–43, 28. 57, 64–65; *ŚP* 2. 5. 42. 14–22; O'Flaherty 1973, p. 272). The sweat of lust is particularly fertile: when Brahmā desired Sandhyā but managed to control his lust, his sweat fell to the ground and produced a multitude of sages, and, at the same moment, the sweat of Dakṣa produced Rati, the goddess of sexual pleasure (whose name also designates female seed) (*Kālikā P* 2. 45–47; *SP* 2. 2. 3. 48; 2. 2. 3. 51). Śiva creates a demon from his sweat to drink the demon-producing blood of Andhaka, himself born of Śiva's sweat (*Matsya P* 252. 5–6; *Vām P* 44. 41–43). These are all negative, demonic creations, perverse creations, not because no woman is involved in the birth (for exclusively male procreation very often has auspicious results) but because sweat is regarded as an inferior, negative form of seed; it is the fluid of emotion (passion, anger, lust), in sharp contrast with the seed that is held back by means of emotional control.

Creation by tears is particularly central to the early mythology of Śiva, for the Rudras are said to be born of Prajāpati's tears (*ŚB* 9. 1. 1. 6–7), and Rudra himself weeps until he is fed (*KP* 1. 10. 22–27). The connection between tears and food is further developed in another context:

> Tears flowed from Atri's eyes, flooding the universe with light. The ten points of the compass, taking the form of a woman, received that embryo in their belly, and after 300 years they released it, and Brahmā made it into a youth, Soma (*Matsya P* 23. 1–10; *PP* 5. 12. 1–13).

The tears, a seed substitute, are ultimately transformed back into Soma, the Upaniṣadic source of all seed.

Blood and Milk

A number of significant tensions are associated with female blood in the post-Vedic period. There is a tension between neutral blood (the source of male semen and female milk) and female blood (contrasted with male semen). A man produces blood when he dies; a woman produces blood when she creates. In this context, it is evident that the menstrual blood is not primarily polluting, as is so often said. Rather, it is taboo or sacred in the broadest sense: because it is the woman's creative power, it is of course dangerous, but it is by no means negative (Gross 1977a, p. 499). In post-Vedic mythology, menstrual blood comes to be a symbol of the passion of women, the cause of the loss of Eden (*MP* 46. 1–35; *KP* 1. 28. 15–40; O'Flaherty 1976, p. 27), or the visible sign of women's share of the guilt of Brahminicide. They accept this stigma in return for the privilege of bearing children (*TS* 2. 5. 1; *BhP* 6. 9. 9–10; O'Flaherty 1976, pp. 157–58.

Milk and blood mingle symbolically within a woman in various ways. The uterine blood that mingles with the male's semen is, by analogy, confounded with the blood that produces milk (distilled, like semen) in the breast: "The blood of women, in the breast, causes the sperm to grow; for the semen of men, in the seed, grows by union with women and is nourished by the blood of the woman. At the time of the falling of the seed of the man, a portion of the soul [*jīva*] grows in the pregnant womb, nourished by the blood" (*H*, app. 1, 2909–15). In mythology, this contrast between blood and milk is clarified and given strong moral overtones: "Pārvatī suckled the Gond gods, but they sucked her right breast until blood came, and they continued to suck blood until the breast shrivelled up. Having sucked her blood, they could not be controlled by anyone on earth" (von Fürer-Haimendorf 1948, pp. 102, 129–37). Again the problem of uncontrollable demonic powers is linked with the drinking of blood, blood that flows instead of the normal milk. In the Brāhmaṇas, an expiation must be performed if blood is found in the cow's milk (*ŚB* 12. 4. 2. 1).

This contrast between blood and milk is heightened by the introduction of yet another related fluid—poison—in a well-known myth:

> The ogress Pūtanā, a devourer of children, was sent to kill the infant Kṛṣṇa. She assumed a charming form and let him suck her breast, which she had smeared with a virulent poison. But Kṛṣṇa, pressing her breast hard with his hands, angrily drank out her life's breath with the milk and killed her, having cut off her breasts (*Bh P* 10. 6. 1–44; cf. *H* 50. 22; *PP* 6. 245; *Viṣṇu P* 5. 5).

Although blood is not explicitly mentioned, it is surely implicit in the "life's breath" that Kṛṣṇa drinks out of her breasts and in the cutting-off of her breasts. Just as Pūtanā reverses the fluid that she intends to give him, changing milk to poison, so he too effects a reversal, changing the poison to blood, which he sucks from her.

Blood is often explicitly said to produce milk in a woman (in contrast with the semen that it produces in a man) or to produce female seed (*rati*) and male seed (*vīrya*) (Yalman 1963, p. 30; cf. Egnor 1978, p. 60; Sinha 1961, pp. 194–96). The first of these models separates the woman's fertile fluid from her sexual base entirely; the second substitutes for the fertile fluid the erotic fluid of that base but defines it as creative as well as erotic. Blood is the source of both of these fluids in the woman. The blood that flows from the breast, however, is an inauspicious milk substitute, an anti-milk substance; for the inverse of the woman whose breasts flow with milk is the demoness who drinks blood. When the gods milk the earth of strength, the demons milk her of blood (*AV* 8. 10. 22–29). This negative correspondence is reflected in the statement of a contemporary Tamil: "We all drink our mother's blood for ten months before we are born, and after birth again we drink her blood in the form of milk" (Egnor 1978, p. 172), a view supported by Āyurvedic texts stating that, since the unborn child drinks its mother's blood, there is a conflict between them. Thus the medical texts points out that during gestation the fetus gains flesh and blood while the mother loses strength and color: the fetus eats the mother (Caraka 4. 4. 22). The demonic implications of the Tamil's statement are clear: "This was M.'s most often repeated speech. And the pre-occupation is not only his own. In Sri Lanka, for instance, there is a large body of mythology about disease demons, several of which were born of a dead mother, surviving by eating her body and drinking her blood" (Egnor 1978, p. 173). The dead mother cannot give milk; this makes her son into a demon who drinks her blood (or, as we shall see, into a yogi who holds back his own fluids).

The intimate connection between blood and milk in a woman is further expressed in a classical medical text:

> With women, the channels of the vessels carrying the menstrual blood, after conception, become obstructed by the fetus. Hence, with pregnant women there is no menstrual discharge. Obstructed below, the blood . . . reaches the breasts. Hence the breasts of pregnant women grow large and projecting (Suśruta 3. 4. 24; cf. Zimmer 1948, p. 185).

According to this text, milk is made, not from nonsexual blood, but from menstrual blood; the most polluting of substances is transmuted into the purest of substances, rising from the genital site as semen rises in a man to become transmuted into Soma.

To drink blood directly is demonic, typical of the evil goddess Kālī and the erotic mare, the inverse of the mother (see below, chap. 6, sec. D, and chap. 8, sec. D); to drink blood when it has been made into milk is natural and good, the defining characteristic of humans (and other mammals); and to feed with milk that has been made from blood is sacred, typical of the maternal goddess Pārvatī and of the cow. Fetuses, a subdivision of the middle category, exist in a liminal state, neither demons nor gods, neither dead nor alive; they drink a fluid that is neither entirely blood nor entirely milk, and so their relationship to the mother is ambivalent. By being filtered through the purifying breast, the blood is transformed into milk (the blood itself had earlier been made out of food filtered through the body). Blood thus mediates between raw food and "cooked" food; for milk is said to be "cooked" by the body, distilled like semen. Blood may be drunk before it is made into blood or after it has been made into something else, but it is dangerous and demonic to eat it in its mediating form. Since blood is closely related to milk but sharply contrasted with it, danger arises when blood and milk are combined or when one is substituted for the other.

Here, as so often, the symbolism of interaction of body fluids expresses a deep emotional ambivalence, extending to the parent-child relationship as well as to the male-female relationship. Another manifestation of the belief that the child feeds on his mother's milk/blood results in yet another "fluid" barrier between husband and wife:

> In rare cases when the husband and wife have the same blood type neither is willing to donate blood to the other. This stems from the belief that whoever receives blood will become the offspring of the other. For example, it is thought that a woman would become the daughter of a man (her husband) after receiving a blood transfusion from him. Any further sexual relations between the couple would be considered incestuous (Howard 1977).

Milk is made from blood; yet blood pollutes and endangers, while milk purifies and engenders.

Milk and Semen

In the sense that milk (rather than uterine blood) is the female equivalent of seed, milk is a directly creative fluid (as well as a nourishing fluid) in the mythology. Milk in the woman comes to be explicitly equated with seed: "In the male the principle of life is in the semen (*retas*); in the female it is in the milk, known as *páyas*, which latter word is also frequently used to mean semen" (N. Brown 1942, p. 87). This statement applies equally well to the Vedic and post-Vedic material. In the same sense that personality qualities and karmic tendencies are transferred from parents to children in the seed, it is believed that the mother's mental faculties, intelligence, and fears and worries are transferred to the child through the milk of the breast (Egnor 1978, p. 146).

The myth of creation from milk can be traced back to the Vedic metaphor of Soma churned or milked from the ocean (i.e., the Soma vats); in post-Vedic texts one encounters the cow, or earth-cow, who is milked of all that one desires—that is, who creates unilaterally, without a male agent other than the milker and the calf. In the epic myths, this milking is transformed into the churning of the ocean (a more direct multiform of the Vedic Soma-pressing): the gods churn the ocean and produce first milk, then butter, then wine, then poison, and, finally, Soma (*MBh* 1. 15–17). In addition, the magic wishing-cow is produced when the ocean is milked, and the ocean of milk flows from her udder (*MBh* 1. 23. 50; *R* 7. 23. 21); thus the cow and the ocean are each other's mothers. This logical circle is stated explicitly: the magic cow was born of the Soma that Brahmā spat from his mouth; from the cow's milk, the ocean of milk arose on earth, and four cows were born from her; when the gods and demons churned the ocean that was mixed with the milk of these cows, they obtained the Soma (*MBh* 5. 100. 1–13). Eating and the reversal of eating produce milk and the source of milk. Like the Vedic Prajāpati, the cow is her own parent.

Milk functions as semen not only in its creative power but in its role in the image of the retentive body. This is based on the analogy, not between the actual fluids themselves, but between their containers, the breast and the phallus, whose similarity is affirmed in such words as *payodhara*, "milk-bearing" or "liquid-bearing," which designates both a breast (filled with milk) or a cloud filled with water (metaphorically called seed or urine, a phallic image). Melanie Klein has advanced a fruitful hypothesis of "the breast that feeds itself," the breast that holds back milk for its own use; this also appears in Indian mythology as the breast that kills with poison instead of milk (the myth of Pūtanā). But in India the image of the self-cannibalizing limb plays a more important role in the male than in the female: the yogi seals his powers within himself by storing up his semen, drawing it away from his phallus (Hayley 1976; Klein 1948, pp. 265 and 357; O'Flaherty 1976, pp. 355–57). In popular folklore in India today, it is believed that when a yogi retains his seed, the seed is transformed into milk: "Semen of good quality is rich and viscous, like the cream of unadulterated milk" (Carstairs 1958, pp. 83–84). The yogi actually develops breasts, just as a pregnant woman does when her "seed" (i.e., menstrual blood) is obstructed. It is also said that the yogi becomes "pregnant" as his stomach swells with the retained seed.[5] The yogi thus becomes like a productive female when he reverses the flow of his male fluids.

The pervasiveness of the image of the pregnant yogi supports the mythological equivalences of breast and phallus, milk and seed, which occur in numerous episodes (O'Flaherty 1976, pp. 341–42). When King Pṛthu milks the earth-cow, she promises to yield her milk, which is the seed (*bījabhūtam*) of all vegetation (*Viṣṇu P* 1. 13. 80). But there is a significant difference in the values placed on the two "retentive" organs, for it is good for milk to flow out but bad for semen to do so. The breast that feeds itself is symbolic of the evil mother, but the phallus that draws up its seed is symbolic of the perfect man. Women are meant to give, men to keep. Or, on another level, maternal flow is good, while sexual flow is bad. It is suggested again and again by the myths that the ideal is to stop the flow, to keep back—or take back—the sexual fluid, which tends always to leave the body. Since semen and milk are literally constructed of one's life-blood, it is clear that to keep them back means to preserve one's very life, to *save* one's life—literally, as one would save money (in a kind of blood bank); whereas to give milk is to give life. In one Hindu view, the loss of semen destroys not only the life of the man who spills it; one informant stated that the Banias regard all sexual intercourse "as sacrilege because so many small creatures must die every time the semen comes out" (Carstairs 1958, p. 117).

Thus Śiva functions like those whom F. Scott Fitzgerald characterized as having "old money"—rich because of what they *have*; while Kṛṣṇa, orgiastically dispensing butter to his friends and to the monkeys and to the participants in his *līlā*, functions like the rich who have "new money"—rich because of what they *spend*. The direct equation of semen with life emerges from the medical texts, where semen is expressly said to promote longevity; therefore, to live long, one must retain semen (Caraka 1. 25. 39). This is merely a reformulation of the Vedic hypothesis: Soma promotes immortality; to become immortal, one must drink Soma.

The Upaniṣads state that a man's soul is transmuted from food into semen; in contemporary Tamilnadu, it is said that a man's power, *śakti*, enters him in food and is stored in semen: "to increase and retain this *śakti*, males must retain their semen and hence lead an ascetic life. Females, while having greater *śakti* of their own, also acquire, in intercourse, the *śakti* stored in the semen, thus further increasing their supply." Men are encouraged to perform asceticism; "females, however, can increase their *śakti* at a faster rate merely by being chaste wives" (S. Daniels 1978, p. 6). The chaste wife is a mother full of milk, the source of a woman's power in Tamilnadu. Thus the female increases her power, not by performing asceticism (for then she would be denied access to her supplementary source in the male), but by remaining "chaste" in the socially sanctioned way: by letting milk flow. Thus, she increases her power by letting her fluids flow freely.

Here one may recall that in the Upaniṣads the man who spills his semen is instructed to place it between his breasts or eyebrows (*BAU* 6. 4. 4–5). These two places are the two most important *cakras* or centers through which, in Kuṇḍalinī Yoga, the seed moves upward from the base of the spine to the tip of the head. The rich supply of semen stored in the yogi's head is symbolized by his high-piled hair (Leach 1958; Obeyesekere 1978); his powers, like those of the seduced Samson or the macho Sikh with his topknot, reside at the top of his head, in the "snake locks," or matted hair, that characterize the Sādhu (Hershman 1974). The highest point for the semen, and the highest *cakra*, is at the very top of the head; but the point on which the mythology usually centers is the more conspicuous *cakra* in the middle of the forehead. The significance of this *cakra*, and its relationship to milk (and, by analogy, to semen), are evident in contemporary South India:

> Each person, says T., has an invisible third eye between his eyebrows. It is at this point that the soul or life (*uyir*) of the person may be perceived, though the soul is spread throughout the body. It is analogous to milk being spread throughout the body of the mother, but only emerging at a certain place on the body, he says (Egnor 1978, p. 24).

The yogi, by drawing his semen to this special point, the site of the third eye, reverses the flow of normal sexuality and hence the flow of normal time; thus he transmutes seed into Soma, converting the fatal act of intercourse into an internalized act that will assure immortality (Eliade 1958, pp. 267–68).

So pervasive is the concept of semen being raised up to the head that popular versions of the philosophy believe that the semen *originates* there:

> Girdari Lal gave another reason for the importance of the head: "There's a sun inside your belly, that keeps your body warm, and there is nectar in your head. It drips down your throat from that point (the uvula) and is caught by the sun inside your umbilicus. . . . There are some holy men who learn the trick of stopping the falling nectar with their tongues; and as long as they do that, they cannot die" (Carstairs 1958, pp. 78).

This concept of the head as the "reservoir in which semen is stored" (ibid.) may be seen either as a distortion of the yogic philosophy or as an extension of other classical Indian ideas, such as the contrast between Soma, representing ecstatic cool religion (above the navel), and Agni, representing world-oriented hot religion (below the navel). Thus the "sun inside your umbilicus" is the internal fire (Agni Vaiśvānara), which converts nectar into mere semen (or food into blood), in contrast with the yogic power (also at the navel, the transition point), which converts semen into Soma. A powerful yogi is said to have an "intact store of rich, uncurdled semen in his head" (ibid., p. 86)—Soma that is *still* milky, in contrast with the more usual view that the yogi's semen *becomes* as rich as cream. The final condition is the same—the yogi's semen is like milk or butter and is stored in the form of Soma in his head—but in the more usual view semen is the original material that undergoes transmutation. The other view, however, lends support to the large body of mythology that equates beheading with castration; if every man, not merely the yogi, stores his semen in his head, every beheading is a castration.[6]

Although the yogic aspiration to transmute semen into Soma is taken literally, and acted upon, by only a small and esoteric section of Indian society, it is known and subscribed to on a theoretical level by most Indians, even nonliterate villagers. This is merely one example of a more general dichotomy between the *mokṣa*-oriented, Vedāntic level of Hindu society and the rebirth-oriented "transactional" level (to use McKim Marriott's term; one might also say Vedic or Purāṇic level), which includes the large majority (L. Dumont 1960, pp. 33–62; O'Flaherty 1973, pp. 78–83). Thus, though most Hindus *say* that a yogi is doing the best thing (an expression of what they think they think), they *act* in a way that belies this belief, by procreating as much as possible (an expression of what they do think).[7] Some Indians have a positive attitude to the process of flow and, indeed, to the world of *māyā*, while others have a negative attitude. This raises the basic question of the general applicability of all the relatively elite, if not esoteric, texts cited in this study; in defense of their general relevance, one can only cite the manner in which they are so frequently mirrored in contemporary folk belief. Moreover, Louis Dumont (1960) has demonstrated brilliantly how the *soi-disant* "renunciation" traditions are in fact a constant source of important new ideas assimilated by the orthodox traditions with which they are supposed to have no contact.

Another significant hiatus between classical theory and folk belief may be seen in a paradox that emerges from traditions about the transmutation of blood into milk or semen. According to general folk belief this transmutation takes place as the result of intimate physical contact: blood is transformed into mother's milk when the baby sucks at the breast, and blood is transformed into male semen during the sexual act. In other words, the transmutation takes place only when the fluid is about to leave the body: the baby makes the milk, and the woman makes the seed. Theoretically, therefore, a woman should not be able to withhold her milk, since it would still be blood if the child had not stimulated the mother to want to give it; if she does not give milk to him, what she is withholding should still be technically classified as blood. Yet clearly it is not blood, for milk does flow without physical contact (as Pārvatī's breasts begin to flow when she merely hears that a child has been born who is technically—though not physically—hers) and can be kept in the body as milk. Similarly, it should be impossible for a man to hold back his seed (since it remains blood until a woman excites him). But this, too, is not the case, for the mere thought of a woman can cause a man to spill his seed, and the seed that is not spilt remains seed within his body (unless it is further transmuted into Soma).

In the absence of physical contact, mere emotion can effect the transformation of blood into either milk or seed; indeed, as we have seen, it is the emotional component of the sexual fluids that contributes the essential spark of life in the act of procreation. Thus the folk view that the fluids are transformed simply as the result of physical contact is superseded by the more subtle view that regards physical contact as secondary to emotional involvement. And since the emotion of maternal love is highly valued and the emotion of lust is devalued, it follows that for a woman to withhold her milk is bad and for a man to withhold his seed is good.

Seed as Food

The identification of the seed with Soma and with milk (or butter) leads to many myths in which pregnancy is brought about by the ingestion of either seed or a substitute for it (usually a milk product). This idea can be traced back to Upaniṣadic views of the birth process, and it persists in contemporary Bengal and Tamilnadu. In Bengal, the man produces seed, the woman uterine blood, from food that is "transformed progressively into digested food (*rasa*), and then into blood (*rakta*)" (Inden and Nicholas 1977, p. 52). This might also be interpreted to mean that food, when eaten, turns into neutral, protean seed (*rasa*) or "food-juices" (Meyer 1930, p. 359), in the Ṛg Vedic sense, and then into blood (and, ultimately, into male seed). In South India the mixing of male and female fluids during intercourse is said to be the mixing of the juice from food and the feeling (*rasa*) of food, for the semen, which is the soul's power, is in the substance of the food (Egnor 1978, p. 61).

The concept of food transformed into seed also survives in modern rituals in which a pregnant woman, to procure a male offspring, eats milk-based and rice-based "seminal foods"; for such foods will be converted within the embryo into semen rather than uterine blood, with the result that semen will prevail and the child will be a male (Inden and Nicholas 1977, pp. 54–55). It is interesting to note that if there are equal quantities of semen and uterine blood in the embryo, the child will be born as an androgyne; in another view, however, the embryo will turn out to be twins (presumably a boy and a girl (*MBh* 1862, 1. 90. 14; *GP U* 22. 18–21), and a Tantric text states that it will be a eunuch (neither a girl nor a boy), not as a result of the equal amounts of blood or semen (as Suśruta maintains [3. 3. 5]) but as the result of the circulation of the progenerative wind *midway* between the left side of the womb (where semen is and female embryos are engendered) and the right side (where menstrual blood is and male embryos are engendered)

(*Saṃvarodaya Tantra* 2. 26–27).

Yet another seed substitute—urine—is sometimes ingested (together with milk) in the ceremony of the "five cow products": milk, curds, ghee, dung, and urine. (Blood, another liquid product of the cow, is conspicuously absent; since blood is nonmilk, or sometimes anti-milk, and is often a deadly symbol, it would be out of the question to drink blood in a milk-based, life-producing ceremony, to say nothing of the problems raised in India by injuring a cow to secure her blood.) Thus, drinking of the stallion's Soma-urine and the Avestan bull's urine was replaced by drinking of the cow's milk-urine. A myth explains this practice:

> The goddess of fortune went to the cows and asked to dwell within them; though they at first refused, since she was so inconstant and fickle, she insisted that no part of their bodies was disgusting, and the cows agreed to let her dwell in their urine and dung (*MBh* 13. 81. 1–26).

The goddess of fortune, fickle and erotic, is consigned to the least attractive parts of the cow, who is the constant mother. Filtered by the body of the cow, even the dangerous goddess may be safely ingested.

Semen is like butter in being the reduced essence of blood or food, as butter is the essence of milk: "As butter is churned out from milk by the churning sticks, so seed is churned out (of a man) by the churning sticks born of bodily desires" (*MBh* 12. 207. 21). The man of continence, who restrains his seed and resists these erotic churning sticks, is said to have seed rich as butter (like Prajāpati in the Vedas). So, too, the Tamil informant says that performing asceticism "is like churning milk for butter, so we churn our bodies to draw out this kind of heat" (Egnor 1978, p. 148). In many myths, a woman becomes pregnant by drinking a man's seed rather than by receiving it into her womb. This is of course a widespread folk belief (cf. Hartland 1909 1:12; O'Flaherty 1973, pp. 276–77), but in India it is strongly supported (as are the other models of sexual hydraulics) by the ritual metaphor; for if the seed is Soma or the oblation of butter, it is natural to place it in the mouth of the woman, just as it is placed in the mouth of the gods—in Agni, the god of fire (O'Flaherty 1973, pp. 277–78).

Indeed, in addition to the many stories in which women are impregnated by drinking the semen of a male (see ibid., pp. 275–76),[8] Agni himself is said to become pregnant as a result of drinking Śiva's seed (*Vām P* 28. 50). Sometimes Pārvatī drinks the seed, too (*Matsya P* 158. 33–50), but she never becomes pregnant. This is surely significant; the myths strongly resist any episode that allows Pārvatī to participate normally in the birth of her child (O'Flaherty 1973, p. 273). Agni, however, not only becomes pregnant but translates this pregnancy to all the gods (as he transfers the oblation itself), so that they all begin to lactate (*Saura P* 62. 5–12). (This is the one act that Pārvatī is usually allowed to perform; when her child is born, far from her and without her agency, her breasts begin to flow with milk [O'Flaherty 1973, pp. 105–7]. Yet even this is often denied her, for her son is given the Kṛttikās as his wet nurses [ibid., pp. 98–103]). Although the male gods do not usually object to being pregnant (this being a very Vedic thing for them to be), they do object to lactating, which makes them a "laughingstock" and is the last straw. Similarly, when King Yuvanāśva accidentally becomes pregnant (by drinking a pot of water consecrated for his wife), the sages arrange for him to give birth to a son without labor pains; this was a marvel, says the text, which easily accepts the fact of his pregnancy. Problems in fact begin to arise only when the boy is born and needs to suck milk. Indra then lets him suck his (Indra's) thumb—Indra being the storm cloud and hence androgynously able to produce semen or milk/rain (*MBh* 3. 126. 1–26; cf. *Viṣṇu P* 4. 2. 12–17). Agastya, a great sage and, like Indra, a notorious drinker, is also said to lactate from his thumb. Thus the male is able to do anything that the female can do, even to produce milk. In South India, on the other hand, the word *karu* (mouth) designates either the male or the female reproductive organ, but its primary reference is to the womb; the penis is thus a small womb. Moreover, "The belief that generativity is essentially a female phenomenon appears again in a Tamil expression for one's own child, 'a child born in my belly' . . . Not only women, but men also, say this of their children, subsuming their male parenthood to motherhood" (Egnor 1978, pp. 143–44). The male participates in pregnancy by imitating the woman.

In the medical texts, it is clear that women can procreate unilaterally but men cannot; in the myths, the situation is reversed, and men, but not women, are capable of unilateral procreation (albeit men do it into a "female" receptable of some sort—any container at all). In the myths, when women become pregnant by drinking seed (or seed substitutes), the outcome is usually less auspicious than when men create in this way. Gaṇeśa is said to have been born to a female demon who had drunk the unguents mixed with the body-rubbings discarded by Pārvatī, i.e., female seed (Getty 1936, pp. 6–7). We have seen that when Yuvanāśva drank the consecrated water by mistake, all was eventually well with him; but when one of the two wives of a king ate a consecrated pot of rice boiled with milk and butter, and the second wife then had intercourse with her in the manner of a man, the child "born without male semen" lacked bones and was a mere ball of flesh (*PP Svargakhaṇḍa* 16. 11–14). "This is the natural consequence of the mating of females," says the modern Indian editor (ibid., p. 44). Even miraculous births follow the logic of the model; indeed, it is here that the model emerges most clearly, for it is *only* the logic of the model (and not the logic of natural observation) that dictates the rules.

In the banal human context, drinking semen is generally regarded as definitely *de trop*; Śiva says to Agni, "You did a perverse thing, to drink my seed" (*ŚP* 2. 4. 2. 46) (though some of the "perversion" derives from the fact that it is a man, rather than a woman, who drinks the seed). The law books prescribe an expiation for a man who has unwittingly swallowed semen (*Manu* 4. 222; cf. *MBh* 7. 51. 35a), and even the permissive *Kāmasūtra* (2. 9) has nothing but blame for this particular perversion, which is confined to eunuchs and prostitutes. Thus it is said, "He who performs sexual intercourse in the mouth of his wife causes his ancestors to eat his seed for a month (*VDŚ* 12. 23; cf. O'Flaherty 1973, pp. 278–79). Here the prohibition on the human level is combined with a parallel description of a reversal in the world of the dead, where the usual *piṇḍa* offering is replaced by the seed that in the birth model is itself an inversion of the "seed" given to the ancestors.

Yet there are certain beliefs about the drinking of semen that echo the mythological texts and doubtless spring from them ultimately. Suśruta recommends that a man who is incapable of erection may remedy this by drinking semen (commentator: of another man), which will expand his semen-carrying ducts (Suśruta 3. 2. 38). In present-day Sri Lanka, men who are anxious about their virility may in pathological cases drink their own semen, though there is probably more fantasy (i.e., myth) about this than actual occurrence (Obeyesekere 1976, p. 214). Equally significant, certain seed substitutes are prescribed in modern folk medicine in Sri Lanka:

> Many young unmarried men, particularly students in the university dormitories, eat raw eggs in the morning to enhance strength and vitality. I interpret this custom, also found in the West, as an unconscious attempt to compensate for loss of vitality due to night emissions, masturbation, or an imagined discharge of semen in the urine. In Sri Lanka the term for egg is *biju*, which is also used for seed, semen, and penis (ibid., p. 208).

To eat seed in order to produce seed is a simple homeopathic method that makes sense in Western terms too. But a more particularly South Asian line of thought appears in yet another proposed Sri Lanka remedy: an Āyurvedic doctor prescribed cow's milk for a man thought to be suffering from semen loss. In Rajasthan, too, the anxieties of men preoccupied over loss of semen could often be palliated by "eating certain exceptionally good, health-giving foods, namely wheat flour, rice, milk and butter, honey and white sugar. These substances have two valuable attributes: they are 'cool' foods, that is to say they give nourishment without inflaming the passions, and they have the property of building pure, unspoiled semen" (Carstairs 1958, p. 166). These foods, which closely resemble the ingredients given to women who wish to conceive male children, have an additional value: not only do they build up a store of semen, they build up the ability to resist the temptation to shed it. Thus they are destined to create an internalized male power, not a form of virility designed to be used in an outpouring of creative energy. It is significant that, in addition to milk, rice, and eggs, butter is regarded as a producer of semen; bridegrooms and other male guests at weddings are encouraged to swallow as much as two pounds of ghee at a single sitting, a feat regarded "as a mark of virility. . . . And the boasting and teasing which attends these feasts make it clear that here ghi is being equated with semen" (ibid.). The Vedic equation of butter and semen on the ritual and mythic level is thus put to use on the medical and psychological level.

In Tantric rituals, where female seed as well as male semen is procreative and magical, the adept drinks not only semen but menstrual blood (Tucci 1969, p. 62).[9] This ceremony, in which the deity is said to enter into the ingested fluids, may be seen as a kind of *prasāda* or eucharist, albeit in an esoteric version (Carstairs 1957, p. 103); but in our context it functions as an instance of sexual power entering through ingested food. The iconography of the Tantric rituals also suggests that the fluid drunk from the skull-cups held by the servants of the Goddess may be menstrual blood.

The drinking of urine is also curiously persistent in *soi-disant* real life as well as in myth. Among the many practices that orthodox Rajasthanis attributed to the "left-hand" (heterodox) yogis was this: "It is a dangerous way, all the time they are breaking the rules of nature, drink their own urine, live in filth" (ibid., p. 232). Among the more respectable eccentrics, India's Prime Minister Desai at the age of eighty-one revealed that he drank a glass of his own urine every morning, and he claimed that this "water of life" was a cure for cancer, cataracts, and tuberculosis. The concept of preserving bodily fluids is clearly at work here, for Desai also prided himself on not having had sexual intercourse since he was thirty-three.[10]

The eating of semen has numerous ramifications in the mythology. One image that we will encounter again and again is that of the devouring female, the woman who eats the man during intercourse. This image pervades not only the explicit instances of oral impregnation in the myths but even descriptions of the normal sexual act, through the image of the devouring womb, the *vagina dentata*. In South India it is said that at the time of union the womb spreads open like the mouth or eye; the *vagina dentata*, as we shall see, often has eyes as well as teeth. The passage to the womb is called *karuvāy*, a compound meaning "womb-mouth," and sexual union is likened to the hand of the mother feeding rice to the child (Egnor 1978, pp. 141–42). The image of rice as seed is one that we shall often encounter in the mythology; the image of the womb as a mouth is also a recurrent one. Through this imagery, every sexual act is an instance of the drinking of semen.

Ambiguous Fluids: Milk, Poison, and Fire

What does all of this indicate about the Hindu image of the fluids of the body? First of all, it is evident that the categories of male and female interact so closely in Hindu thought that one begins to wonder whether they are true categories at all. I think they are; they are certainly grammatical categories, and language forces thought into certain patterns. Male and female are assumed to be complementary opposites in the medical texts as well as in the ritual texts, which use them to express other oppositions. But the myths tell us over and over that things are mixed all the time, sometimes with good results and sometimes with bad results.

Second, it is evident that the woman is far more complicated than the man. She has two sites of sexual fluids to his one, and the one that they share (the genital site) is doubly productive in her (of both seed and blood). Moreover, the fluid that they share—blood—is also ambiguous in her: her blood is in part productive but life-draining (venous blood, producing milk and female seed) and in part dangerous but life-creating (menstrual blood, acting as female seed).

Her milk, issuing from her secondary sexual site, is similarly ambivalent. The ambiguity of milk is heightened when erotic overtones are attributed to this maternal substance, when emotions more appropriate to the genital site are carried to the breast. This happens quite often, of course, for Indian eroticism has always placed enormous emphasis upon breasts swelling like mangoes. Many examples of this appear in the mythology of Kṛṣṇa, who enjoys the gopīs both as foster mothers whose breasts he sucks and as mistresses whose breasts he fondles (Masson 1974; cf. below, chap. 4, sec. C).

The symbolism of ambivalent milk is enhanced by the belief that, since milk is good, an evil woman has either no milk or else poison in her breasts, like Pūtanā. Poison as the inverse of Soma appears throughout the mythology; a fiery poison is said to devour the world—like the doomsday fire—in contrast with Soma or milk, that is itself devoured (O'Flaherty 1973, pp. 278–79). Poison is also thought to reside in the genitals of the destructive erotic woman, the poison damsel (Penzer 1924, pp. 275–313). In the Bengali *Manasāmaṅgal*, Lakhindara is fated to die on his wedding night (the recurrent myth of fatal sexuality); when he flies in the face of the prophecy, he is bitten by the snake damsel and dies of her poison. Snakes (often symbolizing women) perform an alchemy in which milk is transmuted into poison, the inverse of that alchemy that women perform by turning blood into milk. In the village ritual, milk is fed to a snake; the snake then turns this into poison, which in turn is rendered harmless by Soma (or by the shaman, who controls Soma, drugs, and snakes). Yogis, the inverse of mothers in terms of fluid hydraulics, drink poison, which they regard as Soma, and thus have power over snakes (O'Flaherty 1973, p. 279). A yogi can also drink poison and turn it into seed, and he can turn his own seed into Soma by activating the (poisonous?) coiled serpent goddess, Kuṇḍalinī. When the ocean of milk is churned, poison comes out, together with Soma (*MBh* 1. 15–17). Thus, although poison is not literally a bodily or sexual fluid, it forms an important opposition to milk and Soma.

The myth of Pūtanā is significant not merely for the image it presents (which occurs elsewhere) but for the intensity with which the image is depicted and the frequency with which the myth itself is retold in India. This is an instance of the role of mythology in highlighting those psychological concepts that are not merely present but are actively influential in a culture:

> The secret fantasy of poisoned milk, of nourishment that kills, originates early in life when the decisive separation between child and mother takes place. The elevation of this fantasy, which is occasionally encountered clinically, to the status of myth for a whole culture indicates the intensity of inner conflict associated with this separation in the Indian setting (Kakar 1978, p. 147).

We will return to this question of the cultural use of individual fantasy through myth.

Fire is also a kind of ritual fluid in the Indian view, a form of Soma that can be opposed to Soma or identified with it: opposed as a female receptacle for male butter; identified as a male form placed in female water (A. Kuhn 1886; cf. O'Flaherty 1973, pp. 286–89). The view of fire as a female substance into which the male substance, liquid seed, is sacrificed appears in the Brāhmaṇa texts on oblation and the Upaniṣadic imagery of procreation; the view of fire as male substance, liquid seed, which is sacrificed into a female substance or surrounded by a female substance, the watery womb, appears in the Ṛg Vedic image of Hiraṇyagarbha and in the Purāṇic image of the flame *liṅga* in the cooling *yoni*. Here, as so often, the Vedic/Purāṇic symbolism contrasts with the Vedāntic, and both systems of imagery continue to flourish side by side in later Indian thinking, though they are technically contradictory. Fire is an androgynous liquid or the opposite of liquid, an element which, as we have seen in the Agni myths, becomes an anthropomorphic creature who is sexually complex. The Purāṇas use *tejas*, fiery energy, as a euphemism for semen; but Suśruta (3. 3. 3, 1. 14. 3) characterizes semen as moonlike and Soma-like (*saumya*), like its pale color, while female "seed" (menstrual blood) is red and fiery. Only when the male and female unite does the man's seed acquire *tejas*; water belongs to the father, while fire belongs to the mother (*Saṃvarodaya Tantra* 2. 2. 8). Both views of fire merge in the myth of the birth of Skanda: Śiva gives his seed to Agni, who becomes pregnant (cool liquid semen placed in the fiery female, as the oblation is placed in fire); but then Agni places this seed in the Ganges (fiery semen placed in the cool liquid female, as water is poured over the flame *liṅga* to cool it) (O'Flaherty 1973, pp. 286–89).

The Danger of Fluids

The sexual fluids from the breasts of the woman are generally creative and good, while those from her genitals are generally destructive and bad. The "good seed" of a woman (as of a cow) is in her breasts; she creates best with milk; the "bad seed" from the genitals is dangerous. (This distinction may apply to a man as well—good seed from above the navel, bad seed from below [*TS* 3. 25. 1]—but it is less evident in the mythology.) The concept that there is potential danger in a woman's sexual fluids reemerges in Hindu folk beliefs, as is amply testified by E. Valentine Daniel's hilarious interview with a gentleman in a Truchy village, who expressed strong opinions about the manner in which a man's life-fluids would be sucked out of him ("blowing his brains out" or leaving him "with his tongue hanging out") were he to have intercourse with a younger (or, more often older) woman whose sexual fluids were incommensurate with his own (E. V. Daniel 1979, pp. 117–33). As long as there is perfect balance, the sexual act is regarded as a positive source of health in Truchy; but if there is *imbalance*—watch out. We will return to this essential point of balance in the hydraulic systems.

In spite of (or because of) these powerful complexities, the woman is far less significant than the man as an agent of procreation. He is more often unilaterally creative than she is, and it is he who plays by far the more important role in "normal" sexual creation. In the apparent equation of milk and seed, it is evident that seed is the more basic substance; milk is like seed, but seed is not usually like milk. The apparent androgyny of the fluid system does not actually function in truly androgynous fashion; it functions competitively rather than harmoniously. The man imitates the woman (male pregnancy) or the woman the man (creation through the shedding of dirt-seed). There is astonishingly little interaction between these fluids in the mythology of the Purāṇas; even when a man and his wife both participate in producing a child, they may do so in physical isolation from each other; the male seed reaches the female (if at all) through a series of miraculous interventions, which tend to keep the man and woman as far apart as possible; they mate like fishes, one passing gracefully over the place where the other has been before, or like stock animals impregnated with frozen sperm; there is no opportunity for sustained emotional contact.

The fear of losing body fluids leads not only to retention but to attempts to steal the partner's fluid (and the fear that the partner will try the same trick)—yet another form of competition. If the woman is too powerful or too old or too young, terrible things will happen to the innocent man who falls into her trap, a fate often depicted in terms of his losing his fluids.The Indian texts describe this fear in a strikingly powerful and detailed way, but it is a widespread and recurrent anxiety. It underlies the tale of Samson's loss of strength when Delilah cuts off his hair (for hair, as we shall see, may be a symbol of semen), and it is present in the common idiom that describes a seductive woman, particularly a prostitute, as one who "bleeds a man to death" or as "man-eating." In our day, it may be seen in the obsession of the mad general, played by Sterling Hayden in Stanley Kubrick's *Dr. Strangelove*, who was convinced that the enemy was polluting his "precious bodily fluids"; more commonly, it is the basis of the red-blooded American tradition that football players should not have sexual contact with women during their training, particularly on the eve of the Big Game.

In India, it is the older woman who is the primary threat to the man's sexual fluids. An explanation for this emerges from a conversation Carstairs had with one of his Rajasthani informants. When the latter remarked that too much sex is bad for you, Carstairs asked. "Do you believe that the man is weakened and the woman not?" This was the response:

> No, both are weakened, but their weakness is also compensated by the combination of the man's semen (*viri*) and that of the woman

> (*raj*). When these combine properly, both of them are benefited; but for this to happen it is necessary that the woman should be young, younger than the man. . . . [If she is much older] it will be very harmful for him, because her *raj* is thin and watery so it will not combine well with his semen, so he will get no benefit from intercourse, only loss (Carstairs 1958, p. 225).

This statement reveals a number of assumptions: that the woman has seed, like the man, and that during intercourse her seed is transferred to him, as his is to her. An old woman, it is argued, will not have enough seed to make up for his inevitable loss. There are other reasons why there would be greater danger from an older woman, as we shall see in chapter 4 (section C)—dangers stemming from the greater power and greater threat that she represents; but in the Tantric concept of fluid interaction, it is the "weakness" of the older woman that makes her dangerous.

Stopping the Flow

The belief that the sexual act is extremely dangerous is expressed again and again in the mythology. The most notorious case is the story of King Pāṇḍu, who was under a curse to die immediately if "deluded by lust" and seduced by a woman he loved; therefore, in order to beget the *Mahābhārata* heroes, he allowed his wife to invoke male gods to beget his sons by proxy—an instance of the union of a mortal woman with an immortal man, the relatively "safe" combination (*MBh* 1. 109. 1–31; cf. below, chap. 4, sec. C, and chap. 6, secs C–D). In many myths of this type, the man is forbidden to have intercourse with his wife (or a woman he loves) but is not prohibited from having casual sexual relations. This, coupled with the belief that younger women alone are safe, may be part of a general psychological pattern based on fear of the mother (Carstairs 1958, p. 168). Psychoanalysis has much to say about these fears and, even more, about the envy of the "pregnant male," the anal fixation of the "breast that feeds itself," and the terrors of the *vagina dentata*. The parallel between the breast that holds in its fluids and the phallus that holds in its fluids is not merely structural but actually causal, in the psychoanalytic view: the male child withdraws from the mother (later, the wife) as a result of her sexual aggression toward him (see below, chap. 4, sec. C); the phallus holds back in revenge because the breast has held back. This revenge may become manifest in another, related, way in the belief that women should not have pleasure in sex, that it is inappropriate for a woman to be erotic (see below, chap. 9, sec. B): "The double standard or the ideal of chastity is the infant's revenge for oral frustration" (Róheim 1945b, p. 197). In this logic, because the mother has held back milk, denying the son pleasure, he later denies pleasure to his sexual partner by thwarting her eroticism or simply by withdrawing and holding back his seed.

In addition to (or instead of) revenge, it is possible to see simple self-protection at the heart of this causation: the yogi draws up his seed in order to keep his fluids from being drained by the evil mother, who holds back her fluids and will take away his. Asceticism is, moreover, capable of transmuting vulnerable fluids into "safe" substances: semen is transmuted not only into Soma, the elixir of immortality, but also into milk. Thus a Tamil myth tells that the magic wishing-cow performed such intense asceticism that "her body became very hot and much of it was turned into milk," which she poured over a Śiva-*liṅga* (Egnor 1978, p. 70; cf. below, chap. 8, sec. E). We have seen instances of yogis who turned their seed into milk and even began to develop breasts. The udder full of milk is the counterpart of the phallus full of seed; from the myth of the ascetic cow, it appears that the fluids of a man who performs asceticism should be held inside him but that, when a woman performs asceticism, her fluids should flow from her.

The link between the woman's bad breast and the man's withholding his seed may also be seen in Indian hagiographies describing the lives of ascetics. Śaṅkara is said to have suckled the breast of the image of the goddess in a temple (Masson 1976, p. 611).[11] Theologically, this may be taken as a statement that he so completely accepted the goddess as his mother that he sought the quintessential maternal contact with her, even with her sanctified image. But psychologically it may have other implications, such as that Śaṅkara's nursing experience was probably "not very satisfactory" (ibid.), i.e., that retained milk leads to ascetic retention of semen. A psychoanalytically oriented Indologist has compared ascetic fasting and anorexia nervosa, both of which are characterized by the fantasy of oral impregnation and increased fluid intake (ibid., p. 619); we have seen these motifs in the mythology of asceticism. That they represent an actual pathology seems less likely than that they represent the formalization and shared cultural expression of a widespread experience: the fear of the bad breast.

Examples of such mythological expressions of infantile fantasies abound. Freud would have loved the Purāṇas and might have made a great Tantric guru. But it is evident, even without complex interpretations, that the fluidity of the human body is seen by Hindus as a source of danger. If all things flow, as Parmenides said, the Hindu wishes to *stop* the flow or to reverse it (the Taoist would go with it; the

Buddhist would accept it as the nature of an ephemeral life).

Channeling the Flow

To stop the flow, one must construct elaborate meditational techniques, such as those posited in ritual contexts (in which normal social relations tend to be reversed). This is the extreme Yogic or Jaina or Vaiśeṣika view, well known in the West, though it is typically "Indian" only in the limited sense discussed above—on the level of what people think they think. In this view, the Vedāntic ideal is to keep the vital fluids within the indefinable bounds of the human body (in effect, to withdraw from all sexual contact). But for most "transactional," or conventionally interacting, Hindus, the flow was an essential part of the desirable process of life and procreation; this represents more directly what people think. Rajputs, for example, were proud of the flowing of the seed and maximized it to the greatest extent possible. For them, the dangers inherent in the flow of vital fluids might be offset by the construction of elaborate social barriers—the caste system, the most complex system in the world for the selection of the one safe, sanctioned, perfectly balanced and appropriate marriage partner, the woman guaranteed to be in cosmic equilibrium with her husband. With such a complete social equal, the flow would be minimized; for fluids seek their own level. If people are properly matched, their sexual relationship is regarded not only as beneficial to both but far better (in the general dharmic view) than total restraint. In ancient South India, marriage was regarded as a measure for controlling the dangerous powers attached to the chastity and sexuality of women (Hart 1975, p. 111). Nor is this merely a matter of remaining within the caste group, for the institution of cross-cousin marriage makes it "safe" to marry outside the caste. If imbalances still remain to occasion misgivings, astrology may be put to good use: the astrologer can weight his scales with planets to rectify an apparent imbalance, to find the woman who is truly matched in cosmic terms.[12] Similarly, the *Kāmasūtra* ranks men and women according to their sexual dimensions, their force of passion, and their staying power, but it does not merely sanction "equal" unions (though it regards these as the best); it specifies techniques by which unequal unions may be made satisfactory (2. 11; cf. below, chap. 8, sec. G). The problem of mutual control through an ordered ecstasy is also expressed through the mythology of the dance (see below, chap. 5). Thus, imbalance produces a problem—but one that can be overcome by careful, scientific procedures. These forms of control offered a "viable alternative" to yogic semen retention; in this view, each of the partners drew his or her share from the common pool of coded substance, and both were the better for the drawing.

I am certainly not proposing that the underlying cause of the Indian caste system is the idea that the interaction of sexual fluids is dangerous; however, the caste system does seem to be well designed to allay the fears reflected in this ancient and persistent belief. How successful is the attempt to strike a balance? One of Carstairs' informants spoke of the conflict between the desire for chastity (to lead the proper religious life and to preserve one's health) and the opposed claims (the need for normal sexual outlets as well as the duty to beget children). He remarked, "The best they can hope for is to order their lives so that their acts of piety suffice to compensate for the inevitable wastage of soul-stuff and semen." Carstairs' comment is illuminating:

> The clue to this compromise lies in the words *niyam se*—"in proper measure." Appetites may be indulged, feelings given an outlet, sexual relations experienced, provided always that they be subjected to a strict voluntary control: if that is observed, this situation is not too threatening, but the problem is to know what *is* the correct *niyam*. . . . As a mechanism of defence against anxiety, this attempt to confine sensuality "niyam se" too often let them down—hence the widespread pre-occupation with *jiryan* ["a real or imagined spermatorrhoea"], which I would claim to be the commonest expression of anxiety neurosis among the Hindu communities of Rajasthan, and perhaps elsewhere as well (Carstairs 1958, pp. 85, 87).

Control and balance are useful ideals, particularly as theoretical solutions to conflicting claims. But balance and compromise are not the normal Hindu way of dealing with paradox and conflict (O'Flaherty 1973, p. 82), and control is a problem that haunts the mythology, as we shall see. The rules set forth in the Dharmaśāstras, therefore, wisely supplement exhortations about control with suggestions of ways to minimize the damage done by the inevitable loss of control. Instead of boundaries, these rules make channels to keep the fluids flowing—if only in the direction in which they will do the least damage and the most good. But the fluids within the body are basically a pernicious force, as is evident from the etymology of the term used to describe the humors (*doṣa*), whose basic meaning is "fault," "vice," or "crime"; from this comes the meaning of "harm" and then the more specific meaning "disease"; finally, *doṣa* comes to denote the humors of the body as the causes of disease. The stream of life (*saṃsāra*, another fluid image) is a dangerous force. Some Hindus believe that it should not be dammed up; most

Hindus know that it cannot be dammed up; but all of them participate in a system of mythology that suggests that the stream can be shored up by ritual to keep us from being totally overwhelmed by the doomsday flood of our own physical and emotional currents.[13]

III Gods and Goddesses in Opposition

3 The Shazam Syndrome: The Banalization of the Hindu Gods

A. The Dangers of Upward Mobility

In non-Indian religions, a saint is usually someone who, born as an apparently normal human being, develops special powers, often at a very early age, and, much later, is canonized. In the classical Indian texts this could never happen, for reasons that this chapter will set forth; yet, in the late medieval period, we begin to have local stories of saints who fit the non-Indian pattern with which we are familiar, saints such as Caitanya, Kabīr, and many of the Vīraśaivas (Ramanujan 1973, pp. 19–55). The pattern of relationship between man (or woman) and god in classical texts had to undergo certain fundamental changes in order to accommodate these hagiographies, and those changes were to have a profound effect on attitudes toward mortals who sought direct contact with gods—or with goddesses.

In the ancient mythological texts, a kind of *apparent* hagiography appears at a very early period in tales of the great ascetic (*tapasvin*) who, though born as a normal human being (and often, though not always, of a good Brahmin family—Viśvāmitra is certainly a notable exception—but never, to my knowledge, of an outcaste or even Śūdra family), develops superhuman powers and becomes not a saint but a god; he rises to heaven and joins the immortals. Only on the most superficial level can such a person be regarded as a saint; his life lacks the crucial element of spiritual enlightenment (often sudden, though sometimes gradual) and the secondary but usual element of proselytizing or founding an order that is generally characteristic of the saint. These Indian ascetics are after power, not goodness—and they are after it for their own use; they *win* something, but they do not *grow into* anything; they possess something new, but who they are does not become something new. They exist in "nontime" or "collapsed time."[1]

This mythological pattern is crucial to an understanding of later hagiography. The idea of nondevelopment remains basic to the texts, and, in addition to this, a negative line of development begins. From the time of the Brāhmaṇas on, the texts begin to state that serious difficulties arise when a man becomes a god. A sacrificer may win heaven by means of the sacrifice, but it is essential for him to *come back* from heaven, or else he will go mad; he must touch the earth again to remain human (*TB* 4. 3. 5. 6; 4. 8. 9; 15. 17. 2; 18. 10. 10; *ŚB* 1. 9. 1. 29).[2] In the *Mahābhārata*, the ascetic poses a different kind of threat, but a threat nevertheless: he violates caste lines. For he changes from one category to another—a transition strongly opposed by the orthodox tradition of *svabhāva* and *svakarma*, the doctrine that one must perform throughout one's lifetime the duties appropriate to one's nature, which is defined by the group into which one is born (O'Flaherty 1978, pp. 96–106). In terms of Mary Douglas's paradigm, the rising ascetic becomes "dirt"; that is, he is out of place, out of order; he fits no category (Douglas 1966). And in the Hindu paradigm he is polluted and polluting.

In Tulu mythology, too, when an individual is possessed (and hence becomes supernatural) it is because "fundamental categories of the universe are disrupted";[3] that is, the taking-on of supernatural qualities is a reaction against the mixing of categories, not a cause of it. In the *Bhagavad Gītā*, Viṣṇu mixes his categories in the other direction (the god becomes incarnate as a mortal) when forces of good and evil are imbalanced (*BhG* 4. 7). In all of these cases the transition from mortal to immortal or the reverse is accompanied by a dangerous disruption of order.

Indian tradition abounds in stories about such transgressors of boundaries, not only sages but kings with spiritual ambitions, like King Nahuṣa and his son Yayāti. Yayāti's ambivalence is graphically expressed by the statement that he actually remained suspended for some time between heaven and earth while the gods tried to figure out what to do about him (*MBh* 1. 76–91; 5. 118–120). So too, when King Triśaṅku tried to enter heaven, a compromise was reached whereby he remained suspended as a constellation in the sky (head downward, significantly) (*Viṣṇu P* 4. 3. 14–15; *H* 9. 89–100; 10. 1–21; *R* 1. 56–59). That these figures are often kings is, I think, relevant to the fact that the two greatest saints of the ancient period—the Buddha and Mahāvīra, the Jina—are said to have been born in royal families.

These figures pose problems, for when a man becomes like a god in India, there are only two possible resolutions: either he must be made to cease being godlike (i.e., he must be corrupted and reduced to his appropriate mortal impotence—the occasion for numerous ribald tales of seduction and trickery), or he must be actually changed into a god—he must "become an Indra" (O'Flaherty 1976, p. 138). This latter solution produces further problems in the pre-*bhakti* period, where the belief that there really ought to be only one Indra at a time is subscribed to by the gods in general (and by Indra in particular); the metaphor of too many suns in the sky is often invoked at these times, and Indra himself (when challenged by Nahuṣa or Yayāti or Triśaṅku) goes off and sulks in a lotus pond until he is restored to his rightful place. For this reason, the first pattern (seduction and corruption) prevails in the early texts, though the second (deification) becomes favored in the *bhakti* texts.

It is easy enough to see the social motivation for the earlier pattern: the Brahmin authors of the texts were appalled at the thought of losing their monopoly in two simultaneous ways—by individuals treading their own paths of spiritual power without paying priests to intercede on their behalf, and by a few particularly gifted individuals actually leading mass defections from the ranks of Hindu orthodoxy to the fast-growing communities of Buddhists, Jainas, Ājīvakas, and similar riffraff. To nip this movement in the bud, they produced moral tales that depicted the path to heaven as a one-way street: it was impossible to move up (in this life), but it was certainly possible to move down, fast, if one were so foolish as to attempt to engage in spiritual activities above one's station. There are many stories of whole castes who fell in this way.

This one-way street led to other models of human development, made possible by the karmic loophole: it was indeed possible to move up in the next life if one adopted a Looking-Glass pace of spiritual activity—running as fast as one could in order to stay in the same place (in this life). More important, however, it was possible to explain apparent upward mobility in this life in terms of true downward mobility in a previous life. This mobility functioned on the social as well as on the individual and mythological level. A caste could "Sanskritize" itself and appear to rise; but if one knew the truth (it was explained), the caste was merely finally scrambling back to the spot from which it had fallen centuries ago (O'Flaherty 1971, pp. 282–84). For a holy man, too, this was the only explanation: he must be merely regaining the heights (heaven) from which he had previously fallen because of some unknown sin (the karmic loophole).

If, in the ancient Indian context, it was a bad thing, a dangerous, antisocial, disruptive change, for a man to become a saint, how, then, does the mythology deal with the lives of actual saints—that is, with the great historical figures, such as the Buddha, Mahāvīra, and Śaṅkara?

They cannot be allowed to straddle the categories of man and god any more than the mythical figures could. The answer is that they are made into gods, by invoking karma to make it all come out even. They are treated like gods pretending to be men; in effect, they are made into avatars. In this view, saints are *born* saints; they do not achieve sainthood or have sainthood thrust upon them. They are *revealed* as having been saints all along (or, rather, gods).

The traditional Hindu belief that at birth one already contains *in nuce* all the possibilities that time will reveal prevents the pre-*bhakti* gods from having any true life-stories; Kṛṣṇa's childhood is first given attention when he makes the transition from epic hero-god to *bhakti* God, and even then he is not *really* a baby, as his miraculous deeds make clear. This attitude also made it impossible for the myth of Indra's "infancy" in the Vedas to have any currency in post-Vedic mythology (W. N. Brown 1950) or for Viṣṇu or Śiva ever to grow up.[4] It is often said that the gods are all twenty-two years old forever, a sybaritic but not particularly challenging fate. Similarly, when the life-stories of the saints begin to be revised, the hagiographers deny them the possibility of a truly human development; there can be no classical Indian hagiographic *Bildungsroman*.

B. The Shazam Syndrome: Divinity Concealed and Revealed

The idea of concealed divinity being gradually revealed is widespread, and it is particularly apt in the Indian context, with its doctrines of *māyā* (the illusion that conceals *all* truths from us, including the great truth of a special sainthood) and the identity of *ātman* and *brahman* (the belief that *every* man conceals a god—God—within him). Thus, although there may be sequence in the life of a saint, "everything is potential all the time."[5] The God-saint involves himself completely from the very start, but he remains hidden, so that the hagiography is a kind of theological striptease, always hinting at more than is actually seen. This concept is beautifully developed in texts such as the *Bhāgavata Purāṇa*, where the apparently mortal Kṛṣṇa is revealed in his full divinity to the reader (or listener) but not to the participants in the drama (*Bh P* 10. 6, 10. 8, 10. 22; O'Flaherty 1975, pp. 213–31). In Mahāyāna Buddhism, the Bodhisattva often appears to be a simpleton but is really a Bodhisattva—a hidden Bodhisattva.[6]

This is the Indian version of the "Shazam" syndrome, a folk motif that can be traced back to the *Odyssey* (where Odysseus the mighty king masquerades as a feeble beggar) and is still very potent in our day (the little crippled newsboy, Billy Batson, says "Shazam" and turns into Captain Marvel). But whereas in many folk variants of this motif the whole emotional point comes from the feeling of transformation and the taking-on of power (the crippled boy becoming the superhero), in India it is the power of knowledge that is revered: the sudden knowledge that the newsboy always *was* Captain Marvel. In the West, Billy Batson becomes transformed into Captain Marvel; in India, Captain Marvel pretends to be Billy Batson, and we alone know that his secret identity is God.

In fact, Indian saints are really like Superman pretending to be Clark Kent; and it is surely significant that Superman comes "from another planet" (one that is named Krypton, the "secret" place). The Shazam syndrome is not as well fitted to the Purāṇic model as to the *bhakti* model, in which the meek and weak are transformed by love into the exalted and mighty. It is never clear, of course, why Superman pretends to be Clark Kent, why he needs a secret identity at all. To give himself a rest, or to protect himself, or because his superpowers periodically wane —these are unsatisfactory answers. The Sanskrit texts attack the same problem, with more success: why does God bother to pretend to be man? (The usual answers offered for the Christian incarnation are totally irrelevant here, as should be clear from the theological context.) One Hindu answer is *līlā*, divine playfulness: he does it for the sheer hell of it (or earth of it), to experience the bittersweet complexities and sensualities that are peculiar to the life of mortals on this planet. The usual Purāṇic answer, however (and more akin to the one given to account for Clark Kent) is that god cannot *help* becoming incarnate, that his divinity wanes.

Another answer to the question of the Hindu god's masquerade as a mortal is *bhakti*: he does it to make it possible for us to gaze upon him; he presents us with a shaded lens through which we can view his solar splendor without being blinded. Thus when Kṛṣṇa's mother gazes inside his mouth to see if he has swallowed dirt, she sees the universe inside him, and herself, and him, and she faints dead away; in order for her to go on living her life, Kṛṣṇa spreads over her his power of illusion in the form of her maternal affection for him, so that she will forget that he is god and know him only as her little boy (*Bh P* 10. 8. 21–45). Similarly, after the doomsday epiphany in the *Bhagavad Gītā*, Arjuna begs Kṛṣṇa to turn back into his old pal Kṛṣṇa, the wily charioteer (*Bh G* 11. 41–46). It is so much easier to love Billy Batson than to love Captain Marvel; at least in India this appears to be so.

Theologically, this belief in love as the reason for incarnation has implications that we will explore at greater length; but from a literary standpoint, the answer makes good and simple sense. We are dealing with stories, and our literary instincts incline us to the complications brought about by the nonsuper alter ego of the supergod, a character superfluous to the basic plot but essential to the entertainment. We demand a hero who has inconsistencies, weaknesses, problems, personality, and we find this either in a mortal hero or in a god so anthropomorphic as to border on the banal. Lakṣmaṇa, by playing the role of alter ego to the stupefyingly virtuous Rāma (as Sancho Panza plays this role for Don Quixote), supplies the interesting negative qualities that the perfect hero, cast in the dull image of the infallible god, cannot indulge in (Goldman 1977). Both parts are essential, for the omnipotent god lurking in the background serves as a foil to make the fallible mortal all the more fascinating and important; Billy Batson is *not* just a crippled newsboy. But given the need for this split-level incarnation, the text can emphasize the primacy of either the god (the Superman syndrome) or the man (the Shazam syndrome).

One can see the transition from the Shazam model to the Superman model at work in the early biographies of the Buddha and Mahāvīra. The old story of the human prince growing up and undergoing conversion—a true hagiography—is stood on its head by the introduction of classical myths explaining the miraculous birth of the hero, a process which Alan Dundes has also demonstrated in the stories of the life of Jesus (Dundes 1977). The Jainas tell of the manner in which Mahāvīra was transferred from one womb to another (Jacobi 1893), a probable borrowing from the *Harivaṃśa* story of the transfer of Kṛṣṇa in the womb (*H* 47–48; cf. O'Flaherty 1975, pp. 206–13). Although Gautama did indeed undergo a period of enlightenment and conversion—the experience of his first encounters with a sick man, an old man, a dead man, and an ascetic—and although he continued to protest that he was merely a human being, the reality of his mortality was quickly undercut by various supernatural episodes introduced into his early life. Thus the Buddhists tell how Queen Māyā, his mother, dreamed that a white elephant entered her womb when she conceived the Buddha, and at his birth it was predicted that he would be either a great emperor or a great saint.

One result of this process of introducing supernatural elements was that the saint was made into a god, a development fully realized in the case of the Buddha only when the Mahāyāna constructed a more elaborate frame of previous births for the incarnated Buddha. Another result, perhaps equally important, was that a local hero was made into a national saint, and the reason for this is not far to seek. In India, were the saint born a human, he would have to be a *particular* human, a member of a particular caste. It would not be enough to say that he was the son of "a poor carpenter" or the child of "a great king"; he would have to be from a particular *jāti* of carpenters or born into a particular royal lineage. Now this would stand as a barrier to the universalization of the cult; but if the saint is God incarnate, he is a member of *everyone's* family. The fact that heterodox movements, including Buddhism, ignored caste did not prevent them from being integrated into the social fabric as a kind of noncaste caste, outside the rest of the groups; and having a founder from a noncaste, inside all groups, facilitated this process.

The concept that saints are gods who have become incarnate on purpose is further developed and expanded in India by the widespread mythology of gods who, when their powers lapse, fall to earth against their will. This pattern occurs on both the explicit and the implicit levels. Explicitly, the god simply falls: he is put under a curse to become incarnate as a human being. This happens to Śiva when he becomes incarnate as Candraśekhara (see below, chap. 4, sec. C); it happens to Viṣṇu when he precipitously beheads the mother of the guru of the demons (*Br P* 2. 3. 72–73; *Vāyu P* 2. 30. 76–100; *Matsya P* 47; *PP* 5. 13); it happens to the royal sage Mahābhiṣa when he cannot resist looking up the skirt of the heavenly Ganges (*MBh* 1. 91. 1–7); it happens to almost everyone who is anyone, at some time or other. Most often, it seems to happen to Indra, the favorite whipping boy of the Brahmin authors: Indra, the refractory king, who foolishly disobeys his wise Brahmin preceptor and is therefore subject to the ultimate degradation—incarnation on earth.

Incarnation may thus be the result of a curse, or of a willing sacrifice by the god, or of both at once. Viṣṇu is cursed to become Rāma because he has decapitated the evil mother, an act that results in the loss of *his* powers, not of hers (this is a pattern that we will explore in chapter 4). But it is also said that Viṣṇu became Rāma on purpose, because the demon Rāvaṇa had been promised that he could not be killed by gods or demons (he had not bothered to mention men, whom he considered too insignificant to represent any serious threat); so Viṣṇu became a man and killed the demon. Similarly, Devī becomes a woman only in order to kill Mahiṣa, who has been granted immunity from anyone but (insignificant) women (see below, chap. 4, sec. C), and she becomes incarnate as a woman in order to help her husband and children when they have been cursed to be mortals (ibid.). But it is also said that Śiva cursed Pārvatī to roam the earth forever because she briefly entertained thoughts of another man (Beck 1969, p. 6). The pure divinity remains in control in heaven, splitting off an impure aspect that falls helplessly to earth. Here, as so often, mortals and women play structurally similar roles in the myths: those who are supposed to be weak are in reality strong, sometimes to the benefit of mankind (when the strong god masks his strength) but sometimes in a way that brings great danger (when the woman takes on powers that she is not supposed to have).

C. Banalization and Derision of the Gods

In this way, gods may actually *become* men, willingly or through a curse. Perching, then, upon the very top of the human band on the god-man continuum, they become saints, godlike men. But in a very different plane of action the gods are often imagined to *be* men, to be *like* men in character; and here they appear not on the top but rather at the very *bottom* of the continuum, as ludicrous men, men who exhibit all the lowest weaknesses of men. Hindu gods (even uppercase Gods, like Śiva and Viṣṇu) begin, by the medieval period, to become not merely human but banal. A contemporary ritual in Sri Lanka demonstrates how conscious the South Asians themselves are of this process. One of the characters asks, "Do your gods help you to clean up the dishes in the evening . . . and bring firewood?" and the other replies, "No, no, our gods aren't that intimate with us." Obeyesekere interprets this as "an insulting reference to the Brahmanic idea of the husband as a god, and yet also someone who helps the women to wash dishes" (Obeyesekere 1980, p. 407). It is also, of course, a satire on the corresponding idea that the god behaves like a husband—who may be worshiped, but who may also be henpecked.

The intimacy with which the Hindus tend to treat their gods is evident from the care of stone idols in temples: they are carried out to have their teeth brushed and their clothes changed, and little favors are done for them; in the hot season they are set on miniature swings and swung for hours in the forecourts of their temples; their backs are scratched, their finicky appetites tempted. In Bengal, Gopinātha (a form of Viṣṇu) is put down for his nap behind a mosquito net; he has toothpicks and a golden ear-scratcher and earplugs (to muffle the cries of the goats slaughtered for Durgā next door).[7] Occasionally, gods and goddesses who persistently fail to respond to their worshipers' requests are verbally abused; sometimes the idol may be taken down and beaten and thrown into the mud "to teach it a lesson" (Carstairs 1957, pp. 65, 133). This detailed anthropomorphism is a form of devotion, an intimacy that in no way reduces the power or status of the god (though it certainly reduces his awesomeness, his *mysterium tremendum*). On the contrary, the "small things" used for the god are made sacred when taken back into the lives of the worshipers. The majesty of the god flows into the mundane items of the ritual; the banality of these items does not deplete his glory.

But the ritual implications of this apparent banalization do not seem to protect the gods when the same process occurs in myth; there the god really *is* derided for his all-too-human shortcomings. The Bengalis subject Śiva to a slapstick mythology: when all the gods are on parade, going to a wedding, Viṣṇu on his Garuḍa bird buzzes Śiva, whose clothes are held up by snakes; the snakes, shying at the bird, slither away into the bushes, and Śiva's pants fall down.[8] What a bathetic plunge from the awesome figures of the Vedic pantheon! In Purāṇic mythology, too, the gods become pitifully bourgeois. In India, God does play dice with the universe (*pace* Albert Einstein), and it is a game of cosmic meaning and ironic fatality. But when Śiva plays dice with Pārvatī, not only does he cheat, but he is *caught* cheating, and, to make matters still worse, he flagrantly denies it; in an uncontrollable outburst of adolescent bad sportsmanship, he finally pulls rank to end the argument and turns into uppercase God (he burns up the universe with his third eye, or turns off all the light in the galaxy, or flexes his metaphysical muscles in some other excessive way). "All *right*," says Pārvatī; "you win, you win." Whereupon he turns back into the Śiva we all know and love and goes off to commit adultery or beg for alms or smoke hash or do something equally banal (O'Flaherty 1973, pp. 223–24, 247–48). When the gods have come to this sorry state, to say that a man is in fact a god in disguise is not only easy to believe, it is almost an insult.

Mockery of the gods has an ancient pedigree in India. It can be traced back to the Ṛg Veda, where rival poets praised their own gods and abused the gods of the opposing faction (*RV* 10. 71, 10. 86, etc.).[9] Obscene banter of a related sort (often making use of the same abusive phrases) persists in the ritual of the horse sacrifice (see below, chap. 6, sec. B) and in such myths as the story of Dakṣa's sacrifice, in which the devotees of Viṣṇu mock Śiva and the devotees of Śiva mock Viṣṇu (O'Flaherty 1976, pp. 272–79). Finally, in the theology of *bhakti* the devotee subjects the god to a "blame-praise" (*ninda-stuti*), in which apparent insults actually represent great compliments (ibid., pp. 308–9), a phenomenon further related to the "hate-devotion" (*dveṣa-bhakti*) pattern that underlies the myths of the erotic death of the demon (see below, chap. 4, sec. C).

Hindu gods are parodies of men, and the parody often emphasizes the animal nature of the human. As a result, these gods are more theriomorphic than anthropomorphic. Like Dionysus in Aristophanes' *Frogs*, Śiva and Indra are larger than life, Gargantuan and magical in their appetites and flaws; they are Tricksters, self-defeating, self-seeking, pure emotion, primeval in their lack of cultural armor against the experiences of life. In this they are "godlike" in a very different sense from the "godlike" saint, but they are godlike all the same.

The gods who experience lust, fear, and anger are *real* to the Hindus, and this reality was able to serve many surprising theological purposes. The humor and disrespect with which the deities are treated served to relieve various tensions, which were channeled into the myth and ritual—particularly sexual tensions, as we have seen. On a cosmic level, too, humor in myth serves to highlight some rather serious theological components: dimming the opposites, the inverse effect, subjective reserve, and the grotesque (Bolle 1968, pp. 41–72). All of these are present in the myths that satirize the Hindu gods.

The two corresponding rapprochements between man and god—god becoming saint and god imagined as human—combine in a series of myths in which gods become *wicked* saints as a result of their own anthropomorphic inadequacies. This process begins with the antagonism between Hindus and Buddhists, which produced (in the early Gupta period) a myth explaining that Viṣṇu had become incarnate as the Buddha in order to teach a wrong doctrine (preaching noninjury and similar mad ideas) to the *demons*, who had been threatening the gods by performing Vedic sacrifices, which gave them great powers. Viṣṇu became the Buddha (some texts, making a clean sweep of the board, say that he became the Jina too), and did his thing; the demons fell for it, and the gods had a field day with them—killing almost all the demons and incidentally wiping out many (but not all, as history proves) *human* Buddhists and Jainas in India (O'Flaherty 1976, pp. 185–211). Thus the Mahāyāna statement that the Buddha was a god incarnate is taken by the post-Mahāyāna Hindus and twisted into proof that he was *their* god incarnate and that he became incarnate in order to corrupt the demons.

The assumption of bad faith in the Buddha avatar is evident from the manner in which later sects used it as a device to discredit one another. Śaṅkara, the subject of several hagiographies, is said to have been an incarnation of Śiva, sent to earth to combat Viṣṇu's Buddha avatar (ibid., p. 209),[10] or an incarnation of a demon sent to preach Buddhism veiled as Vedānta (ibid., p. 210).[11] The *Basava Purāṇa* says that Nārada reported to Śiva that Śaivism was dying out among Brahmins and other castes; Śiva then asked Nandin to become incarnate as the Vīraśaiva saint Basavaṇṇa to preach Vīraśaivism in keeping with orthodox dharma (Dasgupta 1955, 5:43).[12] Another Vīraśaiva saint, Allama Prabhu, is said to have been an incarnation of Śiva who arrived in the world to combat the force of the incarnation of his consort, Pārvatī, who sent down her dark side, Illusion, to tempt him; Allama and the enchantress are elsewhere said to be mere minions of Śiva and Pārvatī, cursed to be born in the world (Ramanujan 1973, p. 143). The motifs of unwilling incarnation, a yogi sent into the world to destroy orthodoxy, and a wicked woman to spur him on are all familiar from classical Hindu myths about nonsaints.

Sectarian Hindus thus regarded their own founders as incarnations of the true god and the founders of rival sects as incarnations of either the false god or of the true god purposely setting out to delude his enemies. This concept of the negative aspect of the saint as incarnate god is evident from the writings of the philosopher Vyāsatīrtha; in order to counter the usual argument that the Vedas must be accepted because God invented them, he stated that "the Buddha himself is an incarnation of God, and yet he deceived the people by false teaching" (Dasgupta 1955, 4:203). By this time, the bad faith of the gods was so widely accepted that to say that a scripture had been taught by a god was to discredit it. "The devil may quote scripture," we say—in defense of the incorruptibility of scripture despite the corrupt minds that may twist it. "Yes," say the Hindus, "but so may God quote scripture"—in affirmation of the corruptibility of scripture because of (or despite) the incorruptible mind that inspired it.

With gods demoted in this way, it is hardly surprising that saints would quickly come to be regarded as gods. What is more difficult to explain is how the *bhakti* movement was able to overcome this negative tradition. Such a revision must have required major upheavals in basic conceptual attitudes toward man and god and the relationship between them, involving a return to Vedic ideas of symbiosis and away from epic-Purāṇic assumptions of strife between man and god. It presupposes a change in the attitude to scripture and in the concept of the religious community; most of all, it requires a change in the way in which social movement—upward mobility—was regarded and in the way in which it was reconciled with cosmic movement—the circular workings of karma. Only in this way could the *bhakti* cult begin to polish up the sadly tarnished halo of the saint who was a fallen god.

The interaction between the early belief that it is dangerous to try to become a god and the later belief that it is nothing particularly special to be a god had a profound effect on the theological attitude toward potential contact between man and god. Moreover, since many of these contacts were sexual—Indra coming down to earth to seduce a mortal woman in the early corpus, and Pārvatī making fun of her husband Śiva when he was out of his mind on hash, in the later corpus—the shifting status of the gods was often reflected in changes in the nature of hierogamies. If gods were more human than humans, what did it mean for a human to fall in love with a god or for a god to make love to a human? These questions, and some of their implications, will be addressed in different ways in subsequent chapters of this book.

4 The Shifting Balance of Power in Indian Hierogamies

The dominant woman is dangerous in Hindu mythology, and the dominant goddess expresses this danger in several different but closely related ways. She appears as the killer of her demon lover, beheading him in a symbolic castration; she dances on the corpse of her consort, impaling herself upon his still animate phallus. This is the nonmaternal goddess, with whom the worshiper does not dare seek erotic contact for fear of losing his powers. But the dominant woman also appears as the mother goddess, with whom the worshiper does not dare seek erotic contact for fear of incest. On the human level, the dangerous woman is the wife whose sexuality is regarded as a threat to her husband, either as the erotic woman, who will drain him of his life, or as the maternal woman, who conjures up the specter of maternal incest. Indeed, these two roles merge in the figure of the sexually aggressive mother, a recurrent image in myths and a persistent stereotype in conventional perceptions of Hindu family relationships. The dichotomy between male authority and female power on the human level provides new conflicts when it sets a pattern on which divine hierogamies are modeled: any woman, especially a goddess, has power, but this power is tamed by making her subservient to her husband; the dominant goddess, however, adds to her power an authority (by virtue of her divinity as well as by her independent character) that violates the basic Hindu categories of male-female relationships.

Throughout this corpus of myths there is an inequality of power structures between male and female deities. In *bhakti* mythology the worshiper is encouraged to seek an erotic liaison with a male god even if this means that the worshiper must change from male to female, but he is not encouraged to seek such a relationship with a goddess. In classical mythology, the god usually succeeds in commiting incest with his daughter; this is in part because the male is not split as the female is (i.e., he may become a father without ceasing to be a consort) and in part because the system encourages sexual contact between an older, dominant man and a younger, weaker woman but not between an older, dominant female and a younger, weaker man. The mother goddess, by contrast, does not usually succeed in committing incest with her son; the son, however, may initiate an erotic liaison with the mother. This inequality also extends to the problem of love in separation, in which the woman's longing is greater than the man's, just as the worshiper's longing for the god is greater than the god's longing for the worshiper. For in orthodox mythology as well as in *bhakti*, the woman represents the devotee, mediating between the male worshiper and the male god—or the goddess.

These patterns of threatening dominance and imposed inequality are challenged and even reversed in Tantric myths and icons that depict the erotic goddess as a life-giving figure who revives the corpse of her husband and infuses him with her own powers. In this world view, the maternal goddess is depicted either as a negative figure (in contrast with the positive erotic goddess) or as an integral part of the supreme goddess, who is simultaneously erotic and maternal. By reversing the flow of fluids, and hence of powers, from the orthodox pattern (male to female) to the esoteric (female to male), Tantric myth and ritual create a pattern that filters back into orthodox Hinduism to release some of the tensions between male authority and female power.

Gods and goddesses (like kings and queens) are often said to have consorts. "Consort," though literally denoting a partner or spouse, is a heavily loaded term, for a consort is usually implied to be a mere appendage, far inferior in power and status to his or her spouse. Among animals, the ultimate male consort is the deep-sea angler fish, who affixes himself to the female, feeds off her body, and eventually atrophies until nothing is left of him but a bag of sexual organs to service the bloated female (R. Burton 1976, p. 11).[1] In divine hierogamies in India, one of the partners is generally a mere consort, far "less equal" than the other. In several significant cases, the stronger partner is the woman, who is a full goddess of the female angler-fish type; in others, the woman is a mere mortal who expresses, through her joyful subservience to her immortal better half, the theological stance of the worshiper before the god. In this chapter I will trace the rise and fall of the dominant female figures in Indian hierogamies, using the term "hierogamy" in its broadest sense, to denote a ritual or mythic sexual union in which at least one of the partners is a deity and which results in a lasting liaison and/or a child.

A. Male Dominance in the Ṛg Veda

In studies of Indian mythology, the Ṛg Veda is usually taken as the beginning; but it would be misleading here to begin with the Vedas, for by the time they were being composed (1200 B.C.) a major power shift had already taken place. In the earlier, Indo-European, period, there appeared in myth and ritual an important goddess, associated with the moon and with mares, who chose a royal human consort on whom she bestowed various powers, though for a limited period. She survives in the Ṛg Veda in the figures of Urvaśī, Saraṇyū, and Yamī, each appearing in a single obscure hymn (see below, chap. 6, sec. C). No worship is offered to this atavistic triad, for they are already pejoratively represented as immoral, dangerous, and cruel. Urvaśī herself admits that "Women have the hearts of hyenas" (*RV* 10. 95. 15), and the Vedic poet remarks of a sexually aggressive wife, "The foolish woman sucks dry the panting wise man" (*RV* 1. 179. 4).

Besides these obscure figures, there are several goddesses of great power in the Ṛg Veda, though relatively few hymns are devoted to them and they are certainly statistically far less important than the male gods who dominate the pantheon. Dawn and Night are personified and praised as beautiful women and sources of life; Indra is said to have done a heroic, manly deed by slaying Dawn, the woman who intended to do evil (*RV* 4. 30. 8–11). Aditi, personified as a female who gives birth by crouching with legs spread, is the cosmic origin of space itself and of earth, as well as being mother of the gods of the sky (*RV* 10. 72). There is no question, however, that the Ṛg Veda casts goddesses in a secondary role; Indra's wife (simply called Indrāṇī, "Mrs. Indra") boasts of his sexual dimensions and prowess in true locker-room style, but one does not learn very much about *her* (*RV* 10. 86).

B. Transition in the Epics

In the epics, we find both male-dominated and female-dominated hierogamies, that is, Vedic and pre- (or non-) Vedic marriages. The *Rāmāyaṇa* shows traces of both: Rāma, a god incarnate as a mortal king, marries Sītā, daughter of the earth and by implication herself a true earth goddess (Jacobi 1893). But there is a serious ambiguity in the immortality of both partners, for Rāma is merely a mortal king in the early layers of the epic and becomes explicitly a god only in the later portions, whereas Sītā, on the other hand, shows traces of having *been* a goddess but is almost always treated as a mortal woman. (The fact that poetic imagery often likens her to a goddess who embodies beneficent nature is not necessarily significant for the theology of the myth, for it amounts to a poetic set piece in literature of this type.) Thus both Rāma and Sītā have ambiguous claims to divine status, and different parts of the epic bring out different aspects of this ambiguity. The first time that Rāma priggishly rejects Sītā after her long sojourn in Rāvana's palace, he is reminded by the gods that he is a god, like them. Nothing is said here of Sītā's being a goddess, though the text does describe her as having a garland that has not withered, a possible hint of divinity, and she survives the ordeal of fire through divine intervention (*R* 6. 103–6). Rāma the god taunts and rejects Sītā the mortal woman, who is helpless to defend herself against him. But when Rāma tries the trick a second time, the tables are turned; Sītā abandons Rāma and returns to the earth when he mistreats her (*R* 7. 42) (just as Urvaśī abandons Purūravas when he violates his contract with her). At this moment, Sītā is clearly a goddess who will survive in her essential form in the earth, leaving behind a helpless mortal to mourn for her. Significantly, in this part of the *Rāmāyaṇa*, Sītā has borne Rāma twin sons, the usual offspring of the Indo-European goddess; when she is a mother, he no longer treats her as a whore—but *she* rejects *him* (see below, chap. 6, sec. C). A passage interpolated here has Rāma refer to Sītā as being "like Lakṣmī" and to the Earth as his mother-in-law, emphasizing Sītā's divinity (*R* 7, app. 13, 8 and 13); but these phrases do not occur in the earlier layers of the epic. Clearly, Sītā is a transitional figure.

In the *Mahābhārata*, the Vedic model appears in the figure of Kuntī, wife of Pāṇḍu; when he is prevented by a curse from having intercourse with her (*MBh* 1. 109–11), she begs five Vedic gods to impregnate her and produces the five Pāṇḍavas, who all marry Draupadī, a multiform of Kuntī herself (Hiltebeitel 1976, pp. 79–102). Here is a dramatic instance of a mortal woman with five immortal consorts. But the pre-Vedic, Indo-European goddess survives in the form of Śrī, the fickle goddess of prosperity, who plays fast and loose with a number of unfortunate mortal kings (ibid., pp. 144–92). Many volumes have been written about these great female figures; I cite them here only to show that in the epic period the divine-consort game (*līlā*) could still be played with either of two sets of rules.

C. Female Dominance in the Purāṇas

In the Purāṇas, male-dominated and female-dominated couples both occur, and one can occasionally find them side by side in a single text, as in the epics. But, by and large, Purāṇic sectarianism was developed in such a way that it was almost always necessary to stand up and be counted on the side of either the god or the goddess. The dominant female can be traced back to various non-Indo-European origins: to the Indus Valley Civilization of 2300 B.C., with its crude terra-cotta mother goddesses, and, thousands of years later, to Dravidian myths of a goddess who devours her consort (Shulman 1976a, pp. 120–47). On a different plane, one might see a contributing element in some of the basic precepts of Sāṅkhya philosophy that filtered down, on a *Reader's Digest* level, to the Purāṇic texts: the concept of Prakṛti, the female principle, more visible, immanent, and active than her purer but inert spiritual constant companion, Puruṣa, the Male. In Purāṇic mythology (though perhaps not always in Purāṇic theology), the Goddess often comes to affect her consort as Prakṛti affects Puruṣa—animating him and implementing his latent powers.

Beheading and Castration

In certain Tamil texts (which may well underlie the Sanskrit), and in many Greek and Indian myths as well, the Goddess not only dominates her consort but kills him, cutting off his head. In this she resembles the female praying mantis, who bites off her consort's head, and various female spiders who devour those of their suitors who carelessly omit to present the arachnid equivalent of a box of chocolates (a neatly wrapped fly). By eating his head, the mantis removes her consort's inhibitions and frees him to copulate more vigorously; by eating the rest of him afterwards, she nourishes her fertilized eggs (R. Burton 1976, pp. 10–11, 67–68). The parallels are obvious: although the Goddess is not explicitly said to bite off her lover's head, she does behead him, and she is depicted as a creature with gaping mouth and bloody fangs, as well as with another "mouth" that devours the male (O'Flaherty 1973, pp. 186–90). Moreover, Kālī is sometimes represented as a spider.

When this myth appears in the Sanskrit texts, the unwifely behavior of the Goddess is at first masked and justified by the statement that her buffalo consort is a demon whose primary function, vis-à-vis the Goddess, is to be killed by her. Most Sanskrit texts play down their erotic relationship, and some omit it altogether (O'Flaherty 1975, pp. 238–49, 333–34; O'Flaherty 1973, pp. 184–86). The Goddess as *the* central deity first emerges clearly in the *Devīmāhātmya* (a long poem, probably interpolated into the *Mārkaṇḍeya Purāṇa* between the fifth and seventh centuries A.D.). In this text, she is said to be created expressly in order to kill the buffalo demon, Mahiṣa; she is created by a merging of the key powers of all of the most powerful of the male gods (*MP* 80), a significant inversion of the process by which the Vedic Puruṣa creates the universe by means of his own dismemberment.

Another Vedic inversion further highlights the concealed eroticism in the story of the buffalo demon and the Goddess. Richard L. Brubaker has compared this myth to the passage in which Prajāpati's daughter assumes various animal forms in a vain attempt to avoid his lustful advances (*BAU* 1. 4. 4; and see below, chap. 9, sec. C):

> As the Devī pursues and closes in on the *asura* [demon] he repeatedly changes bodily form, from buffalo to lion to man to elephant and so on, escaping to a new form just as the old one is conquered or slain. Thus the two reenact in reverse the Upaniṣadic tale of the origin of creatures: each time the primordial Puruṣa copulates with his female counterpart, she, fleeing his sexual aggression, changes into the female of another species, escaping to the new body just as the old one is impregnated (Brubaker 1978, p. 93).

In one Sanskrit expansion of the *Devīmāhātmya*, the erotic element that is played down in the earlier text emerges quite clearly, only to be challenged and inverted:

> Mahiṣa asked Brahmā to promise that, if he had to die, it would be at the hands of a woman; he asked this in order to ensure that he would not die, since he regarded it as unthinkable that a woman should overpower him. Devī was duly created; she enticed Mahiṣa, who proposed marriage. But she replied that she wanted to kill him, not to sleep with him—that she had become a woman in the first place only in order to kill him; that, although she did not appear to be a man, she had a man's nature and was merely assuming a woman's form because he had asked to be killed by a woman. Moreover, she said to Mahiṣa's messenger, "Your master is a great fool, and certainly no hero, to want to be killed by a woman. For to be killed by one's mistress gives sexual pleasure to a man without balls but misery to a hero." The besotted Mahiṣa, however, was persuaded by a counselor, who suggested that this clearly antierotic speech was the amorous love talk of a passionate woman: "She wishes to bring you into her power by frightening you. This is the sort of indirect speech that enamored women use toward the man they love." Mahiṣa then dressed up in his best suit and boasted to the Goddess that he was a man who could make a woman very happy. She laughed and killed him by beheading him (*DBP* 5. 2–11).

This variant emphasizes the castrating, phallic aspect of the Goddess to such an extent that an actual sex change is suggested. Though she is so beautiful that she inspires the demon with destructive erotic passion, she herself is so devoid of erotic feelings that she insists that she is really a man and, moreover, that her would-be consort is *not* really a man but a mere eunuch (*klība*). Clearly, only one of them has any balls, and *he* is not the one; to clinch this argument, she insists (irrationally) that only a eunuch would wish to experience a Liebestod with a woman.

The explicit connection between the battle and the desired sexual union comes out in the speech of the counselor, who interprets the challenge as "amorous love talk"; he says,

> "When she said, 'I will cause your master [*pati*, also the word for husband] to lie down in the bed that is made of battle,' that was an obvious reference to love play in the 'inverted' position [*viparīta-ratikrīḍā*]. And when she said, 'I will take away your life's breath [*prāṇa*],' she meant (that she would take away) semen, for semen is the life's breath" (*DBP* 5. 10. 32–34; cf. 5. 11. 19–21 and 25–77).

The aggressive woman thus rides astride, like the castrating mare: her sexual supremacy is expressed through a martial image: she holds an erect phallic sword in sculptures depicting the slaying of Mahiṣa. This aggression is immediately coupled with the quintessential metaphor of sexual danger, the draining of life's breath through the draining of semen. The explicit meaning of this text is that the battle that is overtly being proposed is, by implication, a sexual union; but it plays upon the more usual notion (of which it is a self-conscious inversion) that every actual sexual act is, by implication, a fatal battle. In a more positive vein, the fact that Mahiṣa desires to marry and/or battle the Goddess implies that either marriage or battle may be a way of achieving unity; that either may serve as an initiatory death leading to a desired transformation; that strong emotion, be it lust or hatred, seeks a conflict that leads ultimately to the resolution of all conflict in death.

In a still more explicitly sexual variant of this myth, in South India, a Brahmin woman beheads her consort, cuts off his penis, puts it in his mouth, and then enters the fire (as Satī and Sītā do).[2] This myth is related to the myth and ritual of the buffalo sacrifice, in which a man, dressed either as the buffalo demon or as a woman, bites the neck and drinks the blood of the sacrificial animal (usually a lamb or goat) (Hiltebeitel 1980; Brubaker 1978, pp. 226–29). Here is a rare but revealing example of simultaneous beheading and castration, and its close relationship with the buffalo sacrifice supplies valuable support for the hypothesis that Mahiṣa is beheaded and/or castrated by the Goddess.

Throughout the myths of Mahiṣa, beheading is closely linked to castration, and intercourse to the devouring of the penis (or the seed). The Freudians (beginning with Freud himself, in *The Interpretation of Dreams*) regard beheading as a "well-known unconscious device of the upward displacement of the genitals" (Kakar 1978, p. 99), a hypothesis substantiated in a number of Hindu phenomena. We have encountered the Hindu belief that semen is stored in the head. This concept is acted out in myths (as in the episode when Śūrpanakhā's nose is cut off to punish her for making sexual advances [*R* 3. 17–19], a punishment that has been interpreted as a clitoridectomy [Kakar 1978, p. 99]) and in rituals, and Carstairs notes that in quarrels arousing sexual jealousy the opponent's nose might be cut off, a "symbolic castration" (Carstairs 1958, p. 47).

It may appear paradoxical that the Goddess beheads (castrates) her consort in order to free him to copulate with her, but only if the myth is interpreted in rigidly anthropomorphic terms. Death as an erotic release is a recurrent motif in Hindu mythology, on various levels. It appears in the ancient ceremony in which the queen copulates with a *dead* stallion (see below, chap. 6, sec. B), in the medieval myth of Śiva dancing with the corpse of Satī (O'Flaherty 1973, pp. 298–300, and 1975, pp. 249–51), and, closest to the present instance, in the Tantric image of the Goddess holding a severed head while she engages in intercourse with the corpse of Śiva or straddles a copulating couple (Vequaud 1977, plate 58; cf. plate 1, below).[3] In many of the images of the Goddess and the corpse, the only part of her partner that is alive is the erect phallus, which has become animatedly separate from the rest of the body (just as the head that she holds in her hand has become literally separated from its body); in this icon, Śiva has become the quintessential angler-fish consort.[4] (See plate 2.) The Goddess herself provides a further parallel for the motif of the animation of the separate phallus in the myth in which her amputated *yoni* becomes a shrine where Śiva dwells forever with her (*DBP* 7. 30; *BVP* 4. 42–43). Similarly, the severed head of the demon Rāhu not only remains alive but becomes far more powerful than before, able to swallow the sun and the moon (*MBh* 1. 17. 5–10; O'Flaherty 1975, p. 278). A still closer example is the castrated phallus of Śiva, which first wreaks havoc upon the sages responsible for its severance and then becomes the instrument of universal fertility (O'Flaherty 1973, pp. 133–36). The equation of head with phallus is justified not merely on the basis of Freudian observations (though these are instructive) but from the Indian texts, where semen is said to rise into and be stored in the head (see above, chap. 2, sec. B). Moreover, we will soon see that the mythology of the consort as corpse provides ample support for the concept of sexual resuscitation. In this way, castration and beheading are as likely to initiate as to terminate mythical erotic activity.

In the Tantric icons, the goddess stretches out her tongue to drink the streams of blood spurting from the severed heads. The tongue in this context is phallic and life-destroying. As the blood she drinks is, on the explicit level, her own, she presents yet another example of the breast that feeds itself, and she is thus the quintessential evil mother and phallic mother. A significant reversal of this symbolism may be seen in the bowdlerized gloss of this icon given by many contemporary Hindus: "She sticks out her tongue in shock when she realizes that she is trampling on her own husband." This interpretation reduces the dominating demonic goddess to the properly submissive wife.

Whose is the head held by the Headless Goddess, Chinnmastakā? In most paintings, it appears to be her own, for the head matches her headless body in color and other qualities; she decapitates herself in order to copulate with the male figure lying beneath her. Decapitation in this context leads to total freedom and release, for her or for her worshipers (in instances where she straddles a copulating couple). If the image can be related to the myth of Mahiṣa, however, it is his head she holds as she marries/murders him. But in light of the widespread myth of the castration of Śiva, in icons where Śiva replaces Mahiṣa as the consort of the Goddess one may well be justified in viewing the head she holds as Śiva's; for though I know of no myth in which she is said to behead or castrate Śiva, the image of Devī placing her feet on the shoulders and head of Mahiṣa as she beheads him is strikingly similar in its iconic depiction to the image of Kālī dancing on the (ithyphallic) corpse of Śiva, with her sword in her hand. The question remains ambiguous, perhaps purposely ambiguous; captions on the paintings do not offer much help, to my present knowledge, but it is possible that some Tantric texts may identify the head as Śiva's.

One strange variant of the Mahiṣa myth, which appears in South Indian texts in both Sanskrit and Tamil, supports both the contention that the head is Śiva's and the hypothesis that the beheading is a castration. In this myth, after the Goddess has killed Mahiṣa, his head sticks to her hand just as Brahmā's head sticks to Śiva's after that beheading (a beheading that has, in its turn, strong overtones of castration). After bathing in a *tīrtha*, the Goddess discovers that there is a Śiva-*liṅga* on Mahiṣa's headless torso—i.e., in the place where his head had been (*SKP* 1. 3. 2. 18–21; Shulman 1976a). In the context of the story, the main function of this epiphany is to identify Mahiṣa as a devotee of Śiva and hence to plunge the Goddess into an agony of guilt, necessitating a complex expiation; but in the context of the patterning of the variants of the myth, the *liṅga* functions to demonstrate the identity of Mahiṣa and Śiva and, moreover, the identity of Mahiṣa's head and Śiva's phallus. These variants, particularly in the Tamil, abound in implicit and even explicit statements of the identity of Mahiṣa and Śiva.

Yet another possible victim as donor of the severed head is suggested both by evidence we have of a ritual employed in the worship of the Goddess and by the possible significance of the episode in psychoanalytic terms. Both suggest that the head may well belong to the devotee of the Goddess. Purāṇic and Tantric mythology, as well as contemporary local mythology, abound in tales of male devotees who cut off their own heads in an act of devotion to Kālī. In one interesting variant of this theme, a short novel by Thomas Mann, the wife of one of them (the rather epicene Brahmin) "accidentally" places her husband's head on the far more attractive body of his friend (Mann 1941); here, as in the myth of Reṇukā, the sexual tension imposed upon a wife by her husband's asceticism is resolved by the production of two mediating figures; in this myth these two figures combine the personae of the nonerotic husband and the erotic consort. In the myth of Reṇukā, the one who actually performs the beheading is her son (see below, chap. 6), which brings us to a second possibility, a variant of the first: the severed head belongs to the devotee visualized as the son of the mother goddess.

We will soon explore the implications of the relationship between the devotee who plays the role of consort as child and the sexually aggressive mother. But at least one manifestation of this relationship may be seen in the Tantric iconic image of the severed head held by the Goddess, and its value lies in the way that it resolves the tension between the myths in which the Goddess beheads her consort and those in which the consort (devotee) beheads himself for her: in the psychoanalytic view, the sexually assaulted child "sacrifices his masculinity" to the mother in order to escape the unbearable conflict engendered by his sexual excitation by her (Kakar 1978, p. 102). In other words, he castrates himself in order to prevent her from castrating him; the devotee cuts off his head because he knows the Goddess wishes him to do so. Thus the myths of cutting off one's own head, symbolic of self-castration, describe acts of sacrificial worship of the mother goddess. From these myths, it is evident that female dominance is fraught with Freudian dangers. In Indian mythology, the female is truly deadlier than the male.

At this point, a caveat is perhaps in order. Whether or not mythology in general is rife with sexual symbolism, as the Freudians maintain, mythology about sex is certainly rife with sexual symbolism, and, since that is the professed subject of much of this book, numerous forms of destruction and mutilation will here be glossed as symbolic of castration. Nevertheless, it should not be forgotten that these myths are also about the relationship between human and divine forces, and on this level castration, in itself symbolized by various euphemisms and distortions, is in turn symbolic of the loss of other, more general powers. The great forces of sex, god, intelligence, kingship, are all aspects of a central force, spokes of a wheel; though their particular manifestations are very different, in the myths they are *structured* in the same way because they tend to function in the same way. It is possible to move from one spoke to another by crossing at the central nave: castration may be symbolized by beheading, but beheading may also be symbolized by castration, in the sense that the goddess's emasculation of the demon is symbolic of her total triumph over him. The link between the seed in the head and the seed in the groin may be read in either direction: eroticism in the brain, or creative mental power in the groin. Castration may symbolize the loss of the power of imagination; psychoanalysis itself may function in this way, as is betrayed in the idiom for undergoing this particular form of mutilation: getting one's head shrunk.

Thus, although I will tend throughout this study to focus upon the sexual meanings of mutilation, the theological element is always implicitly present (and will become explicit, particularly in chapter 8); for the central nave of all of these spokes is the power to be reborn, and the challenge to survive the threat of the goddess is, therefore, far more than the challenge to surmount the threat to sexual integrity: it is the challenge to survive and to grow.

Change of Sex

Theologically, the concept of the dominance of the female divinity is in some ways a godsend—or, perhaps, a goddess-send. The passionate worship of god required by the *bhakti* movement, which developed simultaneously with the emergence of the worship of the Goddess during the first few centuries of the Christian era, often led the worshiper to imagine himself in an erotic relationship with God. To do this in India was to establish an erotic bond with an Other, a member of the opposite sex—to assume the stance of the consort. *Bhakti* stands here in clear contrast with both Vedāntic and Tantric Hinduism; and the fact that the Purāṇas generally follow the *bhakti* pattern of having the worshiper identify with the consort may be taken as yet one more instance of the generally non-Vedāntic thinking of the Purāṇas. For in Advaita monism, the worshiper *is* the god and cannot possibly approach god erotically; in Tantrism, too, the worshiper occasionally identifies with the consort but more often visualizes himself as the god (or the goddess, as is often the case). But in the qualified nondualism of Rāmānuja it is indeed possible to love god as an Other, and in *bhakti* texts this is the general rule, as it is in most Purāṇic rituals. Indeed, the medieval *bhakti* philosopher Rūpagosvāmin specified that, when the worshiper is selecting a character in the divine *līlā* with whom to identify—or, rather, when he tries to understand which character in the myth of the *līlā* is the one *he really is* —he may choose any character *except* the god (*Bh P* 3. 25. 34).[5] This prohibition holds true, by and large, for the worship of Kṛṣṇa; in the cults of Śiva and Devī, however, the worshiper does tend to identify with the god as often as with the consort. The process of identification is carried even further, in fact, in some forms of Tantrism where the worshiper visualizes himself as both the god and the goddess; here, as in the hagiography of Caitanya, the adept identifies with both the god and his consort simultaneously. Indeed, since Caitanya's religion owes significant elements to both Tantrism and *bhakti*, it might be said that his Tantrism led him to identify with Kṛṣṇa and that his *bhakti* led him to identify with Rādhā.

The devotee visualizes himself as a woman not merely because god is male but because in the Hindu view the stance of the ideal devotee is identical with the stance of the ideal woman:

> The goal of the devotees, who are spiritually female, is to be completely controlled by the male deity. One can also point to evidence in those texts which indicates that this is how the god conducts himself vis-à-vis his divine spouse. Male dominance–female subordination in a marital relationship is an important Tamil social value which also gains expression in a devotional context. . . . As Nammāḻvār in the role of a gopī pointedly says, "Our female nature yields to you" (*Tiruvāymoli* 10. 3. 6). Women yield; proud men don't. Men must renounce their masculinity if they would be devotees (Yocum 1979, pp. 5, 19).

In South Indian *bhakti*, with its emphasis on subservience before god, the meek have a head start and women are well trained to be devout.

One obvious way for the male worshiper to visualize an erotic relationship with a male god would be through homosexual imagery, but in India this never occurred on an explicit level; for homosexuality there is generally regarded as a shameful aberration, known to be fairly common in fact but condoned only if practiced in secret. The erotic bond must be at least superficially heterosexual, and this led to immediate problems. When god is Kṛṣṇa or Śiva, the female worshiper may respond without imagining a change of sex (though with Śiva the erotic relationship leads to dangers that must be hedged with protective ritual); but the authors of most classical texts were male, and the male worshiper must somehow become female. This change of sex is managed in various ingenious ways in the complex theology of Rādhā. It often took the form of transvestism, which may be closely linked with homosexuality (as in the notorious case of the Hinjras, transvestites and homosexual prostitutes); indeed, with or without transvestism, the male worshipers of Kṛṣṇa who imagine themselves as gopīs have been open to charges that their behavior reveals "a thinly-veiled longing for him [Kṛṣṇa] as a homosexual lover" (Carstairs 1958, pp. 60, 163).

As a permanent way of visualizing one's relationship with god, however, change of sex was an extreme step, and one not taken when there were other, more convenient, alternatives. Change of sex remained important for saints of both sexes, but for most *bhaktas* it applied to the man alone; just as androgynes are primarily male, so saints are primarily female: male saints become female, but female saints generally remain female (Ramanujan 1978). This bias toward the female worshiper is in part conditioned by the tendency to visualize god as male, but it is also a result of the nature of the deity when god does happen to be visualized as female.

Some of the emotional connotations of contact with a female deity will have become clear by now from the discussions of the dangers of sexual contact (chapter 2) and the dangers of contact with the gods (chapter 3), but this is merely the tip of the iceberg, as we shall see in the course of the present chapter. These dangers stand in the way of what might otherwise seem a delightfully simple solution to the problem of the male worshiper's erotic relationship with god; it is not merely a matter in which the worshiper can assume that god is a woman so that he himself can remain smugly male. Ironically, the same factors that we will find playing a part in the self-castration implicit in either change of sex or transvestism are brought into even more violent action in the worship of the Goddess, since the bloodthirsty Devī is not the sort of lady to whom anyone but a true masochist would choose to make love. One ironic result of this was that worshipers of the Goddess occasionally became transvestites or even eunuchs, just like the worshipers of the male god; for since it is generally the lascivious demons who are dominated (and killed) by Devī, the worshiper becomes female in order to become her servant or imitator[6] and thus avoid the castration that is an inherent danger in an erotic liaison with her. Here, as so often, the male worshiper is in a no-win situation: he must become female to unite with the male god, and he must become female in order to *avoid* uniting with the female god. By this logic, men become women or homosexuals in order to escape the sexually threatening mother, not (as in the Kṛṣṇa-Rādhā theology) in order to unite sexually with the erotic nonmother.

(In Tantrism, the male worshiper may become female for a different reason: he must identify with the female deity, not with her consort.)

Moreover, the overwhelming prominence of the Goddess as mother made incest a barrier to a hierogamy in this context. We have encountered, and will again encounter, the incest inherent in the worship of the Goddess and responsible for the castration or self-castration of her consort/son. This psychology may well have been at work on an unconscious level (what people think). On a more explicit level, however, incest is denied, and any explicit hierogamy with the Mother is out of the question (what people think they think). Thus, although an incestuous hierogamy underlies much of the motivating force and symbolism of cults of the Mother, the official mythology of hierogamy shied away from it. The resistance to any attempt to combine the images of divine female consort and divine mother may be seen in the mythology of Rādhā, who is almost never said to be a mother; when, on one rare occasion, she does give birth (to an egg), she kicks it away in anger, and her husband places a curse of eternal barrenness upon her (*BVP* 2. 2–3). In this, Rādhā imitates the quintessential evil mother, the mother of the sun, who rejects her son as a "dead egg" (see below, chap. 6, sec. C).

One may therefore distinguish several variants of the motif of change of sex, and these fall into approximately chronological groups. In the ancient period (as we shall see in chapter 6), male worshipers of female divinities experienced themselves as male, and no change was needed. In orthodox Hinduism and the religion of devotion (*bhakti*) to a male god (Viṣṇu or Śiva), the devotee regards himself as a female worshiping a male god, and in more emotional manifestations of this devotion a change of sex is imagined. In Śākta religion (the worship of the Goddess), the male worships a female divinity; but since this is a nonerotic relationship, the male worshiper becomes a female in order to serve the Goddess. In Tantrism, however, the erotic relationship with the Goddess is once again accepted, as in the ancient cult, and the male worshiper may retain and enhance his masculinity in the service of his Goddess (see below, chapter 8).

The Transformation of the Consort: Pārvatī

Indian goddesses can be divided into two distinct categories. The first group are goddesses of the tooth (or of the genitals—the two concepts being linked in the motif of the *vagina dentata*); they are worshiped in times of crisis, such as epidemics, and are ambivalent, dangerous, and erotic figures. The second group are the goddesses of the breast, endemic and auspicious, bountiful and fertile, linked to the life-cycle. Goddesses of the breast provide role models for the wife: they are subservient to the husband. Goddesses of the tooth do not provide such models; though they have consorts, they dominate them and play nonfeminine, martial roles as well.[7] In South India, a similar contrast prevails between the marriages of the goddess Mīnākṣī at Madurai and the goddess Pārvatī at Chidambaram (S. Daniel 1978). To establish an emotional bond with a goddess of the breast (such as Lakṣmī or Mīnākṣī) requires no change of sex for a male worshiper, since as the mother she is gracious to everyone and as the wife she is subservient to her husband. It is difficult, however, to regard her as an erotic object. Therefore, when the tight social structure which the breast goddess embodies breaks down, a looser mechanism for structuring power exchanges is needed; erotic bonds then take over, and the worshiper seeks the goddess who is *not* the benevolent mother.[8]

Another expression of this contrast suggests a distinction between high-ranking goddesses, who are sexually controlled (and whose power lies in their husbands), and low-ranking goddesses or witches, who are sexually free and attack men (Beck 1969). (There is also an intermediary group of unmarried goddesses over whom there is some degree of control and who are not actively aggressive.) Significantly, although food is given to the low-ranking goddesses to placate them, there is no reciprocity in this transaction; but the high-ranking goddesses, by contrast, are able to give back the food given to them, in the form of the *prasāda* distributed to the worshipers. The fact that one cannot accept the *prasāda* from the unmarried, low-ranking female divinities links this hierarchy into the food symbolism of the cycle of fluids and the rituals of the mare: the high-ranking goddess is a mother, a cow, a giver of food, while the low-ranking goddess is a whore, a mare, a devourer of one's essence.

Devī (who in her full form embodies both aspects of female divinity—both cow and mare) is thus split between her maternal persona, which becomes increasingly abstract, and her erotic and martial persona, which becomes increasingly specific. She breaks down into a goddess of the breast and a goddess of the tooth, with cult and myth emphasizing the latter and consigning the former to the realms of pure theology (with some exceptions, such as the cult of Lakṣmī at Diwali). But even when divested of her maternal role and, with it, the incest taboo against an erotic liaison, the goddess of the tooth is a formidable prospect as a consort. Some of her male devotees did indeed seek the divine Liebestod with her, but not many.

Instead, another line was followed, in which a dominant, divine female "consort" was developed by the inversion of an already existing, acceptable, relatively peaceful marriage between a dominant male god and a subservient mortal woman. This took place primarily in the Purāṇic mythology of Śiva and Pārvatī, from which most classical Śākta texts developed (though some were based on the Kṛṣṇa-Rādhā mythology, as C. M. Brown [1974] has shown). In the early layers of this corpus, Pārvatī, the daughter of the mountain Himālaya, is an ambiguous semidivinity, like Sītā. Although poetic metaphors accorded her divine status (Ingalls 1965, pp. 27–29), she is the quintessence of the lowly mortal woman worshiping the lofty male god. She literally worships the phallus, as she is depicted doing on so many South Indian temples and as she is imitated in doing by young girls in Bengal, who make sand *liṅgas* (O'Flaherty 1973, pp. 11, 231); she undergoes physical torture to catch Śiva's attention; she purifies herself to be worthy of him. Like Sītā, she must enter fire (in her first incarnation, as Satī) to be reborn as Pārvatī, establishing the precedent for the very epitome of subservience to the husband: the institution of *suttee*.

Pārvatī's ambiguous status as mortal/immortal is the pivot of the myth, the focal point of transition between male-dominated and female-dominated hierogamies. Below Pārvatī is the figure of the merely mortal worshiper of the God; but above her, and infusing her with power, is the figure of Devī, the Goddess herself, regarded not only as *a* divinity but as *the* divinity. Thus, depending upon the point of view of the particular text telling the story, Pārvatī may act more like her mortal counterparts (totally subservient to Śiva) or more like her immortal alter ego (totally dominant over Śiva). In fact, on all three levels she is a single goddess, but, as the context shifts, different aspects of her are brought into play.

The first aspect, the mortal woman subordinate to the god, is developed at length in many Purāṇic texts. Śiva expounds various Tantric doctrines to Pārvatī, who responds either like one of Socrates' straight men ("Tell me more, O wise one") or by falling asleep. At this, the narrator of the Purāṇa invariably remarks, "Naturally a mere woman could not be expected to understand metaphysical discussions," but Pārvatī is nevertheless punished—usually by being given a curse to become incarnate as a mortal and/or banished from the God's presence, two neatly appropriate fates for the consort who fails to match up to the theological majesty of her husband.

The myth of the Liebestod is removed from the Goddess in another way, as well. The demon who lusts to marry the Goddess and is killed by her in an ecstasy of sexual/martial confrontation appears in a strangely garbled form in several later Śākta Purāṇas that depict Pārvatī as the loving wife even though she is an incarnation of the all-powerful Goddess. In one myth, the demon Āḍi seeks to seduce and kill not her but Śiva; to do this, he must change into a woman (as the worshiper who seeks union with Kṛṣṇa must do), and he places teeth in "his" vagina. Śiva is on to him, however, in more ways than one, and, by placing an adamantine weapon on his own phallus, kills the demon in the most literal of love deaths. It is perhaps significant that during this bizarre episode Pārvatī is out of town at a yogic beauty parlor having her complexion made lighter, to please her light-skinned husband; she does this by sloughing off her old dark persona (the man-eating Kālī, who disappears conveniently into the Vindhya mountains until she is needed again) and returning as Gaurī, the Golden Girl—the pretty wife, the acceptable consort (*Sk P* 1. 2. 27–29; O'Flaherty 1973, pp. 186–90; and O'Flaherty 1975, pp. 251–62).

The Mediation of Pārvatī

Curiously, the assumption of male dominance is maintained even in certain episodes that occur in the great Śākta Purāṇas, in which the Goddess is clearly more powerful than the uxorious divinity whom she deigns to marry. Such an episode occurs in the *Kālikā Purāṇa*. After the Goddess becomes incarnate as Pārvatī in order to marry Śiva, she consents to descend further in order to be born as the princess Tārāvatī, who is later married to King Candraśekhara, an incarnation of Śiva. She does this in part to keep an eye on Śiva (who had been given a curse to become incarnate as a mortal king as a result of trying to rape the goddess Sāvitrī, whom, he lamely insists, he had mistaken for Pārvatī); in part to do him a favor (for he begs her to become Tārāvatī so that he can fulfill the second part of the curse—to beget children on a mortal woman—without being unfaithful to Pārvatī; this is a scruple that did not, apparently, bother him when he was chasing Sāvitrī but one that Pārvatī magnanimously accepts at face value); and in part to do a similar favor for two of her adopted immortal children (Bhṛṅgin and Mahākāla, who had been given a curse to be reborn as monkey-faced mortals in punishment for having inadvertently caught sight of Pārvatī naked; as Tārāvatī, she will, by giving birth to them, fulfill *their* curse as well as Śiva's).

Despite the myth's firm grounding in the female-dominated hierogamy, the old Vedic pattern of male dominance surfaces in the central episode:

> One day when Tārāvatī was bathing in the river, a sage saw her and was overcome by lust for her. He said, "You must be a goddess or a demoness who has become mortal in order to enjoy the pleasures of the flesh. You must be Pārvatī or Śacī, the wife of Indra." But she replied, "I am not a goddess, but merely a mortal

> queen, Tārāvatī, wife of King Candraśekhara." When the sage continued to make unwanted advances, she tricked him by substituting a look-alike sister, but the sage cursed her: "You will be raped by Śiva in his terrifying form and bear him a pair of monkey-faced sons."
>
> Hearing of this curse, Candraśekhara kept Tārāvatī in an inaccessible terrace on the top of the palace, where he himself went to make love to her. One day, when Tārāvatī was worshiping Śiva, she thought of Candraśekhara and did not distinguish between the two of them. Then, at Śiva's request, Pārvatī entered into Tārāvatī and Śiva approached her in the form of a Kāpālika, wearing a garland of bones and disgusting clothing, with a deformed and evil-smelling body. Tārāvatī received him with great joy and then immediately gave birth to two sons with monkey faces. Then Pārvatī left the body of Tārāvatī and deluded her so that she did not recognize herself as an incarnation of Pārvatī. When Tārāvatī saw the two boys, she thought that she had been unfaithful to her husband, and she wept in grief and anger. Then the sage Nārada came to them and explained that they were incarnations of Śiva and Pārvatī, and he said to Candraśekhara, "Take Tārāvatī upon your lap and close your eyes and let her close her eyes, and when you open them you will see your divine nature." They did so; and when they had arrived at perfect understanding, Nārada said, "Now you must close your eyes and return to mortal understanding until you give up your bodies." Then they closed and opened their eyes, and they thought, "We are mortals." And as time passed they neglected the twins that had been begotten by the god (*Kālikā P* 49–54; cf. O'Flaherty 1973, pp. 205–9).

Despite the constant theological reminders that they are gods incarnate, Tārāvatī and Candraśekhara avoid the hierogamy at all costs and abhor the twins, who remain as proof that it has in fact taken place. Tārāvatī is depicted as a trembling, ignorant woman visited by the uncanny, unsavory figure of the orgiastic god, possessed by him (rape, she calls it), and then abandoned—ruined, ashamed, and awkwardly unable to account to her husband for the two monkey-faced infants.

We have seen that Pārvatī generally mediates between mortal women and the omnipotent Goddess. In the myth of Tārāvatī, the Goddess appears on three distinct levels. As Devī, she is the supreme divinity above all other gods and goddesses. As Pārvatī, she pretends to serve her husband Śiva docilely (and helps him out of a tight spot) but in reality controls the event through her higher aspect, Devī; this is a manifestation of the familiar syndrome in which omnipotent gods veil themselves with mortal attributes. And finally she appears as Tārāvatī, the mortal queen. Pārvatī knows that she is Devī and even has conversations with Devī (as is often the case when a Hindu god "becomes" a lower form of divinity while still continuing to exist as the "full" god). Though Tārāvatī experiences a confrontation with Pārvatī, she does not communicate with Devī at all and immediately forgets even her identity with Pārvatī. Pārvatī is therefore the mediator between the omniscient Devī and the ignorant Tārāvatī, who have no contact with each other except through her. Yet there are strong lines tying Devī to Tārāvatī; such motifs as the birth of twins (particularly theriomorphic twins) and their implied incestuous relationship with their mother are remnants of the ancient myth of the mare goddess (see below, chap. 6, sec. C), a role here split (as it so often is) between a goddess and a mortal—Devī and Tārāvatī.

Finally, it should be noted that the three levels on which the Goddess appears have their exact counterparts in the three levels on which men involved with Tārāvatī operate: Śiva (on Pārvatī's level), Candraśekhara (on Tārāvatī's), and the sage, who, by instigating the curse that is the counterpart of the curses set in motion in heaven, is the male figure in control of the event on earth, just as Devī arranges and disposes the curses from above. It is surely significant that it takes three separate men to match the three aspects of a single Goddess, rather like the string of three tenors once needed to play Tristan in three successive acts against Birgit Nilsson's formidable Isolde.

Another point emerges from this complex myth. We have seen in chapter 3 that it is dangerous for a mortal to become an immortal; we have touched upon, and will further discuss in chapter 6, the belief that it is dangerous for a mortal to have sexual contact with an immortal. In the myth of Tārāvatī and Candraśekhara, these concepts merge in the implication that it is dangerous for a mortal to become an immortal and to have sexual contact with an immortal. Although Tārāvatī is reminded of her divine nature again and again, she denies it steadfastly. On one level this is an instance of metaphysical ignorance, lack of enlightenment (O'Flaherty 1973, pp. 206–8); but on another level it is an instance of the human preference for humanity over divinity, of the human fear of contact with the divine, the human inability to accept those moments when the dividing line between mortal and immortal dissolves or is revealed as mere illusion. So, too, Damayantī *prefers* Nala to all the gods who impersonate him, and Sukanyā prefers her decrepit old husband Cyavana to the glamorous divine Aśvins, whose shape he assumes (*MBh* 3. 51–54; 3. 122–23). In each case, the woman rejects an immortal lover who is *exactly like* her human lover in every detail but the essential one—the distinction between human and god. She chooses her true love by spying out the specific qualities that distinguish the mortal from the immortal: mortals sweat, blink, cast shadows, have dust on them, wear garlands that wither, and do not (as the gods do) stand suspended ever so slightly above the ground. In each case, the preference is for the lower end of the continuous spectrum from human to divine—in one's partner as well as in oneself.

One is tempted to see in this another reason for the persistence of the Superman/Clark Kent pattern in Indo-European mythology: only by appearing to be a mortal can the immortal make love to mortal women. Zeus, Odin, Indra—all of them tend to do a bit of slumming when seeking sexual pleasures. But here the mythology tends to distinguish between actual transformation and mere disguise (or the maintaining of a pied-à-terre); Damayantī does not accept the disguise, and, even as Clark Kent, Superman cannot make love to Lois Lane, so powerful is the resistance against this hierogamy (a resistance further bolstered by the related concept of the superhero's need to preserve his vital fluids from the woman who constantly plots to take them from him, as Lois constantly plots to trap Superman—to discover his mortal identity and to marry him). The persistence of this model is sharply evident from a recent statement by Mario Puzo, author of the script for the movie *Superman*: "In the next film he becomes mortal . . . for a brief period of time. . . . I worked that out just so he could get into bed with Lois Lane. I figured you had to have that—well, I had to have that" (*American Film*, May 1979, p. 34). Hollywood may have to have it, but the mythology has done without it for millennia, and it took much revision to make it possible, as Puzo admits ("I worked out a very elaborate, very logical, and, I thought, very skillful way to have him become mortal for a brief period of time" [*ibid.*]).

In India, too, the mythology is sometimes stretched to allow certain types of hierogamy to overcome the underlying resistance to the idea of sexual union with a god. In particular, there are distinct contrasts between traditional Vedic and epic thinking (in which the worshiper does not want to marry the god), Vedāntic thinking (in which the worshiper becomes the god), and *bhakti* thinking (in which the worshiper does indeed want to marry the god). The Vedic line prevails, as usual, in the Purāṇas, but the Vedāntic line reemerges in the mythology of the Tantras.

The complexity of the problem posed by the relationship between the mortal consort and the Goddess may be seen in the cult of the goddess Pattini in Sri Lanka. Pattini originates in South India, where her story is told in a Tamil epic separate from but parallel to the village cults of the terrifying Goddess. When her worship is transferred to Sri Lanka, it poses no problem for Buddhists or villagers, who accept the hierogamy; but when it is then brought (back) to *Sanskritized* Hindus, the fact that the Goddess has a mortal lover necessitates a number of adjustments in the myth and ritual (Obeyesekere 1980, pp. 1233–34). The hierogamy recurs throughout Indo-European culture as an ideal, but always as a dangerous one that most circumspect mortals will shy away from.

The Tantric Triumph of the Goddess

When Śāktism finally effloresces, the pattern of male dominance is turned inside out. Now all the helpless gods prostrate themselves before the Goddess and beg her to help them, not by killing the demon *herself*, as Devī does in the early, non-Vedic hierogamic model, but by becoming incarnate as the lovely Pārvatī in order to marry Śiva and produce a *son* to kill the demon. After subjecting Śiva to a number of sexual and social indignities, she finally stoops to conquer him and to produce the child that is the salvation of the world (O'Flaherty 1973, pp. 151–58). Thus she is able to maintain at least the semblance of the role of the demure woman, the power behind the throne, mother of heroes. The blood is washed from her own fangs and smeared instead on the hands of another generation and another gender. She is restored as the gentle mother and gentle wife, safe for Śiva to marry.

Moreover, just as these myths make the Goddess step back and work behind the scenes to accomplish certain deeds of violence previously attributed to her directly, so too, as her power grows, she is *said* to be working behind the scenes in episodes previously attributed to other deities (usually male) working without her help. Thus, in one Śākta text after another, when Viṣṇu is needed to become incarnate as the Man-Lion in order to destroy Hiraṇyakaśipu, or when Śiva must shoot the arrow to destroy the Triple City—actions that in the earlier texts they were entirely capable of accomplishing on their own—the gods approach *her* first. She then advises them to enlist Viṣṇu or Śiva to do the deed, often remarking that she will of course fill them with her own power so that they will be able to do it. In this way, it is really the Goddess who disembowels Hiraṇyakaśipu or sets the conflagration in the demon cities —though always at such a distance that she does not reinvoke the image of the devouring Mother. The quintessence of this reinterpretation occurs in the *Devībhāgavata Purāṇa*, where the gods ask their wives to give them the *śaktis* to create Devī in the first place, instead of making her out of their own powers, as in the earlier, pre-Śākta texts (*DBP* 5. 8).

Yet another power reversal appears in the Śākta myth in which the

Goddess is sought by the god instead of seeking him, as she does in the earlier corpus. Indeed, she is sought by several gods in competition, an ironic throwback to the old motif of the *svayaṃvara* ceremony, in which the bride chooses her husband from among a number of suitors. The irony lies in the fact that Draupadī, Sītā, Damayantī, and many other *mortal* heroines are wooed by immortal lovers in this way; and the woman, faced with a choice between apparently identical suitors, only one of whom is human, unquestioningly opts for the human and rejects the divine. In these episodes, mortals of both sexes strive to avoid hierogamies, though these do occur. Later, however, Pārvatī grimly and relentlessly pursues the god Śiva, rejecting the more respectable gods, pillars of the divine community, urged upon her by her parents. And in the Śākta Purāṇas, the Goddess in her full aspect of absolute divinity chooses one god from among all the gods who seek her:

> Devī created Brahmā, Viṣṇu, and Śiva. Then she divided herself into three parts and promised to become the wife of each of them. She instructed them to create, preserve, and destroy the universe, and she promised to bear them all children. But Śiva wished to obtain her for his wife alone, and so he began to propitiate her with asceticism and *bhakti*. Viṣṇu and Brahmā then also stopped creating and practiced asceticism, and to test them Devī assumed a terrifying form and appeared before each one in turn. Brahmā became four-faced in order to turn away from her, and Viṣṇu closed his eyes and plunged into the water; but she was unable to turn Śiva from his asceticism, for he was a great yogi. Then she was pleased with him and promised to become Satī in order to marry him (*MBP* 3. 15–70; cf. O'Flaherty 1973, pp. 154–55).

Where previously she had undergone asceticism to win Śiva's love and he appeared to her in an inauspicious disguise in order to test her, in this text he woos her with asceticism and is tested in his turn. True to the pattern of that earlier myth, she still chooses the least likely suitor, the one least susceptible to her; but here she is the manifestation of complete power, the one to whom he turns even when he tries to turn away.

In the earlier myths, the goddess becomes mild in order to wed the god; here she becomes (or remains, depending upon how one looks at it) terrifying and powerful, with the potential to develop into the arachnid male-devourer, though this development is not made explicit in the text. One might view these two patterns as two modes of Śākta elaboration of Purāṇic mythology; and the myths of splitting into two goddesses (the black Kālī and the golden Gaurī) or three (human, immortal, and ultimately divine) might then be viewed as attempts to reconcile them or to mediate between them.[9]

In a variant of the story of the testing of the three gods, Devī uses erotic as well as ascetic means to test Śiva (just as she tempts him, enlisting the aid of Kāma as well as her own ascetic enterprise, in the earlier corpus, where *she* tries to woo *him*) (O'Flaherty 1973, pp. 155–58). This myth also introduces the images of the corpse and the *liṅga* in the *yoni*, images that will undergo several interesting transformations in Tantric mythology:

> After appearing before Brahmā and Viṣṇu in the form of a worm-infested corpse, Devī went to Śiva and was at first unable to shake him from his meditation. She released a perfumed wind, which carried atoms from her body to Śiva's nose. Śiva perceived the perfume, broke his trance, and took the corpse upon his breast. Then he returned to his meditation, and Devī was pleased with him and recognized him as Śiva. He took the form of the *liṅga*, and she the form of the *yoni*. She placed the *liṅga* within her and plunged into the water to create living creatures (*BDP* 2. 31. 16–36).

In these two myths, Devī creates the gods and chooses one of them for her husband. Her power is so absolute, and so abstract, that her act of creation does not seem to lend maternal overtones to her role, and so there is no problem of an incestuous conflict, though this is of course implicit in the material: she does marry her son.

The Consort as Child

Incestuous overtones become fully explicit, however, in a South Indian version of the myth:

> The Goddess in her full primeval form became lustful and created a male to impregnate her. She became a bird and laid an egg, out of which Brahmā, Viṣṇu, and Śiva hatched. When she lusted after them and asked them to satisfy her desire, they protested that she was their mother, that they came from her womb; but she insisted that the egg was their mother, that she was only their grandmother, and that it was therefore all right for them to do as she asked. They fled from her, and ultimately Śiva and Viṣṇu tricked her into giving her third eye to Śiva, thereby causing her to lose both her strength and her desire (Oppert 1893, pp. 465–66 and 472–74, paraphrased).

Here the power of the Goddess is severely undercut; Śiva or Viṣṇu is regarded as the great power, and she is treated like a lustful demon, tricked like Bhasmāsura or Āḍi. The trick used to defuse her—making her give her third eye to Śiva—is a reversal of the actual historical circumstances, in which she took this attribute from him, along with many others.

The eye is often used as a symbol of the phallus, the vagina, or sexual awareness; blinding and castration are closely linked in Indian mythology (O'Flaherty 1969; O'Flaherty 1973, pp. 247–50). Thus, by removing the Goddess's third eye, her unwilling suitor removes her sexual powers; more precisely, he removes her masculine sexual powers: aggressive sexuality unbefitting a consort. Similarly, the goddess loses her third breast, a phallic organ—and stops masquerading as a man—when she meets the god who is destined to be her husband, to tame her into being a woman and a wife (H. Whitehead 1921, p. 54).

But the image of the Goddess as mother (which blocked the use of many Devī myths in the formation of female-dominated hierogamies in the pre-Śākta texts) was used explicitly in order to *avoid* a demeaning sexual encounter proposed by men in many Śākta texts, which exalted the Goddess over the gods. The *Bhaviṣya Purāṇa* tells how Brahmā, Viṣṇu, and Śiva tried to rape Anasūyā, mortal wife of a sage, who avoided a curse (from them or from her husband—a no-win situation) by giving them a curse to be reborn as her children (*Bhav P* 3. 4. 17. 67–78; O'Flaherty 1975, pp. 53–55). In this way she was able instantly to avert a potentially dangerous hierogamy by transforming it into a sexless maternal relationship. Again, a South Indian variant brings out certain hidden meanings in the tale of the sage's beautiful wife:

> One day, when the Ṛishi was away from home, the Trimūrti [Brahmā, Viṣṇu, and Śiva] came to visit her [Anasūyā], to see whether she was as beautiful and virtuous as reported. Not knowing who they were, and resenting their intrusion, she had them changed into little children. They naturally took offense, and cursed her, so that her beauty faded away, and her face became dotted with marks like those of the smallpox (H. Whitehead 1921, p. 115).

As Richard Brubaker comments on this episode, "To see the resented intrusion in the present story in similarly sexual terms [similar to the *Bhaviṣya Purāṇa* myth] requires only a slight reading between the lines in the vicinity of the words 'to visit her, to see whether she was as beautiful and virtuous as reported'" (Brubaker 1978, p. 317). The heroine here is a mortal woman at the beginning (though with great magic powers), and she resists the gods even though she is said not to know who they are; like Anasūyā, she instinctively shies away from a hierogamy. But the myth protects her from this mismatch in two ways:

first she disarms the gods by making them into infants, and then they inadvertently erase the boundary line between them by turning her into a goddess, i.e., by subjecting her to the combination of male aggression and unjust mistreatment that produces epidemic goddesses in South India, as Brubaker has demonstrated.

In a Tamil text, the aggression comes from someone other than the would-be consort:

> When a woman devoted to Śiva married a bigoted Vaiṣṇava and was persecuted by her in-laws, Śiva came down to rescue her. Her in-laws returned unexpectedly and were about to discover her in a compromising situation when Śiva obligingly turned himself into a baby. Eventually he resumed his true form, transformed her into Pārvatī, and carried her away in his chariot (*Tiruviḷaiyāṭar Purāṇam* 23. 1–33).

In these texts, the god—whether dominated, as in the two myths of Anasūyā, or dominant, as in the Tamil story—is made, or becomes, an infant in order to bypass a potential hierogamy.

An inverse of this situation may be seen in the *Bhāgavata Purāṇa* episodes in which erotic overtones appropriate to a mature god are introduced into scenes in which the infant Kṛṣṇa suckles from the gopīs' breasts (Masson 1974, pp. 454–59). Going one step further, other episodes combine the positive erotic relationship with the gopīs with the fantasy of oral aggression underlying the relationship with Pūtanā, the demoness with poisoned milk. These powerful emotions are evident in a Tamil invocation of Kṛṣṇa:

> O you who triumphed over the wrestlers,
> come to me and get on to my lower belly
> and let your chest be on my body.
> Take one of my breasts and suckle
> while holding the other one and gently caressing it;
> one by one suckle both breasts.
> O you who suckled out Pūtanā's breasts,
> suckle gently.
> Let your lips play on my nipples.[10]

Here Kṛṣṇa is asked to play an inverted role, son transformed into lover, but not to do so in the violent manner of Pūtanā, who inverted her role in a very different way (mother transformed into killer); implicit in the poem is the understanding that the mother who loves/feeds the son may desire him, while the mother who hates/eats him must be killed with sadistic desire. Inversions of a similar kind underlie a verse in the

Gītagovinda: "You wander in the woods in order to devour weak young girls—but what is astonishing about that? For Pūtanā herself is witness to your nature as the cruel infant who is a lady-killer" (*GG* 8. 8). Here Kṛṣṇa "swallows" not the milk but the very lives of the gopīs, an erotic consumption, just as he swallowed the life of Pūtanā in an aggressive consumption of the cruel mother.

In these myths of the infant Kṛṣṇa (as well as in the Tamil myth of the Śaiva woman in the Vaiṣṇava household) an omnipotent god, in an erotic relationship with a mortal woman, is merely pretending to place himself in the ultimate situation of impotence—infant vis-à-vis mother (though with the fantasy of infantile omnipotence clearly built in). The positive overtones of the myth of Kṛṣṇa and the gopīs may be contrasted with the negative overtones of the myth of Kṛṣṇa and Pūtanā, and the myth of Devī and her sons, in two ways: Kṛṣṇa is primarily erotic and benevolent, and his role as (foster-) son of the gopīs is secondary, while Devī is primarily maternal and destructive, and her role as wife of the three gods is secondary. Moreover, Kṛṣṇa is the immortal male with mortal consorts, Devī the immortal female with relatively mortal consorts. Another vivid example of the fusion of maternal and erotic motifs in a negative way (initiated by the woman, the goddess) appears in the Tamil mythology of Pattini: in the ancient Tamil epic (*Cilappatikāram* 21. 43–57), the grossly mistreated heroine, Pattini, rips off her own breast and sets a city on fire with it (O'Flaherty 1976, p. 342); in a Sri Lanka ritual, the goddess Pattini says that her adulterous lover tore out her breast and ate it (Obeyesekere 1980, p. 405).

The contrast between positive eroticism initiated by the son and negative eroticism initiated by the mother may perhaps be viewed as yet one more kind of male dominance: incestuous relationships may be tolerated in myth if they are initiated by the male. Thus Prajāpati does seduce his daughter Uṣas, but Yamī fails to seduce her brother Yama. The Hindu female cannot behave in a manner simultaneously erotic and maternal; she cannot be a mother and a whore, a cow and a mare. But the Hindu male can act out his own fantasies of infantile sexuality; though the gopīs are "cows" (in name and function), Kṛṣṇa is able to have an erotic liaison with them (to make them into "mares") because this is a function of *his* behavior, and he is in control. This is an interesting reversal of the normal process hypothesized by psychoanalytic theory, that the son's lust for his mother, being unacceptable to him, is projected onto her, resulting in the image of the castrating erotic mother; in the Hindu texts, the son's lustful fantasies are in fact tolerated, though still balanced by the image of the poisonous aggressive mother (Pūtanā).

The ability of Kṛṣṇa to be simultaneously child and lover was evidently a problem to some Vaiṣṇava theologians, who constructed an elaborate and highly amusing episode in which Kṛṣṇa ceases—for a while—to be a child when he becomes a lover:

> One day Nanda took the infant Kṛṣṇa with him to graze the cows, and he rested with the baby in his lap. A terrible storm blew up, and Nanda wondered how he could take the cows home without abandoning the boy. At that moment, Rādhā appeared in her full, voluptuous beauty, lovely enough to entice even a yogi. She took the child from Nanda and carried him away; passionately excited, she embraced and kissed him again and again, and then she thought of the circle of the *rāsa* [the erotic dance of Kṛṣṇa and the gopīs]. Then, through Kṛṣṇa's power of illusion, she beheld a beautiful house made of jewels and in it a handsome, dark-blue youth in the prime of life, and the baby vanished from her lap.
>
> Kṛṣṇa told Rādhā who he and she were, and then Brahmā appeared and married them. When Brahmā departed, Kṛṣṇa and Rādhā made love passionately; in their battle of love (*rati-yuddha*), they indulged in every kind of love-play; sometimes Rādhā would assume the "inverse" position. Then, suddenly, Kṛṣṇa ceased to be a youth and became an infant again, weeping with hunger just as he had been when Nanda had left him. Deeply disappointed, sighing, Rādhā searched for him everywhere and complained bitterly, suffering from *viraha* (longing for the departed lover), until a disembodied voice assured her that she could always come to the magic house and make love with Kṛṣṇa, leaving only her shadow (*chāyā*) at home.
>
> Then Rādhā took the baby in her arms and went to Nanda's house. She gave the child to Yaśodā, saying, "This rather fat child has been crying with hunger all the time; it was a foul day, and my clothes are soaked through; the muddy ground was very slippery, and I can't carry him any more. Take him and go home; I'm going home. Goodbye." Yaśodā took him and kissed him and gave him her breast to suck. And Rādhā went home and busied herself with housework, but every night she made love with Kṛṣṇa (*BVP* 4. 15. 1–181).

Although this episode takes place in the infancy of Kṛṣṇa, Rādhā is a sexually mature woman; she becomes lustful at the sight of him even though he is still an infant, and she thinks of the erotic circle dance even though, on the superficial human level, it will not take place for several years. At this point she plays the role of the sexual aggressor, desiring him when he does not (apparently) desire her. But the myth immediately removes them from this awkward situation: Kṛṣṇa not only becomes sexually mature but actually marries Rādhā (which he does not do in the sphere of real life). When their love-play ends, however, Kṛṣṇa becomes an infant again, to the evident frustration of Rādhā. The *viraha* she suffers now is even worse than that which she undergoes when he vanishes during the circle dance, but it is short-lived; for to reconcile the roles of mother and mistress, Rādhā is conveniently split into two, and, in keeping with the generally Tantric reversal of orthodox Hindu values that characterizes this text, the secondary shadow is not the nonmother (as it is in the myths of Saraṇyū and Gaurī/Kālī) but the domestic creature, while the "true" Rādhā is the erotic partner of the mature god, the sexually aggressive woman in the dominant, "inverse" position. (Similarly, the true gopīs come to dance with Kṛṣṇa in the moonlight, leaving their shadows at home in bed with their husbands.) That the erotic nature is in fact Rādhā's true nature is evident from her grumpy speech on handing the baby over to his mother and from her refusal to feed the hungry child; she does not want a baby, she wants a lover.

In this episode, Kṛṣṇa is a child who turns into a lover in order to satisfy his erotic consort. The splitting of Kṛṣṇa into two figures, one a baby and the other a young man, occurs elsewhere as well; a text of the *Bālagopālastuti* that describes one of the gopīs "luring" Kṛṣṇa to her and giving him her breast is illustrated by a painting that depicts a baby Kṛṣṇa at the breast and a grown Kṛṣṇa flirting with the gopīs.[11]

In other texts where the Goddess is sexually aggressive (as Rādhā is in the myth of the magic house), her lover may turn into a child in order to prevent her from venting the full force of her passion, sexual or otherwise. Śiva resorts to this device in order to quell Kālī's fury when she has run amuck after killing the demon Dāruka (see below, chap. 5, sec. E). The goddess may also be disarmed by being turned into an infant herself: when Lakṣmī runs after Viṣṇu in the wake of his sudden marriage to someone else, she is turned into a child (Shulman 1976a, p. 291);[12] this device reduces the threatening wife to infantile impotence. Power flows in the other direction, however, when the Goddess participates in Kṛṣṇa's birth: to protect Kṛṣṇa, and to lure Kaṃsa into committing the sin that will mean his death (just as Mahiṣa and other demons are lured to their death by goddesses), the Goddess becomes incarnate as a baby girl. When Kaṃsa murders her, she flies away to heaven, proclaiming his imminent downfall (*H* 48; O'Flaherty 1975, pp. 206–13). Here is another instance of divine strength masquerading as mortal weakness, with no sexual or maternal overtones.

A complex example of the consort as child, and of the motif of self-transformation into a child in order to avoid sexual aggression, appears in one variant of the myth of Brahmā's incest with his daughter, the Dawn. In this version the daughter desires her father as he desires her; then, to purify herself, she immolates herself in a fire (like Satī and Sītā) and obtains from Śiva the boon that she will be reborn as Arundhatī, the epitome of the chaste wife, that her husband will be merely a "close friend" to her, and, finally, that any man who looks upon her with desire will be turned into a eunuch. Moreover, she officially establishes the moral law that creatures before adolescence will not be subject to desire (*ŚP* 2. 2. 5–7; O'Flaherty 1973, pp. 64–65, 118–19). To extricate herself from the immediate situation, she is reborn as a child and, moreover, as a child explicitly protected from any possibility of the infant sexuality from which she has suffered in an unusually blatant way. But, in addition to this, she protects herself by defusing her potential aggressors, not by turning them into children, but by the equivalent (albeit more drastic) measure of unmanning them. In discussing this myth, a psychoanalyst comments on "the castration fantasy of turning all men into eunuchs in the Arundhati myth" and on the daughter's "fantasied erotic wishes towards her father, and her later repudiation of these wishes by transforming them into their opposite, aloofness and chastity" (Kakar 1978, pp. 90, 69).

The Retreat from the Mother

The motif of the consort as child is manifest in a less obvious way in the Indian belief that the husband is reborn in his own son (*Manu* 9. 8; *AB* 7. 13; *BVP* 3. 2. 27). In one Jaina myth based on the doctrine that reincarnation is instantaneous, a husband who dies in the act of intercourse with his insatiable wife (an interesting example of the dangers of sexual intercourse) is immediately reborn in the embryo that he himself creates at that moment. When the child is (re)born, he grows up to torment the wife (now his mother) in punishment for her having killed him (when he was her husband).[13] The incestuous implications of this episode are explicit enough, but they are pale compared with the musings of one late Upaniṣad:

> The breast that was sucked before he presses and finds joy; the vagina from which he was born before—he takes pleasure in that. She who was his mother before is now his wife, and she who is his wife is indeed his mother. He who was his father is now his son, and he who is his son will be again his father (*Yogatattva U* 131–133).

The erotic fantasies that are tolerated and celebrated in the mythology of the infant Kṛṣṇa, the mythology of the flowing of milk, are used here to place an incestuous barrier between the would-be ascetic and any woman—to stop the flow of seed. The ascetic, fleeing from the incestuous aggressions of his mother, retreats into a state of chastity enforced by the perception of all women as his mother.

This state of mind may be, as we have seen, a helpless reaction: because the son sees his mother as a potential consort (i.e., as sexually aggressive or nonmaternal or milk-retaining), he retreats into chastity (by retaining his fluids) or into childhood (thus ensuring that she will remain merely maternal). This may occur on the level of what people think. But explicitly—what people think they think—the culture consciously transforms the potential consort into a mother in order to force the ascetic to retreat into chastity. Because of the cybernetic or synergistic relationship between myth and cultural norms, both patterns are simultaneously at play: the culture uses the myth to instill certain desirable patterns of behavior, and the myth expresses certain inevitable behavioral patterns.

This psychology occurs in many myths.[14] In a particularly explicit episode, Skanda is said to have persisted in committing adultery with all the wives of the gods until they complained to his mother, Pārvatī, who took the form of whatever woman Skanda was about to seduce. Then Skanda thought, "The universe is filled with my mother," and he became passionless and resolved to treat all women as he would treat his mother, though when he found out how his mother had tricked him, he was ashamed (*BP* 81. 1–6). Since the Goddess is regarded by Hindus as the mother of us all, incarnate in every woman, it is easy to see how this pattern of thought could create sexual problems in India.

The image of the female consort as mother can therefore have a positive erotic valence (as in the childhood of Kṛṣṇa), or a negative valence (as in the cautionary tale of Skanda), or no apparent erotic valence at all. Thus, in South India, sexual union is likened to the hand of the mother feeding rice to the child (Egnor 1978, p. 142)—an image that also involves the transformation of the male partner into a woman (the mother who feeds rice/seed to the "child"—the womb/mouth of the female partner). The eating of the seed lends negative overtones to this metaphor, however, as does the change of sex; for, as we shall see, change of sex (self-castration, identification with the female, or homosexuality) is one way to avoid being devoured by the mother. Another way, to transform oneself into a child, is also present in the Tamil metaphor, though in an inverted form (the child being the woman who eats the rice/seed).

The Tamil image of the mother feeding the child has further social ramifications; for in Tamil marriages in which the wife controls her lustful husband (S. Daniel 1978)—a pattern in which she is viewed as unemotional and good (the cow), while he is dangerous and passionate (the stallion) (see below, chaps. 6 and 8)—she dominates him by withholding food. The Tamils say, "If the wife refuses to cook and lies down, what can he do? . . . In fact, he becomes like a chastened child" (S. Daniel 1978, pp. 10, 12). By treating her husband like a child, she makes use of the one legitimate source of female dominance: threatening to behave like the evil mother if he persists in behaving like a naughty child/husband. Significantly, she does *not* withhold the service that women withhold in other cultures under similar circumstances: she does not go on a sexual strike (see below, chap. 9). Indeed, the informant says that she "lies down" in her defiance, leaving the kitchen but not necessarily entering the bedroom. For, by remaining chaste, she is merely being (albeit in an exaggerated form) what a woman *ought* to be. Stated in a different way, a nonerotic woman is perhaps a nuisance but certainly not a danger in India, but, by withholding food, the wife is violating the natural order. By feeding her husband, she revalidates the one and only legitimate form of authority she has: maternal authority, even over her husband.

Before this discussion becomes even more psychoanalytic (as it is about to do), it might prove wise to touch down for one moment in the actual Indian texts. We have suggested a Hindu corpus of texts dealing with classical (and inverted) oedipal encounters; we have noted a Jaina myth explaining the oedipal conflict in terms of an instantaneous rebirth of the father as the son. In Indian and Tibetan Buddhism, as well, the sexual involvement of the child with its parents is attributed to the conscious participation of the embryo in its own begetting; in these texts, the fact that rebirth is *not* instantaneous makes possible the emotional encounter. The creature hovering between death and rebirth sees its future parents in intercourse: "Finding the scene hospitable, its passions are stirred. If male, it is smitten with desire for its mother. If female, it is seized with desire for its father." And, inversely, it hates either mother or father, whom it comes to regard as a rival. Lust and hatred thus arise in the embryo even before it is born; it attaches itself to the place where its future parents' sexual organs are joined, imagining that it is there joined with the object of its passion; in this way it takes on material form in the mixture of semen and blood in the womb (*Abhidharmakośa* 3. 15). The Tibetan texts elaborate greatly upon the precise temptations, musings, imaginings, and actions of the embryo as voyeur, making a particular link between the experience of hatred as based on blood in the left channel (resulting in the birth of a female) and the experience of lust as based on semen in the right channel (resulting in a male) (Stablein 1980).[15] This makes Freud's bold hypothesis of infantile sexuality seem child's play indeed; here we have *pre-embryonic* sexuality.

The concept of the goddess whose son is her consort is of course not confined to Indian mythology, for it is often encountered not only in Indo-European texts but even farther afield (see below, chap. 6, sec. C). The related theme of the evil mother (evil in holding back food and/or in tempting her son) is also universal, but it seems to be especially prominent in India. The myth of Pṛthu and the earth-cow, for example, may be viewed as one in which Pṛthu is not only the calf and son of the earth but also the husband who tames and controls her, turning her from the evil mother who holds back food into the good mother who yields food (O'Flaherty 1976, pp. 321–31; cf. Waghorne 1978). As one psychoanalyst remarks,

> At this most fundamental level of the psyche, no one is entirely free from ambivalent feelings towards the mother. The theme of the "bad mother" merits particular attention in the Indian context not just because it exists, but because it is characterized by a singular intensity and pervasiveness. . . . In all societies the image of the "bad mother" combines both the aggressively destroying and the sexually demanding themes (Kakar 1978, pp. 89–90).

One particularly Indian variant of this theme has already appeared: the image of the yogi who holds back his seed in reaction against the mother who holds back her milk. In this image the mother is neither sexually demanding nor aggressively destroying, on an explicit level, though her failure to feed is, by implication, destructive, and her refusal to play the role of mother (giving milk) casts her by default in the role of whore (stealing male fluids—i.e., being sexually demanding). We have also seen implications of sexual aggression in the Mother in the motif of beheading (or self-beheading) linked to castration (or self-castration or homosexuality). Finally, we have noted the prevalence of incest on an explicit level in myths of creation and hierogamy, and we will encounter far more instances of incest in the mythology of the mare. What would this cluster of motifs suggest to an Indian psychoanalyst?

Sudhir Kakar, working from (though unfortunately not citing) clinical experience in India, suggests a pessimistic pattern similar to one that has been extrapolated from ancient Greek mythology (Slater 1968). He speaks of a

> vicious circle that spirals inward in the Indian unconscious: mature women are sexually threatening to men, which contributes to "avoidance behaviour" in sexual relations, which in turn causes

> the women to extend a provocative sexual presence towards their sons, which eventually produces adult men who fear the sexuality of mature women (Kakar 1978, p. 95).

In the same discussion, Kakar notes the high incidence of "heightened fear, or the actual occurrence, of impotence" in Indian men and attributes it to the prevalence of the incest fantasy in India. We have seen how this leads many men to seek virility cures in the form of ingested sexual fluids, and we will see how another cure is sought, on the ritual level, by taking in the sexual fluids of the Goddess in Tantric intercourse.

Manisha Roy has observed the pattern of avoidance in Hindu men in another context, the romantic longings of educated Bengali women. She expresses the problem from the standpoint of the husband:

> His wife's expectation of romantic love mingled with sexual pleasure does not make sense to him, because he knows he is not supposed to enjoy sexual pleasure with his wife the way he can with a prostitute or a mistress. At the same time, his wife is the only woman at hand who wants and wishes to enjoy him. His understanding of things does not quite fit into this experience. The only way he can explain it to himself is that women in this society have more sexual desire than men do. His colleagues and friends with whom he discusses such topics all testify to this conclusion. This sexual ambivalence that a husband has towards his wife is very deep-rooted in the psychology and personality structure of Bengali men (M. Roy 1975, p. 117).

In Roy's analysis, the avoidance is a cause of, rather than a result of, the man's belief that the woman's desire is greater than his own; in the mythology, as we have seen and will continue to see, the avoidance is more often a reaction against this assumed imbalance.

The avoidance pattern has been substantiated by other clinical studies in India, of which Carstairs' is the most useful. Like Kakar, who drew upon his work, Carstairs commented on the common occurrence of impotence in Indian men and on their preoccupation with and fear of impotence or loss of virility (a form of castration fear) (Carstairs 1958, p. 167). More specifically, Carstairs noted that these fears related only to the men's wives, not to prostitutes, low-caste girls, or younger women in general:

> Significantly, almost every one of my informants told me that it was advisable to have sex relations only with women younger than oneself: to sleep with a woman several years older would destroy a

> man's strength in a short space of time. The older woman is feared because she conjures up the repressed oedipal craving for possession of the mother, and so intensifies the castration anxieties which dog all sexual functions (ibid., p. 168).

We have noted, in the context of the danger of loss of sexual fluids, the repeated statement that the younger woman is less dangerous than the older woman; here, perhaps, is a possible source of that belief. With the younger woman, the man can be a sexual partner; with an older woman, he can only be a son. This is borne out by the mythology of the consort as child; unaware of this corpus of texts, Carstairs nevertheless suggested a similar diagnosis of the worshiper's relationship with the Goddess in general:

> As the Goddess, she [the mother] is seen as a horrific figure, decapitating men and drinking their blood. In order to appease her fury she must be placated with offerings, but what is more important, she must be appealed to in an attitude of complete submission. She becomes kind and rewarding, a mother again and no longer a demon, only when one has surrendered one's manhood and become a helpless infant once again (ibid., p. 159; cf. p. 179).

It is significant, I think, that the male is endangered not only by the incestuous overtones of the mother-son relationship but also by the father-daughter relationship (in which, were there any sort of true parallelism, the female should suffer); this is probably due to the general androcentrism of the entire Indian cosmology. In the myths, males in general are injured as the result of father-daughter incest: the father is beheaded, the future consorts of the daughters are castrated, and her brothers are driven to the self-castration implicit in asceticism, that is, they express their staunch disapproval of their father's incestuous overtures to their sister by withdrawing from sexual creation altogether (O'Flaherty 1973, pp. 70–76, 128–30; 1975, pp. 46–53).

This one-sidedness affects other variants of the myth as well. When the male ascetic protects himself from sexual assault (implicitly by his mother), he undergoes self-castration. When the female ascetic protects herself from sexual assault (from her father), she becomes castrat*ing* rather than castrat*ed*; for her protective asceticism is in itself an act of aggression: she is inappropriately active for a woman, and her actions are explicitly directed against a man. The covert aggression against the male implicit in female asceticism emerges clearly from the myth of Śikhaṇḍin(ī) (see below, chap. 9, sec. B).

The male is also in a no-win situation in terms of the two sets of conditions that make the woman aggressive in this way, conditions that are likely to harm him whether or not he is responsible for bringing them about. We have seen a sexually assaulted woman turn into a dangerous fury (and will see it again and again in chap. 8, sec. N), but it is also evident that the sexually assault*ing* woman (the erotic mother) is transformed into a fury. In the mythology, the first transformation takes place on the explicit level: the raped woman becomes a castrating fury. The second takes place on the implicit level: the aggressive woman is regarded as a castrating fury. Even this level, however, becomes explicit in another realm of myth, when the rejected goddess mutilates her unwilling worshipers. Thus it would appear that the Indian male is trapped: he is castrated either as a by-product of the father-daughter incest or as a direct result of the mother-son incest.

And what happens to the woman in this interaction? She gains power. The assaulted daughter escapes from her father to be reborn as the chaste wife, and the assaulting mother turns into a goddess. In the myth of Reṇukā, the woman neglected by her husband would (by Kakar's analysis) be driven to visit unwanted sexual attentions upon her son. As a result, she is beheaded by that son—but only to be reborn (Brubaker 1977). As Kakar remarks, "another 'defence' in the mythological repertoire against the sexually threatening 'bad mother' is matricide followed by resurrection and deification" (Kakar 1978, p. 99), a pattern that prevails in South Indian village mythology (Brubaker 1978).

We have seen the myth in which the demon Āḍi assumes the form of Pārvatī and attempts to kill Śiva with the teeth inside "her" vagina; while this is going on, the "true" Pārvatī inflicts three parallel nonanatomical injuries upon her son, Vīraka: she refuses to allow him to accompany her when she goes away, though he weeps bitterly and begs her not to abandon him; she stations him at the door to prevent his father from having contact with women (invoking the primal oedipal situation, encouraging the child to challenge his father's active sexuality); and, when, on her return, she thinks, wrongly, that he has allowed a woman to enter Śiva's bedroom, she gives him a curse to become a stone, to become impotent. This is also, significantly, the myth in which she splits into two women, one golden and one black, the good and evil mother (*Sk P* 1. 2. 27–29; O'Flaherty 1975, pp. 251–61).

The corpus of Hindu myths about mothers and sons produces a number of paradoxes. The mother is culturally defined as nonerotic (a cow) and made the female ideal. But the mother becomes (naturally) erotic in the mythology, either in a positive way (when the son dominates the erotic relationship, as in the mythology of Kṛṣṇa) or in a negative way (when the mother dominates it, as in the mythology of Kālī). The cultural ideal is then reasserted all the more strongly by the male authors of the myth because the eroticism of the mother produces intolerable tensions (the gentleman doth protest too much, methinks). The fallout from this massive cultural repression of her eroticism produces the violent image of the nonmother, the erotic woman. Here again we encounter several contradictions. A younger woman is preferred as a sexual partner because, with her, the block produced by the horror of maternal incest does not occur; however, she is also the dangerous woman, who takes fluids, in contrast with the safe mother, who gives fluids. One solution to this conflict is to take a *much* younger woman, one who can be dominated like a daughter (a pattern of father-daughter incest that is far more acceptable than mother-son incest in Hindu mythology), or else a much *lower* woman, equally subordinate (hence the use of outcaste women in Tantric ritual and the prevalence of whores in Hindu mythology).

In a study of the worship of the goddess Pattini in Sri Lanka, Gananath Obeyesekere points out that Pattini is married but a virgin, a combination of Pārvatī (the good wife) and Kālī (of whom she is an actual incarnation, the devouring, evil mother), and that her husband, Palanga, is either impotent or castrated. Obeyesekere interprets this cult in the context of the Sinhala family structure as illuminated by Freudian theory: the women, lacking satisfying sexual liaisons with their husbands, seduce their male children; the men then project their own, and their wives', repressed sex and aggression onto the image of the fierce mother (Obeyesekere 1980, chap. 11). He explains the mechanism of this interaction:

> Since the Hindu female role ideal of "Pativrata" [chaste and obedient wife] pertains to sex and aggression control, the implementation of the ideal in the socialization process entails the radical proscription of sexual and aggressive activity, which on the personality level demands the radical and continued repression of sex and aggression drives (ibid., pp. 877–78).

This pattern, which produces the ambivalent image of the virgin goddess, is, significantly, supported by a parallel cult, that of Skanda and his mistress, Valli, the degraded mother (ibid., pp. 955–56), who is, as Freud pointed out long ago, a logical recipient of the erotic needs deflected from the mother-wife-virgin.

The pattern of retreat from the mother is manifest elsewhere in Sri Lanka in the priests of Pattini. Obeyesekere makes a number of highly relevant observations: the transvestite priests are often impotent (a fact they attribute to the barrenness of the "mother" goddess), and this may be linked to a pattern built into the system of hereditary priesthood. For if the father is a priest, he is often absent from home (or he may reject his wife in various explicit ways: some were said to beat their wives, to frequent whores, etc.); the son is thus extremely close to his mother, even closer than is normally the case in South Asia; he grows up to hate his father and to accept the role of transvestite priest (ibid., pp. 40–45). And so the cycle is perpetuated.

How far can—or should—this pattern of retreat from the mother be taken? How universal is it? Obeyesekere points out that there are significant differences between the Indian and the Sinhala social and family structures and that the relatively relaxed Sinhala structure allows the Sinhalese to combine two female figures who are necessarily separated in India (the chaste wife and the castrating mother). Yet a basic South Asian pattern is clearly at work, and, when one takes into account the Greek and Celtic materials, one begins to suspect that it is Indo-European. Some Freudians (and perhaps many Jungians) would suggest that it is in fact universal, though this is yet to be proved. The Freudian emphasis, however, tends to diagnose the culture as a patient suffering from a sexual neurosis, and there are serious problems when this hypothesis is applied to the Indian materials. For one thing, as we shall see, certain aspects of the mythology and ritual serve to cure or at least alleviate some of the problems arising from the family situation. In Sri Lanka, Obeyesekere notes one particularly dramatic example of the pattern described above; of three brothers, sons of a priest and subjected to the experiences of the priest's family (his absence, his abuse of his wife, etc.), the two who did *not* become priests of Pattini became institutionalized psychotics. The priest's putative self-castration through celibacy is, at least, a realistic survival mechanism and comparatively healthy. The temptation to make correlations between what we regard as aberrant sexual behavior in the service of religion and what we (or the people we study) regard as psychotic behavior is hedged with enormous problems that militate against the use of the psychiatry of pathology in a context to which it is, in any case, peripheral, as in the study of mythology. I would certainly not be inclined to accept Masson's bold formulation that "*all* [his emphasis] ascetics suffered massive traumas in their childhood in one of three ways: they were sexually seduced, or they were the object of overt or covert aggression, or they lost those closest to them early in their lives." There is no clinical evidence to support this contention, nor does it seem reasonable in the Hindu cultural context, which so exalts asceticism (though these sexual tensions may, of course, have contributed greatly to the formation of that context). Moreover, the same psychological underpinnings (a traumatic relationship with a mother who alternatively denies and seduces) may lead to a very different assessment of the ascetic, not as one who suffers from his self-castration but, on the contrary, as one who experiences a sense of bliss likened (in the Indian tradition) to sexual satisfaction, a sense of intense pleasure, which "can be interpreted as resuming possession of one's mother with the intense gratification of infantile sexuality" (Masson 1976, p. 623; cf. Carstairs 1958, p. 161). Two very different world views are at work here: the view from inside, which regards asceticism as sexual satiation, and the view from outside, which regards it as self-castration. This paradox will be encountered again in the image of the androgyne and the doctrine of *viraha*; it turns upon the acceptance or rejection of the process of interiorization that is at the heart of Tantrism, in which apparent celibacy masks true sexuality.

But I would pay heed to Kakar's suggestion that Indian mythology gives a suspiciously prominent pride of place to explicit mythological treatments of a syndrome of incestuous interaction and infantile sexuality (and to the related syndrome of poisoned milk)—a syndrome that appears, generally more modestly veiled, in other cultures as well. Whether this prominence is due to Hindus' being unusually preoccupied with these problems or to their being better taught and encouraged to recognize and articulate their subconscious and/or unconscious symbolism, it is hard to say. In any case, the social context of Hindu myths of infantile sexuality provides a prime example of the cybernetics of cultural psychology and myth: myths told to children influence how they grow up; children grow up with certain cultural preoccupations that lead them to tell certain kinds of myths. Thus Carstairs speaks of shared "nuclear phantasies" transmitted from mother to child and later modified by individual experience; he goes on to suggest that these infantile fantasies are often expressed in myths, that the attitude to the goddess who is alternatively a protective mother and a decapitating adversary is based on the child's relationship with his mother (abrupt weaning replacing a long period of complete gratification). In this view, the actual experience precedes and determines the myth. But Carstairs also suggests that the symbolic castration of a male animal whose blood the Goddess drinks "may be the source of the feeling that sexual intercourse represents a victory for the woman, who must be served when she demands it, and a castrating of the man" (Carstairs 1958, pp. 156, 159, 167). The belief that the woman is demanding, and dangerous when repulsed, is central to the mythology, as we shall see; but Carstairs seems to be saying that the myth is not a reflection of that belief but an important cause of it. Indeed, he goes still farther by suggesting that among the many factors that inhibit the sexual activity of a young married man in India are "his phantasies concerning women, of whom the demon-Goddess is the paradigm." Thus, in Carstairs' view, the fantasy (or myth) may be either a cause or a result of a sexual impasse in actual life; but clearly, it is both at once.

One final, theological aspect of the child consort might be mentioned here. Hinduism has also experienced and expressed a conflict between the desire, as well as the obligation, to have children (attitudes we have characterized as Vedic) and the obligation and desire to renounce family life in order to seek union with god (the Vedāntic heritage). By imagining god to be a child, as in the myths of Kṛṣṇa, the worshiper is able at last to fulfill simultaneously both of these compelling aspirations: to love god and to love one's son. And, on the other side of this paradigm, by imagining himself to be a child worshiping the mother, he is able to revert back to a time before these adult tensions intruded upon his life. In one case, god is male; in the other, female. But both of these encounters take place on the mother-son axis, the basic Hindu affective link between the human and the divine.

The Consort as Corpse

The goddess gives birth to her child but kills her consort; then these two figures merge into one: the Goddess first gives birth, then kills, then gives (re)birth to her consort. This pattern is widespread; we find it in the West Asian cults of the *mater dolorosa*, in the myths of Adonis, so exhaustively studied by Sir James George Frazer, and in syncretistic aspects of Christianity. In Sri Lanka it is manifest in the cult of the goddess Pattini weeping over the body of her dead and/or castrated son/consort (Obeyesekere 1980, chaps. 13–15). We will encounter it at the heart of the Vedic ritual of the queen and the dead stallion (see below, chap. 6), and it is implicit in the myth of the Liebestod and the image of the animate phallus.

The image of the consort as corpse is seen most explicitly in Tantric iconography, where it appears as the culmination of a long line of myths that can be traced back to the Vedic myth of Puruṣa. In that myth, the corpse is dismembered to produce the world; in the Tantric myth of dismemberment, the image is transferred to the Goddess, who is still dismembered (like Puruṣa) rather than assembled from disparate parts (like Devī when she kills Mahiṣa): Śiva embraces the corpse of Satī in necrophiliac ecstasy until it is chopped away piece by piece; in each place where it falls, a shrine to the Goddess arises, and Śiva remains there in some form; where the *yoni* falls, in Assam, he takes the form of the *liṅga* (*DBP* 7. 30; *BVP* 4. 42–43; O'Flaherty 1975, pp. 249–51; see also below, chap. 5, sec. A).

In later Tantric images the role of the corpse is transferred from the female to the male, a reversion to the type of Purāṇic doctrine loosely derived from Sāṅkhya's assignment of active and passive roles to the female and male elements, respectively. Here the ancient myth of the positive encounter between the mortal king and the Goddess reemerges, and the medieval Hindu concept of the contrast between a dangerous divine female consort and a "safe" mother is turned on its head. For the Tantric icons depict the Goddess in her awful form as mother, blood flowing from the stump of her severed head instead of milk from her breasts, while the benign, gentle aspect of the Goddess plays the whore, uniting in a sensuous naked embrace with the corpse of the god, whom she revives with rather more than a kiss (see plate 1). The positive force of her relationship with Śiva is made explicitly by the Tantric texts, which point out that she is the vowel "i" that turns a corpse (*śava*, in Sanskrit) into the god (*śiva*). For this is a significant variant upon the motif of the Liebestod; whereas she killed Mahiṣa by copulating with him (the essence of destructive female sexuality), she revives Śiva by copulating with him.

This reversal is then fed back into the earlier mythology. For many of the later Śāktic texts say that, although she did in fact destroy Mahiṣa's body, the buffalo body, she released his soul; this soul is usually depicted as an anthropomorphic creature (often in an attitude of devotion) emerging out of the headless corpse, the very place where the Śiva-*liṅga*—another symbol of the true, inner nature of Mahiṣa—appears in one variant of the myth. Similarly, the myth of Satī's corpse is rewritten; now Satī is said merely to produce an image of herself (a *chāyā*), which is burnt and dismembered, while the Goddess herself remains intact and in control (*MBP* 9–11). In other words, once she has scaled the peaks of divinity, the Goddess employs a stunt woman to carry out the nastier episodes of her mythology. It is surely significant that the Tantric icons depict the Goddess as literally on top of Śiva, just as the images of the killing of Mahiṣa usually show her crouching or squatting on top of him; this is the inverted or "contrary"—or perhaps even "perverse"—position in sexual intercourse (*viparītam*, as the *Kāmasūtra* describes it [2. 8. 24]). Here at last, after three millennia, she has the upper hand in the Indian game of divine sexual politics.

The Balance of Sexual Power between Divine Consorts

There are various ways in which Indian gods and goddesses divide power, and there are various ways to structure these possibilities. We have already suggested a division between two different kinds of goddesses, based (in part) upon their relationships with their consorts: the dominated breast goddess and the dominant tooth goddess. Devī in her full theological majesty spans both groups, but worshipers tend to emphasize one aspect at the expense of the other.

It might also seem possible to add a third group, consisting of goddesses on an equal level with their consorts, and to redefine the classifying elements of the first two. The first group, in which the goddess is dominated, is epitomized by Viṣṇu and Lakṣmī; this is an auspicious and life-oriented union, in which the woman receives the man's seed. The second group is epitomized by Kālī on the corpse of Śiva, the "inverse" union, in which the man gets the woman's seed: this is inauspicious, abnormal, and death-oriented. Between them is the couple equal in size (iconographically) and in power, epitomized by the adulterous pair Rādhā and Kṛṣṇa, or Śiva and Pārvatī as the androgyne, between whom no exchange of seed takes place (Marglin 1978b).

This tripartite typology is useful for many purposes. It is indeed true in general that Viṣṇu dominates his women, while Śiva allows his to dominate him. Not only is Lakṣmī subservient to Viṣṇu, but Sītā is subservient to Rāma and Rādhā to Kṛṣṇa. Śiva allows the Ganges to flow through his hair, while Viṣṇu touches her with his foot—an indication that Viṣṇu always has to be the boss in his relationships with women, while Śiva is more enlightened in this regard.[16] The foot-head contrast is also manifest in other pairs of myths and icons: Śiva puts Satī's corpse on his head, and Kālī puts her feet on his corpse; but Lakṣmī is most frequently depicted massaging Viṣṇu's feet.

Problems arise, however, with the third group, the "equal" group. As we have seen, and will see further in chapter 9, the androgyne is not the great leveler that it is often said to be; and in most texts, Kṛṣṇa and Rādhā are not treated as equals. The female consorts in the "equal" category have an ambiguous power relationship with their husbands. Soteriologically, the female consort, Rādhā or Pārvatī, may often be greater, but the god is usually ontologically greater. Rādhā has power, but Kṛṣṇa has authority. Authority is male, a kind of seed (*vīrya*), the carrier of social hierarchy, while power (*śakti*) is not inherent in status or rank.[17]

Gods have both power and authority in relation to mankind; human men have authority over human women, while human women have more power than human men. Evidence for these generalizations comes on the one hand from the Sanskrit texts that deal with the theology of devotion, particularly those stemming from the Sāṅkhya distinction between Puruṣa (inert authority) and Prakṛti (active power), and on the other hand from the Dharmaśāstras and anthropological studies of the actual function of power and authority in the Hindu system (studies such as Marriott's investigation of coded substance).

On a purely theological level, the power and authority of the gods stems in part from the degree to which they are unlike us; a male worshiper is therefore strongly drawn to the worship of a female divinity. But in actual worship this great gulf between god and worshiper is felt to be dangerous; it is too wide, represents too great a power differential, and so it is minimized or at least mediated: the male worshipers of the goddess dress as women.

This great ambivalence, this tendency to drive with one foot on the accelerator and the other on the brake, is further exacerbated by a paradox arising not within the conflict between power and authority but within the concept of authority alone: how can a goddess have authority, being female, but how can she not have authority, being a goddess? Attempts to resolve this paradox (which adds further fuel to the tension between the goddess's power and the male worshiper's authority) have produced a seemingly endless series of variations in the myths. To be given female authority, the goddess must have sons (the legitimating factor for a human woman); but she does not always have sons; so perhaps she may adopt sons, or the worshiper may become her son. For the Hindus, a female divinity is a square peg to be fitted into a round hole, and the rich diversity of patterns in her worship is testimony to the constant irritation that generates a series of flawed attempts to solve it, like sand making pearls in an oyster.

Authority is the social force (male) needed to tame, control, and channel pure power (female); to say that he has authority and that she has power is to say that he directs and shapes the life force that comes from her. This is yet another reformulation of the relationship between Puruṣa and Prakṛti. On another plane, the subordination of power to authority has been seen (by Louis Dumont) as the very basis of the Indian social system: impure power resides in the king, pure authority in the Brahmin. If we continue to equate power with the female and authority with the male, we will not be surprised to encounter a positive attitude to the myth of the queen (power) and the divine stallion (authority), contrasting in India (though not in ancient Indo-European culture) with the negative attitude to the myth of the king and the divine mare—a hierogamy in which the king *should* have both power (by virtue of his office) and authority (by virtue of his gender) but in fact lacks both when overpowered by the mare goddess, who has power (by virtue of being female) and authority (by virtue of being divine).

Thus the "equal" partners are unequal in two different ways, which may tend to balance out. But, as in Orwell's *Animal Farm*, one is usually "more equal" than the other. This dichotomy applies to the ideal of all human marriages in India, where, to be "balanced," authority must allow the male to dominate; and human marriages provide the model for the divine hierogamy. Thus one anthropologist refers to the "desired asymmetry between the god-husband and the consort-wife" (Yalman 1967, p. 351), and another characterizes the union in which the unmarried goddess dominates her consort as "sinister," while that in which the married male dominates is "divine" (Babb 1970, p. 142). In Bengal, as in Tamilnadu, only in private can husband and wife treat each other as equals; in public, there must always be a clear hierarchy (Inden and Nicholas 1977, p. 58; Egnor 1978, p. 78). The demonic tooth goddess is usually unmarried, and her divinity may be challenged, her authority denied; but her power is immense. The breast goddess, by contrast, is married and is assured of her divinity only by virtue of that marriage; she is inferior in power, but she is given *his* authority. This is the divine ideal.

This complex interlacing of power and authority in human and mythological marriages is reflected in yet another typology of marriage revealed by field work in Tamilnadu. In this analysis, the "dharmic" view of marriage is that the male is self-controlled, the female an untamed locus of power (*śakti*) and emotion (particularly *kāma*, lust) (S. Daniel 1978, pp. 1–2); she is the quintessential mare (see below, chap. 7). But against this, and active in the minds of the same people, is a "nondharmic" view of marriage: the woman controls the man, who is full of lust and extravagance. Both models may pertain to the same marriage, viewed in different normative lights by the same observer: he *ought* to control her, or she *ought* to control him. A corollary of this theory is the observation that in some marriages she actually *does* get the upper hand and that in other marriages she does not. In any case, the male-dominated model prevails on the level of authority, though the authority may be superficial; the female-dominated model may come into play on the underground level, where true power functions (S. Daniel 1978, p. 4). The male-dominated model functions on the level of what people think (and say) they think (i.e., that the male dominates the marriage); the "underground" level expresses what people really think. A compromise on the first, normative level is distinct from the actual resolution of the struggle for power on the second level. This tension between power and authority is also a tension between private and social interactions: "The husband's awkward position of having to control a person on whom he is dependent and who possesses a greater means of physical force [*śakti*] than he himself possesses, is a reversal of the usual link between status and *śakti* in the caste hierarchy" (ibid., p. 8).

In the human sphere, each marriage is capable of being interpreted normatively in either of two ways, but the actual power goes one way or the other. In fact, Tamils maintain that female-dominated marriages prevail, though this type must manifest its true colors only underground (ibid., p. 6). The female-dominated marriage is an actualization of the "nondharmic" view of all marriages, the male-dominated marriage expressing the "dharmic" view. These concepts are expressed mythologically: the first type is called a "Meenakshi marriage," since in the Meenakshi temple the goddess is primary, and Śiva, while honored as the husband, is not the main deity; the second type is called a "Chidambaram marriage," since, in the Chidambaram temple, Śiva, not Pārvatī, is the central deity.

Significantly, in all marriages, the wife's *śakti* was said to be put to her husband's use—to be actually transferred to him when she "felt lovingly disposed to him" but lost when she "turned her affections to another man" (ibid., p. 11). If these expressions are euphemisms for sexual contact, the analysis explains at least two phenomena: it supplies the basis for the hierogamy in which the goddess's power flows to her human consort, enriching him as the wife's *śakti* enriches her husband when she is "affectionate," and it also supplies the basis for the fanatical emphasis on the wife's chastity: her *śakti* must be transferred to the husband and to no one else. Moreover, in keeping with this model (and with the contrast between male and female withholding of fluids), it is believed that the husband can increase his own small amount of *śakti* by performing asceticism but that the wife can best increase hers simply by remaining chaste, that is, by containing her powers (fluids) or giving them only to her husband.

As goddesses playing the role of mortal women, Pārvatī and Rādhā (and, to a lesser extent, Sītā) serve as mediators who intercede between the worshiper and the god, playing the role of docile and accessible servants. It is difficult to assess the precise components of mortality and immortality in any of these figures at a particular time; Rādhā is unknown to the *Bhāgavata Purāṇa*, is a very human figure in the *Gītagovinda*, and is the essence of the great female godhead in the *Brahmavaivarta Purāṇa*. Subtle shifts may take place within a single text; thus, despite her generally inferior position in the *Gītagovinda*, Rādhā triumphs in the end, placing her feet on Kṛṣṇa's head (as Kālī does to Śiva), and assuming the "inverse" position in her love play with Kṛṣṇa; at this point she is called Caṇḍī (a name usually given only to Devī), a possible indication that she has transcended the bounds normally assigned to Rādhā (*GG* 12. 10).[18]

Pārvatī, too, may be regarded either as an appendage of the great god Śiva or as his controller. Similarly, as Satī and Sītā assume higher theological status, the same technique is used to distance both of them from embarrassing episodes in their predeified past: Satī no longer actually burns herself on her husband's pyre but merely creates a "shadow" Satī (*MBP* 9–11), just as Sīta creates a "shadow" Sītā to be burnt when Rāma abandons her (*RCM* D. 23–24 and 108–9). Both of these incidents are in imitation of the earliest Indian split goddess, Saraṇyū the mare, who leaves a "shadow" image behind when she abandons her mortal husband (see below, chap. 6, sec. C).

Despite these variations, it is usually clear at any given moment what the emphasis of the text is, and this emphasis bears strongly on the balance of power between the two members of the unequal partnership. Richard Brubaker has discussed this problem with reference to the consorts of the village goddess: "The antagonists [of the Goddess] are sometimes gods rather than men or demons, but the antagonist . . . is the one who *responds* to the hierophany; his relationship with it therefore parallels the human relationship with the divine and, in so doing, has theological implications for human behavior" (Brubaker 1978, p. 153). If Kṛṣṇa or Śiva is God, and if he is supplicated by his consort, the consort is *thereby* cast in the role of a mortal even if she is technically a goddess. This becomes explicit in the frame episodes of several Tantras, which take the form of a conversation between Śiva and the Goddess, both of whom are regarded as divinities in the Tantric context. The text opens with a statement by her to him: "How is it that you are immortal, while I am merely mortal? How may I too become immortal?" And his answer to her is the subsequent Tantric doctrine (cf., for example, the *Gorakṣa-vijaya*).

The relationship between the mortal and immortal partners, or between the devotee and the object of worship, may vary in different texts with different theologies. Thus the image of dancing on the prostrate body of a devotee or dancing to control and dominate a consort (see below, chap. 5) takes two forms in the mythology of Śiva: in the image of the Naṭarāja, Śiva (the god) crushes the body of the lover (the devotee); in the Tantric image of Kālī, the Goddess crushes the body of her lover (Śiva) (Egnor 1978, pp. 172, 198). In the first image, the relationship between God and devotee is primary, the sexual (or martial) relationship secondary (for no one is sure whether the image under Śiva's foot is a demon or a devotee); in the second image, the relationship between Goddess and devotee is secondary, for the image is usually described in purely sexual terms. Nevertheless, Śiva is on top in the first and on the bottom in the second, changing from God to devotee. This tendency to depict the consort as the devotee is enhanced by the overlapping patterns of devotion to a god, service to a husband, and supplication of a lover—particularly a lover who remains aloof and distant, as Kṛṣṇa distances himself from Rādhā through erotic teasing and Śiva withdraws from Pārvatī through his ascetic meditation.

Viraha: Longing in Separation

This brings us to the motif of *viraha*, or the suffering of separation from the beloved. Usually it is the woman who suffers in this way, not the man, for in the orthodox tradition (Śaivism or Vaiṣṇavism) she is the worshiper longing for the (male) god, and the god is a *deus absconditus* or *otiosus*. As Professor Godbole explains to Mrs. Moore, the worshiper imagines that he is a gopī who sings to Kṛṣṇa, "Come to me," but the god refuses to come:

> "But He comes in some other song, I hope?" said Mrs Moore gently. "Oh no, he refuses to come," repeated Godbole, perhaps not understanding her question. "I say to Him, Come, come, come, come, come, come. He neglects to come" (Forster 1924, p. 80).

He may come in "some other song" but not in *our* song, not now.

Does the god long for her as she longs for him? *Bhakti* theology tells us that he does, that he must, that devotion is by its very definition mutual. But the emotional stance of the myth does not always jibe with the general theology that is often read into it; and if we look at what the myths *say* they mean, it is evident that her suffering is greater than his. The woman's greater suffering in separation may be a reflection of human social conditions in India, where the woman marries out of the family and is penned up at home, while the man has outside diversions; female *viraha* is thus a hierarchical and agnatic fact as well as a psychological reality. Moreover, since women are usually much younger than their husbands in India, for reasons that we have discussed at some length, women are more often widows than men are widowers, and the life of an Indian widow is one of separation not only from her husband but from many other parts of society.

But the overriding meaning of *viraha* in the myths must be theological: the worshiper suffers more than the god does, and woman (as worshiper) more than man (as god). Sītā in Laṅkā misses Rāma more than he misses her—or, rather, she can *do* nothing but miss him, while the whole *Rāmāyaṇa* is the story of what he does because of his inability to tolerate her abduction. Thus her mood is portrayed as *viraha*, while his is anger, heroism, and all the attendant male qualities. To be sure, several passages in the *Rāmāyaṇa* express his extravagant sadness and longing when, in her role as earth goddess, she disappears from him forever (*R* 7. 88, app. 1. 13). But Rāma is cursed that he will undergo separation from his wife at the same time that he is cursed that he will become mortal in the first place, which strengthens the hypothesis that *viraha* is primarily a human emotion, not a divine one (*R* 7. 50, app. 1. 7. 13). Rāma (or Viṣṇu, as he is at the moment of the curse) magnanimously agrees to accept the curse "for the sake of all creatures" (the usual face-saver); but even here there is no evidence that he will suffer *viraha*, merely that he will experience separation (*viyoga*). Moreover, the scenes depicting Rāma's excessive longing are late interpolations, which may well have been influenced by the set piece that recurs in many Sanskrit poems and plays, in which the man expresses his grief at the departure or death of his beloved. All of these instances gain their power from the fact that they are reversals of the normal situation, in which men do *not* usually experience the pangs of *viraha*, which is regarded as a primarily feminine weakness.

When we come to Śiva, the situation is somewhat different, as we might expect. Śiva allows women to dominate him more than Viṣṇu does; so, too, he misses them more when they go away. Indeed, Śiva is credited with having created the fever of *viraha* himself when attacked by the god of desire. Although the mythology of Śiva does contain important examples of the woman as worshiper longing for the god—Pārvatī in her lonely asceticism suffering an agony of desire for the god, who hardly thinks of her at all (*Kumārasambhava* 5)—Śiva suffers in his turn. He undergoes *viraha* for the city of Benares and for the goddess who is the city incarnate; he is expressly said to ache with longing for Benares even as he ached for Satī, to experience an erotic agony that even cool sandalwood paste cannot allay (*Sk P* 4. 44). In later texts, however, the goddess of Benares herself is said to experience equally great suffering in separation from him and to undergo violent asceticism in order to win him back (*Mudgala Purāṇa* 1. 50–51). In this way, the inappropriate suffering of Śiva in the earlier text is set right, in the Hindu view, by the more conventional suffering of the female. Yet in Śiva the pangs of *viraha* are not truly out of character; when Satī commits suicide, Śiva goes literally mad with longing for her, even to the point of a pathological attachment to her corpse and a series of violent sexual encounters undertaken in the vain attempt to quench his longing for her (O'Flaherty 1973, pp. 173–75).

There are other, more general, examples of men suffering from *viraha*. Kālidāsa's *Meghadūta* is based entirely on the words of a demigod driven to commit a poetic fallacy by longing for his wife (esp. v. 5); but, even here, more of the poem is devoted to his image of her longing for him than to his expression of his own sorrow. South India provides a double twist: classical South Indian poetry presents the image of a man who undergoes public suffering when he fails to win the woman he loves: he rides naked on a palmyra horse (a palmyra mare, one would expect), whose sharp fronds slash his body as her cruelty cuts into his heart. In South Indian *bhakti*, however, when the man imagines himself to be a woman, the devotee likens himself to a woman riding a palmyra horse (Nammāḻvār, *Tiruvāymoli* 5. 3. 9; Yocum 1979, p. 15). Thus the inversion is inverted, and, once again, it is the woman who suffers *viraha*.

South Indian devotional texts make great use of the concept of *ūṭal*, "quarrelling between lovers, sulking, particularly feigned aversion in order to enhance the pleasure of union" (Yocum 1979, p. 16). To this day, religious festivals in Tamilnadu enact such lovers' quarrels between Śiva and his wife or Viṣṇu and his wife (ibid., p. 17). One of the most sacred Tamil texts, the *Tirukkuṟal* (v. 1326) establishes this taste as canonical (while, incidentally, relating sex to eating): "Digesting food is better than eating. Fighting is more fun than fucking" (ibid., p. 18). When the gods quarrel in this way—or the devotee quarrels with the god, mocking him for his all-too-human banality—the anger and humiliation are expressed primarily by the woman. For the fire that Śiva distills into the flame of *viraha* in one text becomes the underwater mare in another—the symbol of thwarted female emotion (see below, chapter 7, sec. F).

Viraha remains an important theological metaphor when god is female. In the mythology of the mother goddess, the abandoned consort (and son) experiences desperate longing for her; here, as in the Sanskrit plays, it is the man who suffers (as Rāma suffers for his abducted goddess, Sītā). But when god is androgynous, *viraha* takes on new meanings to express the paradox of separation in union. Here, when one might expect an equal balance of suffering, it is again the woman who suffers most; for the basic equation of woman as devotee overrides the archaic pattern of goddess and consort, and the image lapses back into its primary impact: *viraha* experienced by the woman who is the devotee. In any case, *viraha* is regarded as essential to the most passionate love, human or divine (Dimock 1966, p. 17).

The Union of Mortals and Immortals

The theoretical model of pairs ranked according to male/female dominance interacts with another model, which ranks them according to the mortal or immortal status of each partner. Several different patterns may be simultaneously present at any moment, though one is usually emphasized. First is the mating of a god and a goddess, the classical hierogamy, in which he may be dominant (Viṣṇu and Lakṣmī, Oberon and Titania) or she (Śiva and Devī). Second is the mating of the mortal and his mortal mistress, in the tradition of Sanskrit court poetry; here there is usually no marriage at all but merely an illicit liaison. In this group, as in the first, the male is usually dominant. This human pattern pervades much of the mythology of Kṛṣṇa and Rādhā, and it is interesting to note that when it was applied to that of Śiva and Pārvatī (in the eighth canto of Kālidāsa's *Kumārasambhava*, many centuries before the myth of Kṛṣṇa and Rādhā) voices were immediately raised in protest, for it was thought unseemly to depict in such human terms the love play of gods (as unseemly as describing that of one's own parents).[19] Even Kṛṣṇa's love play proved an embarrassment to many a devout commentator once Kṛṣṇa came to be regarded as God incarnate; Śrīdhara goes to great lengths to explain why, since Kṛṣṇa is God, he could not actually have committed adultery with the gopīs (though other commentators went to even greater lengths to explain why, precisely because he *is* God, he can do things that mortals had better not imitate [*Bh P* 10. 33. 30–35]).

Third is the mating of a mortal with an immortal. The dominated female figures in this group occupy a twilight zone, supplicating the god as a mortal would but assuming a quasi-equality with the god when the marriage actually takes place. This pattern may be seen in many of the myths of Sītā with Rāma and Śiva with Pārvatī, and it is relevant to the understanding of many manifestations of the cult of Kṛṣṇa and Rādhā as well. This third group raises certain theological problems. We have seen that any sexual interaction is fraught with dangers; sex is auspicious (life-connected), but it is impure and dangerous even when the partners are well matched (Marglin 1978a). Indeed, when they are well matched, and both are powerful gods, the cumulative power of their sexuality places the entire universe in danger. Thus Śiva's seed must be kept away from Pārvatī when she is treated as a mighty goddess, lest the two forces together reach a kind of radioactive critical mass and blow up the universe (O'Flaherty 1973, pp. 300–301). When the partners are badly matched, the dangers are also great; and what could be more unequal than the mating of a mortal with an immortal?

When the goddess is the dominated figure, the mating is regarded as auspicious (i.e., hypergamous) and no danger is seen, for power flows the way it is supposed to, from male (divinity) to female (worshiper).

Thus the worshipers of Kṛṣṇa imagine themselves to be Rādhā, for the consort is identified with the mortal worshiper and mediates on his behalf with the god. The Purāṇas abound in instances of such mediation on a very literal level; when Śiva is angry, for example, and wishes to destroy or punish a mortal, Pārvatī often intercedes and persuades him to be lenient. This means that the male worshiper must imagine himself to be the (dominated) female, and *bhaktas* seem often willing to do this, though Śiva-*bhaktas* usually identify with Śiva rather than with Pārvatī (O'Flaherty 1976, pp. 286–91). The correspondence between the devotee and the woman is made explicit in a Tamil text that puns on the word that can mean either "husband" or "God" or both (here translated as "Lord") and the word "ripeness," which can designate either sexual or metaphysical maturity:

> Even though he marries every year, Śiva is still called a chaste student and Śakti is known as a virgin. . . . Further, just as women are called "eternal virgins," and just as they need a post to cling to as creeping vines do, so all life must unite with the ultimate, which is the Lord (Husband/God). The holy wedding ceremony teaches that the Lord will take unto himself living creatures of the nature of women when they are mature in devotion.[20]

In hierogamies, therefore, the female is the devotee. In human marriages, too, it is believed that deities respond to the compelling power of the *śakti* of the woman, and so the wife is better able than the husband to prevail upon the deities to intercede on behalf of the husband and family (S. Daniel 1978, p. 7). Thus the consort of the god, lower than him in authority, and the consort of the human husband, higher than him in power, form a doubly mediating chain to connect the two male figures between whom religious authority and power must flow.

When the Goddess is dominant, the worshiper need undergo no change of sex in order to identify with her consort, but there are other problems inherent in this process, problems arising from the forbidding nature of the Goddess. Ancient Indo-European mythology abounds in object lessons of this type, as we shall see. As one observer drily remarked of this corpus, "Cohabitation with a goddess (= mother figure) usually weakens, unmans or even paralyses the mortal man" (Devereux 1976, p. 305 n.). In addition, there are dangers inherent in the worshiper's identification with Śiva even when Śiva is not regarded as the all-powerful deity; though Indian myths and ritual texts, like so many others, state explicitly that the worshiper should think, "I must do what the gods did" (*ŚB* 7. 2. 1. 4), they also emphasize the dangers of overstepping the boundaries between the human and the divine, as we have seen (chap. 3). Thus the Vaiṣṇava commentator's warning that one should not imitate Kṛṣṇa might be taken as an orthodox objection to Tantric visualization, in which the worshiper imagines himself to be the god; but the Tantras themselves are careful to specify that the average mortal cannot imitate the god, that "Quod licet Jovi non licet bovi" (O'Flaherty 1976, pp. 286–91), and it is perhaps worthy of note that the god, the Roman equivalent of the orgiastic Indra (or Śiva), is here contrasted with the bull, the animal whose virility compares unfavorably with that of the (divine) stallion (see below, chap. 8, sec. F).

Moreover, there are complex problems arising from the flow of power in the "perverse" direction, from female to male. The primary danger is that the male worshiper will be overpowered by his Goddess. For this reason, though the worshiper of divine couples in which the female is dominant may identify with the consort (as the Tantric worshiper of Devī may identify with Śiva), other alternatives are usually preferred: the worshiper identifies with *both* the Goddess and her consort or even with the Goddess herself. Often the Tantric visualization makes use of a human woman who is identified with the Goddess, a woman who is, moreover, explicitly required to be of a *very low caste*. In this way a balance of power is restored between human and divine powers and, on each level, between male and female. Despite the danger to the male worshiper of the Goddess, benevolent forces flow to him. Another way in which the danger is offset is by splitting the spheres of ritual and myth: power does not flow merely vertically, from the female divinity to the male worshiper; it is also split so that it flows horizontally on two levels: in heaven, it flows from Śakti to Śiva, and on earth it flows between their two human incarnations, from female to male. Authority, however, still flows from Śiva to Śakti and from (high-caste) male adept to female Untouchable, in the accepted pattern of male dominance. The flow from Goddess to worshiper, transcending the boundaries of this split-level flow, is also welcomed in this cult as a way in which the male becomes enriched and energized by receiving power (female semen) from the female while retaining authority (male semen) within himself.

These reversals or inversions occur in several forms in the myths and icons. The inverse position in sexual intercourse, with the woman on top, is a reversal of hierarchical patterns of authority; it is therefore significant that the goddess is "on top" when she kills Mahiṣa or dances on Śiva's corpse, that the erotic Yoginīs carved on medieval Hindu temples are on top of the yogis with whom they are copulating, and that, as we will see, the hag of the night-mare rides the man whom she destroys. The same Sanskrit term used to describe this position (*viparītam*) is also used to describe the "reversed" or "backward" direction of the flow in the Tantric ritual, where the female gives the male her fluids (semen or menstrual blood); though auspicious, this is called the "fierce recitation" (see below, chap. 8, sec. L). Clearly, the two processes are related as well as analogous: when the woman is on top, her fluids can flow downward naturally. That the native tradition explicitly calls these processes "inversions" substantiates our attempt to analyze the structure of the myths and rituals both in terms of cosmic inversions of the type that Eliade has explored so deeply and in terms of the simple inversions of plot and process (stallion replacing mare, copulation replacing slaughter) that are at the heart of structural analysis.

In some texts the flow of erotic power from the Goddess is further controlled and made safe by raising her to such a high and abstract plane that eroticism is no longer significant (the same process also made the human implications of her "motherhood" insignificant and thus made possible in the first place an erotic relationship in which incest was irrelevant). As *bhakti* grows, the emphasis shifts from the emotion in which one imagines god as a lover (*śṛṅgāra rasa* or *madhurya bhāva*) to one in which god is loved as a master is loved by a slave.[21] In such a relationship, as in the maternal, it no longer matters whether the worshiper is male or female.

The Rewards of Living Dangerously

This material raises a basic hermeneutic question: Are the activities of the gods and goddesses meant to serve as models for human behavior? Gods do many things that men do not do, acts that serve many purposes: wish fulfillment, a negative moral lesson, or a symbol of human potential. It is difficult to sort out the elements of a myth, ostensibly about a god and a goddess, that correspond to normal fantasy, to pathology, and to theology. But something of a balance between these categories may be achieved when we examine myths in which gods and mortals interact and in which the behavior of mortals is explicitly compared with the behavior of gods.

On the most basic, orthodox level, the question of identifying with the god's consort is met with a blatant prohibition: Don't do it. This is the philosophy underlying the myths in which mortals shun contact with the gods, as Damayantī prefers Nala over her divine suitors. But both *bhakti* and Tantra challenge this model and suggest ways in which such contact—though admittedly *dangerous*—is a source of power for the worshiper willing to take the chance, to expose himself to such enormous forces.

Many of the transformations in these myths involve the transfer of power from one sex to the other. The Goddess is the incarnation of the power of the god (*śakti*), but she derives this power from the authority of the male gods in the first place, when they create her out of their own powers. So, too, though she "milks" her husband of his strength sexually or even kills him, she is the corpse-reviver par excellence. The exchange of male virility for female powers of revivification may also be seen in some of the episodes of sex reversals: the god turns himself into a woman in order to siphon off male powers (often demonic powers), ultimately to return to his male condition newly invigorated.[22] Similarly, Kṛṣṇa-worshipers become *temporarily* female and then return to being males—but fuller and better males; this process may be regarded as a kind of serial androgyny (see below, chap. 9, sec. B). The epitome of this Śākta development appears in a myth in which the Goddess turns all three male gods (Brahmā, Viṣṇu, and Śiva) into females in order to teach them how to create; she then turns them back into males, after giving them their three *śaktis*, Mahālakṣmī, Mahākālī, and Mahāsarasvatī (*DBP* 3. 4. 6–8; 3. 6. 83). If one is willing to take the chance of losing one's sexual identity, one can not only survive but return, stronger than before.

Thus, although sexual contact with divinity is dangerous, it holds the possibility of salvation. In yogic thought, duality is death and nonduality is the conquest of death; the merging of male and female is immortality. So, too, any contact with divinity—the closer the better—is an experience that promises a taste of immortality. The worshiper willing to risk this doubly hazardous encounter may achieve realizations and powers that can be won in no other way.

5 The Dance of Śiva with Kālī and Pārvatī

A. The Dance of Śiva in Poetry and Myth

The carrion-eater dances:
he produces day and night by successive opening and
closing of his eyes.
He covers heaven with his quill-like hair that flies in all directions
from the openings of the skull he holds within his hands.
He breaks our eardrums with his mighty roar.
(*SRK* 1541, trans. Ingalls)

"Pretty eyebrows, put your arm like this
and take your posture so.
Stretch not too high, but bend your toes.
See? Just look at me."
Thus Śambhu teaches Pārvatī
with voice-drum sweet as thunder.
May what he adds for rhythm of her dance,
the clapping of his hands, protect you.
(*SRK* 60, trans. Ingalls)

Śiva is the dancer in both of these verses, yet how different the two dances are. The first is the dance of death, the *tāṇḍava*, appropriate to Śiva in his destructive aspect; the second is the dance of creation, a gentle, erotic dance (*lāsya*). Are they two aspects of the same dance, or two different dances? Daniel H. H. Ingalls has addressed this problem:

> While the image makers represent several different dances, it is almost always to the *tāṇḍava* that the poets of our anthology refer. . . . While our poets speak of Śiva as creator of the world . . . they seem not to associate this function with the dance. In one

> verse . . . the *lāsya* dance is mentioned, which should be a gentle dance, but the poet actually gives it symptoms as violent as the *tāṇḍava*. Only when teaching the dance to the mountain princess . . . does the divine dancer grow mild (Ingalls 1965, p. 73).

In both classical mythology and poetry, the *tāṇḍava* prevails overwhelmingly, but in late medieval and modern Indian literature, and in works of Western scholarship, the image of Śiva as the graceful, creative dancer is far more frequently encountered. In a parallel development within the mythology, Śiva's dance changes from a solitary act to a dance with a consort. Often his dance becomes gentle when she is present; on the other hand, her dance may be as violent as his own. To understand the power balance in their union, and in particular to understand how they control each other, it is essential to understand how they dance, both together and apart.

Coomaraswamy (1971, p. 67) has distinguished three main variants of Śiva's dance: the dance performed in the midst of the gods at twilight; the *tāṇḍava*; and the dance of Śiva Naṭarāja in Chidambaram. The last, as we shall see from the underlying mythology, is clearly a dance of aggression and destruction. The twilight dance, too, is a dance of death (*SRK* 50 and 52); it frightens Śiva's wife, Bhavānī, who watches it with eyes paralyzed with terror and is grateful when a red cloud takes the place of the usual gory skin of the flayed elephant draped around Śiva's shoulders (*Meghadūta* 36). And the third form, the *tāṇḍava*, is by definition the dance that destroys the universe. What, then, is the occasion for the *lāsya*, the gentle dance? Coomaraswamy ignores it, and with good reason, for it is of very little significance in the mythology, despite its popularity in iconography.

Only when Śiva is in loving union with Pārvatī (or with another subservient woman) does he perform a gentle dance—which is, implicitly, an erotic dance. Thus Śiva dances to assuage Pārvatī's anger; and when Menā, the mother of Pārvatī, hesitates to allow her daughter to marry Śiva, he appears to Menā as a charming dancer:

> Śiva danced before Menā and Pārvatī, and when Pārvatī heard his beautiful song she fainted, and in her heart she saw Śiva smeared with ashes and garlanded with bones. She chose him for her husband, and the vision passed. Then Menā, who saw only the graceful dancer, was enchanted by him and offered him jewels, but he refused them and asked for Pārvatī as alms, and then he began to sing and dance again. Menā was enraged, and she abused him and tried to throw him out, but no one could touch the beggar, who blazed like a great fire. He changed his form into Viṣṇu and

> then into the sun, and into the androgynous form of Śiva with Pārvatī, and then finally he turned back into a beggar asking for Pārvatī as alms. When this request was refused, the beggar vanished, and then Menā and her husband Himālaya realized that this had been Śiva, and a great devotion was born in them (*ŚP* 2. 3. 30. 25–54); cf. *BVP* 4. 40. 71–111 and O'Flaherty 1973, p. 216).

Śiva's Dionysian aspect appeals to Menā when she fails to be won by any rational argument; yet even here there is an edge of terror in his dance, and when this other, darker side becomes dominant, Menā fears him again. Superficially, Menā sees the graceful dancer before her, while Pārvatī has the inner vision of the graveyard dance; in their theological attitudes, however, Pārvatī sees him as the handsome dancer, while Menā sees the doomsday dancer blazing in defiance against her. Unlike Tārāvatī, who resists the vision of the gruesome, fully divine aspect of Śiva even as she resists her own divinity, Pārvatī joyfully accepts the full implications of the hierogamy. She is as deeply stirred by the *tāṇḍava* as she is by the *lāsya* dance.

Another of Śiva's in-laws, Dakṣa, the father of Satī, is similarly troubled by the antisocial aspect of Śiva, epitomized by his wild dance. When Satī marries Śiva, Dakṣa takes Satī upon his lap and complains, "Śiva always wanders about dancing and singing and doing other despicable things, and this embarrasses me" (*PP* 1. 5. 41). On the other hand, Śiva's tamer dance may also arouse scorn precisely because it is too tame—because it is banal:

> When the gods were harassed by the demons, they sought refuge with Śiva, who agreed to slay the demons. But just then the Goddess said to him, "See how Skanda is playing," and Śiva embraced Skanda and danced with him, crying, "My son, my son," and the little boy danced and played, and all the world danced, and Pārvatī was full of joy. But the gods stood beside the door in misery, and, though they praised Śiva, they looked at one another as if to say, "But . . . ." And they said, "We are unlucky. The demons have all the luck." Aloud they said, "Honor to Śiva," but they honored him less in their hearts (*LP* 1. 71. 119–41).

Śiva dances here in joy rather than in anger or lust, but the dance still frustrates the purposes of the cosmos. The gods take exception not to his dancing per se but to his delay in fighting, his neglect of his social duty; similarly, he is said to be the laughingstock of the gods for singing and dancing to please Pārvatī (*PP* 6. 11. 7). Śiva's uxorious nature may be satirized in an episode in which he dances with the celestial nymphs (*apsarases*), becomes sexually aroused, and then sends for Pārvatī and becomes cross as a bear when she delays too long in putting on her jewelry (*ŚP* 2. 5. 51. 35–45; cf. O'Flaherty 1973, p. 146).

An important variant of the *tāṇḍava* that we have already encountered in another context is Śiva's dance with the corpse of Satī:

> When Satī had killed herself, Śiva took up her corpse and, balancing it on his head, danced fervently. The earth trembled, and the tortoise and serpent supporting the earth could not bear it; but Śiva kept dancing in mad joy, his eyes whirling. All the gods wondered how he could be made to calm down, and then Viṣṇu cut the body of Satī into pieces with his discus, and, as Śiva continued to dance, he felt the body become light, and he realized that all the limbs had been cut off, and he stopped dancing (*BDP* 2. 40. 18–54; *DBP* 7. 30. 44–50; *MBP* 11. 32–118).

This destructive *tāṇḍava* explicitly inverts the qualities of the erotic *lāsya*; for Śiva, bereft of the living Satī and tortured by *viraha*, embraces her dead body in necrophiliac frenzy. This is a manifestation of the general pattern: with Pārvatī (or another subservient woman), the dance is gentle; without her, it is destructive. The two dances, the erotic and the deadly, are often interchangeable from a cosmic point of view, and in the classical texts they are both inauspicious: excessive energy, whether overtly destructive or purely erotic, endangers the universe (O'Flaherty 1973, pp. 296–313). Moreover, the scorn of the dancing Śiva expressed in the texts cited above stems from a deep-seated mistrust of dancing. This mistrust—which is characteristic of the majority of the medieval and many of the ancient texts—is based in part on earlier Upaniṣadic attitudes of ascetic misogyny.

B. Death as a Dancer

Dance is closely associated with death in the earliest post–Ṛg Vedic texts. A vivid example appears in the *Jaiminīya Brāhmaṇa*:

> Prajāpati (the creator) and Death were competing in sacrifice. Prajāpati's weapons were praise, recitation, and ritual; Death's weapons were song accompanied by the lute; dance; and what is done for no point [i.e., no ritual point, or art for art's sake]. The two were equally great, and for many years there was no victory. Then Prajāpati wished to conquer Death, and he saw numerical equivalence and computation in the sacrifice [i.e., the precise formula of the ritual]. With that he conquered Death, who

> retreated for refuge. The parts of the sacrificial ritual—praise, ritual, the instruments of sacrifice—became the music of the lute, and dance, and what is done for no point, and the various parts of the lute (*JB* 2. 69–70).

At the end of this myth, musical instruments become ritual instruments; Prajāpati absorbs Death; fear of death is replaced by fear of ritual error (Heesterman 1962, p. 20). This is the Apollonian aspect of religion typical of the Brāhmaṇas—a static, ritualized sublimation of the creative spirit. The secular arts (for dance in the Vedic period was not yet a part of formal religion) are conquered and absorbed by the priestly crafts.

A closely related myth from the same period depicts a conflict in which dancing is associated with another form of death:

> The Gandharva Viśvāvasu stole Soma from the Gāyatrī. The gods said, "The Gandharvas are fond of women; let us send Vāc [Goddess of speech] to them, and she will return to us, together with Soma." Vāc did this, but then the Gandharvas tried to woo her back by reciting the Vedas to her; the gods created the lute and song, and she turned to the gods. She turned to them in vain, since she turned from those who were praying to those who were engaged in dance and song. And so, even to this day, women are given to vain things and are most attached to the man who dances and sings (*ŚB* 3. 2. 4. 1–6).

The word translated here as "in vain" is the same as the term used in the previous myth to refer to nonritual action; in this second passage it refers to an action explicitly contrasted with prayer and the recitation of the Vedas. Dance is thus the opposite of religion, but here, in addition, it is associated with women, on three different levels: the Gāyatrī (a poetic meter, or a bird), here regarded as a female; the goddess of speech; and women in general. All three of these females are instruments of loss: Gāyatrī loses Soma; Vāc loses the Vedas; and women in general lose (by implication) good men in favor of profligates. Finally, the fact that the woman causes the gods to lose Soma, the sap of life, may imply a sexual loss; and the fact that, through dance and song, the goddess of sacred speech—the goddess who dwells in the mouth—is lured back again implies the possibility of using dance in the service of higher forms of nonecstatic religion. Thus the instrument of loss becomes the instrument of restoration.

In the Upaniṣads, death is a dancer. When Naciketas visits the world of Death in order to obtain knowledge about dying, Death tempts him with many boons and, finally, offers him lovely women with musical instruments; but Naciketas scorns them as objects that cause one's powers to wear out with age (*jarayanti tejas*), and he says to Death, "Dance and song are yours" (*Kaṭha U* 1. 25–26). The association of the dance not only with aging but with death persists in many later texts, where Indra sends dancing girls instead of Death to destroy would-be immortals (O'Flaherty 1973, pp. 87–89).

In epic mythology, Śiva appears in the role of the ascetic, opposed to the dance (though he also appears as an erotic dancer):

> The sage Maṅkaṇaka, seeing some vegetable sap fall from his hand, began to dance. To stop his dancing, Śiva broke off his own finger, which turned to ashes. Seeing this, the sage realized, "One's own body is made only of ashes." Because of this, Śiva is called "Made of Ashes" [Bhasmabhūta] (*MBh* 13. 17. 92; *MBh* 1862, 13. 17. 95, with Nīlakaṇṭha's comm.).

This is the typical Upaniṣadic view of the dance as the epitome of emotional chaos, as the greatest obstacle to the Apollonian spirit of classical Indian religion.

The significance of the dance in this brief myth is clarified and emphasized in a Purāṇic variant that adds another dance and an erotic dancer to offset the ascetic Śiva:

> The sage Maṅkaṇaka set out to bathe in his bark garment, and the celestial nymphs bathed there with him. Then the ascetic sage became excited and shed his seed in the water, and seven sages were born from it. One day, Maṅkaṇaka was wounded in the hand by a blade of sacred grass, and plant sap flowed from that wound, and he was filled with joy, and he began to dance. And then everything that was moving or still started to dance; the universe started to dance, for it was bewitched by his energy. The gods asked Śiva to do something about the sage so that he would stop dancing. When Śiva saw that the sage was filled with joy to excess, he struck his own thumb with the tip of his finger, and from that wound ashes shining like snow came forth. When the priest saw this, he was ashamed, and he fell at Śiva's feet and begged him to let his ascetic power be preserved, and Śiva granted this (*Vām P* 5. 17. 2–23; cf. *MBh* 3. 81).

When Indra wishes to destroy an ascetic, he sends a celestial dancing girl (a nymph, or *apsaras*) to seduce him; these nymphs are also described as "Graspers" who carry off embryos—the quintessence of the whore who destroys children (*MBh* 3. 219. 38). In the myth of Maṅkaṇaka the seduction seems to take place without the agency of

Indra, for Maṅkaṇaka's own Dionysian frenzy is sufficient to destroy his ascetic power, first in the presence of the nymphs (whereupon he sheds his seed) and then at the sight of the primeval sap, symbolic of that same seed. As the god of ascetics, Śiva is the enemy of dancers, the enemy of the dancing Maṅkaṇaka, and the benefactor of the contrite Maṅkaṇaka. But in later mythology, Śiva himself becomes a dancer.

Śiva's aspect as god of dancers comes from several different sources, and one of these is Indra; for Indra is often portrayed as a dancer in the Ṛg Veda (7. 68. 7; 8. 92. 3), a role that Śiva inherits from Indra along with many other orgiastic qualities (O'Flaherty 1973, pp. 84–89). Indra is a dancer and the enemy of ascetics; Śiva is an ascetic and the enemy of dancers—but he is also a dancer, though not the enemy of ascetics. On the contrary: Śiva's dancing may serve the same function that his *yoga* serves.[1] As the epitome of culture inflicted upon nature, of form superimposed on passion, of society riding herd on instinct, dance serves to control sexuality—even as *yoga* does; but it produces dangerous activity when it gets out of control itself. Like *yoga*, dance channels violent but useful forces; and, like *yoga*, it both heightens sexual powers and internalizes them through the use of techniques of elaborately pinpointed physical control and deep concentration. At the end of the myth describing the origin of Śiva's *tāṇḍava*, the narrator remarks, "But there are others who maintain that the dance of the lord takes place because of the bliss of *yoga*" (*LP* 1. 106. 28).

Indra is not the only dancer in the Ṛg Veda nor the most important one: Uṣas, goddess of the Dawn, is described as a beautiful dancing girl who puts on bright ornaments and uncovers her breast. But the same hymn reveals another side of Dawn that is less charming and more in line with the concept of the dance of death:

> The ancient goddess, born again and again dressed in the same color, causes the mortal to age and wears away his life-span, as a cunning gambler carries off the stakes. . . . Shrinking human generations, the young woman shines as her lover [the sun] gazes at her (*RV* 1. 92. 4, 10–11).

The central metaphor evidently refers to Dawn as a measure of time, appearing day by day to mark the steady approach of old age and death; but the secondary metaphor is that of a courtesan who wears men out and destroys them by aging them (*jarayanti āyus*, like Naciketas's accusation of dance). Moreover, it is implied that this siphoning-off of vital forces not only harms human generations but is of benefit to her: she remains young forever, living on the forces that she has stolen from us like a cunning gambler. The sun, her consort, is mortal; she is the immortal woman who will be the death of him—and of us.

This sinister aspect of the dancing girl persists in Purāṇic literature as well. At Indra's instigation, Old Age (*jarā*, a feminine noun) takes the form of a beautiful young woman to dance before a king who has been granted eternal youth. Assisted by Kāma, the god of lust, as stage manager, and by Rati, Kāma's wife and the goddess of sexual pleasure, in the role of another dancer, Old Age deludes the king and enters him: "And when the dance was over, and the dancers had gone, the virtuous king was overcome by Old Age, for his mind was sullied by desire" (*PP* 2. 76. 18–30; 2. 77. 1–4). By succumbing to the demonic charms of dance, song, and emotion, the king loses the powers of self-control that have kept him immortal. Here the dancers are not Death but his minions, Old Age and Desire; when the dance is over, Old Age is exposed as the hag she really is, even as Śiva's dance before Maṅkaṇaka ends in a display of ashes, the stuff of death.

The image of Death as a dancer occurs in two Baiga myths; these tribal tales, though technically non-Hindu, show strong Hindu influences. In the first myth, Death is the seductive dancer:

> In Koeli-Kacchar lived a Baiga and a Baigin. When Bihi Mata saw that nobody was dying, she was troubled; she made from the dirt of her body a Sahis and his wife and sent them to the Baiga, saying, "Make a drum of earth and go and dance in front of these Baiga." The Baiga could not help it, he fell in love with the Sahis woman. Now, before that time, man and woman had never been to one another, and that was why there was no death in the world. But when the Baiga met the Sahis woman alone in the forest, there was an earthquake. Mother Earth trembled, and the Baiga died immediately. From that time there has been death in the world (Elwin 1949, p. 414; O'Flaherty 1976, p. 244).

The dance is here equivalent to sexual intercourse, as in the Sanskrit texts; the image of the earthquake translates the dangerous act into the epitome of violent, destructive movement. Death here is a drummer as well as a dancer, a role that he also assumes in Tamil texts (Thurston 1909, 2:116).

In a second Baiga myth, a demon is tricked into dancing himself to death, like the Demon of Ashes, Bhasmāsura, or the ballerina in *The Red Shoes*:

> A demon had a magic amulet that burnt people to ashes. He was in love with Pārvatī and tried to seduce her. Viṣṇu took the form of Pārvatī and said, "My Mahārāja first dances, then he does it [i.e.,

> copulates]." The demon danced, and Viṣṇu told him to place his hands on his head. The demon did so and burnt himself to ashes (Elwin 1949, p. 348).

As in the myth of Maṅkaṇaka, the dance is associated with ashes; here the anti-dancer is not Śiva but Viṣṇu in the form of a woman, the form he often assumes in order to rescue Śiva.[2] And the woman whom he impersonates is Pārvatī, the right woman to calm down a dangerous dancer—in this case not Śiva but a demon with Śiva's power to burn people to ashes.

C. Dance as the Conquest of Death

When dance was eventually transformed into a ritual activity, it took back some of the functions that had been stolen from it in the *Jaiminīya Brāhmaṇa*; specifically, it became a way to conquer death. The purpose of the Hindu liturgy was to ritualize death in a sacrifice that Jan Heesterman has described as "controlled catastrophe" (Heesterman 1977, p. 87). It was precisely to safeguard this element of control that the priests banished the Dionysian elements of music and dance, replacing them with dry, precise rituals. But in Tamil religion "music and dance are highly ordered and can help keep under control the forces of disorder. . . . It is important that such behavior [as dancing in trance] did and does not take place at random, but rather in carefully controlled situations" (Hart 1975, p. 135). It is possible that the positive attitude to the dance of Śiva, the concept of a graceful, beneficial dance, stems from Tamil literature. That ecstatic dancing was common in Tamil worship is recorded in early texts (ibid., p. 29); dancing girls were usually courtesans, and "music and dancing had religious significance in ancient Tamilnad. It seems natural therefore that dancing girls, who continued to be courtesans, should later come to be associated with temples" (ibid., p. 142).

Whatever its source, the idea of a dance of Śiva that not only does not cause death but controls and counteracts it became accepted in Sanskrit texts and in South Indian iconography. Specifically, Śiva in his form of Kālāntaka ("the Ender of Death") is a dancer who dances on the body of Death (O'Flaherty 1976, pp. 231–36). In particular, he kicks Death in the chest, an effortless motion, regarded as a dance step (Sivaramamurti 1974, pp. 25 and 86). One interpretation of this image gives credit for the conquest of Death not to Śiva but to Pārvatī, arguing that, since Śiva used his left leg to kick Death (the inauspicious leg, as befitting contact with one so impure), and since Pārvatī occupies Śiva's left side when he is an androgyne (see below, chap. 9, sec. C), it must have been Pārvatī who actually gave the kick: "It was your left leg, O Mother, that destroyed death; Śiva's power did not accomplish this" (Sivaramamurti 1974, p. 25).[3] In this way, the dance of Pārvatī subdues Death, just as she subdues Śiva in his own dance of death.

D. The Dance in the Forest

The sexual overtones of the dance that render it fatal in the eyes of Vedāntic Hinduism are a positive factor in the Purāṇic myths that celebrate the Dionysian aspects of Śiva. An example of this shift in emphasis can be seen in the difference between the Sanskrit and Tamil traditions of the dance in the forest. In Sanskrit texts, Śiva enters the Pine Forest and dances there with the wives of the sages; he does not dance alone. In the form of a beautiful dancer, he seduces (or is seduced by) the women; the sages castrate him but become terrified by the consequences of this act; they recognize the god and worship his *liṅga* ever after (O'Flaherty: 1973, pp. 172–209; 1975, pp. 141–49; 1976, pp. 310–17). This is the version of the myth that appears in most Sanskrit texts and is implicit in the earliest variant of all, in the *Mahābhārata* (although it is rejected in the critical edition): Śiva laughs, sings, and dances charmingly, sporting in ithyphallic nakedness with the wives of the sages (*MBh* 13, app. 1, no. 4, vv. 55 and 66–67). Although the Pine Forest is not mentioned here by name, the pattern is clearly apparent; here is an early example of the erotic dance of Śiva, described in a hymn of praise and therefore regarded as a positive aspect of the god.

When the Pine Forest myth appears in Tamil texts, however, a notable change takes place: Śiva enters the Pine Forest (Taragam) and the women flock to him, but he is not castrated (which was the point of the myth in the Sanskrit texts); rather, when the sages attack him, he dances in such a way that their attacks are useless, and the sages and gods witness the dance of Naṭarāja there and worship him (Kulke 1970). In these texts, Śiva does not usually dance with the women at first; but at the end, in place of the castration episode of the Sanskrit texts, he dances all alone, and it is a dance of aggression and danger, as violent as the castration that it replaces. As Śiva dances, he presses the tip of his foot upon an evil dwarf sent to kill him; he breaks the creature's back, so that it writhes upon the ground (Coomaraswamy 1971, pp. 68–70; Gopinatha Rao 1968, 2:113–14, 304–7). Thus the history of the Pine Forest myth demonstrates a Tamil tendency to translate a purely sexual image of violence into an image of the solitary dance. Significantly, the image of Naṭarāja as ithyphallic appears in Orissa but not in South India (Daniélou 1964, p. 29; Sivaramamurti 1974). In the Tamil myth and icon, the dance is used to control enemies (the sages), just as it controls dangerous women in ancient Tamil culture. The basic paradigm still holds true in the South Indian variants of the Pine Forest myth: when Śiva dances with dominated women, his dance is beautiful; when he dances alone, it is terrible.

E. The Control of Śiva and Kālī through the Dance

Gentle, dominated women thus represent a calming influence upon Śiva, but dominant, powerful women not only fail to control him but drive him to wilder extremes. The Goddess herself, in her aspect as Kālī, is represented (particularly in Bengal) as dancing a dance of death in the ashes of the burning-grounds (Coomaraswamy 1971, p. 74; Kinsley 1975, pp. 114–25).[4] Kālī dances in a wild frenzy, inviting her devotees to dance with her; she endangers the world when she dances out of control (Kinsley 1975, p. 157). In a typical Tantric reversal, Kālī dances over the corpse of Śiva as he danced with the corpse of Satī.

Another reversal occurs in two texts of the same myth. In the first variant, Kālī is said to have made a body out of the poison in Śiva's neck in order to kill the demon Dāruka; but after she killed him, she went mad. Śiva became a little boy in order to drink away her anger with her milk; she suckled him and thus was made calm, and then he danced to please her, and she danced with him (*LP* 1. 106). Śiva drinks away Kālī's milk when she goes mad because she has been transformed into the evil mother whose milk is poison; by suckling at her breast, he turns her back from a goddess of the tooth into a goddess of the breast. To do this, he himself changes into a child, a standard way to defuse a dangerous consort (see above, chap. 4, sec. C). The episode of the dance then reinforces this pattern; it may have been attracted to this myth via the Pine Forest corpus, for the demon's name (Dāruka) is closely related to the name of the forest (Dāruvanam or Dārukavanam).

In the second variant of this myth, the sexes and their powers are reversed:

> A demoness named Dārukā threatened the gods until Pārvatī created from her own substance a black maiden who destroyed the demoness. Śiva appeared as an infant in a cemetery, and when Kālī took him up and gave him her breast he sucked but became angry; to divert and pacify him, Kālī clasped him to her bosom and danced until he was pleased and happy (Kennedy 1831, pp. 337–38, citing *LP*).

Here the gender of both the demon and the source of the black goddess is changed from male to female, and Śiva appears as deadly rather than charming; so she must dance to calm him, as he had danced to calm her. Because of these reversals, the suckling alone is insufficient to stop the chain reaction of violence: although *she* becomes calm when he suckles at her breast (as in the first variant), her ever-present anger now is transmitted through the milk, and *he* becomes furious. The dance, which in the first variant was a superfluous reinforcement of the calming through the breast, is here necessary to accomplish what the suckling failed to do: to calm both him and her.

From these inversions, it is evident that Śiva and Kālī may each use the dance to control the other. Yet another graphic example of the manner in which Śiva alternates as controlling or controlled by dance is apparent in the variation between the South Indian Naṭarāja and the Tantric images of Śiva and Kālī: in the first, Śiva crushes the devotee (or demon) under his foot; in the second, Kālī crushes *him* under her foot (Egnor 1978, pp. 172, 198).

F. The Dance Contest

In South India, Śiva and Kālī are often said to compete in a dance contest, and Śiva is always victorious; when Kālī goes mad, he dances with her to keep her from killing (Rangaswamy 1958, 1:442–45).[5] But the dance itself is dangerous and destructive, a dance of battle rather than an Indian version of the tango. The union of the two mad dancers ultimately results in the domination of male over female and the subsequent restoration of peace, though the dance itself is not peaceful.

One South Indian tradition of the dance context centers around Tiruvālaṅkāṭu:

> Gods and mortals, harassed by wicked demons, sought help from Devī. She created Kālī, who killed the demons but upon drinking their blood became intoxicated and ranged through the forest near Tiruvālaṅkāṭu, madly devouring living creatures. At Nārada's request, Śiva agreed to quell her fury; he came down from Kailāsa and engaged her in a dance contest. Kālī excelled at the *lāsya*, but when he began his *tāṇḍava*, the worlds shook, constellations fell to earth, and Kālī fainted upon the ground. When she revived, she shyly admitted defeat, for Śiva had done the *ūrdhvatāṇḍava* with one leg lifted high above his head, and modesty prevented Kālī from imitating this step. Śiva granted that she was the second-best dancer in the world, but he himself continued to dance violently

> until the gods begged Umā to help them calm him down in order to avert any calamity to the universe. Finally calm, Śiva said that he danced in order to give a vision to the sages in the forest (Shulman 1976a, pp. 206–9).[6]

The final remark identifies this myth as yet another variant of the Pine Forest myth, but with several significant developments. It is marked by a chain of violent dances, two individual *tāṇḍavas* (first Kālī's and then Śiva's) bridged by a dance contest. Violence is transferred from the demons to Kālī to Śiva, each episode more dangerous than the one before, as if to show the futility of any direct attack upon violence; only by channeling it can one hope to attain peace. The contest is an attempt to domesticate and formalize the wild solitary dance, and there are comforting overtones of banalization in it: Śiva's victory is the result of cheating (reminiscent of his cheating at the dice game with Pārvatī; see above, chap. 3, sec. C), for he exploits her sense of feminine modesty by lifting his leg; she loses because she is a woman, not because she is an inferior dancer.

It must be noted in passing that there are variants of this episode, depicted in South Indian temple carvings and in the local texts associated with these temples, that *do* allow Kālī—or even Pārvatī—to perform the *ūrdhvatāṇḍava*, to outkick Śiva and win the contest; there are even depictions of Viṣṇu performing the step.[7] Indeed, as we have seen, the statement that it was Pārvatī's leg that kicked Yama (when she was the left side of the androgyne) implies that she performed this high kick on at least one highly significant occasion. But that verse is, to my knowledge, unique, and the dominant, classical image is of Śiva's monopoly of this particular dance step.

For the fact that Kālī is defeated—or, rather, disqualified—because she will not sacrifice her feminine *pudor* (*lajjā*, in Sanskrit) is precisely the point of the myth: by affirming her subservience *as a woman*, she ends the contest. Indeed, the position that she refuses to assume, with thighs spread wide, is precisely the position (called *uttānapad*) that characterizes the creative goddess in the Ṛg Veda (10. 72. 3–4) and in early Indian sculptures. But by rejecting the stance of the goddess with gaping womb mouth, Kālī gives up her own intoxicated bloodlust. Yet this ends merely the contest; it does not end the dance, for Kālī's subservience is not enough. The gods must appeal to the higher female authority above Kālī—and, by implication, even above Śiva—to calm him down. This aspect of the Goddess, however, is here identified as Umā, another name for Pārvatī, the quintessential peaceful bride. Only her intervention can break the rhythm of the dangerous solitary dance and restore Śiva to calm domesticity (Yocum 1977).

Because the dance is a metaphor for sexual intercourse, it is a natural (and therefore auspicious) act when performed by male and female together, but it is twisted into a dangerous act of solitary ascetic destruction when performed alone. Although dancing, like sexuality, is dangerous, it is auspicious (Marglin 1978a), and it is less dangerous when controlled than when denied (see below, chap. 6, sec. D); this is one lesson that we learn from the *Bacchae*. But who is the partner best fitted to control Śiva's dance? Is it the equally wild Kālī or the contrasting, mild Pārvatī? In the Tiruvālaṅkāṭu story, both goddesses appear as distinct personae, but only Kālī dances; Pārvatī is a spectator, though an essential one. So, too, when Kālī dances a mad *tāṇḍava* that threatens to destroy the triple world, her dance terrifies Pārvatī until Śiva comforts her (*Mālatīmādhava* 5. 23). The union of the god with his subservient consort relaxes the dangerous tension created by the dance; the union with his dominant consort spells trouble.

G. Pārvatī as Spectator of the Dance

Many texts say that Śiva controls Kālī, but the icons do not depict a "becalmed, docile Kālī"; on the contrary, Śiva and Kālī incite each other, or Kālī dominates Śiva (Kinsley 1978). But when Pārvatī looks on, modestly refraining from challenging her husband, Śiva comes round. The one form in which Pārvatī may participate is as half of the androgyne, and even then she does not do the *tāṇḍava*; on the contrary, her function in this particular icon is to provide a peaceful contrast to his wild dance. For when the androgyne dances, the male half, on the right, performs the *tāṇḍava* and expresses the "horrific" emotion (*raudra*); the female half, on the left, performs the *lāsya* and expresses the erotic emotion (*śṛṅgāra rasa*) (Sivaramamurti 1974, p. 4).[8]

One late and almost certainly Tamil-influenced Sanskrit text combines the Pine Forest myth with the motif of the dance that pacifies Pārvatī:

> One day, Pārvatī became mad at Śiva and shouted tearfully that he was immoral and reviled by the gods, that he was an Untouchable because he ate poison, an evil beggar who had no right even to talk to her. Then she cursed him so that he would be attacked by Brahmins [i.e., the Pine Forest sages]. Śiva pacified her with sweet words, offering to do whatever she wanted; somewhat appeased, she replied, "If you take a vow of chastity and then dance the *tāṇḍava* before the gods and then make half of your body into

Viṣṇu's body, then I will revoke my curse." Śiva was pleased; he took the vow of chastity, and all the gods and sages assembled to see the dance of Śiva. Bhavānī came there, surrounded by her sixty-four female attendants, rejoicing to see Śiva; and the goddesses with Pārvatī sat on golden chairs and looked on.

Then Śiva assumed his terrifying form, loosing his matted locks, and he danced as he dances to destroy the universe. Everyone threw flowers, and the mountains whirled as his feet struck them, and the earth shook. Then Pārvatī was pleased, for Śiva had kept his word and completed his vow, and she said to him, "When the Brahmins curse you so that your *liṅga* falls, everyone will worship it." Then she praised Śiva and asked him to forgive her for having been angry, and he was pleased with her. He made the left side of his body Viṣṇu's, and Pārvatī embraced him. Half his necklace was a garland of headless torsos, half was of pearls; he wore an animal skin on one side and on the other side a silk cloth; he rode a bull on one side and a fish on the other. When the gods saw him in this form and realized that Śiva and Viṣṇu were one, they rejoiced and went home rejoicing (*Sk P* 6. 253. 1–37; 6. 254. 1–104).

This is a marvelous potpourri of earlier motifs, taken from other myths. They appear one by one, sometimes slightly altered but unmistakable: the myth in which one goddess gives Śiva a curse to be castrated but another promises him that his *liṅga* will be worshiped (*PP* 5. 17. 141; cf. O'Flaherty 1973, p. 301); the myth in which Śiva and Viṣṇu join in one body when Śiva dances before the yogis (*KP* 2. 5. 2. 18–19) or after Viṣṇu appears as a female dancer to trick the demon Bhasmāsura into dancing himself into ashes (Oppert 1893, p. 508) or to assist Śiva in the Pine Forest (Dessigane et al. 1967, pp. 84–85); the many myths about the quarrels between Śiva and Pārvatī (O'Flaherty 1973, pp. 221–29); and, of course, the Pine Forest myth itself, describing the origin of the dance.

At first, as in the other South Indian variants in which the dance replaces the castration, Pārvatī gives him a curse merely to be attacked by the sages, not castrated; later she says that they will castrate him, as in the Sanskrit texts. In any case, he must be chaste, for he dances alone. Śiva appears in two forms: first as the fierce *tāṇḍava* dancer and then in the peaceful form that he shares with Viṣṇu. This second form, which harks back to the dancing androgyne, Śiva with Pārvatī (see below, chap. 9, sec. C), is symbolic of reconciliation and satiation, but it is also symbolic of ambivalence and tension. Translating the image from the realm of sexual opposition to that of sectarian opposition serves to defuse much of this tension, but it also obscures the point of the myth. Like Śiva, the Goddess appears in two forms at the dance; for though it is Pārvatī, the gentle goddess, the wife, who requests the *tāṇḍava* and watches it from a golden chair, along with the other wives of the gods, the fierce Bhavānī, here designating the dark goddess, appears with her entourage of sixty-four Yoginīs. Finally, the dance itself appears in its full ambivalence; for though it is clearly destructive and is even said to be like the doomsday dance, no one seems worried about it at all. The gods just throw flowers, as if Śiva were a Bolshoi Ballet star executing the Bluebird variation with extra *panache*. The dark dance is at last fully integrated into the classical Indian tradition; Dionysus has merged with Apollo.

But the Dionysian aspect of the dance continues to threaten the peace of the gods. It is all very well to say that the "solution" to the dangerous dance of Śiva is to pair him with a submissive woman; the mythology of Pārvatī supplies such a woman, and the myths of the dance of Śiva with Pārvatī present an Apollonian balance. But the Dionysian Kālī has a dance of her own, and the attempts to make her submissive in order to tame either her or him produce explosions far in excess of the original force of the fires which the explosion was meant to put out. The problem of controlling the unsubmissive woman is expressed, not resolved, by the mythology of the dance, and it is this problem that underlies the myths of the mare, to which we must now turn.

IV Cows and Mares

6 The Indo-European Mare

A. Introduction: The Mythical Prototype

Striking parallels between the ancient Indian and Irish horse sacrifices have been discussed since 1927,[1] most recently by Jaan Puhvel, who has called attention to the significance of the reversal of the sexes in the two rituals (mare and king in Ireland, stallion and queen in India), a reversal which, he maintains, "provides us with a wedge for penetrating from the ritualistic to the mythological level in dealing with Indo-European equine tradition" (Puhvel 1970b, p. 164). By driving that wedge into some previously overlooked Irish, Indian, and other Indo-European mythlogical and ritual materials, it may be possible to extract from them certain structural and psychological patterns and so to answer three riddles:

1. Why did the Irish ritual involve a mare and a king, while the Indian ritual involved a queen and a stallion?
2. Why was the horse killed in the ritual but rarely in the myth?
3. What was the meaning of it all?

The ritual began with symbolic copulation between the royal figure and the equine figure and ended with the slaughter of the animal and the eating of its flesh or fluid. The myth reveals other details of this equine Liebestod:

> A goddess in the form of a white mare or a water bird assumed human form and mated with an aging sun king. Impregnated by him through her mouth, she gave birth to hippomorphic twins, male and female, who incestuously begat the human race. The goddess or her evil black alter ego injured or threatened to devour her children or the king. She then disappeared.

The myth ends there, but the ritual elaborates upon the simple disappearance of the mare and the simultaneous mutilation of the king or the stallion or the son: in the ritual, the king killed the mare and ate her, to restore his waning powers.

This is not a true Indo-European prototype; that is, I do not wish to suggest that there actually was an ancient proto-Indo-European myth that contained all the elements I have included in my summary. I am not an Indo-Europeanist, though I enjoy playing with Indo-European materials; thus I lack faith in the reconstructed prototype that is the sine qua non of any formal study in this field. I produced the pseudo-prototype above with some misgivings, largely in response to the urgings of true Indo-Europeanists (Jaan Puhvel and Bruce Lincoln), to whom I showed an early, prototype-less draft; and it does clarify and structure certain features of an otherwise rather untidy approach. It enables us to isolate the mythemes, to distinguish the recurrent elements from those superimposed by a few individual cultural variants (see chart 2). In this

Chart 2. Recurrent Motifs in Indo-European Myth and Ritual

	Indian		Irish		Greek	Welsh	Gallic	Roman
	myth	rite	myth	rite				
King mates with mare	X	(X)	X	X	X	X	X	
Mare is killed (set free)		(X)	X	X	X	X		
Queen mates with stallion	X	X			(X)			(X)
Stallion is killed		X			X			X
White horse	X	X		X	X	X		
Chariot race	X	X	X		X			X
Flesh/seed is eaten	X	X	X	X	X		(X)	
Witch eats/abandons child	X		X		X	X	(X)	
Mutilation of horse/father/son	X	(X)	(X)		X	X		X
Transformation of woman into bird		(X)	X		X	X	X	
Sun as bird or horse	X	X			X			
Goddess mates with mortal	X	(X)	(X)		X	X	X	
Chastity of king		X	(X)		(X)	X		
Wicked (step) (split) mother	X	X	X		X	X	X	
Hippomorphic twins	X		X		X	X		
Brother-sister incest	X		X		X			
Father-daughter incest	X		X		X			
Queen mates with bull	X				X			

NOTE: Parentheses indicate veiled or merely implicit occurrence of the motif.

sense it may represent the core of the myth, but it is a thematic rather than a historic core. It may indeed turn out to be the historical core, but I am not prepared to prove this, nor is it relevant to my study of the meaning of the myth. Proto-Indo-Europe, the country east of the asterisk, is a never-never land less real to me than the world of the enduring cluster of motifs on which variations are struck, but the prototype is a heuristic intellectual construct.

The "core" myth appears with many variations in different Indo-European texts (Indian, Irish, Greek, Roman, Gallic, Welsh, Russian), but the Irish and Indian variants are the most detailed and are best supported by ritual. The more significant variations, which can be explained by the historical development of Indo-European attitudes toward women and mares, include the omission of the ritual slaughter from the end of the myth, the reversal of the order of copulation and killing in the Indian ritual, and the reversal of the sexes in that ritual and in some late forms of the Indian and pan-European myth (in which a god, in the form of a stallion or bird, mates with a mortal woman, the opposite of the pattern of the Irish ritual and the prototypical myth, in which a mortal man mates with a goddess in the form of a mare or a water bird).

There are a number of significant variations here, which are barely indicated by the word "inversion." There are variations between the myths in different Indo-European cultures, between the rituals in different Indo-European cultures, and between the myths as a whole and the rituals as a whole. There are, in addition, historical variations in each of the elements as they develop through time, sometimes parallel to one another and sometimes divergent. Details, often minor but offering clues to major changes, will emerge from the analysis of the materials presented in this chapter, but certain overarching patterns may be suggested at the start, patterns that integrate the wide range of myths and rituals.

The incident at the heart of it all involves two basic processes: a sacrifice and a marriage. The sacrifice brings gods and humans together through food that is obtained by slaughter. The marriage brings men and women together through sex (here, as elsewhere, expressed through metaphors of food and eating). The emotional components of lust and fear/aggression, which we have seen to underlie so much of the mythology of the Goddess, are present in this compound ceremony, as is the theme of the Liebestod, which unites these emotions on the narrative level. Upon this basic structure are grafted variations in sequence (the killing preceding or following the copulation) and gender (of the sacrificial victim and the equine partner) which invert the direction of the flow of power that is the dynamic force of the myth and ritual alike.

B. The Ritual

The Irish Rite: The Mare in the Cauldron

In the Irish ritual (recorded A.D. 1185 by Giraldus Cambrensis), a white mare was led before the king in the presence of the people. Then, "He, seeking to elevate himself not into a prince but a beast, not into a king but an outlaw, approaching like an animal, professes as shamelessly as irrationally that he too is a beast" (ad quoad sublimandus ille non in principem sed in beluam, non in regem sed exlegem, coram omnibus bestialiter accedens, non minus impudenter quam imprudenter se quoque bestiam profitetur). That is, he behaved like a beast (mounting her on all fours and from the rear) and wanted to express the animal within him (a monkish euphemism for copulation with the mare). The mare was then killed, cut into pieces, and boiled, and the king bathed in the broth, drinking it by lapping it up directly with his mouth, not using a cup, and he also ate the mare's flesh (see Brewer 1861, p. 169; cf. Pokorny 1927; Hoare 1905, p. 138).

This brief text suggests far more than it states, but even here one sees *in nuce* three essential elements: the mating of the king with a white mare; the slaughter of the mare; and the eating of her flesh and the drinking of her essential fluids. Moreover, in the attempted bowdlerization implicit in the monk's shocked description of the ritual (which he characterizes as barbaric and abominable), we encounter the Indo-European tendency to deny the divinity of the mare, a theme that will haunt these myths and rituals, and the suggestion that the king, too, is a beast—a concept that becomes acted out, as a result of that same squeamishness, when the king is actually replaced by a stallion in other variants of the ritual.

Though the Irish text is late, brief, and problematic (having been recorded by a monk who could scarcely believe, let alone understand, what he had seen), there are several good reasons for according it great weight. For one, it is a truism in Indo-European studies that the Indo-Iranian and Irish extremes of the Indo-European area preserve in vocabulary and myth many archaic elements that are found nowhere else. The isolation of the Irish, perhaps reinforced by their notorious pigheadedness, has produced a society that preserves an enormous number of archaic features, particularly manifest in Irish attitudes toward cows and horses (Vendryes 1918; Piggott 1950, chap. 7; Dillon 1947 and 1975). Moreover, the medieval Irish ritual is supported by so much other fragmentary Indo-European material that it may be taken as an enactment of a widespread and perhaps ancient myth. The one element unique to the Irish ritual, the eating of the mare's flesh, appears elsewhere only in its inverted forms: the stallion is eaten and/or the mare eats—two motifs that jointly form a clear structural contrast to the Irish text. But since the mare is also killed (though not eaten) in some Irish as well as Indian and Greek myths, and since the stallion, when killed, is often devoured; and since it is in general the fate of sacrificial animals to be eaten, it seems reasonable to suggest that the eating of the mare was also once an actual event. That the texts do not record this ritual can be explained by the suppression of positive mare myths and rituals in androcentric Indo-European tradition.

In support of this hypothesis, Robert Graves has marshaled considerable material relating to myths of taming winged horses (Perseus and Bellerophon), in Danish and Irish as well as Greek traditions, which he relates to a hypothetical rite in which the Triple Muse or Goddess of the Mountain made the candidate for kingship capture a wild horse that was "sacramentally eaten by the king after his symbolic rebirth from the Mare-headed Mountain-goddess" (Graves 1955, 1:255). Still, many problems remain, not least the unexplained contrast between the gender of the wild stallion captured in the mythology and the divine mare represented in the ritual. But when these figures are assigned to two different myth-ritual cycles, one in which the mare goddess is both devoured and devouring (for the king's symbolic rebirth is a result of both processes, as we shall see) and one in which a stallion comes to replace the mare in the former (though not in the latter) role, much of the confusion disappears. To sort out the elements in this way will be the burden of the rest of this chapter.

The Celtic Cult of Epona and the Foals

Close to the Irish in theme as well as geography is the Gallic cult of the goddess Epona, almost the only goddess worshiped in the same guise by both continental and insular Celts (Dent 1965, p. 9). Intimately connected with the Welsh Rhiannon and the Irish Mácha, and thematically connected with the horse-headed Greek Demeter (ibid., pp. 9, 10), Epona is often depicted as a woman riding on a mare, or as a mare, or with a mare's head; she is also associated with a male horse god, Rudiobus (Le Roux 1955, p. 122; Koppers 1936, p. 288). Epona's name comes from the proto-Indo-European *ékwo-s, "horse" (Latin *equus*, Sanskrit *aśva*); significantly, she is associated with birds (Benoit 1954, pp. 105–12; cf. Reinach 1895, de Jubainville 1906, Magnen and

Thevenot 1953).

Epona is particularly concerned with pregnant mares and with foals (Dent 1965, p. 10). One of the oldest representations of her shows her seated on a throne with her hands on the heads of two foals (Reinach 1895, pp. 313–16); others depict a woman feeding apples or hay to pregnant mares (Dent 1965, p. 10). Epona was believed to preside over the mating of mares and the birth of foals and to exercise a benevolent influence over human birth as well (ibid.). But like many another true mother goddess, her relationship with children was ambivalent; sometimes a child is depicted crouching under the raised leg of the mare (Hubert 1935, p. 193; Reinach 1895, p. 310), a threatening pose. One notably misogynist myth is related about her: "A certain Phoulouios Stellos, who hated women, had intercourse with a mare. In time, she brought forth a beautiful maiden whom she named Epona, a goddess of horses" (Pseudo-Plutarch, parallel 29).[2] This may be the only ancient record of a Celtic hierogamy, and it rounds off a useful group of motifs in the cult of Epona: the mare-headed goddess associated with a mortal lover and a horse, who presides over the birth of foals (significantly, *two* foals—perhaps twins), feeds mares, and threatens children. Epona's association with rivers (Macculloch 1918, p. 129) further assimilates her to the submarine mare.

The Indian Ritual of the Queen and the Dead Stallion

When we turn to ancient India, we have far more (and far older) material. Here the main *personae dramatis* are the chief queen (Mahiṣī) and a consecrated white stallion, who is killed. The queen lies down beside the dead stallion and entwines her legs with the hind legs of the horse, saying, "Let us two lie down here together, entwining our four legs" (*AŚS* 20. 17. 17–20; *TS* 7. 4. 19c–e; *VS* 23. 20; *ŚB* 13. 2. 8. 5). A commentary on this text adds helpfully that they extend their legs "in order to achieve coupling" (*KŚS* 20. 6. 14–2; P. Dumont 1927, pp. 178–82). The significance of this emphasis upon the horse's legs or feet will be illuminated by the Indian mythological materials.

Feeding the Stallion and Eating the Mare

Just as the king in the Irish text ate the mare's flesh and blood (to restore his virility, as we shall see), so the queen in the Indian text symbolically eats the stallion's seed to ensure fertility and/or pregnancy, the female equivalent of virility. Some texts say that union with the stallion bestows long life on the queen. The first consecrated act performed by the sacrificer consists of offering the priests gold and a ball of rice, and the texts spells out this symbolism:

> The Adhvaryu cooks the priests' mess of rice; it is seed he thereby produces. . . . For when the horse was immolated, its seed went from it and became gold; thus, when he gives gold (to the priests), he supplies the horse with seed. . . . For the ball of rice is seed, and gold is seed; by means of seed he thus lays seed into that (horse and sacrificer) (*ŚB* 13. 1. 1. 1–4).

Food is also given directly to the stallion by the wives of the sacrificer, who offer him "rice which is seed" (*AŚS* 20. 16. 19–20; P. Dumont 1927, p. 274). And it is said that the four women participating in the ritual (including the Mahiṣī) throw grains of fried rice to the horse, as well as barley and milk: "She (of the wives) whose food the horse eats (when she throws it) will have a child who will prosper" (*BŚS* 15. 25–26).

The ball of rice as a metaphor for a ball of seed occurs in many Vedic contexts, notably in the parallel model of feeding the dead ancestors and "feeding" the unborn embryo (Knipe 1977, pp. 111–17; O'Flaherty 1980, chap. 1). Rice remains part of a horse ceremony in Assam, where an image of a horse is used in a night-long dance and then taken to a stream; the body is thrown into the water, but the head is preserved for another year. (The beheaded horse under water is a variant of the image of the doomsday fire, with its mare's head, under water; see below, chap. 7, sec. A.) Frazer, noting that rice is consumed on the banks of the river by all the participants, speculates:

> Can it be that the horse whose effigy is thus made at rice-harvest and thrown into the water, while the head is kept for another year, represents the spirit of the rice? . . . on the same theory the horse's head would be comparable to the horse-headed Demeter at Phigalia as well as to the head of the October horse at Rome (Frazer 1963, pt. 5, 2:338).

And, one might add, to the head of the Vedic sacrificial horse, who is hardly a "spirit of the rice" but is indeed the spirit of fertility and rebirth.

The correspondence between eating and sexual intercourse is explicit throughout the texts of the horse sacrifice. In the obscene banter between the queen and the priests, it is said, "When a deer eats the barley, (the farmer) does not think that the beast has been nourished; when a Śūdra woman has a noble lover, she does not become enriched" (*VS* 23. 30–31). The feeding of the stallion represents a partial transformation from the Irish ritual: in both cases, it is the male participant (the Irish king, the

Indian horse) who is actually fed; but it is the human participant (the king or the queen) who derives the fertility benefits at the expense of the sacrificed equine (divine) partner; and there are *two* human participants in the Vedic rite. Thus the queen is said to become pregnant, not by eating the stallion, but by feeding him—a symbolic inconsistency in the extant rite; moreover, the true beneficiary in the Indian ritual is the king, who takes on the powers of the stallion, rather than the queen, whose increased fertility is of peripheral importance to the ritual. The mantle of immortality passes from a male divinity to a human king; the mare has only a vestigial role, and the human queen acts as a mediary between male figures, human and divine. Thus the king grows strong, not by eating the mare, but by having the stallion (his alter ego) eat the seed that must, symbolically, be the stallion's own—a substance drained from him during his intercourse with the queen but immediately transferred back to the king. These overlapping models suggest the possible loss of an intermediary rite in which the queen ate the flesh, not of the mare, but of the dead stallion (just as the Irish king ate the flesh of the mare); for *she* feeds *him* the ball of seed/rice and is, as a result, "blessed with a child who will prosper" (as one would expect if *he* gave *her* the seed), but in the ancient Vedic offerings to the ancestors and in later Indian rituals this ball of rice is fed to a woman who wishes to become pregnant —a more obvious and logical symbolism (O'Flaherty 1980, chap. 1).

The manner in which the chief queen mediates between the two male protagonists in the Vedic ritual has analogues in other aspects of Vedic and Hindu worship. By her intercourse with the stallion, the queen siphons off his powers and gives them to her husband, just as the adulterous woman in the Upaniṣadic text may serve as a medium through which the husband's powers are transferred to the lover (see above, chap. 2, sec. A). On the theological level, since the stallion is the divine alter ego of the king, the woman mediates between the male god and his male worshiper, providing a means by which sexual power may flow from the former to the latter without forcing the worshiper to assume a homosexual attitude (see above, chap. 4, sec. C).

The Vestigial Mare

Evidence in support of the hypothetical mediating ritual, in which the queen ate the flesh or seed of the stallion, may be seen in the fact that the king and the mare (the Irish protagonists) play an important role in the Indian ceremony, despite the fact that the stallion and the queen are ostensibly given the central place. Thus one begins to see in the Vedic ritual a conflation of two sacred models rather than the simple replacement of one by the other. Such conflation is well documented in Hinduism; we have already seen examples of it in the simultaneous belief in the two different models of embryology examined in chapter 2 (male semen and female blood, male semen and female seed) and in the two different pattersn of hierogamy discussed in chapter 4 (male-dominated, female-dominated). Both of these double-image models are relevant to the mythology of the mare because of their specific ideas about sexual interaction, but they are also relevant because of the mere fact that they coexist in the minds of individual Hindus.

The king and the mare appear to be vestigial, to become involved for no apparent logical reason, as if they had been there before and were kept on, emeritus, even when their roles had been usurped. This, plus the appearance of the Irish pattern in Vedic myths and in other Indo-European materials, tempts one to regard the Irish as the older ritual and the Indian as a development out of it, despite the fact that the Irish ritual is first described in a text dated some two millennia after the one in which the Indian rite is set forth. Technically, one can speak only of two separate patterns; but thematically it is convenient to regard one as a development out of the other, and to do so may in fact be historically justified.

At the beginning of the Vedic rite, a group of mares is shut into an enclosure on the north and kept hidden (*BŚS* 15. 17–18; P. Dumont 1927, p. 317). Later, the mares are shown to the stallion, who whinnies (*KŚS* 20. 5. 4; P. Dumont 1927, p. 136); the mares whinny in response (*AŚS* 20. 6–7, *ŚB* 13. 2. 3. 27), a sign of desire that is regarded as a good omen (P. Dumont 1927, pp. 266 and xii). The mares are then set free. In many rituals of this type, the animal may be either set free or slaughtered at the end of the sacrifice; in either case, it disappears from the ritual. In this context, one may see a parallel between the treatment of the mares in the Irish and Indian rituals.

The king's role in the ceremony is in at least one important aspect the mirror image of that of the stallion: while the contact between the stallion and the queen involves (mimed) sexual union, the contact between the king and the queen emphasizes the lack of sexual union (as did the "contact" between the stallion and the mares, who are kept apart, "enclosed," from the stallion and then set free). That is, the ritual protects the king from sexual contact with the dangerous woman, who is, as we shall see, symbolized by the mare. For while it is the chief queen, the Mahiṣī, who lies with the stallion, it is the favorite wife (the Vāvātā) with whom the king lies but does *not* have contact. Here we may see an early example of the splitting of the woman into two halves, one fertile (the Mahiṣī, the queen with the stallion), and the other erotic (the Vāvātā, the "mare" with the king), each reversing her normal role (the queen behaving obscenely, the favorite chastely.)

> When the evening offering has been performed, (the king) lies down with his favorite wife behind the Gārhapatya [householder's] hearth, with his head toward the north [where the mares are penned up]. At the same place, the other (wives) also lie down. He lies in her lap without embracing her, thinking, "May I, by this self-control [*tapas*], reach successfully the end of the year" (*ŚB* 13. 4. 1. 9).

The stallion is also required to remain chaste during his year of wandering before the sacrifice (*BŚS* 15. 8), and at the final sacrifice his virile powers are transferred to the chaste king (Gonda 1966, p. 23). Another specific parallel between the sexual behavior of the king and the stallion may be seen in a later ritual text in which, when a man has died and his body has been placed on the funeral pyre, his wife performs with him the rites of "sexual union, etc." (*saṃveśanādi*) (*Bh S* 1. 5. 14).[3] The union of the queen with the dead stallion or the dead husband is perhaps the earliest example of the Indian motif of the consort as corpse (see above, chap. 4, sec. C). The *live* king or stallion, however, must remain chaste. Thus the powers (royal, divine, and sexual) of the dead stallion are drained from him through sexual intercourse and transferred to the chaste, living king.

Other texts state that the sacrificer lies down between the thighs of his favorite wife without uniting with her, remaining chaste (*brahmacārin*) (*ŚB* 13. 4. 1. 9; *KŚS* 20. 1. 18; P. Dumont 1927, p. 18). One text is still more specific: "They say, 'The sacrificer should lie down naked with his naked wife, with nothing between them, though he must not unite with her.' But they also say on this subject, 'He should lie naked with his naked wife (etc.); this is a form of the state of wakefulness.' Thus he lies near her and remains wakeful" (*Vādhula Śrauta Sūtra*, frag. 70; P. Dumont 1927, p. 358).

Wakeful Chastity and Sleeping Sexuality

This wakefulness in the night, guarding the chaste king against the seductive goddess, occurs in another related text:

> The sacrificer and his wife place precious metals in their mouths—the sacrificer a piece of gold, his wife a piece of silver (or several pieces of silver, if there are several wives). . . . The sacrificer gives (the priests) a cow that has not yet calved but is of the right age to calf and that desires the bull. They spend the night cooking it,

> keeping the sacrificer awake. The next morning, the sacrificer and his wife rinse their mouths and breathe on the two pieces of precious metal (which they had put in their mouths for wakefulness). The son of a prostitute receives the two pieces of metal (*BŚS* 15. 3; P. Dumont 1927, p. 296).

This is a strange and rich text. The sacrificer places gold—the symbol of seed—in his mouth to avoid spilling his true seed (and losing his virile powers) during the night spent with his favorite wife (just as the Irish king takes the mare's "essence" into his mouth). The priests then cook a cow (another displacement of the cooking of the Irish mare) to keep the king awake—as if destroying a cow "who desires a bull" will protect the king from the insatiable queen. This particular cow is a perverse image; for although the cow is usually contrasted with the mare as the epitome of the good mother in contrast with the whore (see below, chap. 8, sec. E), this cow has not yet calved, though she might have, and she lusts in a manner that is atypical for cow mothers. She is, in effect, a mare and is eaten, like the Irish mare. Finally, the gold (seed) is given to the son of a prostitute (the human equivalent of the son of the mare); he also kills a black dog and throws it under the feet of the horse (P. Dumont 1927, p. 298). The prostitute in her own right plays an important role in the closely related ceremony involving the Brahmacārin (the chaste student) and the prostitute (*puṃścālī*)—the Mahāvrata ceremony, which includes an obscene dialogue between the pure male and the impure female that is strikingly similar to the dialogue between the priests and the queens in the horse sacrifice (*DŚS* 11. 3. 9; Eliade 1958, p. 257; O'Flaherty 1973, p. 51).

The prostitute represents yet another aspect of the erotic alter ego of the fertile queen. Indeed, the split aspects of the queen proliferate in these texts. In addition to the two primary figures—the Mahiṣī, who lies obscenely with the stallion, and the favorite, who lies chastely with the king—three other women participate in the ceremony, women who are sharply distinguished in moral and social quality: the despised queen (Parivṛktā or Parivṛktī, the obverse of the favorite) and a woman from an inferior caste (Pālāgalī) or a kitchen maid (Mahānasī, the obverse of the consecrated queen) (*BŚS* 15. 25–61; *ŚB* 13. 4. 1. 8; *KŚS* 20. 1. 12). According to one text, only the chief queen, the favorite, and the despised queen prepare the horse (*AŚS* 20. 15. 7–13); they adorn the stallion and feed him, and the one whose food is accepted will have a prosperous child (*BŚS* 15. 25–6).

In several texts, all of the wives complain that the horse is neglecting them: "O mother, dear mother, dear little mother, no one is leading me (to the horse). The little horse is sleeping" (*AŚS* 20. 17. 12–20. 18. 16; *TS* 7. 4. 19a–b; *ŚB* 13. 2. 8. 3–4); or, more explicitly, "No one is fucking me; the little horse is sleeping" (*TS* 7. 4. 19h; *BŚS* 15. 29–30). (In Coomaraswamy's euphemism, *yabhati* becomes "No one is consummating a marriage with me" [Coomaraswamy 1936, p. 309], but *yabh* is the basic Indo-European obscene term for copulation.) It is surely significant that, whereas wakefulness for the king was a protection of his chastity against the (equally wakeful) mare/queen, wakefulness in the stallion is a desired state of sexuality. Moreover, the reference to the stallion's sleep serves to explain how one can have sexual union with a dead creature: he is not dead, merely asleep. More specifically, he is temporarily impotent. Not only is this a useful mechanical device for glossing over a physical and logical inconsistency in the ritual; it also serves to underline the concept of resurrection and rejuvenation that is at the heart of the ritual.

For, as Coomaraswamy points out, the queen complains that the stallion is inactive, a complaint voiced (as we shall see) by many other ancient Indian goddesses in other texts, several of which are closely connected with this ritual:

> If the solar horse is "dead," or more correctly, "gone to heaven," to its rest, and is "asleep" and "impotent," there are innumerable Vedic precedents for that. . . . If she complains that the horse is ineffectual, this is also the fundamental grief of the Vedic Vadhrimatī, "She whose husband is unmanned," who nevertheless by the Aśvins' aid, that is to say at dawn, becomes the mother of Hiraṇyahasta, Savitṛ, the new-born Sun, by her husband Śyāva, Śyāvaka, or Śyāvāśva (the "Dark Horse") . . . who is rejuvenated by the Aśvins (*RV* I. 116. 13; I. 117. 24; X. 62. 5, etc.). . . . It is likewise pertinent that in *RV* X. 69. 10. Jātavedas [Agni, or the Sun] is addressed as the "son of Vadhryaśva"—either the "Gelded Horse" or "Whose steed is gelded"—and is said to be honoured by his father (Coomaraswamy 1936, pp. 309, 312–13).

The sleeping horse is thus directly linked with other Vedic horses who are ritually transformed from impotence to virility and, in particular, with solar horses, like Vivasvant, who undergo this transformation. The Aśvins (who are, as we shall see, central to the myth of the mutilated sun god) are also credited with restoring virility to an ancient sage who bore the epithet Saptavadhri ("Seven Times Impotent"), enabling him to make love to his young wife and to satisfy her desires (*RV* 1. 116. 10; 5. 74. 5; 5. 78. 5–6). In this context, what the sleeping stallion symbolizes is not the dying and resurrected god but the impotent mortal revived by contact with immortals—reflecting in this the ancient Indo-European model of king and mare.

The Female Bird and the Sun Stallion

Besides the obscenities connected with the word *yabh*, the women in the Vedic horse-sacrifice engage in obscene banter with the priests, but it is the chief queen—the one who lies with the stallion—who is subjected to the most extensive obscene mockery. Much of this ribaldry draws upon imagery comparing the woman to a bird, an animal closely associated with the mare in Indo-European mythology. When the queen lies down beside the stallion, the Adhvaryu priest says to the maiden (Kumārī), "The female bird [*śakuntikā*] moves back and forth, making the sound 'āhalak'; the penis enters the vagina, and the vulva swallows it up with a gurgling sound" (*VS* 23. 22; *ŚB* 13. 5. 2. 4; 13. 2. 9. 6). The commentary explains that the term "female bird" indicates a vagina of a finger's breadth (the *śakuntikā* being a small bird); in the next verse, the maiden replies to the priest, "The male-bird moves back and forth, making the sound 'āhalak,'" and the commentary suggests that the term indicates a penis of a finger's breadth. The use of the verb "to swallow" for the action of the vagina is surely significant in this context.

The authors of these texts apologize for their obscenity and make sure that at the end the participants rinse out their mouths with the soap of a "perfumed" Vedic verse—a verse about a stallion, Dadhikravan (see below, chap. 7, sec. C). It is this bowdlerizing tendency that excluded the mare from the ceremony in the first place and, in later times, ensured that the ritual was seldom performed, though political and financial considerations also played a part in its demise. But the ritual copulation of the queen and the stallion was often mocked by later texts and later myths (see below, chap. 7, sec. B).

The ritual texts themselves give several explicit hints about the symbolic meaning of the rite, in addition to the aspects of fertility already discussed. The stallion is identified with the god Prajāpati, the creator, in his role of sexual procreator; but he is also explicitly identified with the sun (*ŚB* 13. 4. 2. 16). The image of the sun driving his chariot across the sky may be reflected in the ritual when the king drives a chariot drawn by the sacrificial horse and three others (P. Dumont 1927, p. v), a probable survival from a chariot race that formed part of the older ritual, since it occurs in the Greek and Roman parallels. In this connection it is to be noted that the horse must be white (ibid., p. 22), the color of the horse traditionally sacrificed to the sun god in India (Hillebrandt 1891–1902, p. 391) and in other Indo-European cultures, as we shall see. Prajāpati is sometimes said to have a two-colored horse (Schwab 1886, p. xvii), and the forequarters of the sacrificial horse should be black, the hindquarters white (P. Dumont 1927, p. 32). This splitting of the image into black and white is also reflected in the mythology.

The ritual texts present on a fairly overt level an inversion of the theme of the goddess mating with a mortal man, just as the stallion represents a god mating with the mortal queen. The theme of the mutilation or castration of the (mortal) sun god also appears in the symbolic castration of the stallion who represents the sun; for at the moment when the horse was killed (by suffocation), he was struck upon the testicles (Koppers 1936, p. 345; Schwab 1886, p. 106). The whiteness of the mare has moral overtones; the whiteness of the stallion may also function as a symbol of the light of the sun king. Finally, the bicolored horse (as well as the black dog thrown under the horse's feet) introduces the possibility of an ambivalence in the equine character, supported by the ambivalence (perhaps also expressed through color, in the form of a low-caste woman set in contrast to the queen) of the female character. The casting of this female in the role of mother is supported only loosely, by her fertility role (and the reference to the children she hopes to have as a result of her liaison with the stallion) and by the fact that the priest murmurs in the ear of the sacrificial horse, "You have been strengthened by the mother" (P. Dumont 1927, p. 67). These fragments are structured and given meaning by the myth.

The Death of the Stallion/King and the Survival of the Goddess

Although the explicit Indian ritual involves copulation between the queen and a stallion and the feeding of the stallion by the queen, one can detect from other parts of the ritual another, probably older, form of the rite in which the king united with a dangerous mare to gain virility; this union is then bowdlerized in the commentator's more typically Indian statement that he lies chastely beside her in order to preserve his virility. Moreover, the fact that the queen is said to become fertile as a result of her contact with the stallion, together with the use of a ball of rice to express this, indicates the possibility of a lost transitional rite in which the queen ate some part of the stallion. Finally, the contrast between the consecrated fertile queen and the dangerous erotic mare is highlighted by the proliferation of other women in the ritual, explicitly contrasted in terms of their erotic powers and social roles.

Two striking contrasts with the Irish ritual may be seen in the reversal of the sexes of the participants in the central ceremony and in the fact that in the Indian ritual the stallion is dead when copulation takes place, whereas the Irish mare is alive. The first inversion must be understood in the context of Indo-European mare mythology as a whole, but the second may have some basis in simple practicality as well as in religious inclinations. For given the first reversal, mare into stallion, the sexual role of the equine *in the ritual* must become active rather than passive, and this produces immediate practical problems: one cannot easily persuade the stallion to perform on command. In the Indian *myth*, however, the mare is the active sexual aggressor (a factor represented in the ritual by the penned-up whinnying mares and the concubine against whom the king must be wakeful). To resolve the conflict between the stallion's theoretical physical activity (as the one who covers the mare) and his mythological and actual passivity (for in the myth he is said to be seduced by the mare, and in the ritual he is actually dead), the ritual is able to invoke yet another powerful and ancient mythological and ritual pattern: the stallion is treated throughout the copulation ceremony as if he were still alive and temporarily sleeping. He is *not* alive, for two very different reasons: first, there are very practical problems inherent in handling a live stallion under the circumstances; second, copulation with a *dead* horse is essential to the mythology of resurrection through sexual contact. Here, as in the inversions of the corpse motifs in the myths of Mahiṣa and the icon of Kālī, the Liebestod may work in either of two ways: the live consort may be killed through sexual intercourse (as in the Mahiṣa myth and the Irish ritual, in which copulation precedes death) or the dead consort may be revived through sexual intercourse (as in the Kālī icon and the Indian horse sacrifice, in which copulation follows death).

The myth and ritual of the consort as corpse plays a significant role in the Vedic ceremony. This motif is further enriched by the greater complexity of the treatment of the stallion: where the mare is merely killed, the stallion may be castrated instead of (or in addition to) being killed. This had repercussions in the mythology, which tended to substitute for the slaughter of the mare the mutilation of her (mortal) human partner.

This interchange between the mare's equine and human victims has its basis in ancient Indo-European rituals. At some point, horse and man may have been interchangeable as sacrificial victims. It may be argued either that man came to replace stallion or that stallion came to replace man (Puhvel 1970b; Sauvé 1970); the evidence is difficult to sort out chronologically, but it is at least plain that both the sacrifice of a man and the sacrifice of a stallion were of great importance in Indo-European culture. Since both horse and man were identified with the creator in the

Vedic texts, the theological valence of both ceremonies was the same. But when a sexual ritual is combined with the killing, the theology becomes more complicated; for if the god is present in the equine member of the partnership, who is killed, and the worshiper plays the role of the human consort, who is revivified, it matters greatly whether one kills a man (with a mare) or a stallion (with the queen). The same contrast (copulation with the living animal as opposed to the dead one) obtains between the horse sacrifice and the buffalo sacrifice: in the former, copulation occurs *after* the slaughter; in the latter, *until* the slaughter (Hiltebeitel 1980).

In this typology, the determining factor is the gender of the immortal participant, not that of the theriomorphic participant; for in the horse sacrifice the female is a mortal who kills—and revives—her immortal consort, while in the buffalo sacrifice the female is an immortal who kills her mortal consort. In either case, the woman is the killer and her partner is the animal; these are the two consistent factors in the two great Indian sacrifices, where all other factors (mortality or immortality of the woman and of her theriomorphic partner; killing of the latter before or after the ritual intercourse) vary, not only between horse sacrifice and buffalo sacrifice but even within variants and levels of the horse sacrifice itself. It is perhaps worthy of note that the queen in the horse sacrifice is the Mahiṣī, or "she buffalo"; this name appears throughout the literature to designate the first-married queen. She is said to be called Mahiṣī because the earth (regarded as the wife of the king) is a she buffalo (or a cow) (*ŚB* 6. 5. 3. 1); thus the Mahiṣī, the official queen, is explicitly a cow who lies with a stallion, in contrast with the temptress who lies with the king (the immortal mare who lies with her mortal consort).

Both the Irish model (mare and king) and its inverse (stallion and queen) are implicated in the Indian ritual, for all four members of the quartet play essential roles, though the queen and stallion are preeminent. This overlapping of contrasting ritual models is evidence of tension arising out of historical transition. The fact that the myths, like the rituals, describe the killing or mutilation of the king but not the queen may indicate that, by the time the mare-king pattern had been juxtaposed with the stallion-queen pattern, human sacrifice was no longer practiced; on the other hand, it may indicate that the human queen had already become so sharply differentiated from her immortal counterpart, the mare, that she was regarded as simply not worth killing. More positively, the special Indo-European taboo against killing a woman (or, later, a cow) may be at work here (see below, chap. 8, sec. C).

Other Indo-European Rituals

Materials from Indo-European civilizations other than Ireland and India are more miscellaneous, but combined they strongly support a proto-Indo-European horse sacrifice; that is, many scattered details of the ritual in its various forms flesh out the skeletal structure that has emerged from the Indian and Irish rites.

Among the ancient Norse, a white horse symbolizing the sun and accompanied by women was killed in a ritual involving obscene references to the phallus of the horse, ritual castration (Johansson 1917–19, p. 97), and an intoxicating drink (Koppers 1936, pp. 286–87). In the Roman October festival, a horse was killed and a chariot race took place (ibid., p. 298); in the Pales festival, a horse was mutilated (perhaps castrated) (Dumézil 1956, pp. 232–45). Among the Greeks, white horses were sacrificed to Poseidon and to the sun (Koppers 1936, p. 292); a white mare was sacrificed at the grave of a maiden who had been raped and committed suicide; black horses were inauspicious (ibid., p. 360). Both Roman and Greek sources indicate a fertility cult associated with the horse (Puhvel 1955, p. 354), often closely resembling the Vedic cult. The Persians tell of a battle between an evil black horse and a good white horse whose victory released the fertilizing rains; and the Iranians regarded white horses as symbolic of the sun (Pausanias 3. 4. 20; Xenophon *Cyr.* 8. 3. 11; Koppers 1936, p. 294). Among the Indo-Europeans in general the white horse was sacred (Frazer 1963, pt. 1, 2:174; cf. Jung 1967, pp. 259–60). Most of these rituals involve variations on the Indian prototype, using a stallion rather than a mare, often in a sexual ritual; the white mare of the Greek ritual (and of the Irish) are conspicuous exceptions.

A final link between far-flung Indo-European cults of the horse is supplied by linguistics, the darling of Indo-European studies. The Gallic proper name Epómeduos may be cognate with the Sanskrit *aśvamedha*, both royal names, possessive compounds designating kings who have (performed) horse sacrifices (Puhvel 1955, pp. 353–54). The first element of the compound simply means "horse"; the second element is more difficult to pin down, but it has the connotations of a ritual drink (like mead) or an intoxicating drink. Thus the term as a whole may mean "intoxication with the horse" (Jaan Puhvel [ibid.] notes that "The early Indo-Europeans were undoubtedly 'crazy about horses,' and so were the Gauls") or "one who has performed a ritual involving a horse and a sacred drink." In the light of our knowledge of Indian and Irish horse rituals, a third meaning may be suggested: the term may designate a ritual in which a horse supplied the substance of the sacrificial food and drink for the king, a ceremony in which a horse was ritually eaten. The widespread evidence for horse sacrifices in Greece (Herodotus 7. 113; Xenophon *Cyr.* 8. 3; Ovid *Fast.* 1. 385), as well as among the Armenians and Massagetes (Xenophon *Anab.* 4. 5; Herodotus 1. 216) and the Irish (Dillon 1975, pp. 106–10), supports this hypothesis, for sacrificial animals are usually ritually eaten. The facts that the rituals say nothing about eating the horse and that the Greeks had a strict taboo against the eating of horseflesh (Koppers 1936, p. 292), as do most Indo-Europeans to this day, need not prove decisive, for the sacrificial animal is often taboo in other contexts or at later times. A prominent example of this phenomenon is the Indian cow, which was sacrificed in Vedic times because it was sacred and was *not* killed in Hindu times because it was sacred (Alsdorf 1962; cf. below, chap. 8, sec. C). Moreover, the devouring of a part of the stallion recurs with impressive frequency in the myths.

One final element of "other" Indo-European rituals might be mentioned here, and that is the evidence from archeology for Europe before 3500 B.C. (that is, before the major Indo-European dispersals). Although equine imagery is absent (probably because the horse was not domesticated until the end of this period), other elements of the pattern of the mare are prominent. In particular, there is a bird goddess who shows signs of bisexuality; her neck is phallic, in part as a reflection of the juxtaposition of two theriomorphic images, bird and snake, which are opposed in enough ways (both here and later in India) to allow us to characterize this goddess as a symbol of the coincidence of opposites. In addition to the bird goddess, there is a nontheriomorphic goddess who appears in numerous clay images; she has female breasts and male genitals (Gimbutas 1974, p. 135 and pl. 111). Lastly, the goddess is associated with the moon and with the processes of fertility and regeneration (ibid., pp. 152–57). The birds, androgyny, and lunar symbolism all loom large in the mythology of the mare, to which we must now turn.

C. The Myth of the Mare

To move explicitly from the ritual to the myth may imply that there is a clear separation between the two; but in fact the separation is a purely artificial construct. We cannot understand the ritual without the myth, for the ritual survives in India not in the form of a mare sacrifice but in the form of a Vedic myth about a mare sacrifice. Moreover, the ritual material (with the exception of the Vedic) is far too scanty to allow the reconstruction of a convincing prototype, but when one tackles the mythology one faces the opposite problem: the *embarras de richesse* makes it impossible to reconstruct a skeletal Urtext with any confidence. The myths also tend to lead us away from the material evidence of archeology and the traditional evidence of etymology onto the shifting chronological sands of undatable texts arising out of a fluid oral tradition. This need not deter us, however, if we are interested in essences rather than in origins, in things that survive in many late versions rather than things that may have been present in a nonsurviving early version. Thus, although it is foolhardy to place any real faith in the likelihood that a prototypical myth was ever actually told in that form, the recurrent elements of the myth of the mare do shed light on the ancient Indo-European ritual of the mare.

The Irish Myth: Mácha and the Birth of Cuchúlainn

The Mare and the Birds

The closest Irish mythological parallel both to the Irish ritual and to the Indian myth and ritual appears in the story of the birth of Cuchúlainn, which is told in at least two significantly different versions (Kinsella 1970, pp. 6–7, 21–23).[4] The first version may be summarized for our purposes as follows:

> A supernatural woman named Mácha agreed to marry Crunniuc on one condition: "Our union will continue only if you do not speak of me in the assembly." . . . But one day King Cónchobor heard that Mácha's husband had boasted that she could run faster than the horses of Cónchobor. Though she protested that she was too pregnant to race, he forced her to race against his chariot. Just as the chariot reached the end of the field, she gave birth beside it, bearing twins, a son and a daughter. The name Émain Mácha, the Twins of Mácha, comes from this episode and remains the name of that plain. . . . Years later, Cónchobor mounted a chariot with his sister, the woman Deichtíre, who drove the chariot for her brother; they chased a flock of birds from Émain Mácha until they reached Brug and took shelter in a solitary house, where they ate and drank. Later, the man of the house told them that his wife was in her birth pangs in the storeroom. Deichtíre went in to her and helped her bear a son. At the same time, a mare at the door of the house gave birth to two foals. The Ulstermen took charge of the baby boy and gave him the foals as a present, and Deichtíre nursed him.

The story continues, with further details that we will examine in other contexts. For the moment, let us merely note that the two birth stories—

one about the birth of Mácha's twins, the other about the son and foals born at Brug—are clearly related. Cónchobor in his chariot is prominent in both, and he plays a closer part in both births than is at first apparent, as we shall see. In each story a mare appears as the alter ego of the heroine. Both episodes begin at the plain called the Twins of Mácha (a reference to the two forts on the plain), and both result in twins (*émain* being cognate with Latin *geminus* and Sanskrit *yama*). The contract that Mácha's husband violates is a significant motif in the myth of the immortal wife of a mortal husband, a woman who often takes the form of a bird—though birds appear here only in the second birth, in which Mácha has no obvious role.

The birds in this episode are of scant importance, but their meaning becomes clearer in another variant:

> Cónchobor and some of his men chased a flock of birds from Émain Mácha. Now these birds were the avatars of Deichtíre, the sister (or half-sister or daughter) of Cónchobor, and of fifty young girls with whom she had lived for three years. When Cónchobor and his men chased the birds to the house at Brug, Deichtíre and her companions assumed human form again, and Deichtíre appeared as the mistress of the house. Cónchobor, not knowing that it was Deichtíre, demanded to use on his hostess the *droit du seigneur* that was his well-known prerogative. Deichtíre begged for a postponement, for she was pregnant, and that night she brought forth a boy who looked just like Cónchobor, though Cónchobor did not learn until the next day that the woman who had received him was his sister. The child, the future Cuchúlainn, was named Sétanta; he was brought to Émain Mácha to be nursed by Fínnchoem, the mother of Conall (Gricourt 1954, pp. 75–79).

This variant connects the birth of Cuchúlainn thematically with the story of Mácha and the chariot. The link is Deichtíre's protest that she is pregnant and therefore cannot sleep with Cónchobor—a protest he here *apparently* respects (in contrast with the episode in which he overrides Mácha's protests), though he manages nevertheless to be on the spot when the boy is born "who looks just like Cónchobor"; for, as we will see, the boy is indeed Cónchobor's son. The birds are Deichtíre and her companions, swan maidens whom we will meet in Indian variants of this myth (and who are adumbrated in the Indian ritual). The importance of the birds is evident from the fact that in a later episode of the *first* variant, in which the birds are *not* identified with Deichtíre and her maidens, the god Lug appears to Deichtíre and tells her that it was he who had "kidnapped her with her fifty companions in the form of birds" —an episode that, since it has no logical place in this variant at all, must have been kept from an earlier variant in which it was truly essential.

The Drinking of the Seed

Another important theme, the drinking of seed, or impregnation by mouth, appears in the first text, after the child born at Brug has been brought back to Émain Mácha:

> They reared the baby until he was a boy, but he caught an illness and died. Deichtíre's grief was great at the loss of her foster-son. She came home from lamenting him and grew thirsty and asked for a drink, and the drink was brought in a cup. She set it to her lips to drink from it, and a tiny creature slipped into her mouth with the liquid. As she took the cup from her lips, she swallowed the creature and it vanished. She slept that night and dreamed that a man came toward her and spoke to her, saying that she would bear a child by him—that it was he who had brought her to Brug to sleep with her there [an episode not yet mentioned in this text], that the boy she had reared was his, that he was again planted in her womb and was to be called Sétanta, that he himself was Lug mac Ethnenn, and that the foals should be reared with the boy. The woman grew heavy with child, and the people of Ulster made much of not knowing its father, saying it might have been Cónchobor himself, in his drunkenness, that night she had stayed with him at Brug. Then Cónchobor gave his sister in marriage to Sualdam mac Roich. She was ashamed to go pregnant to bed with her husband, and got sick when she reached the bedstead. The living thing spilled away in the sickness, and so she was made virgin and whole and went to her husband. She grew pregnant again and bore a son, and called him Sétanta. He was given to Fínnchoem, another sister of Cónchobor, to be nursed, and raised at Inrith Fort, in Cónchobor's court (Kinsella 1970, pp. 21–23).

This is a tangled tale, and many of the twists are inspired by the desire to gloss over the incestuous relationship between Cónchobor and Deichtíre. Deichtíre becomes pregnant by mouth (as do both Cónchobor's own mother and Fínnchoem, as well as other Irish heroines [Macculloch 1918, p. 140]). But Deichtíre also miscarries that way, and this introduces the motif of the erotic mother who destroys her child (for Deichtíre aborts in order to sleep with her new husband), which we will encounter again in this corpus. Often the mother is said to eat the child;

here she kills it by vomiting it forth. Another new element in this episode is the union between a god (Lug) and a mortal woman. This motif is an inversion of the older Indo-European theme of the union between a goddess and a mortal man.

Too Many Mothers

The mare runs as a leitmotiv throughout this complex myth. Mácha becomes a mare in order to race with the king's horses; the child born at Brug is the "twin" of the (two) foals born simultaneously and reared with him, destined to become his chariot horses (Gricourt 1954, p. 79), as are the "twins" born to Mácha after the chariot race. Further resonances with Indo-European equine mythology, particularly with the Indian corpus, may be seen in the episode in which Cuchúlainn captures an underwater horse named the Grey of Mácha (Macculloch 1918, p. 128). In the original myth, not only must there have been but one mother, but the boy and a *single* colt must have been twins. Only later, when the mare goddess had been divided into a mare *and* a goddess (or queen) (Gricourt 1954, p. 83) are there two distinct births.

Thus Deichtíre is another form of Mácha, and Cuchúlainn may be the second "twin" of the pair born after the chariot race (ibid.). The identity of Cuchúlainn's mother is further complicated by the introduction of yet another stepmother (and also a sister of Cónchobor), named Fínnchoem, of whom it is rather fatuously said, "He [Cuchúlainn] will be raised with Conall Cernach, because Fínnchoem, the mother of Conall Cernach, has two breasts" (ibid., p. 167). Thus Mácha, Deichtíre, the woman in the house at Brug, and Fínnchoem are all forms of the same woman.

Why the smoke screen? It serves, in part, to conceal the relationship between Deichtíre and the father of Cuchúlainn, a figure easily as elusive as the mother. If Mácha is a form of Deichtíre, then Cuchúlainn's first father is Crunniuc—though Cónchobor already appears on the scene in this episode, forcing the pregnant Mácha to race (even as he threatens to force his *droit de seigneur* on the pregnant woman at Brug). Cuchúlainn is then engendered in the womb of Deichtíre or the woman at Brug—engendered by the latter's husband (first version) or by Cónchobor (second version). That the first is a bowdlerization of the second is evident from the fact that the child "looks like Cónchobor" and is regarded as Cónchobor's by the court gossips. Simultaneously, the mare gives birth to foals, and so, in a sense, Cuchúlainn has a stallion for a father, too. Later, the child born at Brug dies but is reborn when engendered by the god Lug mac Ethnenn; he is then lost again; and finally he is successfully fathered by Sualdam mac Roich, who, though he has fairy blood on his mother's side, is a convenient stranger; and the child is raised at court with Cónchobor himself.

It is evident that at least one cause of this multiple parentage is the need to disguise the fact that Cuchúlainn's parents are sister and brother (or half-brother) or, alternatively, father and daughter (Sjoestedt-Jonval 1940, p. 82). This unsavory fact is denied, either by the blatant statement that these people are *not* his parents or by the much lamer assertion that Cónchobor didn't know that the woman in the house was his sister (Gricourt 1954, p. 175). Cónchobor's involvement in Cuchúlainn's parentage may reflect the ancient Irish tradition of a special favor granted to the son of the king's daughter or sister, as though the king were a royal godparent (ibid., p. 180).[5] This special favor may have had something to do with the fact that in Celtic, alone among Indo-European languages, the term *nep(ō)t* is restricted to the meaning "sister's son" (Old Irish *nia(e)*, Welsh *nei*) instead of meaning "nephew" in general, as most other Indo-European cognates do, or even extending to the still looser meanings of "grandson, descendant," as in Indo-Iranian and Latin; the Celtic usage may reflect the proto-Indo-European meaning.[6] Thus Cónchobor may have the right to treat his sister's child as his own even if he does not physically father the child. But the physiological parentage is also accounted for by political tradition in Ireland, the *droit de seigneur* that looms large in two episodes of the Cuchúlainn myth.

Multiple parentage is a common characteristic of gods and heroes, particularly in epics: Oedipus, Skanda—there are so many. Indo-European mythology is rife with them, and they serve multivocal symbolic purposes: to express a child's psychological need to deny his parentage (in order to deny his own emotional involvement with his true parents); to set the stage for the myth in which the apparently lowborn hero is in fact a prince; to express the various sources of different powers inherited by the child. In some cases there may be actual conflation of two myths of parentage; thus Skanda is said to be the child of Agni, then the child of Śiva, and finally the child of Agni *and* Śiva. All of these facts are at play in the myth of Cuchúlainn, in addition to the more specifically Irish traditions and certain subtraditions associated with the mare, such as the motif of the good mother and the evil stepmother.

The three principal mothers of Cuchúlainn are Mácha, Deichtíre, and the woman at Brug. Mácha is a goddess, Deichtíre is a queen, and the woman at Brug is the wife of a peasant or farmer. These three levels correspond with Dumézil's hypothetical three functions of Indo-European culture: sacred, martial, and agricultural (the priest, the warrior, and the cultivator) (Le Roux 1963, p. 132). Since all three female figures are aspects of a single woman, the mother of Cuchúlainn, she appears to be a trifunctional goddess who splits into three synonymous heroines (as the Goddess splits into Devī, Pārvatī, and Tārāvatī). Although the Irish goddess is an integrated figure, the men with whom she interacts have sharply distinct functions; there is one of her, but there are three of them. The Goddess is complex: when worshiped in her own right, she spans all aspects of human culture; when translated into an androcentric culture, she is split apart into manageable units, each of whom is overpowered by a single male.

Another element of the myth of Cuchúlainn raises a point that is significant for the Indo-European mythology of mares. This episode occurs at the end of the race between Mácha and the horses of Cónchobor:

> As she gave birth she screamed out that all who heard that scream would suffer from the same pangs for five days and four nights in their times of greatest difficulty. This affliction, ever afterward, seized all the men of Ulster who were there that day, and nine generations after them. . . . Only three classes of people were free from the pangs of Ulster: the young boys of Ulster, the women, and Cuchúlainn (Kinsella 1970, p. 8).

This is a fine example of the *couvade*, of birth pangs experienced by men, a motif that has been related to pregnancy envy and the myth of the pregnant male (Dundes 1962; cf. above, chap. 2, sec. A, and below, chap. 9, sec. B). At the moment when Mácha gives birth, the men of Ulster become mothers—thus adding an incalculable number to the already large group of substitute mothers of Cuchúlainn. (Cuchúlainn, be it noted, is the one sexually mature male who is free of the curse; furthermore, he is famed for his chastity [Koppers 1936, p. 382]—the only reliable protection against the furious mare—though this chastity is sometimes denied.) More precisely, the dying "mare," Mácha, who is killed by Cónchobor just as surely as the white mare in the Irish ritual is killed by that king, puts a curse on Cónchobor and his ilk to become women—to be mutilated or castrated—a theme that plays a more significant role in other variants of the myth.

The Irish Bull

Mácha's curse upon the men of Ulster and Cuchúlainn's exemption from it play an important part in the great cattle raid, to which the story of Cuchúlainn's birth is merely a prelude:

> Two cows, who had been magically impregnated by mouth, gave

> birth to the Brown Bull of Ulster and the White-horned Bull of Connaught. The former belonged to a king in Ulster; the latter originally belonged to Queen Medb but, unwilling to belong to a mere woman, went over to her husband's herd. In order to equal him, Medb asked to borrow the Brown Bull for a year; when this was refused, she attacked Ulster at the time of the year when all the men were suffering under Mácha's curse. But Cuchúlainn, unaffected by the curse, fought single-handed against Medb's army. She offered her favors to Cuchúlainn if he would forsake Cónchobor, but he refused, whereupon Medb stole the Brown Bull. Then Mórrigu, the war-goddess who drove a chariot drawn by red horses, fell in love with Cuchúlainn; when he spurned her, too, she cursed him and transformed herself into a crow. During the battle, she appeared in various disguises and fought against him, but later she came to him as an old woman, and he healed her wounds that he himself had inflicted, and then she became his friend and helped him. At last the Brown Bull of Ulster entered Connaught and killed the White-horned Bull; he dismembered him and carried off pieces of his body on his horns, dropping them in various parts of Ireland. Then he himself turned mad and killed his own people, until he dropped down dead (Kinsella, 1970).

Despite the switch from equine to bovine (and from female to male animals), many of the motifs of the Irish mare cycle reappear in this part of the story, together with motifs familiar from myths found in the broader corpus of hierogamies. The birth from two cows who conceive by mouth and give birth to dark and light offspring combines Irish and Vedic motifs of the good and evil mother. The competition between husband and wife is a motif that we have seen in the story of the dance of Śiva and Pārvatī and will encounter again in the folk variants of the androgyne. The strife between them is heightened in two episodes in which the hero fights a love battle with a spurned goddess (first Medb, then Mórrigu), whom he wounds and then heals; unlike the variant we have seen in the story of Devī and the buffalo (where the male opponent was a demon), the battle does not result in a death. The conflict, however, is part of a larger theme of the immortal woman spurned by the mortal worshiper, a theme that is familiar from Hindu mythology and assumes even greater importance in the Greek and Vedic corpus, as we shall see. The woman who turns into a bird (here a black bird—a crow) and drives a chariot of flaming horses is the fiery mare goddess, who assumes the role of swan maiden.

The nature and fate of the twins of Mácha is channeled into the history of the one human son, Cuchúlainn. But another Irish myth elaborates upon the theme of the twins:

> Lir married Eve, the oldest of three foster-daughters of King Bodb Derg, and Eve bore him two sets of twins (first a daughter and son, then two sons), but died in giving birth to the second pair. Lir then married Eva, the younger sister of Eve, who was jealous of the affection that the children received from their father. She ordered her horses to be yoked to her chariot and set out for the house of her father, taking the four children with her. On the way, she turned the children into four snow-white swans. When Bodb Derg found out what she had done, he transformed her into a demon of the air (Joyce 1962).[7]

The two sets of twins, the good woman who dies in childbirth and is replaced by an evil stepmother who attempts to kill the children, the transformation into birds (here applied to the children as well as to the wicked woman, who becomes a flying demon), and the flight (by chariot) of the woman to her father are all motifs that loom large in the Irish and Indian myths of the mare.

The Indian Myth: Vivasvant and Saraṇyū

In the Vedic myth of Saraṇyū, as in the Indian ritual, several different models overlap. We have the mare as well as the stallion and the king as well as the queen, but in the Vedic myth there are no cross-matched pairs. Instead of mare paired with king and queen with stallion, we have mare paired with stallion and anthropomorphic god with goddess. One might think that these rearrangements would cancel out the contrasting levels, that there would be no conflict between one mortal and one immortal partner of either species or gender. But this is not the case. Rather, the two patterns are juxtaposed, with either female or male being regarded as immortal on different levels of the myth.

The Vedic myth is brief and cryptic; later variants present a full expansion, but with certain reversals of the hypothetical prototype. The myth revolves around the birth and marriage of the sun:

> Aditi, the mother of the gods, brought forth eight sons. Seven were well-formed, but the eighth miscarried and came forth an unshaped lump, as broad as it was high, the size of a man. The other sons of Aditi became gods; but she pushed the eighth away, to propagate and then to die.
>
> His brothers, however, shaped him so that he was not lost; they

> cut the flesh away from him and threw it into a lump, and in this way they fashioned Vivasvant, the sun. He is called Mārtāṇḍa, "Dead in the Egg," because he is a bird and because he was born of a dead egg.
>
> Vivasvant married Saraṇyū [or Saṃjñā, "bright image"], the daughter of Tvaṣṭṛ, the artisan of the gods. But she substituted for herself another, identical female, Chāyā ["dark shadow"], and went away, leaving the substitute behind her. Vivasvant begat upon the substitute a son, Manu, the ancestor of the race of men. Thus they [the gods] concealed the immortal woman from mortals.
>
> Saraṇyū took the form of a mare when she fled, but then Vivasvant took the form of a stallion and followed her. In their haste, the semen fell on the ground, and the mare smelled that semen because she desired to become pregnant. Thus the twin Aśvins were born, and Saraṇyū abandoned them (*RV* 10. 72. 8–9; 10. 17. 1–2; *ŚB* 3. 1. 3–5).

This is the story as it is told in the Ṛg Veda and the texts immediately following the Ṛg Veda. Vivasvant is abandoned first by his mother and then by his wife, who also abandons their twins; his wife has two forms, dark and light; the dark form begets a mortal child, the light form, immortal twins.

The precise manner in which Aditi conceives and mutilates her son Vivasvant is further illuminated (though also somewhat confused) by other Brāhmaṇas:

> Aditi wished to have offspring, and so she cooked a Brahmin's rice offering to the gods. When they gave the remains to her, she ate it and became pregnant, giving birth to the four Ādityas. Then she cooked a second rice offering, and, thinking that her children would be stronger if she ate before the gods did instead of merely eating the remains, she ate first, became pregnant, and gave birth to an egg that miscarried. Then she cooked a third time, this time for the Ādityas, saying, "Let this work be for my enjoyment," and, as they granted her request, Vivasvant was born, an Āditya whose offspring are men (*GB* 1. 2. 15; *TS* 6. 5. 6).

In this text, Aditi becomes pregnant by eating rice offerings. The first time, she is satisfied with her proper share; but when she becomes greedy and eats first (violating not only the Indian tradition that a wife eats only after her husband but also the belief that woman becomes pregnant by eating the remnants of the *piṇḍa*, the offerings to the ancestors, or, indeed, by eating the *prasāda*, the remnant of the offering to the god), she gives birth to a dead egg (distinguished, in this text, from Vivasvant). Thus she has two sets of healthy twins and a third set of deficient twins—the dead egg *and* Vivasvant. The twin-ness of her offspring emerges in another, closely related text, which states that she gave birth to *four* sets of twins: three sets by eating the remains of the rice offering and then one set after eating but before making the offering—one of these latter twins being born dead (hence the traditional seven Ādityas plus Vivasvant) (*MS* 1. 6. 2, 4. 6. 9). These supplementary Brāhmaṇa texts greatly strengthen the parallels between Aditi and Saraṇyū: two groups of twins are conceived by mouth and are eventually born as immortal and mortal children as a direct result of the mother's restraint or greed in devouring the seed.

The psychological motivations and theological implications of these events may be surmised even from these early, often obscure texts, but they become clearer when analyzed in the context of later, far more explicit expansions of the myth—despite the fact that these expansions often introduce new points of view at direct odds with the Vedic viewpoint. Indeed, it is precisely at the point where these manipulations become most blatant that we can begin to discern the problem posed by the earlier texts. The Hindu reworking of the Vedic myth presents several significant changes:

> Before Saraṇyū abandoned Vivasvant, she bore him twins, a boy and a girl, named Yama and Yamī; she left him then because she was "unsatisfied with her husband's form." Meanwhile, Chāyā, the shadow wife, mistreated her twin stepchildren, and the boy, Yama, kicked her, whereupon she uttered a curse that his foot might fall off. When Yama reported this to his father, Vivasvant realized that Chāyā was not his true wife, for a mother could not harm her child that way; he modified the curse so that Yama did not lose his foot but became the first mortal, king of the dead in the underworld. Then Vivasvant went to Saraṇyū's father, Tvaṣṭṛ, who told him that Saraṇyū had fled because he blazed too fiercely; Vivasvant asked Tvaṣṭṛ to place him upon his lathe and trim his form, and this was done; when Vivasvant had been given a handsome body by Saraṇyū's father in this way, he went to seek his wife. He found her in the form of a mare; taking the form of a stallion, he approached her. She turned to face him, to protect her hindquarters, and his seed entered her nose. In this way the twin Aśvins were born. Then Saraṇyū resumed her own form and went back home with Vivasvant and the Aśvins (*MP* 103–5; *Matsya P* 11; *PP* 5. 8; O'Flaherty 1975, pp. 15–16).

How has this version changed the myth? The initial mutilation of Vivasvant because of his mother's dissatisfaction with him is now duplicated, and he is mutilated again, this time because of his wife's dissatisfaction. Moreover, his son, Yama, is mutilated as a result of being abandoned by one mother and abused by a second, and the mortal twins, Yama and Yamī, are abandoned while the immortal twins, the Aśvins, are not. Finally, a reason is given—at two different points in the myth—to explain why Saraṇyū deserted her husband, and a new reason is given for the abnormal mode of her impregnation: where the first text implied that the Aśvins were conceived through the nose because Saraṇyū *wanted* to become pregnant, in the later variant it is said that this happened as a result of her attempt to *avoid* becoming pregnant.

Behind this complex myth we may discern a few repeated, familiar themes. In the first version, the ambivalent Indo-European mare goddess is already split into several female figures. Saraṇyū has two doubles (her "shadow" and the mare that she becomes) and two natures (the loving mother and the wicked stepmother or rejecting mare mother). Although she is not explicitly identified as a mare in the oldest text of the myth, the Ṛg Veda, it is reasonable "to regard Saraṇyū's metamorphosis into a mare as an integral part of the story; . . . our theory that the version of the Rig-Veda is a *brahmodya* [riddle] makes it more than natural that her change into a mare (*aśvā*) be left to be inferred from the designation of her second pair of twins as 'the horsemen' (*aśvins*)" (Bloomfield 1893, p. 178). Saraṇyū is a white horse (always thus represented in paintings of the myth; see plate 3), and her alter ego is black.

The alternation between light and dark, together with the relationship with the sun, may suggest that Saṃjñā is a riddle term for Sandhyā, dawn; the Doppelgänger woman is then evening twilight, and the sun has two wives (Lommel 1949, pp. 243–57). The connection between Saraṇyū and Dawn (Uṣas or Sandhyā) is indeed striking. Like Saraṇyū, Uṣas is the wife of the sun; her ambivalence, too, is a match for Saraṇyū's, as Coomaraswamy demonstrated long ago, pointing out the identity of Uṣas and Saraṇyū and their shared characteristics of double motherhood (of Agni), of light and dark, and of incest (Coomaraswamy 1935). For Uṣas is not only the daughter with whom Prajāpati attempts to commit incest (an episode in which she assumes the form of a mare, and he becomes a stallion to cover her, just as Saraṇyū flees from Vivasvant [see above, chap. 4, sec. C]); she is simultaneously the wife (or, rather, the wives) of the sun and the daughter of the sun (*RV* 4. 5. 13, 7. 69. 4). Her mare nature emerges in other ways, as well: she is, as we have seen, a dancer and a killer, the dangerous whore, the immortal wife of a waning mortal husband (*RV* 8. 75. 4; 1. 124. 8;

3. 2. 2; 3. 55. 4; cf. above, chap. 5, sec B). As an equine, she is said not only to be a prize-winning mare but to lead a white horse and to drive a horse-drawn chariot (like Mácha in Ireland, Mudgala's wife in India, and so many Greek mare goddesses who draw the chariot themselves) (*RV* 1. 113. 4; 3. 61. 1). Moreover, there is a chariot race implicit in her story: Indra (who in later Vedic literature is said to have Night and Dawn as his consorts [*VS* 3. 10]) destroys the chariot of the evil woman, Uṣas; "the bright Uṣas was afraid of the destructive thunderbolt of Indra; she departed and abandoned her chariot" (*RV* 10. 138. 5; 4. 30. 9; 2. 15. 6). The mare goddess is incestuously attacked by her father and retaliates by inflicting injury upon him in his character as her husband; she is then attacked by the phallic thunderbolt of her husband in the course of a chariot race that destroys her own chariot. The tale of Saraṇyū, fragmented and reassembled, is told again, even to the final point of the incestuous child; for Agni is said to be not only the child of the two mothers, Uṣas and Night (*RV* 6. 1. 4; cf. 10. 116), but the lover of Uṣas (*RV* 1. 69. 1 and 9). Saraṇyū/Chayā and Uṣas/Ratri (Dawn/Night) function as good and evil mothers, examples of the type epitomized by Hāritī, goddess of children, symbol of nourishing mothers and simultaneously an ogress who devours children (Hubert 1925, p. 198; Foucher 1950–51, 2:130; cf. *MBh* 1. 3. 70).

The Mutilating Mare

The image of the destructive mare applies to Saraṇyū in three ways within the second version, though two of the episodes are transferred to other mothers: first, Mārtāṇḍa's mother miscarries him and tries to kill him (a danger from which his brothers rescue him by trimming his form); then the "shadow" mother causes Yama's leg to be mutilated (a danger from which his father rescues him by making him fall to the underworld); and finally Saraṇyū's desertion causes Vivasvant to be trimmed again, this time (significantly) by his wife's father. The third episode, the trimming of the mature sun, appears only in post-Vedic texts and is clearly a development of the first episode, the trimming of the embryonic sun. In early versions of the third episode, in which the first episode still exerts a strong influence, it is said that Saraṇyū left her husband because he had "no form at all" or was perfectly round (*H* 587; *Vāyu P* 84. 70); but as the myth develops, it is said that the sun had an unbearable brilliance, that he was *too* majestic for her, and so he had to be "trimmed down" (i.e., be made round, as he is today) before he could be a suitable companion for his little bride (*Bhav P* 1. 79. 21; Blau 1908, pp. 354–55). The shift from a husband unacceptable because of his inferiority to one unacceptable because of his superiority is highly significant in the history of the mare and the shift from hypogamous to hypergamous hierogamies in India. But, whether she is stronger or weaker than her husband, Saraṇyū injures him; the sun is mutilated by two women, and his son, Yama, is mutilated by a third. In all three cases, a father or brother minimizes the damage.

The mare injures Vivasvant in a more directly sexual way, as well, by drinking his seed. That this drains his power while simultaneously increasing her power is evident from at least one ancient text:

> From the creatures seized by Prajāpati the mule went forth; he went after the mule and took away its seed. He wiped the seed off on the mare. Therefore the mare has double seed (for it brings forth both horse and mule), and therefore the mule is barren, for its seed had been taken away (*TB* 6. 1. 4; cf. *ŚB* 6. 3. 1. 23).

The seed is "wiped off" on the mare as sin is "wiped off" on various scapegoats in Vedic texts (*AV* 7. 65. 2). In the closed karmic universe, if one gains, the other loses; sexual power is a limited good (O'Flaherty 1976, pp. 141–43).

Yama's mutilation takes the form of a threatened loss of a leg, which is not only a fairly obvious euphemism for castration but has strong equine resonances in Indian mythology. For the hoof of the horse is treated symbolically with much of the imagery associated with the phallus: imagery of water, butter, and gold. In Vedic ceremonies contemporaneous with the horse sacrifice (including the Agnicāyana that underlies the horse sacrifice itself), water is poured into the horse's footprint, an oblation of butter is made to the footprint, and gold is pressed against the frog (see O'Flaherty 1978a) on the inside of the horse's hoof (*BŚS* 10. 2–3; cf. *TS* 4. 1. 2o–p). This imagery is found in the Ṛg Veda as well: the Aśvins gave one of their worshipers a horse, rich in seed, from whose hoof a hundred potfuls of wine flowed, as from a sieve (*RV* 1. 116. 7). In the context of this symbology (which is not limited to India), the mutilation of the leg of the sun stallion's son surely has overtones of the loss of a more general power of life.

Even more significant for our hypothetical proto-Indo-European model of the dismemberment of the *mare* is a closely related Ṛg Vedic image: when the leg of the racing mare Viśpalā was cut off like the wing of a bird, the Aśvins replaced it (*RV* 1. 117. 6; 1. 116. 15). Dumézil has connected the mare Viśpalā with the horse mutilated in the Roman Pales festival, disregarding the change of gender (Dumézil 1956, pp. 54, 232–45; Puhvel 1970b, p. 381). Although, as we shall see, it is by no means meaningless to speak of the castration of the mare, we might be better advised to read this, and the other myths of mutilation of an equine leg, as basic images of the loss of special powers, whether sexual or divine. For Viśpalā's leg is likened to a wing; her mutilation foreshadows that of the flying horses whose wings were cut off by Indra to make them useful to gods and men (*Aśvaśāstra*, pakṣacchedakathā; cf. *MBh* 1. 16. 34–35)—i.e., to tame and control them, to take away their divinity (see below, chap. 8, sec. A). These are myths about winged horses, about sun symbols that are simultaneously horses and birds.

Immortal Woman and Mortal Man

The sun is called a bird (Mārtāṇḍa), and, although Saraṇyū is not a bird, another close Ṛg Vedic parallel provides us with the quintessential swan maiden: Urvaśī, the heavenly nymph who sleeps with King Purūravas and abandons him after bearing him a son (*RV* 10. 95). In a later variant of this myth, she has two theriomorphic children as well, two lambs that she refers to as her sons (*ŚB* 11. 5. 1. 2–3). The gods take Urvaśī away from her mortal husband just as they take Saraṇyū from Vivasvant, though the device is reversed as the myth develops. Just as the gods conceal Saraṇyū from Vivasvant, so in the Ṛg Veda the nymphs and Urvaśī shy away like excited gazelles when Purūravas approaches them at a time when they have laid aside their veils (*RV* 10. 95. 8). But in a later version of this myth, Urvaśī makes Purūravas promise that she will never see *him* naked, a promise that the immortals force him to violate when they flash lightning to reveal him to her in his nakedness (*ŚB* 11. 5. 1. 1–4); the occasion for this is the theft of the theriomorphic sons, another theme familiar from the Indo-European mythology of mares such as Rhiannon, whom we shall soon encounter.

The myth is also transformed in transition from the Vedic to the Brāhmaṇic text in other ways that are the inverse of the pattern of transition in the Saraṇyū myth. For in the Ṛg Veda, Urvaśī complains that Purūravas "pierces her with his rod" three times a day, filling her even when she has no desire (*RV* 10. 95. 5); and she also says that the "drop of butter" that she had swallowed among mortals once a day even now more than satisfies her (*RV* 10. 95. 16), a possible euphemism for the swallowing of his seed. In the Brāhmaṇa, however, she makes him *promise* to strike her three times a day with the "rod." Here the first text implies that his desire (or capacity) is greater than hers, while the second implies that hers is at least as great if not greater. The final transformation, in keeping with these shifting elements, is that in the Ṛg Veda he is left longing for her, with a vague promise of reunion in heaven, whereas in the Brāhmaṇa she loves him so much that she teaches him how to become immortal (a Gandharva) by cooking rice (*odanam*) and churning fire—the first element familiar from the tale of Aditi, the second an important component of the birth of the underwater mare (see below, chap. 7, sec. E).

In both texts, Urvaśī is a water bird, discovered by her husband among other water birds. But she is also a mare: Purūravas says that immortal women who shy away from mortal men are like horses grazed by a chariot (*RV* 10. 95. 8), a further resonance with the theme of the mare goddess harnessed to the chariot; he also says that Urvaśī is as hard to catch as a winning racehorse (10. 95. 3), and Urvaśī admits that immortal women, when they respond to a mortal's caresses, are like water birds or like horses who bite in their love play (10. 95. 9), an allusion to both the aggressive and the oral motifs of the erotic mare. Finally, another animal serves as a metaphor: Purūravas threatens to let the wolves eat him, and Urvaśī admits that women have the hearts of wolves or jackals (10. 95. 14–15). These images of devouring animals appear in striking combination in the story of Urvaśī, the classic form of the myth of the union of a mortal man and an immortal woman, of which the myth of Saraṇyū is an early variant.

The immortal woman's mare nature is frequently replaced with that of a bird or a deer (the latter recurring as the white hind or doe of Celtic and Russian mythology). One myth of this corpus separates deer, bird, and woman:

> One day, when Gaurivīti had shot a deer for a sacrifice, the magic bird Suparṇa came flying to him. Gaurivīti put his arrow on his bow and aimed at him, but the bird begged him not to shoot, in turn promising to help him win the woman he loved, the daughter of a jealous demon, who guarded her in a palace in the middle of the sea. The bird took Gaurivīti to her every night; she became pregnant and bore him a son, but the demons tore the child apart and threw him away. Then the bird taught him a magic spell by which he revived the child (*JB* 3. 197 and 3. 18).

The bird is the alter ego of the demonic woman whose father threatens the hero (and we shall see the fathers of many Greek mares threatening their suitors, just as Tvaṣṭṛ threatens Vivasvant) and whose kinsmen destroy their child (as the Gandharvas steal away the lambs). In her beneficent aspect, however, she teaches him the secret of revival, the secret of immortality.

The deer and the swan are more delicate and "feminine" female images, frail and vulnerable, in need of male protection. But even the swan maiden remains morally ambivalent, as every balletomane knows:

the good, chaste Odette opposes the evil (erotic) Odile, who is in thrall to her jealous, deadly father (Rothbart). In Norse mythology (and Wagnerian opera), the Valkyries ride horses or become swans. Another example of the ambivalent bird woman in India is Pūtanā, who is described as a bird (*śakuni*) perched on the wheel of a wagon before she assumes the form of the beautiful woman with poisoned breasts (*H* 50. 20). The evil bird is the woman with an active, phallic, clitoral beak (to use D. H. Lawrence's image), in contrast with the white bird, who is "feathery" in her internal, passive sexuality.

The myth of the immortal woman as bird is a broader form of the Saraṇyū myth. The two patterns of that myth—the one in which she flees from him because he is superior and the one in which she flees because he is inferior (both mirrored in the texts of the myth of Urvaśī)—are based on contrasting perceptions of the power balance between the two main participants. This in turn is a reflection of the conflation of two contrasting ritual images: Saraṇyū is the divine mare with a human consort (the Irish ritual), or she is the human queen with a divine stallion as her consort (the Vedic ritual). The two levels of the myth may be chronologically discrete (the mare goddess of the ancient Indo-European world preceding the stallion god of Vedic India), though this is difficult to prove; in any case, the two patterns appear to be fully integrated in the transmitted versions that we have. But by sorting them out and separating them, we can see the process of their interaction. Moreover, many of the ambiguities of the Hindu myth are the result of a constant tension between two palpably discrete historical levels of the myth, in which the goddess first abandons the king (Ṛg Veda) and is then abandoned by him (Purāṇas). Originally, the mare was an immortal creature who had both power and authority; in the Hindu myth, she loses her authority but keeps her power.

In the myth of Saraṇyū, the sun (whom we would normally regard as an immortal, and who is definitely a god in the Vedas) is a mortal. This is emphasized by the story of his birth, for he fails to reach the gods and is born "to die" (*RV* 10. 72. 8–9). Saraṇyū, on the other hand, is immortal; this immortality, and its role in causing her to leave Vivasvant, is one of the very few things that we learn about Saraṇyū in the Ṛg Vedic verse that is the earliest source of her story: "They concealed the immortal woman from mortals" (*RV* 10. 17. 1–2). In the Purāṇas, Saraṇyū flees from Vivasvant of her own will, but for the same reason, as Bloomfield pointed out long ago:

> Saraṇyū presents Vivasvant with the twins Yama and Yamī, but after this the feeling that she is the victim of a *mésalliance* gains

> ground more and more. The poet at Harivaṃśa 547 has a true sense of the situation when he says: . . . "Saraṇyū, endowed with beauty and youth, took no delight in the form of her husband." Possibly the story aims to convey a more special form of Saraṇyū's dissatisfaction, which peeps out not only in her abandonment of her husband, but more clearly in *her metamorphosis into a mare* [italics added]: Vivasvant in his human capacity may have failed to satisfy the instincts of the goddess, which were probably laid out on too large a scale for his mortal capacities. Without desiring to imply any genetic connection, we may bear in mind the prevalence of similar features in ancient novel-literature: e.g., in the story of Pasiphaë and in the *onos* of Lucian (Bloomfield 1893, pp. 177–78).

Bloomfield states the case with nineteenth-century delicacy but with unmistakable insight: the metamorphosis into a mare reveals the woman's "large-scale instincts." These instincts drive her to leave Vivasvant in the early, Vedic variant; but when her status drops, in the post-Vedic period, she is said to flee from him, because he is "too brilliant," and to have him "cut down to size" by her father.

A similar inversion of the Saraṇyū myth (or, more directly, a mythological version of the already inverted Indian ritual) may be seen in the later tradition that the lascivious god Indra impersonated the consecrated stallion during a horse sacrifice in order to seduce a certain mortal queen whom he fancied (*H* 18. 11–17).

The fact that the Saraṇyū myth is a hierogamy between a mortal and an immortal accounts for both Saraṇyū's desertion of her husband and her "trimming" of him: either the sun is impotent and abandoned by the goddess or he is *too* powerful and is therefore castrated, a no-win situation if ever there was one. This is a pattern that one might regard, in Lévi-Straussian parlance, as a dialectical alternation between underrating and overrating marital relations (Lévi-Strauss 1958, p. 55). It also accounts for some of the elaborate gymnastics which the storytellers went through in order to explain the dual maternity/paternity of the child/foal twins. Later variants of the myth give Manu a sister, too, and attribute yet another Manu (a "look-alike" Manu) to Saraṇyū herself. Yet originally the Aśvins must have been the first set of twins, with Manu the third child. Yama then was added, to form a pair of twins with Manu, and Yamī is a relative latecomer to the myth, though already present elsewhere in the Ṛg Veda (Lincoln 1975, pp. 129–36; Puhvel 1975, p. 153; Ward 1970b). The theme of the immortal woman and the mortal man can then be read into the dialogue between Yama and Yamī in which Yamī unsuccessfully entreats Yama to make love to her (*RV* 10. 10); Yama may be objecting to the union not because he and Yamī are too close (i.e., incestuously related) but because they are too distant (i.e., because she is a goddess while he is merely a mortal) (Goldman 1969, pp. 273–303).

Incest and Abnormal Procreation

The tale of Saraṇyū contains even more incestuous relationships than the tale of Cuchúlainn's birth reveals. It is a family drama to bring tears to the eyes of any Freudian: Saraṇyū leaves her husband and runs home to daddy (Electra complex), who "cuts" her husband down; she gives birth to a son and a daughter who are the primeval Indo-European incestuous couple. It has even been suggested that the marriage alluded to in the Vedic riddle of Saraṇyū (*RV* 10. 17. 1–2) might refer to the connection of Tvaṣṭṛ with his own daughter (Bloomfield 1893, p. 181, citing Weber 1850–98, 17:310; cf. A. Kuhn 1886, p. 448; Bergaigne 1883, 2:318). Tvaṣṭṛ is indeed guilty of some oedipal underhandedness toward his male offspring (O'Flaherty 1976, pp. 102–4), but he seems to have a clean slate as far as Saraṇyū is concerned (though not, perhaps, as far as her husband is concerned). Incest is endemic to the solar nuclear family, however, for the Ṛg Veda states unequivocally that the Aśvins, the two brothers of Sūryā (the daughter of the sun—perhaps another form of Uṣas), are, as we have seen, both her suitors and her joint husbands (*RV* 10. 85. 8–9; 4. 43. 6; 1. 119. 5).

A final factor in the Saraṇyū myth that ties it to the Indo-European corpus of mare mythology is the episode of drinking the stallion's seed. Saraṇyū absorbs through her nostrils the seed of the sun stallion; the children born of this union are therefore called Nāsatyas ("nose-born") (*Nirukta* 6. 13), an ancient etymology often ridiculed but recently brought back into favor (Lommel, 1951; Puhvel 1970b, p. 381). In the first text, Saraṇyū abandons her husband *before* she has children and then returns to him in order to become pregnant; in the second, she abandons him *after* she has children and flees from him in order to avoid becoming pregnant again. In the first text, she sniffs the semen in order to become pregnant; in the second, she turns her hindquarters away from her husband because she does not wish him to cover her and is therefore accidentally (forcibly?) impregnated by mouth. In the first text, she is a figure of fertility, the goddess who unites with the king in order to produce immortal progeny; in the second text, she is an erotic figure who rejects her mortal progeny. This transition from good mother to evil mother is highly significant in the Indian context; indeed, some Purāṇic texts tried to restore a modicum of maternal spirit to Saraṇyū by stating that she turned away from the stallion because she feared that he might be some man other than her husband (*MP* 103–5). This gloss makes good sense in the light of emerging concepts of caste marriage and the importance of controlling the "field" in which the seed is planted (or in maintaining a monopoly on the *śakti* of the wife), but it is untrue to the original spirit of the myth.

The Welsh Myth: Rhiannon and the Disappearing Foals

Almost all of the themes that emerge from the Indian and Irish myths persist in the story of Rhiannon, found in a twelfth-century Welsh redaction but undoubtedly a much older tale:

> One day Pwyll was out hunting and met Arawn, King of Annwfn in the Otherworld. In order to help Arawn conquer an enemy, Pwyll agreed to take Arawn's shape (through Arawn's magic powers) and live in his place for a year, sleeping with the queen, while Arawn lived in Pwyll's place; at the end of the year, Pwyll would fight in Arawn's stead and kill his enemy. Pwyll did as they had agreed, but every night as he got into bed with the queen he turned his back toward her, and so spent the year. At the appointed time, he killed Arawn's enemy and they took back their own shapes; when Arawn returned to his queen he was surprised to learn that Pwyll had not touched her.
>
> Some time later, Pwyll saw a beautiful woman riding on a great white horse. He pursued her and captured her, and she became his wife, Rhiannon. After three years, she bore him a son. Now, on the night of his birth six women were brought in to look after mother and child, but these women and Rhiannon all fell asleep before midnight and only woke at dawn. Upon waking, the women searched but found no trace of the boy; then they found a deer hound with pups, and they killed the pups, smeared Rhiannon's hands and face with the blood, threw the bones before her and insisted that she had destroyed her own child. The nobles asked Pwyll to separate from his wife because of the terrible outrage she had committed, but he refused, asking that she be merely punished instead. Rather than haggle with the women, Rhiannon accepted her punishment, which was to sit every day by the mounting block near the gate, telling her story and offering to carry guests to the court on her back.
>
> At that time, Teyrnon had a mare in his house who foaled every

> May Eve (Walpurgisnacht), but no one ever knew anything of the colt. So Teyrnon finally had the mare brought inside on May Eve and armed himself and began to watch. At night she foaled, and Teyrnon heard a noise and saw a great claw come through the window and seize the colt by the mane. Teyrnon hacked off the arm at the elbow and rushed outside, but the night was so dark he could see nothing. He returned and found the foal inside; and by the door there was a small boy in swaddling clothes. He gave the boy to his wife, and they agreed that she would pretend that she had been pregnant and borne him. At the age of four, he was given the colt to ride.
>
> Meanwhile, they heard the news of Rhiannon and her punishment, and Teyrnon saw how the boy resembled Pwyll. He realized that it was wrong for them to keep a boy whom they knew to be another's son and to allow Rhiannon to be punished, and so they brought the boy back to Pwyll and Rhiannon. When they arrived, Rhiannon was sitting at the mounting block; she offered to carry them, but they all three refused. Then they told Rhiannon who the boy was, and there was great rejoicing, and Rhiannon and Pwyll took the boy back (Ford 1977, pp. 37–56; cf. Hubert 1925, pp. 189–90).

Rhiannon's mare nature is revealed not only by the parallel births of her son and a colt but by her position "at the mounting block" and her task of carrying guests on her shoulders, as a horse would. Teyrnon's wife, too, has strong ties with stables and colts. Like Deichtíre, Rhiannon is a double mother, simultaneously goddess and mare (Gricourt 1954, p. 79). The goddess (on horseback) and the mare (together with yet another theriomorphic stepmother, the deerhound) give birth simultaneously but in different places, while Teyrnon's wife fakes yet another pregnancy and claims the child as hers. The disappearance of the mother after the birth (as in the tale of the swan maiden) is here transformed into an accusation of infanticide, murder replacing mere abandonment. This, like the theme of multiple mothers, is a widespread Indo-European theme; although the infants survive, the heroines suffer greatly; their story has been called "a tragedy of maternity" (Hubert 1925, p. 197).

The prelude to the story of Rhiannon is highly significant in the light of the Indian horse sacrifice. Pwyll sleeps for a year beside a woman described as "the fairest woman anyone had ever seen," but he does not make love to her; he is like the stallion who remains chaste for a year, especially beside the mare, and like the king who lies between the thighs of his favorite queen without making love to her. In addition, Pwyll and Arawn, together with Arawn's wife, form three-fourths of a double pair: the mortal sleeps with the immortal woman, while the immortal man (Arawn) takes the place of the mortal man. Pwyll then repeats this pattern when he marries Rhiannon, the mare goddess. The theme of Pwyll's wakeful chastity is also carried over into the episode of Rhiannon and the foals: Rhiannon loses her child when she fails to remain awake, and Teyrnon, by contrast, saves his child by remaining awake, like the Indian king. To keep the child, Teyrnon must mutilate a limb of the fiend (as the solar horse is mutilated); this fiend is Rhiannon's evil alter ego, the witch who rides on Walpurgisnacht.

The tale of "The Adventure of the Mare and the Boy," as the episode of Rhiannon and the foal is referred to by Teyrnon, was probably an ancient Welsh myth about a horse goddess and fertility deity, related to the cult of Epona as well as to the myth of Mácha and Cuchúlainn and the Irish ritual of the king and the mare (Ford 1977, pp. 4–6). When the horse goddess fails to guarantee fertility and to generate a hero (or a foal), she is punished by being deprived of her equine divinity and reduced to the function of a beast of burden (ibid., pp. 6, 13). But Rhiannon is never out of control of the situation, never truly lacking in divine power; it is she who first speaks of her love to Pwyll before he has had the courage to speak of his own love for her; it is she who tells Pwyll how to win her, in a long episode that reveals Pwyll's foolishness (Rhiannon does not mince words on this occasion; when Pwyll falls silent, Rhiannon remarks archly, "Be silent as long as you like. . . . Never has a man been more feeble-witted than you have been" [ibid., p. 46]) and her cleverness: it is she who deigns to accept the punishment meted out to her, knowing full well that she has been falsely accused. Pwyll's inadequacy toward Rhiannon (his inability to protect her) is foreshadowed in his sexual inadequacy toward Arawn's wife, an equally sharp-tongued lady; she remarks to Arawn after finding out that it was Pwyll, not Arawn, who lay so chastely with her for a year, "I confess to God, as far as fighting temptations of the flesh and keeping true to you goes, you had a solid hold on a fellow" (ibid., p. 41).

Pwyll's weakness is further highlighted by the way he is contrasted not only with the virile Arawn but with Teyrnon, who is both the "foster father" of Rhiannon's child and, through the same distortions that characterize the Irish myth, the consort of Rhiannon. For the myth may preserve "the detritus of a myth wherein the sea-god mated with the horse-goddess"; Teyrnon has an epithet meaning "Tempestuous Flood," and Rhiannon later marries a third man, Manawydan, Son of the Sea, the third foster father of Rhiannon's son (ibid., pp. 12, 15). Just as

Pwyll changes places with Arawn, so by implication he changes places with Teyrnon, another supernatural figure. Now, Epona is associated with a hippomorphic sea god; Mácha is the daughter of a man called "Nature of the Sea" and is also the mother of a horse who returns to the sea and mother of a son—Cuchúlainn—engendered by Lug, the foster son of the Irish sea god (ibid., pp. 5–10, 70–71, 144); and the Indian mare is tamed by the ocean. Like all of these, Rhiannon is a mare goddess married to the sea, and, like so many mares (like Medb, who boasts of her string of lovers and fights against her husband), Rhiannon overpowers and cuckolds her husband. Finally, like Epona and many other immortal women with mortal lovers, Rhiannon is closely associated with birds, the Birds of Rhiannon, who come from the ocean (ibid., pp. 70–71).

A modern retelling of the myth of Rhiannon, sophisticated in the scholarship with which it links her to Epona, Mácha, and the mare in the cauldron, makes explicit many motifs that may be implicit in the Welsh tale and others that are at least part of its Celtic frame (see Walton 1971–74).[8] In Walton's version of the story, Pwyll has the *ius primae noctis* in his land (as Cónchobor has in his) but does not dare use it on the wife of Arawn, his own superior (ibid., 1:20); on the contrary, he asks Manawyddan (who in the Welsh text is merely the foster father of Rhiannon's child) actually to father a child upon Rhiannon by virtue of his (Manawyddan's) *droit de seigneur* (ibid., 3:41–43). Furthermore, the two incidents are causally linked: by lying beside the woman in the Otherworld, Pwyll has lost his virility and/or his ability to beget children and so must ask the king to produce a child for him. Though Pwyll insists over and over that he lay beside the woman, not with her (ibid., 1:128), she drained his mortal strength (ibid., 1:107). Indeed, when he boasts that he never gave her his seed, the Druid replies, "The seed you denied her has shriveled within you" (ibid., 1:104). Pwyll is in the now familiar no-win situation of the consort of the goddess, damned if he does (drained of his strength by even his chaste contact with her) and damned if he doesn't (punished by being made impotent for rejecting her).

To cure this disability, which Pwyll at first denies ("I do not hoard my seed," he reminds the Druid, pointing to all the children he has begotten on *other* men's wives through his *droit de seigneur* [ibid., 1:103), the Druid commands Pwyll to lie with the White Mare and give her his seed, then slay her and drink the broth made of her blood. Union with this goddess will restore the sexual powers that the first goddess (Arawn's wife) took away: "What one Goddess has taken, Another must be able to give back" (ibid., 1:107). The goddess herself assures Pwyll that this will be so, particularly commenting on his fears of being too old and weak to do her justice: "Have no fear. If we two come together, it will be as young man and young woman. Your loins will still be mighty" (ibid., p. 39). This restoration of youth and virility is a function of the ritual encountered also in the Indian myths. But Pwyll resists the ritual aspect of this restoration, even as he resisted Arawn. And Rhiannon herself, in her aspect of full Goddess, applauds his action and regards the rite as sacrilegious:

> "Man, had you done their will—gone on all fours and given your seed to a beast—you never could have drunk from My cup! The mare would have been as defiled as you. I would take no shame in putting on her flesh to meet any stallion in your fields, for all that lives and breathes in Dyved is part of Me. But man and mare—bah!" (ibid., p. 38).

Rhiannon regards Pwyll as heroic in disdaining this "holy horseplay," as he calls it; he has passed a test. And the parallels between this achievement and his chastity in the Otherworld are again made explicit, for Rhiannon says that she took the form of Arawn's wife and tried to seduce him in order to test him (ibid., pp. 72–74).

Within the context of the Welsh myth, Pwyll's action is consistently in character, but he is caught in the double bind of two sets of values inherent in the hierogamy. He is allowed (nay, encouraged) to beget children on the Goddess in the form of Rhiannon and to sire children throughout the kingdom on the basis of his special royal fertility, which is dependent on his union with the Goddess; he is therefore proud that he "does not hoard his seed." This is the ancient set of fertility values. But he is forbidden (by Her, in this text) to have contact with her in her immortal forms, queen of the Otherworld and White Mare; he is therefore proud that he does *not* give his seed to Her. (Even in the Welsh text, these attitudes begin to interact; Arawn and his wife mock Pwyll for his chastity—"Lady, do not blame me," says Arawn, when speaking of the chaste year—but Arawn also praises him for his courtly "strong and unwavering friendship.") For Pwyll, caught in the middle, one set of values blocks the productivity of the other: though he is encouraged to beget children on Rhiannon, his power to do so is ruined by his rejection of Arawn's wife. His strength is drained from him by contact with the Goddess in the Otherworld, but he is not allowed to participate in the ritual union with her as the White Mare, which would restore that strength.

In the context of the Indo-European history of the myth of the mare and the goddess, Pwyll's and Rhiannon's attitude to the ritual in this modern text demonstrates the debasement and devaluation of the ancient hierogamy; when the Goddess says that Pwyll would not have been able to drink from "her cup," she forgets that the direct and primal nature of the archaic rite specifically required the king to drink without the use of any cup at all. Rhiannon accuses the Druids of debasing the true religion of the mare, but the history of the cult indicates that this is exactly the opposite of what has happened: the later Indo-European value laid on chastity (ancient wakeful chastity as well as the chastity of the medieval courtly tradition, by which the Welsh text has been influenced) has been the undoing of the archaic rite.

The Greek Myths: Demeter and Hippolytus

The Greeks do not "disappoint the comparativist" (*pace* Puhvel [1970b, p. 168]). They were, if anything, even horsier than the Vedic Indians, and their literature presents an equine mythology of dazzling complexity. Despite the well-known pitfalls of using Greek materials in an Indo-European context, we can clearly discern a pattern that resonates strongly with the Irish and Indian texts dealing with mares and stallions. And though one perhaps compounds a felony by using such problematic scholars as Robert Graves and Sir James George Frazer in interpreting these problematic texts, it is possible to separate the texts themselves from the speculations upon them in order to see what the myths say and then allow ourselves the luxury of listening to Graves and Frazer tell us what they may mean. It may be objected, too, that there is a potentially equally grave danger in drawing on texts ranging from Homer through medieval Greek; but clearly the Greek tradition is self-consciously continuous.

Horse-headed Demeter and Poseidon

Demeter (who is often depicted with a mare's head) took the form of a Fury and had intercourse with Poseidon (god of the sea, to whom horses were sacrificed, and himself called Hippios, "equine"); from this union, Arion was born (Apollodorus 3. 6. 8; Pausanias 8. 42; see also Gricourt 1954, p. 166). The Furious nature of this mare is elaborated in a myth in which she resists Poseidon, a myth regarded with great suspicion by the fastidious Pausanias, who is our only source for the full version:

> The goddess (Demeter) has the surname Fury, for the following reason. When Demeter was wandering in search of her daughter, she was followed, it is said, by Poseidon, who lusted after her. So she turned, the story runs, into a mare, and grazed with the mares of Oncus. Realizing that he was outwitted, Poseidon changed into a

> stallion and enjoyed Demeter. At first, they say, Demeter was angry at what had happened, but later on she laid aside her anger and wished to bathe in the Ladon. So the goddess has two surnames: Fury because of her avenging anger, because the Arcadians call being wrathful "Being furious"; and Bather because she bathed in the Ladon. . . . Demeter, they say, had by Poseidon a daughter, whose name they are not wont to divulge to the uninitiated, and a horse called Arion (Pausanias 8. 25. 4–8).

The Greek goddess thus has both a double physical nature (mare and goddess) and a double emotional nature (fiery and watery—the latter corresponding to the mare in whose broth the king bathes in Giraldus' report). She also has dual offspring: a horse (male) and a human (female). The second version of the myth, in which she resists Poseidon, adds a moral overlay to the first; it corresponds to the Indian myths in which Saraṇyū becomes a mare in order to avoid the embraces of Vivasvant or in which Prajāpati's daughter becomes a mare in order to avoid his incestuous advances. H. J. Rose suggests that both Demeter and Poseidon are equines in this union (Rose 1959, pp. 66–67). Robert Graves goes much further, asserting that when Poseidon conquered "the Goddess . . . he celebrated by calling himself the Mare-tamer" (Graves 1959, p. 390); this hypothesis is to some degree substantiated by the concept, widespread in Indian mythology, of the taming of a dangerous woman or a mare (see below, chap. 7). The dark side of Demeter is portrayed in a cave painting described by Pausanias as being in Phigalia in Arcadia, the locus of the myth of her pursuit by Poseidon: to escape from him, she hid in a cave in Phigalia, where she is portrayed as Black Demeter, with the head and mane of a horse on the body of a woman (Pausanias 8. 42; Ovid *Met.* 6. 406). Frazer speculates that the rites of Demeter at Phigalia might have included a dance by women wearing masks of horses' heads; in support of this, he notes a statue of Demeter or Persephone adorned with semibestial figures of women with the heads, paws, and feet of horses—figures that may be related to the troops of horse-headed Maenads (Frazer, pt. 5, 2:21, 338).

Poseidon and The Rape of the Mare

Although Demeter herself does not (*pace* Graves 1959, pp. 427–29) destroy children—she is, on the contrary, noted for her perseverance in attempting to rescue her daughter—she is said to have devoured some of the flesh of Tantalus's son, Pelops, when she was dazed by the loss of Persephone (Pindar *Ol.* 1. 49). Moreover, she is linked, through Poseidon, with a corpus of myths in which mare goddesses do behave destructively toward their offspring, myths in which rape plays a part (as it does in the story of Demeter's daughter and in the myth of Demeter herself). These stories are often brief; but some more elaborate versions include episodes in which male children are harmed by mares, thus establishing a wider base of mare mythology that reinforces the Demeter pattern. Moreover, the stallion who rapes the mare is strongly analogous to the mare who destroys her child (or lover), rape (or defloration) being for the female the counterpart of castration.[9]

Seven representative versions of the myth of Poseidon and the mare touch upon the major leitmotivs relevant to our wider inquiry. The protagonists in many of these myths have names that are usually translated as possessive compounds ("one who has a white stallion" for Leucippus, for example), appropriate epithets for royal mortals; but in the present context one may perhaps see a deeper significance in these names, a reference to the actual nature of the man or woman.

1. When Rhea gave birth to Poseidon, she offered Cronus a foal to eat instead of the child, whom she hid among the horse herds (Pausanias 8. 8. 2). The foal is clearly a multiform of the child (as in the myths of Mácha, Rhiannon, and Saraṇyū) and becomes explicitly so in the following, related, myth.

2. Cronus fell in love with Philyra and begat upon her the centaur Chiron, having turned himself into a stallion either by way of disguise—to fool Rhea, who surprised them *in flagrante*—or because Philyra had turned into a mare to escape him. Loath to suckle her monstrous offspring, Philyra begged Zeus to change her into something else, and he made her into a lime tree (Hesiod *Theog.* 1002; Pindar *Pyth.* 3. 1; Hyg. *Fab.* 138; Apollonius Rhodius 2. 1231–34). Here the child is *both* foal and son; the conflicting rationalizations for the conditions of his birth (that Philyra was willingly seduced, merely fleeing from the righteous wife, or that she was taken against her will) are strikingly similar to the contradictory rationalizations given for Saraṇyū's conception of semiequine sons. The metamorphosis of the raped goddess is also, as we have seen and will often see again, a common technique to appease her and to assuage the guilt of her violators. Philyra's refusal to nurse her child is also typical of raped mares.

3. Poseidon seduced Melanippe ("black mare"), who bore him twin sons; they were exposed on the mountains, but a cow found them and raised them (Pindar *Nem.* 10. 55; Euripides, various fragments, cited by Rose 1959, p. 289). That the mare abandons her children should be unsurprising by now; that the cow nourishes them will become an equally familiar theme in the Indian and Irish texts, though it is not a line that we will pursue in this sampling of the Greek parallels.

4. The daughters of Leucippus ("white stallion") were raped by the Dioscuri (the Greek equivalents of the Aśvins). Each bore a set of twins, who were bitter rivals (Apollodorus 3. 11. 2). The Dioscuri may also have had a "polyandrous, incestuous" relationship with Helen (Ward 1968, p. 11).

5. Alcippe ("mighty mare") was raped by Poseidon's son Hallirrhothius ("roaring of the sea"), whom her father, Ares, then murdered (Eur. *El.* 1258; Apollodorus 3. 180; Pausanias 1. 21. 4).

6. Alope was seduced by Poseidon and bore a son, Hippothous ("impetuous stallion"), whom she exposed twice on a mountain; each time, he was raised by a mare who suckled him, while Alope died in prison (immured by her father's command) and Poseidon transformed her body into a spring (Hyg. *Fab.* 187, 252; Ael. *V.H.* 8. 42). Here the mare appears as the nurturing mother as well as the murderous mother, and in the now familiar pattern she is made murderous as a result of rape, is destroyed by her father, and is deified—in her safe, watery form—by her seducer. Instead of giving birth to twins in the usual way, she has one son who is abandoned twice.

7. Poseidon raped Medusa and begat upon her twins, the winged horse Pegasus and the warrior Chrysaor (Pindar *Pyth.* 10. 31; Ovid *Met.* 4. 780; Apollodorus 2. 4. 3; Hesiod *Theog.* 280). Here there are obvious parallels with Indian myths about the taming of winged horses[10] and the birth of these horses from mares impregnated against their will. Moreover, the entire cycle of myths in which Poseidon rapes the mare recalls another important motif in the Irish and Indian myths: the mistreatment of the mare. Saraṇyū is raped by Vivasvant, Rhiannon is falsely accused, Mácha is killed, and Deichtíre is impregnated by force. We will return to this important theme.

The Father of the Mare—Hippodameia

The myth of Alcippe and Hallirrhothius combines two themes: the rape of the mare by Poseidon and the father's revenge for this rape. This second theme is also apparent, in a distorted form, in the myth of Alope, who is herself the victim of her father's desire for revenge; her compensatory deification is also typical of this pattern. The theme of the father's revenge, of which we have seen a variant in Tvaṣṭṛ's "trimming" of Vivasvant after the rape of Saraṇyū (thinly masked by the statement that Vivasvant asked to be trimmed), has incestuous overtones, which are far clearer in the Greek corpus.

1. Alcippe had a daughter, Marpessa, by Euenus (a son of Ares and hence Alcippe's half-brother). In an attempt to keep Marpessa a virgin,

Euenus invited each of her suitors in turn to run a chariot race with him; the victor would win Marpessa, and the vanquished would forfeit his head. He killed many in this way, but Idas, the son of Poseidon, begged a winged chariot from his father and carried Marpessa away. Euenus pursued them in vain, killing himself and drowning his horses. But when Apollo took Marpessa away from Idas, the god and the mortal fought for Marpessa, who chose Idas because she feared that the immortal Apollo might leave her when she grew old (Homer *Il.* 9. 557; Hyg. *Fab.* 242; Apollodorus 1. 60–61; Pausanias 5. 18. 2; Plutarch *Par.* 40). In this myth, as in the myth of Alcippe and Hallirrhothius, Poseidon and Ares come into conflict over the affairs of their mortal offspring. In addition to the theme of the jealous father of the mare, this myth includes the closely related themes of the death or mutilation of the mare's suitor and the parallel death of the horses (stallions, one assumes) and the correlative theme of the mortal who avoids a hierogamy. The fear that the immortal will abandon rather than rejuvenate the aging mortal lover is evidence that this myth has already been well integrated into the Indo-European corpus, in which the proto-Indo-European Goddess no longer plays a positive role. That she does not do so is also indicated by the fact that the immortal is male, the mortal female.

2. Hippodameia ("horse-tamer") was the daughter of King Oenomaus, who made suitors for Hippodameia engage in chariot races against him, the loser to forfeit his life. Since the king's chariot was drawn by wind-begotten mares, he always won, and he occasionally murdered the challengers' mares as well. Pelops fell in love with Hippodameia and obtained from Poseidon a winged golden chariot drawn by winged, immortal horses; Pelops also promised Myrtilus, Oenomaus's charioteer, that, if he betrayed his master, he would be allowed to spend the bridal night with Hippodameia. Hippodameia, who had fallen in love with Pelops, bribed Myrtilus to remove the linchpins from the axles of Oenomaus's chariot and to replace them with others made of wax; she herself stood beside Pelops as his charioteer. In the race, Oenomaus's chariot was wrecked and he was dragged to his death; but when Myrtilus attempted to possess Hippodameia, in keeping with what had been promised to him, Pelops killed him (Pindar *Ol.* 1. 69; Apollodorus 2. 3; Hyg. *Fab.* 83).

This myth contains, in an expanded form, many of the themes of the myth of Marpessa and Idas. In both stories, as in the cycle of myths in which the mare is raped, Poseidon plays a part in the taking of the equine girl. In both, the father is killed (in the myth of Hippodameia this is the direct result of the daughter's collusion with her lover), and the first successful suitor is removed (killed, in the case of Myrtilus). But the myth of Hippodameia shifts the emphasis in several significant places: here the horses that are killed are the suitor's, not the father's, and they are female horses. The mare is far more dangerous in this second myth than in the tale of Marpessa; she is directly responsible for the deaths of Hippodameia's father and her suitors, in both their human and equine forms. Hippodameia also plays the part, familiar from the Irish myth, of the woman charioteer and the mare harnessed to the chariot; the killing of the mares takes on a new meaning when viewed in the context of the tragedy of Mácha. Another striking parallel to this episode appears in a Vedic hymn: the wife of Mudgala acted as charioteer and substituted a bull and a piece of wood for the usual chariot horses; she won both the race and the affection of her husband (*RV* 10. 102).

3. Hippomenes ("might of horses"), king of Athens, caught an adulterer with his daughter. He outraged (castrated?) the man and then killed him. He then shut his daughter in a building with a stallion. The horse, starving, devoured the wretched creature and later perished of hunger.[11] In this late variant, the theme of being eaten by a horse is added to that of starving or killing a horse or being killed by one. Again the Greek myth emphasizes the incestuous tie between father and daughter, a theme present in the Indian myth as well as the Irish (in the variant that regards Deichtíre as the daughter of Cónchobor).

A further episode in the saga of Hippodameia, recorded in a still later text, yields many motifs related not to the cycle we have just examined but to the more basic Indo-European corpus of myths about destructive mares who become birds:

4. Hippodameia married Autonous, the son of Melaneus, and had four sons and a beautiful daughter. They had many herds of horses. One day Anthus, one of the sons, drove the mares out of the meadow; they became enraged at this, attacked Anthus, and devoured him. The father, though out of his mind with grief, was afraid to drive off the mares; the mother kept struggling against the mares but was too weak to avert the calamity. As they were lamenting Anthus, they were pitied by Zeus and Apollo, who changed them all into birds: they made Autonous into a bittern (*oknos*) because he had shrunk back (*okneō*) from driving off the mares, and they made Hippodameia into a crested lark (*korudos*) because she had put on a helmet (*korus*) when fighting against the mares to defend her son.[12] Hippodameia is the good mother who defends her son; but the mare, the evil mother, devours him after he has mistreated her, and the father shrinks away in fear of the mare.

The myths of Hippodameia are linked, through Pelops (who wins her away from her father, Oenomaus), to another equine cycle, since Pelops is eaten (at least in part) by Demeter. Oenomaus is another such link, for he is the father of Leucippus, whose daughters are raped by the Dioscuri and who is himself the subject of another myth only loosely related to the cycle of Hippodameia but more closely related to the myth of Hippolytus:

5. Daphne, in devotion to Artemis, wanted no lovers, but Leucippus made love to her, disguising himself as a girl in order to be near her. Apollo, who was jealous, gave Daphne the idea of bathing with her companions; Leucippus was discovered and killed by Artemis. When Apollo pursued Daphne, she fled and was changed into a laurel (Ovid *Met.* 1. 452; Pausanias 8. 20). In this tale, Daphne is doubly assaulted, by a mortal and by an immortal; unlike Marpessa, however, she is not allowed to keep her mortal lover (who first unmans himself [becomes a transvestite] for her sake and is then killed by her goddess) but is pursued and destroyed by her immortal lover (a fate that Marpessa foresaw and was able to avoid but that Alope fell prey to, being transformed by Poseidon not into a tree but into a spring). That Daphne's lover is Apollo is highly significant for the contrast with the myths of Dionysus (himself a transvestite) and Hippolytus, as is the fact that her patroness (like Hippolytus's) is Artemis, in contrast with Aphrodite.

The Man Eating Mares of Glaucus and Diomedes

Yet another group of man-eating mares is associated with the suppression of women and with a chariot race imposed upon the mares against their will by male charioteers, a theme reminiscent of the Irish cycle.

1. Glaucus, who had been made immortal by a magic herb, scorned the power of Aphrodite and refused to let his mares breed, hoping in this way to build up their power to win chariot races. But Aphrodite became angry and complained to Zeus that Glaucus had even fed the mares on human flesh. With Zeus's permission, she secretly allowed the mares to graze on a herb called *hippomanes* ("maddening horse"); when Glaucus then yoked them to his chariot, they bolted, dragged him entangled in the reins, and ate him alive (Homer *Il.* 6. 154; Apollodorus 2. 3. 1; Pausanias 6. 20. 9; Aesch. *Glaucus Potnieus*, cited by Rose 1959, p. 227 n.).

2. Diomedes of Thrace had four savage mares, whom he kept tethered with iron chains to bronze mangers, and he fed them on the flesh of his guests. As one of his labors, Heracles captured the mares, stunned Diomedes, and allowed the mares to devour Diomedes alive. It is also said that Diomedes' minion, Abderus, was killed when the man-eating mares wrecked a chariot to which he had harnessed them (Apollodorus

2. 94–97; Diodorus Siculus 4. 15).

In both stories the mares are made savage by being denied sexual freedom or freedom to roam—by being pent-up. This is done by men who wish to harness the mares' powers for their own uses, either in mock war (the chariot race) or to destroy actual enemies. In both cases, the mares devour their tormentors and destroy the chariots that are the symbols of their oppression. A psychoanalytic view of the myths of Glaucus and Diomedes (and of Hippomenes) suggests that they may represent a small child's fantasy of being devoured by his mother, an expectation simultaneously terrifying and erotically exciting (Devereux 1975, p. 204). If one views the mares as goddesses, and therefore couples the psychological apprehension with the theological, one recognizes the *mysterium fascinans et tremendum*; the mare suppressed and transformed is both the woman whose powers are feared by very virtue of their suppression and the erotic goddess (explicitly thwarted, in the myth of Glaucus) who devours a mortal if he fails to pay heed to her claims upon him.

The Mare and Her Son—Hippolytus

A less straightforward but ultimately more powerful story of a mare goddess who destroys her son appears in the myth of Hippolytus and Phaedra, well known from Euripides' tragedy. Hippolytus ("torn apart by horses") worshiped Artemis and denied Aphrodite; his stepmother conceived an incestuous passion for him and, when repulsed, falsely accused him of raping her. Hippolytus's chariot horses were frightened by a monster (some say a white bull) sent from the sea by Poseidon; they dragged the boy to his death (Eur. *Hippolytus*; Ovid *Met.* 15. 492; Seneca *Phaedra*).

The theme of incest is veiled in this story by the statement that Hippolytus was merely Phaedra's stepson, not her son; but a parallel situation is instructive in this regard.[13] Phoenix's father, Amyntor, took a mistress and dishonored his wife, who continually entreated her son to lie with his father's mistress so that the latter would come to hate the old man. Phoenix was persuaded and did it, and his father called down the Furies upon him and cursed him to be childless (later sources say that he blinded him as well) (Homer *Il.* 9. 445–95; Apollodorus 3. 13. 8; Eur. *Phoinix*, cit. Rose, p. 241). The mother herself is implicated in the son's sexual transgression; Phoenix's own oedipal perception of his mother's dishonor is enhanced by her explicit exhortation. Moreover, the punishment (castration and blinding) and the instrument thereof (the Furies) are typical of the Greek reaction against true incest.

In the myth of Hippolytus, as in many mare myths, the accusation is false but the accused is punished by a horse. Hippolytus is punished ostensibly for his (falsely reported) sexual excess, but in the gods' view he is punished for his lack of sexuality, for his rejection of the erotic goddess. Frazer has speculated upon other possible implications of the myth:

> We shall probably be doing no injustice either to Hippolytos or to Artemis if we suppose that the relation between them was once of a tenderer nature than appears in classical literature. We may conjecture that if he spurned the love of women, it was because he enjoyed the love of a goddess. . . . We may discern an analogy with similar tales of other fair but mortal youths who paid with their lives for the brief rapture of the love of an immortal goddess (Frazer 1963, pt. 1, 1:38–39).

If Frazer is right, Hippolytus belongs in the company of Vivasvant and all the other hapless suitors of the Goddess; he is thus punished for two passions: his mother's for him, and his for Artemis. However, if we take the myth at its face value, Hippolytus belongs with a different group of mortals, which we are soon to encounter: men who are punished for denying rather than accepting the sexual Goddess, for denying their own sexual nature. In this setting, Hippolytus is cursed because he does *not* reciprocate his stepmother's passion and because his goddess, Artemis, is chaste. He is entangled with two goddesses, one positively and one negatively: he loves Artemis (and was killed for this, in Frazer's view) and spurns Aphrodite (and was killed for this, since our texts explicitly state that it is Aphrodite who makes Phaedra fall in love with him; Phaedra is the incestuous human counterpart of the erotic goddess and serves as her instrument of revenge). Hippolytus is thus trapped between two aspects of the Goddess, one chaste and the other erotic; he is in the familiar no-win situation. Both lines are developed in other important Greek myths and are worth examining one by one.

Mortal Man and Immortal Woman

Both Aphrodite and Eos (like Uṣas in India) "arise daily from the arms of a much older man about whose sexuality there is considerable ambiguity" (Friedrich 1979, p. 43); one of these men (Hephaestus) is, significantly, lame (his leg is mutilated, like Yama's and perhaps like Oedipus's, whose "swollen leg" may be interpreted as ithyphallic or wounded) and rejected by his mother (Hera) and wife (Aphrodite).

The aging of the mortal lover presents a problem for the goddess,

> not only the obvious one of the lascivious Eos, but also those revealed in the complaints of Thetis. In any case, these Dawn and Dawn-descended figures are themselves the cause of the passage of the days, and so of aging. . . . Greek and Indic, that is Indo-European, mortal lovers differ fundamentally from those of the Near Eastern Great Goddesses, for whose lovers three elements are predictable and critical: violent death, ritual mourning, and rebirth. . . . [The Greek triads contain:] (1) a beautiful mother/lover/wife, (2) an aging, mortal lover/husband, and (3) a beloved son (ibid., p. 44).

The central motif, the death of the aging mortal lover, is the cornerstone of much of the mare mythology. In the archaic myth he is revived by the dying mare; in later variants she kills him. The Greek myths represent a juxtaposition of these two patterns: the goddess first causes her lover to age and then rejects him because he is old, the usual no-win situation for the mortal lover of an Indo-European goddess.

The Denial of the Erotic Goddess: Pentheus and the Maenads

Whatever the role of Artemis in the death of Hippolytus, it is clear that Aphrodite is the direct cause of his demise, and for an obvious reason: Hippolytus denies her worship. Aphrodite therefore arranges to have him torn apart by horses—horses incited by a monster sent by none other than Poseidon, the raper of mares. Horses were not allowed into the sacred grove of Artemis and Hippolytus at Aricia, and Frazer's remarks on the reasons for this—explicit and implicit—are suggestive, though certainly purely speculative:

> If we knew the ritual of the Arician grove better, we might find that the rule of excluding horses from it . . . was subject to an annual exception, a horse being once a year taken into the grove and sacrificed as an embodiment of the god. . . . This conjecture . . . derives some support from the similar sacrifice of a horse which took place once a year in Rome [at the October festival]. . . . By the usual misunderstanding the horse thus killed would come in time to be regarded as an enemy offered up in sacrifice to the god whom he had injured (Frazer 1963, pt. 5, 2:41–42).

In this view, the horse was originally Hippolytus himself, sacrificed as a god (Virbius); the divine horse was killed to benefit mankind. Then a shift occurred: the horse became negative (and female: the horse sent by Aphrodite must be symbolically a mare), and Hippolytus was regarded as the mortal killed by a horse goddess. We will see a similar shift taking place in the Indian texts: first the mare is killed to benefit mankind; then the mythology shifts so that mortal men are killed by mares.

Another Greek development of this theme appears in Euripides' story of Dionysus and Pentheus. When Dionysus came to Thebes, Pentheus, king of Thebes, tried to arrest him and his wild maenads; but Pentheus went mad (capturing a bull whom he mistook for Dionysus), and the maenads escaped and tore him limb from limb. Pentheus' mother led the riot and herself tore off his head. (See Eur. *Bacchae*; cf. Dodds 1951 and 1960; Ovid *Met.* 4. 1).

The maenads are often likened to cows in the Greek texts, but there are also strong equine overtones to their behavior. They are likened to fillies (*Bacchae* 106, 1056) and are replaced by horses in other variants of the myth. In one of these Lycurgus opposes Dionysus, is driven mad, so that he kills and dismembers his son, and is eventually blinded or mutilated (Homer *Il.* 6. 130), but in another variant he is torn apart by wild horses (Apollodorus 3. 5. 1), just as Pentheus is torn apart by the maenads. In still another myth of Dionysus, Leucippe ("white mare") and her sisters kill and devour her son, Hippasus ("horseman"); they then roam the mountains until they are turned into bats or other nocturnal flying creatures (Hesiod frag. 27, cited by Rose 1959, p. 153; Apollodorus 2. 26–29; Ovid *Met.* 4. 1). The horror of the story derives precisely from the Kafkaesque reversal when the cows turn into mares; for there is a violent contrast between the chaste, maternal maenads in one scene and the ferocious madwomen in the next. Though they are said to nurse wolves and fawns (*Bacchae* 700) (the inverse of the Indo-European wolf-cow who nurses the human twins), they are also said to induce women to kill their children (Apollodorus 2. 2. 2). These cow-mare women in the myth of Leucippe and Hippasus are finally changed into winged creatures, flying night-mares—witches and vampires. So, too, the maenads are described as birds (*Bacchae* 748–50, 1090) and lustful birds (957).

The episode of Leucippe and Hippasus is strongly reminiscent of the tale of Rhiannon, as Graves notes, though he also sees in it (on very questionable grounds) an explicit historical transition that borders on euhemerism:

> The meaning of the myth is that the ancient rite in which mare-headed Maenads tore the annual boy victim . . . to pieces and ate him raw, was superseded by the more orderly Dionysian revels; the change being signalized by the killing of a foal instead of the usual boy (Graves 1955, 1:110).

There is indeed evidence that the maenads were originally more violent (mare-like) and later came to be more subdued—hence the two contrasting groups in Euripides' play; but the Indo-European context also encourages us to view the two groups synchronically as ambivalent, still-integrated figures who are simultaneously mares and cows. So too, the implication that the foal came to replace the human victim may have a parallel in India, where the king is replaced by a stallion. But neither of these transitions—from violent to subdued, from human to equine—has been established. Moreover, whatever the historical sequence may have been, in the extant myths (in Wales and India) both a foal and a son, both a king and a stallion, are endangered by the mare. To take this (as Graves does) as evidence that both sacrifices took place in actual ritual, let alone that one superseded the other, seems unjustified.

The ties between Dionysiac orgies and the myth of the mare who devours her son are compelling. Like Hippolytus, Pentheus is destroyed by his mother, who actually beheads him and (by implication) eats him—the most brutally bald statement of the nightmare of the castrating mother and devouring goddess. The relationship between the denial of sexuality (the sin of Hippolytus) and being devoured by the goddess is stated in the myth of Pentheus in two forms, straight and inverted. In the first, straightforward, form, the maenads accept the deity and their own passionate nature; they dismember and eat the deity and gain great powers. Dodds remarks on the logic of this eucharist:

> The practice seems to rest in fact on a very simple piece of savage logic. The homoeopathic effects of a flesh diet are known all over the world. . . . If you want to be like god you must eat god (or at any rate something which is θεῖον) (Dodds 1951, p. 277).

Therefore the maenads eat Dionysus. But when Pentheus refuses to do this, he is forced to experience the inverse of the eucharist: Dionysus (through the maenads and his mother) eats him. When Pentheus denies the orgiastic deity, he denies his own erotic nature; the deity dismembers and eats him, and he loses all powers; he loses life.

Before Pentheus is killed, he is emasculated: Dionysus forces him to wear women's clothing. This is in part a fitting revenge, for Pentheus had mocked Dionysus for being so woman-like. Dionysus is not only androgynous in appearance and function (as the deity presiding over the liquid element and the procreative powers of the earth and nature) but is himself the child of an androgyne, for he was born from the thigh of Zeus (*Bacchae* 94–99, 242–97, 523–28)—thigh-born like so many Vedic and Hindu gods. But by making Pentheus dress as a woman (against his will at first), Dionysus reduces him to a sexless child, groveling before his mother ("Will my mother carry me back from the mountains?" he asks Dionysus, who promises him that she will—knowing that she will carry back his severed head [*Bacchae* 966–69]). It is the female aspect of Dionysus that destroys Pentheus through his female instruments of vengeance: Agave and the maenads. Thus the male god (Dionysus) or his male worshiper (Pentheus) is eaten, but the eaters are female. The devoured male and devouring female form a significant pattern in mare mythology, as we have seen; and its inversions are equally significant, as we shall see when we examine later Indian parallels to the myth of Pentheus and Dionysus (see below, chap. 8, sec. N).

Miscellaneous Mare Myths

It is hardly necessary to delve further into Indo-European mythology to establish the range of the mare; but it is perhaps worth mentioning that, on the evidence of the Aarne-Thompson index of tale types (not exhaustive, but always highly suggestive), the pattern with which we are concerned is almost exclusively Indo-European.

The theme of the Banished Wife or Calumniated Wife (Aarne 1961, TT 706 c and 707) is particularly widespread: a queen's children are killed by her father, who wants to marry her; when she is falsely accused of the murder, her husband condemns her to death; the children are resuscitated, and her innocence is established. In one variant, her older sisters substitute a dog for the newborn children and accuse the wife of giving birth to the dog (Thompson 1955–58, motif K 2115). Examples of this myth, which closely resembles the story of Rhiannon, are known from Irish, Greek, Indian, and American Indian sources (the latter apparently brought from Europe [Thompson 1919, p. 387]). Several of these family dramas involve horses. The accused woman's brothers are transformed into ravens; she sets out with a mare, and the wicked fairy who calumniates her is torn to pieces by a horse (Aarne 1961, TT 451). The unfaithful wife transforms her husband into a dog; she is then transformed into a mare (like adulteresses in the *Arabian Nights*, as well as in Finnish, Russian, and Italian tales [ibid., TT 449; Penzer 1924, 6:8]). Witches are closely associated with mares: the witch may be accompanied by a horse (Thompson 1955, G 225.2); she may appear as a horse (G 211.1.1); she may transform a man into a horse and ride him (G 241.2.1); or she may become a man-eating mare (B 16.1.3.1; cf. Apollodorus 1. 200. n. 1). The mare appears consistently as the villain in Indo-European folklore, as the female fiend who eats children and rides her victims (an image with psychological overtones of fear and sexuality —the latter expressed through the element of rhythm), or the black maiden from hell, riding on her white horse (Reinach 1895, p. 329), or the leader of the wild chase of the witches on their phallic broomsticks—the horses of death (Le Roux 1963, pp. 134–35).

The "nightmare," though etymologically unrelated to the word for the female horse, comes to assume explicit equine overtones from an early period in European mythology, in part through the attraction of assonance and in part through the attraction of an already developed mythology (cf. Reinach 1895, p. 329). The true etymology is from OE *mare*, "hag," and a nightmare is a "female monster . . . supposed to settle upon people and animals in their sleep producing a feeling of suffocation" (*Shorter OED* 1964, p. 1328). The prototype of "the nightmare who presses down on the sleeper or has intercourse with him while lying on top of him" (*Concise OED* 1964, p. 814) is the mare who rides perversely astride her son/husband instead of being ridden. It is perhaps for this reason that the *Kāmasūtra* labels the position with the woman astride the "perverse" position; the designation of this technique as "riding St. George" is a further folk inversion of the myth in which the hero on the white horse pierces the dragon's maw (the devouring womb) with his sharp lance.[14] In modern reinterpretations of the image of the nightmare, in literature and art, the cluster of meanings related to the several homonyms often merge: mother (F. *mère*), female horse (E. *mare*), ocean (Lat. *mare*, F. *mer*), death (IE **mer*, **mor*), and the underlying OE etymological meaning, "hag."

These meanings are diffused throughout Indo-European culture and may be seen even in such ancient and classical episodes as the Norse myth in which the Trickster, Loki, turns into a mare in order to lead astray a giant's horse (J. Young 1954, p. 67).[15] Here, as usual, the mare is false (she is really a Trickster transformed into a mare), seductive, and destructive; she is also androgynous, for Loki undergoes a change of sex to take her form and even gives birth to an eight-legged horse by the giant's stallion. A vivid example of an adulterous mare is Tolstoy's portrait of Anna Karenina; though her lover, Vronsky, is never described making love to her, his mare is presented in highly sensual images; Vronsky caresses the mare, in a passage full of tactile detail, and then proceeds to ride her to death in a race which he loses, a foretaste of Anna's death because of him and of his own ruin because of her.

The theme of foster parents and the hero transferred at birth is not confined to the bounds of Indo-European civilization (Gricourt 1954, p. 167), but the emphasis on the horse distinguishes the Indo-European variants. This is also true of the closely related theme of twins: dual paternity of twins is a universal folk motif, and often one of the fathers is a god (ibid., p. 168); but the twins are associated with horses in most

Indo-European versions of the myth (Ward 1968, pp. 11–12). Baltic, Vedic, and Greek systems share the motif of twins who are brothers and lovers of a female solar figure (Friedrich 1979, p. 34).[16] In Iran, the myth of the incestuous twins, Yama and Yima, assumes greater importance than in India, perhaps because brother-sister marriage is canonically endorsed in Iran;[17] in the Iranian myth, the king's glory departs from him in the form of a bird, just as the swan-maiden goddess departs from her mortal royal consort.

We have seen birds in many of our variants, and we are all familiar with the ballet figures of the Firebird (the magic sun bird) and Odette-Odile. The swan-maiden myth may very well be more than Indo-European, for it appears in numerous forms among North American Indians and Eskimos, perhaps more than can be accounted for by cultural contact.[18] In the Indo-European corpus, however, the equine influence makes its mark here as usual, and the swan maiden often usurps the place of the (swan-necked) mare goddess.

To account for this, and for other variants in mare mythology as a whole, we must turn our attention first to the psychological implications of the myth, then to its possible historical development and to the thematic pattern of its many meanings.

D. Interpretations: From Mare to Stallion

We have seen at least three levels on which the myth and ritual function: the divine (the hierogamy of goddess or god with a mortal), the royal (the renewal of the powers of the king), and the domestic (a conflict between a father, a mother, and twin children). We have seen that these three levels correspond to Dumézil's three functions, and we have encountered the trifunctional goddess in various guises. The stallion and the mare also appear on all levels: as symbols of divinity, royalty, and parenthood (or twinhood). What is it that links all three levels, and how does the equine symbolism serve to color each level in a particularly Indo-European way?

The Freudian Myth

The Freudians, most notably Ernest Jones and Géza Róheim, have offered their own versions of the Indo-European myth of the mare, which, as Lévi-Strauss tells us (1958, p. 57), are every bit as valid as the versions of the ancient Greeks or medieval Celts; but whether they are telling the *same* myth as that told by their Indo-European ancestors is perhaps arguable.

Castrating the Sun/Father

The stallion rather than the mare is regarded as typical of the genus *Equus* in most Indo-European cultures. "Horses" serves as the generic term for both male horses and mares, while the feminine "cow" seems to serve the same function for cows and male cattle. Horses are by nature male animals:

> That the male horse is mythologically to be regarded as a phallic animal is . . . widely recognized. Our psychoanalyses fully explain this by disclosing how significant for the imagination of the child is this big aggressive animal, with his habit of biting and trampling; the earliest impression of sexual acts may date from witnessing the copulation of stallion and mare (E. Jones 1971, p. 260).

So much for horses in general; now for *sun* horses. We begin with the sun:

> The themes of impotence and castration . . . play a most important part in sun mythology, and indeed probably furnish the main reason for the role of the sun in early religions. The identification of the waxing and waning sun with the phallus, and particularly with the father's phallus, brought with it the projection of repressed wishes and fears relating to this organ. . . . The decrease of the sun's power after midsummer was felt as a symbolic or portending castration, and indeed still is so in the unconscious (ibid., p. 285).

Here then is our missing link: both the sun god (on the divine level) and the horse (on all levels, but particularly on the royal) are symbols of the father (on the domestic level). The phallic/seminal nature of the sun in ancient India is evident from a late Vedic text: "When the father emits him as seed into the womb, it is really the sun that emits him as seed into the womb" (*JUB* 3. 10. 4–5). The phallic nature of the sun may be extrapolated from the solar nature of seed, a double correspondence that occurs not only in Indian texts but in Avestan, Manichean, Egyptian, and South American texts as well; though the association of the seed with the moon is stronger in India, the identification of male with sun and female with moon is also well known (Eliade 1976, p. 95; cf. below, chap. 8, sec. G). The fact that the sun is often said to be "swallowed" (at the time of the eclipse) adds yet another layer of meaning to the sun god's encounter with the wife who eats his seed/phallus, for the sun is always reborn again after his ordeal.

Although Ernest Jones does not deal at all with the royal or political myth (as Frazer does, relating it to royal ritual), it needs no Procrustean analysis to suggest that the king is a "paternalistic" figure par excellence, and that God is our father. All levels of the myth, therefore, express fears of the loss of (sexual) powers by the male hero, the sun/king/father/stallion.

Frazer remarks on the idea of the sun's loss of power and relates it to the theme of the horse in the sea, which we have so often encountered and will meet again, in chapter 7, in the submarine mare.

> The ancient Greeks believed that the sun drove in a chariot across the sky; hence the Rhodians, who worshipped the sun as their chief deity, annually dedicated a chariot and four horses to him, and flung them into the sea for his use. Doubtless they thought that after a year's work his old horses and chariot would be worn out (Frazer 1963, pt. 1, 1:315).

The ritualist is optimistic, and speaks of the renewal of the sun (just as the Vedic *aśvamedha* speaks of the revival of the stallion and the rejuvenation of the king). The Freudians are more pessimistic, emphasizing the loss, and the fear of impending loss, of power.

How does this loss take place? By castration, the Freudians answer, of course. Explicit castration is rare in our myths, but the sharp-eyed analyst will quickly detect at least two classical distortions or euphemisms: change of sex and mutilation of a limb. Both are generally characteristic of Indo-European sun gods (E. Jones 1971, p. 285); the second looms large in the myths of the mare. The first distortion appears in the episode of *couvade* in the myth of Mácha and in the Indian myth of the birth of Purūravas: his father, King Īḷa, was transformed into a woman (and his stallion into a mare); the woman married a king and gave birth to Purūravas (see below, chap. 9, sec. C). The magic leg of the horse—seed-giving, wine-producing, winglike—is restored by the Aśvins, who grant immortality and virility to mortals on many occasions (O'Flaherty 1973, pp. 57–62). Ernest Jones suggests a bright, if predictable, explanation for this phenomenon: the horse's leg is a phallic symbol, and "we know ambrosia to be a symbol for semen; this again shows how the leg and foot must have a phallic meaning" (E. Jones 1971, pp. 297, 299; cf. Schröder 1926, p. 312).

If, then, the sun/king/father/stallion is indeed castrated, who wields the knife? The mare-mère, of course; "cherchez la femme," say the Indo-European myths. Here we begin to have an inkling of the reason why the myth denounces the mare, goddess though she may be:

> There is . . . no sharp difference of sex in these various associations [of the horse with demonic and divine powers], but a study of

> extensive material inclines me to the conclusion that the female connotations are more often associated with the terrifying and erotic, while the noble and divine connotations have more often male associations; it should be observed that these two statements are not counterparts (E. Jones 1971, p. 248).

In India, this distinction is sharply observed: stallions remain symbolic of life, royalty, and power, while the mare is the symbol of lechery, danger, and brute appetite (see below, chaps. 7 and 8).

The Phallic Mother

The mare in Indo-European mythology becomes symbolic of the evil mother, the dark mother, the erotic and devouring mother, the whore, in contrast with the good mother, the white mother, the milk-giving chaste cow (O'Flaherty 1976, pp. 346–53). Instead of feeding her child (as the cow does), the mare eats her child. Moreover, like the female praying mantis, she devours her husband as well; she eats his substance and power even as she drinks his seed. In extreme cases, the furious goddess actually devours the testicles of the god, as an alternative to devouring young children and pregnant women, her usual food (*PP* 5. 26. 91–125).

Rhiannon (accused of devouring her child), like her mare doublet, gives birth on Walpurgisnacht; like so many others, she is accused of witchcraft, of being a mare. This also accounts for a recurrent element of the castration syndrome: by taking away the male's powers, she becomes a male herself, the female of a male species; she becomes inappropriately equine. The erotic goddess is doomed to masculinity; she becomes "Aphrodite, or The Woman with a Phallus" (Róheim 1945b). Thus Devī, when beheading (castrating) Mahiṣa, insists that she is really a male deity merely pretending to be a woman (see above, chap. 4, sec. C).

The masculinity of the mare is also manifest in the motif of change of sex; Jones remarks on the "remarkable interchangeability of the sexes" in the nightmare myth:

> Female night-fiends ride on horses, become horses, acquire masculine attributes, and so on [the broomstick, the pointed hat, etc.]. The same is equally true of their descendants, the mediaeval witches. The explanation of this state of affairs is that the forbidden wishes that furnish the driving force behind all these beliefs and myths are the repressed sexual desires of incest, and one of the most characteristic defences against the becoming conscious of such desires is to repudiate them and conceal them through the

> mechanism of identification with the opposite sex (E. Jones 1971, p. 260).

The witch is male because her erotic nature has become unacceptable to the Indo-European image of woman. Jones, however, sees in her masculinity a means of expressing incestuous desires. A far more relevant disguise, in this context, may be seen not in the witch's gender but in her species. For the transformation into animals, particularly horses, in dreams and myths usually occurs because "the human being in question is in most cases specifically a parent; . . . the presence of an animal in such contexts always denotes the action of an incest complex" (ibid., p. 246). Either as a male or as a mare, the witch expresses incestuous desires; Freudians never lose.

The mare is a projection of the child's oral aggression onto the image of the devouring mother—a projection that is, as we have seen in the Freudian analysis of the myths of Glaucus and Diomedes, simultaneously erotically exciting and terrifying (*fascinans et tremendum*). The relative primacy of the oral, sexual, or theological levels of this process is a matter of some dispute; as Jung summarizes the Freudian view, "Fear of incest turns into fear of being devoured by the mother" (Jung 1967, p. 419). But clearly there is *some* symbiosis between these various powerful instincts, and the value of the Freudian insights is apparent when one notes the remarkable prominence of the theme of incest in the mythology of the mare.

However, the Freudian analysis totally ignores the social, political, and economic levels with which Indo-European analysts usually deal (conjuring them up by ingenious linguistic reconstructions). Of course, the myths and rituals in question are at least *in part* about kings; and this fact is also highly relevant to the theology of the myths, as we shall soon see. One of the main purposes of the ritual is to make the king a king: "The goddess selects the man most deserving of the office of king and 'marries' him, thereby insuring his success" (McKnight 1977, p. 686). But this aspect of the material has been more than amply analyzed by Dumézil and his tribe, and I am disinclined to beat a dead horse. Despite the wealth of analysis, however, it seems worth pointing out that the royal nature of the king is not utterly central to the myth. After all, Rex (Tyrannus) was Oedipus's second name; it is his first name that identifies a problem shared by prince and pauper alike. Indo-European myths tend to have kings as their protagonists; part of the reason for this is that the myths are usually composed or recorded by bards or scribes employed by kings; but they are not only about kings.

The Cretan Connection: The Queen and the Bull

The Freudian theory offers one explanation for the transition from mare to stallion that can be applied to the history of the culture rather than to the history of the individual: the change is the result of a gradually increasing emphasis upon a negative affect in the image of the female (mare) and a positive value for the male, the stallion. Another historical explanation, is, however, possible:

> The Indo-European pattern of the theriomorphic hierogamy was clearly King and Mare, the Near Eastern and Aegean one Queen and Bull (e.g., Europa, Pasiphaë in Cretan saga, wife of Archon Basileus in Greek religion, and so on). The Indic *aśvamedha* is thus a halfway house of transformation (Puhvel 1970b, pp. 168–69).

This ingenious suggestion is well supported by the sharp contrast between the Indo-European pattern of goddesses mating with mortals and the Near Eastern pattern of myths of the Great Goddess (Friedrich 1979, p. 44). Bloomfield, as we have seen, noted the parallel between Saraṇyū and Pasiphaë. However, Puhvel's hypothesis that the *aśvamedha* priests had to borrow some bright ideas from Crete in order to "synthesize" their new couple (queen and stallion) is undercut by three factors: the previous existence of bull-and-queen myths already on Indian soil; the internally consistent development of queen-and-stallion myths from king-and-mare myths in the context of Indo-European psychology; and the importance of the bull, as well as the stallion, in Indo-European myth and ritual. The third of these factors will be discussed at length below (chap. 8, secs. F and H); the second has been developed in the preceding section. Let us merely take a glance at the first.

An intriguing parallel to the Mácha myth may be seen in the myth of the bull and Mudgala's wife; the possibility that Mudgala is an old man, perhaps an impotent ascetic, whom the bull replaces would establish this myth within the cycle of rejuvenation and sexual restoration (*RV* 10. 102; see the commentary on this text in Geldner 1951, 3:316–19). In the Mudgala hymn, woman and bull pull together in the traces; both of them replace the horses that would normally do this work, and so it may be inferred that he becomes a stallion while she becomes a mare. Other implications of the Vedic conjunction of woman and bull emerge from a strangely garbled later version of this myth. According to this version, Manu (son of the sun) had a bull whose voice killed demons; the demons tricked him into sacrificing the bull, but its voice entered Manu's wife; he was about to sacrifice her, but Indra saved her (*ŚB* 1. 1. 4. 14–17;

MS 4. 8. 1; *KS* 2. 30. 1; *TS* 6. 6. 6. 1). Here the power of the bull enters not the man but his wife; when this power is needed by Manu, he is willing to sacrifice the woman who has the rejuvenating power—to sacrifice the mare, to whom the bull's power has been transferred, even as the *aśvamedha* stallion's power reaches the king through the intermediary of the queen. The Vedic god (and great bull-and-stallion figure) Indra prevents the sacrifice; euhemeristically, one might see an explicit refusal to indulge in the now archaic sacrifice of the mare.

Another series of parallels occurs, as we have seen, in the ancient Irish tradition that Queen Medb (whose name is linked with the *aśvamedha* as well as with the Indian queen Mādhavī [Dumézil 1973, pp. 85–107]) tried to steal a magic bull in order to prove her superiority over her husband. Here, as in the Mudgala hymn, the theme of competition between man and woman (as in the chariot race) is linked with the motif of the theft of the sacred and virile animal; for Mudgala's bull was harnessed to the chariot when thieves had stolen all the rest of his cattle (*RV* 10. 102, with Sāyaṇa's commentary).

This is by no means to say that the Near Eastern cult of the bull and the queen is irrelevant to the development of the myth of the mare; far from it. But the evidence suggests that the Indo-Europeans could look far closer to home for a model of theriomorphic-god-with-mortal-woman, using their own ancient myths of bull and queen or, indeed, stallion and queen to replace the ritual of mare and king. On Indian soil, too, the invading Aryans might have found raw materials from which to draw their contrasting mythology of bull and queen. For the bull is a powerful presence in the Indus Valley Civilization that flourished in India before the time of the composition of the Ṛg Veda, and it may very well be possible to account for a transformation in Indo-European materials by reference to the influence of contacts with the culture of the substratum with which it interacted. We have seen how Tamil concepts played an important role in the transformation of Indian ideas about the fate of the Goddess's consort and the value of the dance, and it is tempting to see a similar process at work here. Despite the enormous span of time between the Indus Valley Civilization and the first Tamil texts, let alone the problem raised by the unproved hypothesis that the undeciphered Indus Valley script is in fact a Dravidian language, it is quite possible that the pre-Indo-European cult of the bull in South Asia did in fact survive to influence the Indo-European myth and ritual. The great continuity of Indian culture, as well as the parallel phenomenon of linguistic petrefaction, inspires confidence in such survivals.

Simultaneous Models and Historical Development

There are two different patterns of flow in the myth of the mare, and one may conjecture that the positive pattern (good power flowing from above) is earlier than the negative pattern (evil power flowing from above, or power being drained from the mortal—flowing in the "perverse" direction). However, both models come to exist side by side at a very early period and produce a theology that must be confronted as an integrated problem: the Goddess who can destroy or bless, the ambivalent Goddess whose presence is always desired even when her essence may be disease and death (Brubaker 1978; Dimock 1978).

The simultaneous existence of two other paradigms (present in early layers of both the Indo-European and the substratum of non-Indo-European cultures) produces complex moral conflicts in the mare mythology. The myth of the mortal male and immortal female (the king and the mare, the swan maiden and the prince) confronts the myth of the immortal male and the mortal female (the stallion and the queen, Leda and the swan). As the patterns interact, the immortal female often mimics the behavior of the female in the other model—the mortal female; thus Pārvatī may be subservient to Śiva even when she is the more powerful Devī, and Śiva may be henpecked by Pārvatī even when he is God and she is a mere consort. Saraṇyū also vacillates, as we have seen, between mortality and immortality. As divinity shifts to and fro in equine-human couples, friendly gods may turn into demonic enemies. Frazer sees this process at work in the cult of Hippolytus, and it is the story of the demise of the mare in India (see below, chap. 7, sec. B).

In some myths (notably the Greek), the consort of the goddess ages; in others (notably the Indian), he is sexually mutilated. In both cases his loss of power is the result of her overpowering immortality: he ages either in contrast with or (as in the case of Eos/Uṣas) as a direct result of her agelessness, and he is emasculated by her insatiable because divine appetites. But the rituals, both Irish and Indian, restore what the myths threaten; he is renewed, restored, reinvigorated. And when we look back at the myths, we can see that this archaic, positive ritual function of the mare is reflected there too, in many places.

The distinct levels in the myth of the mare present a tantalizing appearance of a historical chronology. At first there is one mare goddess, an awesome and dangerous creature (sacred in Otto's sense of the word [R. Otto 1923, pp. 24, 36]) who was sought by the king, captured, and wooed. She is a source of power who invigorates the aging king by her annual ritual copulation with him; she dies in a sacrifice of her immortality to his mortality. At this period, the mare (and the image of woman) is still whole, integrated; the proto-Indo-European goddess of dawn is also simultaneously maternal, sororal, and erotic (Friedrich 1979, p. 46). In Semitic and Babylonian myths she is manifest in the figures of Inanna and Ishtar, both of whom were said to copulate with horses (ibid., p. 14). In Greece she survives in Leda, herself a bird goddess as well as the victim of a bird god, for the Dioscuri are said to have hatched from an egg laid by Leda after she was raped by Zeus (Rose 1959, p. 248). Aphrodite, too, is associated with the goose or swan or winged horse (Friedrich 1979, pp. 11, 33, 50) and is both a danger and a benefactress to her mortal lovers:

> [Usually] a mortal man who has sexual relations with a goddess is punished by death or castration. . . . Aphrodite, on the other hand, is the potential lover of any god or hero and, like her cognate, Dawn, is sometimes seized by a desperate longing. . . . By seducing mortals and providing a transcendent image of such seduction she mediates between the human and the divine in a way that gives man exceptional intimations of the immortality he can never attain (ibid., p. 136).

This is the integrated aspect of the dangerous mare.

But under the influence of a steadily increasing Indo-European androcentrism (or, to put it more bluntly, male chauvinism) the mare goddess was split into two parts, the good mother and the evil mother. Here we begin to have proliferations of women in the rituals and the myths; now it is feared that the mare will take away her lover's powers, and so the auspicious (albeit dangerous) white mare must be given a malevolent evil black alter ego who can be destroyed because she threatens to kill or mutilate the king. At this time, also, the image of the mare was overlaid by another already available Indo-European image of the goddess who mates with a mortal—the swan maiden. Finally, as the model of mortal woman and immortal man rose above the model of immortal woman and mortal man, the goddess was demoted to ignominous mortality and passivity. Now the helpless female was left hoping against hope that the great horse/swan god would deign to visit her (riding on *his* white horse). Now Leda awaits Zeus, awaits the moment when she may, in William Butler Yeats' words, "put on his knowledge with his power / Before the indifferent beak could let her drop."

7 The Mare beneath the Sea

"United with Pārvatī, Śiva passed the days and nights of a thousand years as if it were a single night. But the joys of lovemaking did not satisfy his thirst, just as all the floods of the ocean do not quench the fire blazing within" (*Kumārasambhava* 8. 91). With these words, Kālidāsa ends his poem about the marriage of Śiva and Pārvatī. The verse celebrates the endless passion of the ideal lovers, perfectly balanced so that the water does not quench the fire nor the fire scorch the water. But the particular image chosen to express this balance carries a heavy burden of less auspicious symbolism; overtones of danger resonate from the myth of the mare beneath the sea, even in the hierogamy in which the fire is attributed to him.

A. The Doomsday Mare

The fire of doomsday is said to have the form of a mare at the bottom of the ocean; inextinguishable flames issue from her mouth. The destructive fire that cannot be quenched can at least be made to wait for the moment appropriate for destruction; the fire that blazes from Śiva's eye to burn Kāma is the fire of untimely doomsday, which yawns wide to burn up the universe; Śiva cannot quench it, but he can place it beneath the sea—for the time being (*ŚP* 2. 3. 19. 15; *Matsya P* 154. 251–52). The fire of the mare's mouth drinks the waters of the ocean and lets them out again; eventually this fire of the underworld will destroy the universe, at the end of the Kali age (*MBh* 5. 97. 3). The fire is in her mouth because the mare is the great devourer.

The destructive nature of the mare-fire allows it to be associated with the demon powers lurking in the underworld that is its home. The sage Ūrva (eponymous author of the fire, called the Aurva fire) gave it to the demon Hiraṇyakaśipu, who used it to dispel Indra's magic darkness during a battle; Indra then sent Soma and Varuṇa (gods of water) to extinguish the demon magic of the fire (*H* 1. 45–46). The mare-fire is also associated with Death; in one myth it is said that the mare (*vaḍavā*) was a river named the Vaḍavā and that the river was given to Death as a wife; in gratitude to Śiva for this gift, Death established a great *liṅga* known as the Mahānala (the Great Fire) at the *mouth* of the Vaḍavā River (*BP* 116. 22–25).

The metaphorical value of the image was quickly noted by Indian poets and sages. In the *Bṛhadāraṇyaka Upaniṣad* the universal fire is said to be the open mouth of the sacrificial horse in the sea (*BAU* 1. 1. 2). A commentary on the lawbook of Manu says, "Fire is born of water, as is seen in the case of lightning and the mare-fire" (Rāghavan on Manu 9. 321). It is frequently used as a metaphor for a voracious or insatiable energy: "Not by anything can the fire of hatred be assuaged; it is inextinguishable, like the submarine fire" (*MBh* 12. 327. 41). Significantly, the mare is considered to be a particularly apt metaphor for the insatiable appetites of a flirtatious woman (*ŚP* 5. 24. 29; *MBh* 13. 38. 25–29), though it was also applied to male passion: a character in a play boasts that he has crossed the ocean of passion, escaped from the whirlpool of affection, and dispelled "the mare-fire of anger" (*Prabodhacandrodaya* 6. 8). The elements of the submarine mare (fire, water, and death) are piled one upon the other in a tirade against the danger inherent in a lustful, seductive women:[1]

> Fire is never satisfied by fuel, nor the ocean by rivers; death is never satisfied by living beings, nor attractive women by men. The minute she sees a man, a woman's vulva becomes wet immediately. . . . Death, hell, the mare-headed (fire), a razor's edge, poison, a serpent, and fire—women are all of these in one (*ŚP* 5. 24. 29–34).

In noting the popularity of this proverb, one psychiatrist remarked upon "a secret conviction among many Hindu men that the feminine principle is really the opposite [of the chaste ideal—the cow]—treacherous, lustful and rampant with an insatiable, contaminating sexuality" (Kakar 1978, p. 93).

In one version of the myth, in which Śiva cuts off the fifth head of Brahmā, it is said to be a horse's head (*Bhav P* 1. 22. 14–16; O'Flaherty 1973, pp. 111–40); in another, the Fury of Brahminicide, who pursues Śiva after the beheading, is likened to the fire of the mare (*Sk P* 3. 1. 24. 30–67); the Ocean fears that, if the terrible head is placed within him, he will be burnt dry (*BP* 113. 13). When the Goddess instructs her female servant to drink up the inexhaustible flood of the demon

Raktabīja's blood, she says, "Open your mouth and drink his blood as if your mouth were the fire of the mare" (*Vām P* 30. 27). Since the demon's blood is seed, the Goddess is behaving like the man-eating, castrating mare; since it is an unending flood, she is behaving like the insatiable fire in the ocean.

When the gods and demons churn the ocean to obtain the elixir of immortality, a terrible poison emerges and threatens the gods until Śiva swallows it (*Sk P* 1. 1. 9. 90); the poison is merely another aspect of the destructive fire waiting to come forth from the sea, a devouring poison that can be destroyed only by being devoured in its turn—by the great yogi and drinker of poison, Śiva, who holds in all his fluids. The Kālakūṭa poison from the ocean and the fire of the mare appear together in this verse (*SRK* 1045):

> The goddess Śrī is fickle, . . .
> and the Kālakūṭa is a deadly poison.
> It is pondering these vices of his family
> that burns the ocean's heart
> and not the underwater fire.

The promiscuity of the Goddess and the "family problems" implicit in the ocean's relationship with his daughter and consort, the mare, are themes familiar from the Indo-European corpus of mare myths. Here they are used to explain, or rather to replace, the underwater mare-fire.

The circle of the sun, surrounded by clouds in the rainy season, is likened to the mare's head in the ocean (*ŚP* 2. 2. 22. 10), a simile given greater depth by the Indian belief that the sun's horses place his chariot in the western ocean at night (*Kumārasambhava* 8. 42). The sun, which emerges from the clouds to destroy the universe at doomsday, is an obvious prototype for the mare-fire, particularly since, as we saw in chapter 6, he is himself entangled with a very destructive mare. The image of the mare is often used to emphasize the greatness of the ocean (*Pañcatantra* 5. 2. 32); the element of latent power is beautifully expressed in a verse that describes the ocean stirring the submarine fire as like a lion that roars and shakes his mane in rage when he is roused from deep sleep when pierced by an arrow (*Rāvaṇa Vaha* 5. 34). But most important for the symbolism of sexual conflict and matching of powers is the frequent emphasis on the perfect balance between fire and water, mare and ocean:

> How marvellous the underwater fire!
> How marvellous the blessed sea!
> The mind grows dizzy thinking of their greatness.

> The first keeps drinking greedily its dwelling
> and yet its thirst by water is not quenched;
> the other is so great it never suffers
> the slightest loss of water in extent.
> (*SRK* 1198; cf. 1210–12)

B. The Post-Vedic Symbolism of the Mare

The particular form that the fire assumes, the form of a mare, is of Indo-European significance. In post-Vedic Hinduism, the connotations of the mare as a dangerous seductress begin to pollute the reputation of the stallion. The ancient horse sacrifice, the *aśvamedha*, becomes the object of ridicule; Bṛhaspati, author of the Cārvāka heresy, is said to have mocked the Vedic ritual in which "the sacrificer's wife takes the phallus of the horse" (*Sarvadarśanasaṃgraha* 6–7). An element of satire is also present in the episode in which Indra, overcome by desire for the sacrificer's wife, enters into the stallion and unites with the queen during the ritual (*H* 3. 5. 11–17). Some aspects of the ritual may have survived in later Hinduism, for medieval friezes and paintings depict ritual orgies or scenes in which a woman is mounted by a stallion (see plate 4). The turnabout also occurs: a man couples with a mare (see plate 5). But the satirical attitude behind these depictions is clear from the gestures of the spectators (who cover their eyes or stare in disbelief).

The image of the lascivious, destructive mare appears even in the Ṛg Veda as the goddess of Dawn (see above, chap. 5, sec. B). Horse-headed celestial musicians named Aśvamukhas or Kiṃpuruṣas (Horseheads or Wrong Men) are depicted with human bodies and horse's heads and the reverse, respectively; their women are erotically described (*Kumārasambhava* 1. 11). Horse-headed women appear on an erotic frieze at Aihole, apropos of which Philip Rawson remarks, "The horse-headed female [Yakṣa] is a familiar Indian night-time bogey, who carries men off for sexual purposes" (Rawson 1968, p. 73 and pl. 42).[2] Buddhist sculptures depict lascivious horse-headed women carrying off terrified men to a fate worse than death (see plate 6), and Buddhist literature warns about them: A horse-faced Yakṣinī was in the habit of eating the men she captured until she fell in love with one, whom she then forced to marry her (*Padakūsalamāṇava Jātaka* 432). Another Buddhist Yakṣinī, a beautiful mare named Vaḷavāmukhī ("Mare-mouth," the same term used for the underwater doomsday fire), had a white body and red feet; pursued by a king, she plunged into a pond, but he grasped her mane, subdued her, and rode her into battle (*Mahāvaṃsa* 10. 53–62). Here the mare plays a more positive, controlled role (going back into the water instead of emerging from it like the mare at doomsday); she is pursued and captured, as Rhiannon is, and the king, instead of being overpowered by her, channels her aggression into martial power. In this usefulness she is more like the proto-Indo-European mare. Indeed, Buddhist sculptures from the second century B.C. and the fifth century A.D. depict men happily mounted on creatures with the heads of women and the bodies of mares, as well as women happily mounted on creatures with the heads of men and the bodies of stallions (see plate 7).

These Buddhist oppositions may be seen as survivals of the two different models of ancient mare myths, one positive and one negative (see above, chap. 6, sec. D). The changing distribution of head and body may also demonstrate a shift in attitudes resulting from emphasis or deemphasis of the mare component, for the head of the creature carried its primary symbolic meaning in the ancient sacrifice and in later myths of horse-headed gods (Heesterman 1967, pp. 22–43); thus a creature with the head of a mare and the body of a woman is more mare than woman, while one with the reverse pattern is more woman than mare. The mare-headed figure actively attacks and carries off men, while the mare-bodied figure is pursued (running swiftly with her equine body) and is passively ridden by men. The mare-headed creature overpowers; the mare-bodied one is conquered. Significantly, the latter usually has not only the head but the top torso and therefore the breasts of a woman—the element that makes her "safe," cow-like.

The negative connotations of the mare are tied to her Vedic origins. An explicit link between the ancient horse sacrifice and the mare-fire may be found in the belief that the submarine fire devours the offerings of the horse sacrifice (Hooykaas 1964, p. 109, citing *Kauravasrama* 78); in this one may see a transition from the ancient ceremony of eating the mare to the Vedic ceremony of feeding the stallion and finally to the concept of the devouring mare (see above, chap. 6, sec. D). Many elements of the myth of Saraṇyū contribute to the image of the submarine fire: the control of excess energy (Vivasvant's, in the old myth, but Saraṇyū's, by implication, in the still older myth) and the fiery seed in the mare's mouth. The myth of Saraṇyū is linked to Śiva by the belief that Śiva's own creative-destructive energy (*tejas*), released when he was castrated in the Pine Forest, was placed in the sun; in return, Śiva receives from the sun a portion of that same destructive energy for the making of his weapon, the trident (*ŚP Dharmasaṃhitā* 49. 78–81). We will see this pattern behind the myths of the origin of the mare-fire. Moreover, Śiva, like the sun, is said to have difficulty in finding a wife capable of bearing his extreme energy (*ŚP* 2. 2. 16. 38). And the Seven

Sisters, who play an important role in the birth of Śiva's son Skanda, are described in the Ṛg Veda as seven bay mares who pull the chariot of the sun (*RV* 1. 50. 8–9; 9. 86. 36).

Even Lakṣmī, usually depicted as the model of the submissive and subservient wife, follows in the footsteps of Saraṇyū:

> Lakṣmī, the daughter of the ocean, married Viṣṇu. One day she saw Revanta, the child of Saraṇyū and Vivasvant [born right after the Aśvins—*MP* 105], when he was mounted on the marvelous horse Uccaiḥśravas, and she lusted for him. Viṣṇu cursed Lakṣmī so that she became a mare, but then he promised that she would be released from the curse when she had a son. Lakṣmī went to the very place where Saraṇyū had wandered as a mare, at the confluence of the Kalindī and Tamasā rivers. She meditated upon Śiva and performed asceticism for a thousand years, in the form of a mare. Then Śiva came to her and promised that Viṣṇu would appear to her in the form of a stallion and beget a son upon her. Śiva then vanished and sent Viṣṇu to Lakṣmī; Viṣṇu begat a son upon her, stallion mounting mare; and when Lakṣmī gave birth to a handsome child, they resumed their normal forms and returned home, giving the child to a king who had performed asceticism in order to have a son (*DBP* 6. 17–19).

The parallels with the Saraṇyū story are explicit, and the psychological overtones are almost so: the heroine becomes a mare because she is lustful; for this quasi sin she is given a curse to be half theriomorphic—to become half mare, half woman—just as Reṇukā is made half Untouchable, half high-caste woman in punishment for a similar transgression (Brubaker, 1977). The horse that Revanta rides is Uccaiḥśravas, the horse of Indra, who appears when the ocean is churned—the occasion on which the poison bursts forth; he is thus the positive male counterpart of the negative mare-fire from the sea. Finally, the goddess is released from marehood when she has a son—when she is transformed from a lustful woman (a mare) into a fertile woman (a cow). The fact that the son is then given to a king may be a simple plot device (for Viṣṇu and Lakṣmī do not have a son) or a vestige of the elements of abandonment, kingship, and foster parenthood from the ancient myth.

C. The Myths of Search: Dadhyañc and Sagara

The horse's head is connected with the myths of the search for lost fire and stolen Soma, perhaps because of the natural image of swift flight that the horse suggests. Moreover, since the horse is an essential part of the Soma sacrifice, it is associated with the drinking of Soma in the Vedas; just so, in later Hinduism, the submarine mare is the great drinker of water (and of blood):

> Dadhyañc knew the secret of the mead and the secret of the sacrifice: how the head of the sacrifice is put on again and becomes complete. Indra threatened to cut Dadhyañc's head off if he told this secret to anyone. The Aśvins asked him to tell them the secret and made this provision: they first cut off his head and laid it aside, and then they placed the head of a horse on his neck; then he told them the secret through the horse's head. Indra cut off that head, the Aśvins brought back his own head and restored it, and all was well (*ŚB* 14. 1. 1. 18–25).

Dadhyañc is the sacrificial stallion who is beheaded and restored; his head is the source of the mead, the Soma, and the secret of resuscitation. The fiery stallion with elixir in his mouth is the inverse of the oceanic mare with fire in her mouth.

The later fate of Dadhyañc's head connects his myth more closely to the story of the origin of the mare. The Ṛg Veda is enigmatic about this:

> With the bones of Dadhyañc, Indra slew ninety-nine enemies; as he sought the head of the horse, which was hidden in the mountains, he found it in Śaryaṇāvat (*RV* 1. 116. 12; 1. 117. 22; 1. 84. 13–14).

Soma is hidden in the mountains and sought by the gods in many hymns of the Ṛg Veda. But later tradition, perhaps influenced by the submarine mare, shifts the hiding place of the horse's head to a lake:

> When Dadhyañc died, he left behind the horse's head. The gods sought it and found it in Lake Śaryaṇāvat, a lake in Kurukṣetra. With the bones of this head, Indra slew the demons (Sāyaṇa on *RV* 1. 84. 13–14).

The bones of Dadhyañc appear in Purāṇic mythology as the bones of Dadhīci, which are a direct cause of the birth of the submarine mare. The skull used as a weapon recurs in the mythology of Śiva beheading Brahmā and in the iconography of the Goddess holding a skull full of blood. Here Indra seeks the horse's head in a lake, where it will remain until the end of the Kali age, like the mare (*Bṛhaddevatā* 3. 24). In the earlier version, about the Aśvins, Dadhañc functioned as a combined image of fire (his body) and water (the "Soma" head). The later episode, about Lake Śaryaṇāvat, uses only the head of Dadhyañc, which is fiery (in contrast with the water in which it is placed) and destructive (it kills the demons, in contrast with the horse's head that gives life to the Aśvins). Thus, in response to a shift in context, the head changes from cool to hot.

We saw in chapter 2 that fire and water have a related ability to change not their qualities of cold or heat (for these remain constant) but their male or female natures; they function androgynously, in tandem, one changing in response to the other, adjusting in response to context in order to maintain an overall balance of qualities. Their interaction also plays a part in the variation of the Dadhyañc myths, for Soma, a property of the head of Dadhyañc, is both fire and water, and the search for Soma has a close parallel in the Ṛg Vedic myth of the search for Agni (O'Flaherty 1975, pp. 97–104). Agni changes himself into a horse on many occasions, sometimes in order to deceive demons who are searching for him (*RV* 1. 58. 2; 1. 149. 3; 1. 60. 5; 2. 4. 4; 2. 5. 1; 3. 2. 7; 3. 27. 3; etc. cf. *AB* 15. 5. 1–7), and Prajāpati takes the form of a white horse to seek Agni when he hides from the gods; when Prajāpati enters the water in this form, Agni burns the horse's mouth (*ŚB* 7. 3. 2. 14). Here again is a positive male counterpart to the negative submarine mare. The search for Soma, the search for fire, and the Sun's search for his wife—all are associated with the flight of the horse.

The search for the horse itself is the central theme of the myth of Sagara, of which there are several different versions:

> King Sagara had two wives. In order to obtain sons, he performed asceticism for a hundred years; then, by the favor of Śiva [or by propitiating Aurva, the creator of the submarine fire] he obtained sixty thousand sons from one wife and one son, named Aṃśuman, from the other. After some time, the king performed a horse sacrifice; as the horse wandered over the earth, protected by the king's sons, it reached the ocean, and there it disappeared [or: it was snatched away by a wave as it wandered by the ocean; or: Indra took the form of a demon and stole the horse, for Indra was jealous of his own reputation as the one who had performed the most horse sacrifices]. The king sent his sixty thousand sons to search for the horse; they dug with spades in the earth, destroying many living creatures, digging out the ocean that is the abode of sea demons. They reached down into Hell, and there they saw the horse wandering about, and they saw the sage Kapila haloed in flames, blazing with ascetic power. The sons were angry and behaved disrespectfully to Kapila; infuriated, he released a flame

> from his eye and burnt all the sons to ashes. Then Aṃśuman came and propitiated Kapila and obtained the horse, with which Sagara completed the sacrifice. Sagara made the ocean his son, and thenceforth it has been called Sāgara. The ocean took the horse and worshiped with it and thus became the ocean. Years later, after Sagara's death, Bhagīratha, the grandson of Aṃśuman, propitiated Śiva and the Ganges; the Ganges fell from heaven to earth, breaking her fall upon Śiva's head; and as she flowed over the ashes of the sixty thousand sons she revived them (*MBh* 3. 104–8; *R* 1. 38–44; *Vāyu P* 2. 26. 143–78; *Br P* 3. 46–53; *Viṣṇu P* 4. 4. 1–33; *Bh P* 9. 8–9; *ŚP* 5. 38. 48–57).

The myth begins with two mothers, one good (the mother of the virtuous Aṃśuman) and the other evil (the mother of the destructive sixty thousand). But Sagara himself has double mothers, who connect his story even more closely with the tale of the origin of the mare:

> King Bāhu had several wives. When one was pregnant, her jealous rival queen gave her poison to prevent her delivery; the poison prevented the child from being born but did not kill him. When Bāhu grew old and died, the pregnant queen prepared to mount his funeral pyre, but the sage Aurva forbade her, saying that she would give birth to a great king. The child was born in Aurva's home, and along with him came the poison; therefore Aurva named him Sagara [from *sa* ("with") *gara* ("poison")] and gave him the magic fire weapon with which he later conquered the barbarians (*Viṣṇu P* 4. 3).

The poisonous mother, like Pūtanā with her poisonous breasts, is contrasted with the good mother, who is totally subservient to her husband. The child is born "along with poison," just as the Soma comes forth from the ocean along with the Kālakūṭa poison. More specifically, the fire weapon that Aurva gives to Sagara is the same mare-fire that he gives to the demons in the myth of the mare's birth. The submarine mare appears in other, less explicit forms in the Sagara myth, too: first, as the horse that vanishes into the ocean, to be churned out of it again, like Uccaiḥśravas; then as the submarine fire of Hell, blazing from the eye of Kapila, just as the doomsday fire blazes from Śiva's eye; and finally as the ashes of the sons, revived by the floods of the Ganges, just as the doomsday fire in the doomsday flood is ultimately transformed into the seed of life in the cosmic waters of the womb.

Many of the elements of the myth of Sagara appear more briefly and simply in the story of the demon Dhundhu:

> King Bṛhadaśva had a thousand sons, of whom Kubalāśva was the eldest. When the old king handed over his throne to Kubalāśva and entered the forest, he met the sage Uttaṅka, who told him that a demon named Dhundhu was performing asceticism there by his hermitage, in the sands of the ocean, burning like the doomsday fire, with flames issuing from his mouth, causing the waters to flow about him in a whirlpool. Bṛhadaśva asked Kubalāśva to subdue the demon; he and the other sons dug down into the sand, but Dhundhu appeared from the ocean, breathing fire, and he burnt all but three of the sons with his power of asceticism. Then Kubalāśva drank up the watery flood with a fiery arrow, quenched the fire with water, and killed the demon Dhundhu, burning him up (*MBh* 3. 192–95; *Vāyu P* 2. 26. 30–60; *ŚP* 5. 37. 1–36).

The end of the myth expresses the final destructive balance of the powers: the fire is quenched by water, but the water is "drunk" by fire. The submarine mare is explicitly likened to the demon Dhundhu and is also present in the names of the kings: Bṛhadaśva ("possessing great horses") and Kubalāśva ("possessing fodder horses"). The story of the burning of the king's sons by a fire in the ocean ties the stories of Sagara and Bṛhadaśva together; this tie is further strengthened by the *Mahābhārata*'s remark upon their similarity: "Dhundhu burnt the sons of Bṛhadaśva with the fire from his mouth, just as Kapila had burnt the sons of Sagara" (*MBh* 3. 195. 25).

D. Viṣṇu as the Horse's Head—Hayagrīva

Dhundhu is yet further related to the mare cycle by the cycle of myths revolving around Viṣṇu as the horse-headed god Hayagrīva, for Dhundhu is said to be the son of Madhu and Kaiṭabha (*MBh* 3. 193. 16), two demons who were killed by Hayagrīva. This myth undergoes several significant reversals; it begins with the story of Madhu and Kaiṭabha in the *Mahābhārata*:

> Two demons, Madhu and Kaiṭabha, stole the Vedas and took them to the Hell beneath the great ocean. Brahmā told Viṣṇu what had happened, and Viṣṇu took a horse-headed form and entered Hell. He took the Vedas back to Brahmā, and then he resumed his own form, leaving the horse's head in the ocean; then he killed Madhu and Kaiṭabha. Viṣṇu is the horse's head that lives in the ocean, devouring oblations (*MBh* 12. 335. 1–64; 3. 193. 16; *Viṣṇu P* 5. 17. 11; *Bh P* 5. 18. 1–6).

Viṣṇu assumes the form of a horse's head in order to save the Vedas; this makes good sense, since the Vedas are "contained" in the head of the sacrificial stallion Dadhyañc. The demons themselves, however, have Vedic overtones, for the first one is named "mead," the Vedic secret that Dadhyañc told to the Aśvins. This, plus the growing importance of the myth of the *demonic* horse's head (mare's head, to be precise), caused an interesting turnabout in the myth: A horse-headed demon stole the Vedas, and Viṣṇu took the form of a fish to steal them back again. The name of this demon, Hayagrīva, is the epithet taken by Viṣṇu in his horse-headed form (*Bh P* 8. 24. 7–57; *AP* 2. 1–17; van Gulik, 1935). In order to rescue Viṣṇu from his equine role when it becomes a negative one, the Paurāṇika draws upon an already available avatar: the fish who rescues the Vedas from the doomsday flood (*ŚB* 1. 8. 1. 1–6; *MBh* 3. 185, 12. 300; *Matsya P* 1–2, 164–65; O'Flaherty 1975, pp. 179–84). So the fish who was the enemy of the doomsday mare now becomes the fish who is the enemy of the demonic underwater horse.

No female appears in any of these variants, but two (one good, one evil) are introduced into a late variant of the first pattern (divine horse, demonic Veda-stealers):

> Madhu and Kaiṭabha, aided by Māyā, cast a spell on the gods, took the Vedas, chopped them into pieces, and hid them at the bottom of the ocean. Without the Vedas, the gods were unable to perform rituals, and Brahmā was incapable of creation. Śiva's female power, Śakti, helped Viṣṇu recover the Vedas (O'Flaherty 1976, pp. 100–101).[3]

The demons, aided by the Goddess of Illusion (Māyā), steal the Vedas; the gods, aided by Śiva's Śakti, get them back. In this way the tale of Viṣṇu and the Vedas is attracted to both of the ancient equine models: the good stallion and the demonic mare. The demonic Goddess steals; the divine Goddess restores.

Yet another late variant of the Hayagrīva myth elaborates on the theme by incorporating material from the Brāhmaṇas, where it is said that Viṣṇu's head was cut off by a bowstring and became the sun; the vital sap [*vīrya*] flowed from him. Since Viṣṇu is the sacrifice, the gods went on sacrificing with the headless sacrifice and so did not obtain heaven until the Aśvins replaced the head of the sacrifice (*ŚB* 14. 1. 1–17; *TB* 7. 5. 6; *TA* 5. 1. 1–7). Although this text does not say what sort of head the Aśvins gave Viṣṇu, it is followed *immediately* by the story of Dadhyañc, whose head the Aśvins replace with that of a horse. Thus Viṣṇu is cast here in the role of the solar stallion who is mutilated, loses his vital sap (or seed), and finally is restored—just like Vivasvant. These elements are made into a complex Purāṇic myth:

> Once, when Viṣṇu was in a deep sleep, the gods began a sacrifice. But although Viṣṇu is the lord of sacrifices, they hesitated to wake him; for, as Brahmā said, it is a great sin to rouse one from deep sleep or to interrupt a married couple in their pleasure. Nevertheless, they snapped his bowstring to wake him, and it cut off Viṣṇu's head, which fell they knew not where. At this the world was plunged into darkness; Brahmā reminded the gods that this must have been fated to happen, just as it was fated for Śiva to cut off Brahmā's head, and for Śiva's *liṅga* to be cut off by a curse, and for Indra to be marked with a thousand *yonis*. He suggested that they ask the Devī to help them.
>
> The gods propitiated the Goddess, who told them why Viṣṇu had been beheaded: "Once upon a time, Viṣṇu laughed while looking at Lakṣmī's lovely face, and she feared that he thought her face ugly or that he had taken another beautiful woman as her co-wife. Then Lakṣmī became angry, and a ferocious Power of Darkness (*tāmasī śakti*) possessed her, and she said slowly, 'May your head fall off.' Thus because of the nature of women, and because of fate, Lakṣmī thought that having a co-wife would be more painful than being a widow. For falsehood, trickery, stupidity, rashness, excessive greediness, impurity, and cruelty are the faults that every woman is born with by her nature. Because of that curse, Viṣṇu's head has fallen into the ocean of salt.
>
> "I will put it back on—and for another reason, too. For the demon Hayagrīva performed great asceticism and won from me the boon that he could be killed only by someone horse-headed. Therefore, have Viśvakarman take a horse's head and place it on Viṣṇu's headless body, and Viṣṇu as Hayagrīva will slay the wicked demon."
>
> The gods did as she commanded. Viśvakarman took an axe and cut off the head of a horse; Viṣṇu became horse-headed and killed the horse-headed demon (*DBP* 1. 5. 1–112; cf. Shulman 1978, pp. 109–12).

The sexual nature of Viṣṇu's mutilation is indicated here by a number of factors: the gods regard their act (which culminates in his beheading) as a sin tantamount to interrupting a couple in intercourse; when his head falls, they are plunged into universal darkness, as they are when Śiva is castrated—a parallel that Brahmā immediately makes explicit by linking Viṣṇu's mutilation with the sexual mutilations of Śiva, Indra (who is castrated in other variants of the myth of the thousand *yonis*), and himself (the victim of Śiva's oedipal attack). Finally, the horse's head is chopped off by Viśvakarman, the Purāṇic form of Tvaṣṭṛ, the artisan of the gods, who "trims" Vivasvant.

It would appear that it is the gods who cause Viṣṇu's mutilation. Not so, says the Devī; it is really all the fault of a woman. And she proceeds to narrate a tale of female vanity and jealousy in which a woman would rather destroy her husband than share him; just as Gaurī becomes the black Kālī when Śiva teases her about her dark skin, so Lakṣmī becomes possessed by a Black Fury when Viṣṇu laughs at her beauty. This fierce female curses her husband to be beheaded. The head falls into the ocean, of course, and the demon Hayagrīva performs his asceticism on the banks of the river Sarasvatī: these are the loci of the birth of the mare beneath the sea. Thus the myth of the horse-headed sun stallion and the myth of the horse-headed demon combine. Although there is no female equine, Lakṣmī, overcome by the female fury of sexual jealousy, mutilates her husband; and Lakṣmī has been previously prone to unseemly lust—which turned her into a mare. In this late Śākta text, however, another, positive, Goddess intervenes to undo the damage done by the shadow of Lakṣmī; this ritual restoration is of great significance in the history of the dangerous Goddess.

Viṣṇu's negative equine associations do not stop here. In Mahāyāna Buddhism, Hayagrīva, previously associated only with the positive Hindu concept of saving the Vedas, is made into a fierce god with terrific features, a possible resurgence of his demonic character; in China and Japan he is a horrific Tantric deity (Mahalinga 1965, p. 193). Within the realms of Hinduism itself, during a later period, when the image of the demonic mare had been more fully developed, it was reapplied to the earlier image of Viṣṇu as Hayagrīva to become the most destructive of Viṣṇu's avatars: Viṣṇu comes, mounted on a white horse (sometimes even depicted as a white horse himself, or as a centaur [*MBh* 3. 188–89; *Viṣṇu P* 4. 24. 25–29; *Bh P* 12. 2. 16–63]) in the form of Kalki. Kalki's mission is to exterminate barbarians, an act initiating the destruction of the universe at the end of the Kali age, which is also accomplished (on another level, or immediately afterward) by the mare-headed fire. In other Purāṇic texts, another form of Viṣṇu—Kṛṣṇa—fights with a horse demon named Keśin; significantly, Kṛṣṇa kills this demon by injuring him in the mouth and splitting him in half right down the middle (one eye, one ear, two legs, and half a tail on each side) (*Viṣṇu P* 5. 16). The mouth is the focus of the destructive powers of the horse or mare, and the vertical split is characteristic of the demonic androgyne.

E. The Origin of the Submarine Mare-fire – Aurva

The submarine fire is often called the fire of Aurva or Ūrva, from the name of the sage whose anger was its source. The Vedic term *ūrva* can denote the ocean (*RV* 2. 13. 7; 2. 35. 3; 3. 30. 19), particularly the part of the ocean into which many rivers flow (Grassmann 1955, p. 277), for the mare-fire arises at the confluence of a river and the ocean. Sāyaṇa glosses *ūrva* as the mare-fire in the ocean, a metaphor for the fire of lightning in a cloud (*RV* 3. 1. 16; 4. 50. 2; cf. Sāyaṇa on *RV* 2. 35. 3) or for unsated desire (Sāyaṇa on *RV* 3. 30. 19). It has also been interpreted as a wide, empty space (Grassmann 1955, p. 277), a *yoni* (source) of water or of cattle (Oldenberg 1901, pp. 361–21), and a name of the divine life-source in which the sun and the dawn remain during the night (Lüders 1951, 2:238, on *RV* 5. 45. 2). All of these concepts are motifs in the cycle of mare myths.

The myth of Aurva is in many ways an inversion of the myth of Dadhyañc (Bosch 1961, pp. 144–45). A brief prediction of Aurva's birth appears in the *Mahābhārata*:

> A sage named Aurva will be born, blazing like a fire, and he will create a fire of anger to destroy the three worlds and reduce the earth to ashes. After some time he will extinguish the fire, throwing it into the mouth of the mare in the ocean (*MBh* 13. 56. 4–6).

The myth is expanded and rationalized elsewhere in the epic:

> The sage Aurva was born from his mother's left thigh, blazing with anger toward the warrior class because they had killed his father. He performed asceticism in order to destroy the worlds and the people, and the heat of his asceticism heated all the gods until they begged him to be merciful and restrain his anger. Aurva said, "My vow of anger cannot come to naught, or I could no longer live. For my undispersed anger would burn me, as fire burns a forest, if I were to restrain it with my own energy." The Fathers said, "Release it into the waters if you like; and since the waters are the people, this will fulfill your vow to burn the people." So Aurva placed the fire in the ocean, and it became the horse-headed fire, which vomits fire from its mouth and drinks the waters of the ocean (*MBh* 1. 169. 16–26; 1. 170. 1–21; 1. 171. 1–23).

Aurva states well the problem of controlling emotional forces: they cannot be obstructed, for the fluid must flow; they cannot be taken back (except in later, Tantric mythology, and in the yogic process of seed retention) or they will destroy the body that contains them; they must be placed *somewhere safe*—in the body of the waters, which receive fire as the woman receives the seed.

The importance of chastity in this context is indicated by a more explicit description of the asceticism involved in the birth of Aurva:

> The sage Ūrva was performing asceticism; the gods asked him to stop and begin family life. He replied, "I will not take a wife, but I will create a son nevertheless." Then, by his ascetic power, Ūrva placed his thigh in the fire and churned it; a halo of flames broke out of his thigh and became a son, named Aurva.
>
> Aurva blazed so fiercely that he terrified the universe. He said, "Hunger binds me. I will eat the universe." He grew great, burning all creatures, until Brahmā said to Ūrva, "Restrain your son's fiery energy for the good of all people. I will give him a dwelling place and a food like Soma: he will dwell in the mouth of the mare in the ocean, and he will live upon an oblation of water. This water-eating fire will burn all creatures at the end of the Kali age." "So be it," said Ūrva, and he threw the fire into the ocean (*Matsya P* 175. 23–63; *H* 1. 45. 20–64).

The force of chastity here becomes dangerous when it is released to become productive; the sexual power that refused to associate with a woman (i.e., to place a seed in her, to allow her to devour it) produces a child who threatens to devour everything; this is an inversion with which we are familiar from myths of the mare. Moreover, Ūrva produces a child by "churning his thigh" in the manner typical of unilateral male creation or male androgyny (see above, chap. 2, sec. A, and below, chap 9, sec. B); similarly, Dhundhu is mysteriously born of two male demons, a process never fully explained. But Ūrva's thigh-churning is taken from the *Mahābhārata* text in which Aurva's *mother* churns *her* left thigh; in this, she behaves like a male androgyne and hence assumes a masculine role in keeping with her association with mares. Another, and more basic, sex reversal is never openly discussed in the myth: though the fire beneath the ocean is a mare, the story of its origin tells of the birth of a male child. Indeed, the control of this child by his father, Ūrva, amounts to a reversed oedipal conflict (what Devereux calls a Laius complex): the father destroys the son.

This is an inversion of the earlier variant, where the fiery child, born from a woman alone, destroys the killers of his father. This first pattern persists in some later versions of the myth that return to an emphasis on female chastity rather than male but at the same time reintroduce the Vedic model of *male* equinity, Dadhyañc (here called Dadhīci);

> The gods placed their weapons in the hermitage of Dadhīci for safekeeping, and Dadhīci made them into liquid and drank their essence. One day Subhadrā, his wife, put on his loincloth for a menstrual cloth, and she became pregnant by the seed that was on the cloth. When she brought forth a child, she cursed the father, not knowing who he was, saying, "I swear by my chastity: let the man who engendered this child die." At this time, the gods returned to take back their weapons, and Dadhīci abandoned his body so that the gods could make their weapons of his bones (*Sk P* 7. 1. 32. 1–128).

This is a brief summary of a rather long myth in the *Skanda Purāṇa* (over two hundred verses), consisting of three closely juxtaposed episodes, of which the first is the text just cited and the others will be discussed subsequently. This text changes the abnormal birth from thigh-churning, typical of male androgyny, to seed-swallowing, typical of the mare. Dadhīci swallows the essence of the gods' weapons; the male pregnancy that he undergoes as a result of this eventually causes his death, since the weapons he must give back to the gods are contained in his bones (the element of the fetus contributed by the father). Then Subhadrā, when menstruous, becomes pregnant without having direct sexual contact with her husband. She is ignorant of the actual paternity of her child, as Tārāvatī is; and Saraṇyū, also, is said not to recognize her own husband, Vivasvant, when he covers her and she takes in his seed abnormally—again like Subhadrā.

The motif of the woman's remorse for an abnormal impregnation appears, moreover, in another, very similar, version of the myth of the birth of Pippalāda; here, the mother conceives by bathing in a garment on which there is semen. She, however, knows whose semen it is: it belongs to her brother; for this reason she is overcome with shame, and he, too, is ashamed, for the seed was spilt on the garment when he dreamed of a beautiful woman. Her shame is too much for her, and she dies. The child, Pippalāda, wishes to kill himself when he learns the circumstances of his birth, but his shame and anger (against the planet Śani, whom he blames) are turned aside by the sage Nārada, and so there is no mare in this story (*Sk P* 6. 174–75; cf. Shulman 1978, pp. 121–22).

In the tale of Dadhīci and Subhadrā, however, Dadhīci plays the role not only of the father of the angry child but of the sacrificial stallion, willingly giving up his limbs to be dismembered, just as the mare does in her sacrifice. This generosity contrasts with the self-protective care taken by Dadhyañc when dealing with the Aśvins, where he makes sure that he will *not* be killed. But Dadhīci's sacrifice functions in this text as a replacement for the unavenged death of Aurva's father in the *Mahābhārata*; for Dadhīci is the great-grandfather of the mare-fire, which is called the Aurva even when it is no longer related to Aurva. Dadhīci himself does not appear in the second episode of this myth (for the first ended with his death), but many aspects of his role are transferred to his son, who is called Pippalāda:

> When Subhadrā learned that Dadhīci was the father of her child, she rejoiced. But the child, named Pippalāda ["eater of the fruit of the fig tree" or "enjoyer of sensual pleasures"], wished to kill the gods who had killed his father. He performed asceticism to propitiate Śiva; then he churned his left thigh with his left hand, and from it a mare appeared, followed by a stallion. The mare was covered by a stallion, brought forth a child, and disappeared. Pippalāda then told the child to devour the gods. The gods sought help from Viṣṇu, who tricked the fire-child into eating the gods one by one, beginning with the waters. The mare-fire, haloed in flames, asked to be brought to the waters, and no one but Sarasvatī could bear to do this (*Sk P* 7. 1. 33. 1–50).

The vacillating gender of the equine element of the fire is ingeniously solved in this text by making it androgynous: it is a mare *and* a stallion, though it continues to be called a mare-fire (the first half of the compound being feminine, the second masculine). The parentage is greatly complicated here, for the dangerous fire that was directly sired by the murdered sage in the *Mahābhārata* is here sired in a mare by a stallion sired (through unilateral male androgyny) by the child sired (through apparent female unilateral androgyny) by the wife of the murdered sage. The child's name is significant: he is an eater (and he tells his offspring to devour the gods); more precisely, he is an eater of the fig tree, a tree associated with horses (another name for it being *aśvattha*, "under which horses stand"). The term *pippala* also denotes sensual pleasure, and the eater of sensual pleasure is likely to be associated with mares, who symbolize the sullied chastity of his mother. The theme of chastity is brought out in the continuing story of Sarasvatī and the fire:

> As Sarasvatī carried the fire to the waters, a mountain saw her and asked her to marry him. She refused, and he threatened to abduct her by force. She then agreed to marry him if he would hold the mare-fire while she bathed; he did so and was burnt to ashes. She took up the fire and set out again for the ocean. When they

> reached the ocean, the mare-fire was full of joy and offered Sarasvatī a boon. Sarasvatī said, "Promise that you will drink the waters through a mouth no larger than a needle." Then she threw the fire into the ocean, and that was the birth of the Aurva fire (*Sk P* 7. 1. 33. 50–103).

Sarasvatī's steadfast chastity enables her to control the fire. Subhadrā's chastity was inadequate; this is implicit in her wearing her husband's loincloth while menstruous. In short, she behaved like a mare, erotic and masculine, and this was the beginning of all the trouble. In contrast, when Sarasvatī is threatened, as the mare Goddess is so often threatened, with rape, she escapes by a trick, by playing on her attacker's lust (the same trick that is used on the lustful demon Bhasmāsura).

Thus Dadhīci and Sarasvatī epitomize successful chastity, while Subhadrā epitomizes dangerous lust. In one early variant of the myth, however, Dadhīca (*sic*) and Sarasvatī are both implicated in the lustful creation of a child:

> The sage Dadhīca performed excessive asceticism until Indra became worried and sent an Apsaras to tempt him. Dadhīca succumbed to her charms and shed his seed, which fell into the Sarasvatī River. She held the seed in her womb and gave birth to a son, whom she presented to Dadhīca. Dadhīca rejoiced and accepted the child. Years later, during the battle between gods and demons, Dadhīca gave up his life so that Indra could use his bones for weapons; and when, after the battle, there was a great drought, the river Sarasvatī nourished her son, who was a great sage and preserved the Vedas when all the Brahmins had forgotten them (*MBh* 9. 50. 5–50).

Dadhīca appears here as an enemy of the gods (as his son does in other variants), but his son is virtuous: not only does he not have the destructive power of fire, but he alone saves the Vedas during a great drought. Sarasvatī conceives and bears a child to the sage just as the Ganges conceives and bears Skanda to Śiva or Agni; Skanda is clearly a child born of fire in water, as Dadhīca's child is, by analogy. It is surely significant that these two sons, born of seed shed, because of male lust, in a nonlustful female, are virtuous, productive, calm, and useful to the gods, whereas the children conceived because of a *woman's* lust, and despite a man's chastity, play the role of the destructive mare-fire, suppressed and insatiable.

In addition to the trick played on the lustful demon, two tricks are played on the lustful mare-fire: first she is tricked by Viṣṇu into devouring only waters, and then she is tricked by Sarasvatī into devouring them very slowly. This double bridle, limiting her scope, supplies an explicit rationalization of the eternal balance of food (water) and eater (fire)—an essential balance, for the ancient ritual concept of water as food for fire is central to this myth.

Sarasvatī provides a multiform of the ocean: she is a watery receptacle for the fire. But she cannot be its final resting place, for she is the wrong gender. We have seen how fire and water are given varying assignments of gender; but the Vedāntic concept of (male) water as food for (female) fire causes the scales to tip in favor of the distribution in which woman is the devourer, man the devoured: the fire is a mare. Since rivers are feminine and the ocean masculine, the mare remains a mare when "married" to the ocean but becomes a stallion (or is at least half stallion) when "married" to Sarasvatī.

The plight of Sarasvatī is explained in another text, which omits the whole story of the origin of the mare-fire:

> Once in the past the gods said to Sarasvatī, "You must take this mare-fire and throw it into the ocean of salt so that the gods will be relieved of their fear; otherwise the mare-fire will burn everything with its fiery energy." Sarasvatī asked Brahmā what she should do, and Brahmā told her to protect the gods. She wept bitterly, but she set out, accompanied by Yamunā and Gāyatrī, and went to Uttaṅka's hermitage. There she received the fire in a golden pot and took it to the ocean (*PP* 5. 18. 159·98).

Nothing is said here about the origin of the fire, but it comes from the hermitage of Uttaṅka, the place from which the submarine fire of Dhundhu originates; there may be a confusion between the two myths here.

This same episode is retold in the *Brahma Purāṇa* in a version of the story of Pippalāda and Dadhīca that supplies a more specific rationalization for the presence of the mare in the story:

> Pippalāda, the son of Dadhīca, performed asceticism in order to kill the slayers of his father. When he was able to see the third eye of Śiva, he gained from Śiva the power to kill the gods. The fig trees [*pippalas*] said, "Your mother was called a mare." When Pippalāda heard this, he became angry, and from his eye an evil spirit came forth in the form of a blazing mare with a deadly tongue; she had the form of a mare because he had been thinking of a mare. He told her to eat the gods, but she began to eat him, since he had been made by the gods; in terror, Pippalāda fled to Śiva, who told

> the spirit not to attack any creature within a league of that place. Then the mare set out full of fire to burn the universe, terrifying the gods, who sought refuge with Pippalāda; but Pippalāda could not restrain the mare. When she came to the confluence of the Ganges, the gods begged her to begin with the waters of the ocean and then to devour everything. The fire said, "How can I reach the ocean? Let a virtuous maiden place me in a golden pot and lead me there." The gods asked the maiden Sarasvatī to do this, and she asked them to join her with four other rivers, the Yamunā, Ganges, Narmadā, and Tapatī. The five rivers put the fire in a golden pot and brought it to the ocean; they threw it into the ocean, and it began to drink the waters little by little (*BP* 110. 85–210).

Here, as in the long Pippalāda variant in the *Skanda Purāṇa,* the sage wishes to kill the gods, not the class of warriors, whom Aurva sets out to destroy; this is a fight between man and god, mortal and immortal. The slur against Pippalāda's mother makes it plain that "mare" is a term of opprobrium, probably implying insatiable sexual appetite; it is reminiscent of the mother's own fears about her chastity in the other version. Moreover, Sarasvatī's chastity, which in that version is important though only implied, is here made explicit: only a maiden can carry the fire. A further difference between the two versions resides in the fact that here the fire undergoes a change of gender: it is a mare as long as it is the possession of the sage Pippalāda; but as soon as the chaste maiden and the four rivers appear on the scene, the fire is called a fire (masculine), is placed in the golden pot that is the female receptacle of the golden seed of Śiva, and, like that seed, is submerged in the Ganges (*ŚP Dharmasaṃhitā* 11. 28–35). Pippalāda's connection with Śiva is also stronger here than in the earlier version: he becomes able to see Śiva's third eye and then produces the fiery mare with his own eye; the gods then beg Śiva to protect them from the mare created by the fire of *his* eye (*BP* 110. 124. 136). Clearly the two eyes function as one, and Pippalāda and Śiva are one; elsewhere, too, Pippalāda appears as an incarnation of Śiva (ŚP 3. 24–25). The theme of being destroyed by your own destructive creature—in particular, of being eaten by your own hungry creature—is taken from the mythology of the birth of Agni, the omnivorous male force (*ŚB* 2. 2. 4. 1; 9. 1. 1. 1; O'Flaherty 1976, p. 31). Because the mare is both Pippalāda's mother and his daughter, her intention to devour him bears implications of dangerous, incestuous sexuality.

Śiva participates in the action of the myth of the underwater mare in iconic forms more often than he appears anthropomorphically, though it is he who makes possible the birth of the mare-fire in both Pippalāda stories (the long *Skanda Purāṇa* version and the shorter *Brahma Purāṇa* version) and who first controls her in the second version. However, in yet another version of the myth (one that centers around Aurva rather than Dadhīci and entirely omits Pippalāda), Śiva not only fails to control the mare but is himself endangered by her (as Pippalāda is in the *Brahma Purāṇa*):

> The sage Aurva performed asceticism until he began to burn the universe. The gods were frightened; and so one day, while the sage was performing asceticism, Śiva looked in anger on Aurva's hermitage and burnt it up. When Aurva saw that it had been burnt, he said, "Let the one who has burnt this hermitage be burnt by sorrow and wander over the world." And so Śiva himself was burnt by a great fire and wandered about without finding rest. Finally he went with Pārvatī to Aurva, who promised that Śiva would be released from the curse if he performed the ritual of bathing a herd of cows; and he did so and was cured (*Var P* 147. 1–27).

Aurva's curse upon an unknown enemy, like the unwitting curse Subhadrā places upon her own husband, results in the creation of a fire. Śiva is both the immediate source of this fire (burning the hermitage with his third eye and causing havoc, as the demon Dhundhu caused havoc in Uttaṅka's hermitage) and its first receptacle; he wanders in torture, the way he wanders under the influence of *viraha* after the death of Satī. Finally he is released from pain when, soothed by his meek wife, he bathes cows; the fire ignited by a mare is quenched by cows.

F. Śiva and the Mare

In some texts, Śiva engenders the mare-fire with the blaze of his third eye. In the battle between Śiva and Kāma, the fire of anger that shoots forth from Śiva's third eye to burn Kāma to ashes is expressly said to be the fire of doomsday; there is therefore but one ultimate resting place for it: the ocean.

> When Śiva burnt Kāma to ashes with the fire from his third eye, the fire could never return to Śiva; moreover, Brahmā had paralyzed the fire in a vain attempt to shield Kāma. Śiva vanished, and the fire began to burn all the gods and all the universe. The gods sought refuge with Brahmā, who made the fire of Śiva's anger into a mare with ambrosial [*saumya*] flames coming out of her

> mouth. Then Brahmā took the mare to the ocean and said, "This mare is the fire of Śiva's anger, which burnt Kāma and now wishes to burn the whole universe. I gave it the form of a mare; now you must bear it until the final deluge. Then I will come here and lead it away from you; but until then it will devour your water, and you must make a great effort to bear it." The ocean agreed to this, and the fire entered and was held in check, burning quietly with its halo of flames (*ŚP* 2. 3. 20. 1–23; *MBP* 22–23; *Kālikā P* 44. 124–36).

The fire that Brahmā makes into the mare is the fire of suppressed passion and anger; it is the destructive force of rigid chastity breaking out in lust and hatred, like the murderous self-suppression of Reṇukā's husband, Jamadagni (Brubaker 1977). That the fire is in fact composed of equal parts of lust and of anger directed against lust is clear from another variant of this episode:

> Śiva reduced Kāma to ashes, and the fire from his third eye soon yawned wide to burn the universe. But then, for the sake of the world, Śiva dispersed that fire among mangoes and the moon and flowers and bees and cuckoos—thus he divided the fire of Kāma. That fire that had pierced Śiva inside and outside, kindling passion and affection, serves to arouse people who are separated, reaching the hearts of lovers, and it blazes night and day, hard to cure (*Matsya P* 154. 250–55).

The full power of Kāma is augmented by contact with Śiva's own antierotic force and is therefore all the more compelling. The interaction of the two supposedly opposed fires—the fire of desire and the fire of asceticism—is clear: the ascetic fire from Śiva's eye merges with the fire with which Kāma pierced Śiva and serves as the flame of *viraha*. The phrase "the fire of Kāma" is a pun, denoting the fire used *by* Kāma and *against* him as well, a flame composed of two sparks, "sparks fanned by the flames of Śiva's glance from the coals of burning Love" (*SRK* 171). Thus, when Śiva attempts in vain to disperse his erotic fever, he is said to be aflame with the fire of Śiva, Kāma, and Agni (*Sk P* 3. 3. 26. 4).

This is the fire that Śiva places in the ocean in the form of a mare, the fire of thwarted passion. Ironically, the mare-fire is also the source of Śiva's own *viraha*, for the fire in which Satī immolated herself is called "Jwala Mukhi" ("Mouth of Fire"), the name of the mare (Elwin 1942, p. 119). The fire of Śiva's anger, the mare-fire, and the fire of Kāma are combined in a verse addressed to Kāma (*Abhijñānaśākuntala* 3. 2. alt.):

> Surely the fire of Śiva's anger still burns in you today
> like the fire of the mare in the ocean;
> for how else, Kāma, could you be so hot
> as to reduce people like me to ashes?

Here the fire is masculine—the creation of a male sage and expressive of a male god's anger and lust. There is therefore an element of irony in the application of this image—the expression of lust's ultimate triumph over the angry suppression of lust—to the insatiable appetite of Śiva for his Goddess, Pārvatī.

Śiva's connection with the mare makes good sense on another level of the myth as well. For the mare is born either when a woman violates her vow of chastity and becomes pregnant in an abnormal manner (the myths of Subhadrā) or when a yogi (Śiva, the greatest of all yogis) violates his vow of chastity, a violation that ultimately results in an abnormal pregnancy and the birth of Skanda. In the first cycle, the submarine mare is a symbol of a woman's thwarted power; it is the image of resentful, unwilling chastity imposed on the female by terrified males; it is passion denied and suppressed, divinity denied and devalued. In the second cycle, the mare is a symbol of yogic power thwarted and rebounding against itself.

The yogi is a positive image of powers held in and controlled (though the myth of Śiva and Kāma reveals hidden reefs even in those quiet waters), in contrast with the woman who holds back her milk, the evil Goddess. The myth of the mare implies that a man may voluntarily hold in his powers (though this may have destructive results when these powers break out against his will) but that a woman will do so only under compulsion (see above, chap. 2, sec. B).

Yoginīs, who do undergo voluntary self-control, are quickly assimilated to the herd of mares. Servants of the ambivalent Kālī, they are very dangerous and highly erotic females (O'Flaherty 1973, motif 27ea, erotic Yoginīs) and, like other forms of the mare, are regarded as dangerous because they act like men; they are in many ways androgynous.

Indeed, that is one of the basic reasons for the rejection of the mare and everything she symbolizes: a female androgyne is unacceptable. By straddling polarized categories of female (equated with maternal) and divine/erotic (equated with male)—categories that were once integrated in the figure of the Indo-European mare goddess—the Hindu mare poses a taxonomic problem similar to that posed by the figure of the good demon (O'Flaherty 1978, pp. 96–106). Figures that transcend categories or mediate between them are usually sacred in either a positive or a negative way; if they are taken in a negative sense, regarded as dirt ("matter out of place"; see Douglas 1966), the taxonomic problem may be solved by reclassification: the demon either ceases to be good or ceases to be technically a demon; the mare goddess becomes a demon, appropriately evil and grotesque. But if this transcending, mediating character is taken in a positive sense, one experiences the *coincidentia oppositorum*, the deity who is wonderful because she shatters all categories; this is the theology of the Indo-European mare.

For the mare is the quintessential female androgyne, the phallic woman, and androgynes, as we shall see in chapter 9, are regarded as grotesque and dangerous as often as they are regarded as beautiful and beneficient; indeed, female androgynes are comparatively rare but, when they do occur, are deadlier than the male. In the Sri Lanka cult of Pattini, the virgin/mother/wife of Palanga, the problem of reconciling her status as wife with the need to keep her (as a goddess) pure is solved in various ways, usually by the statement or implication that Palanga is impotent or castrated. In rare cases, however, it is said that Pattini is a hermaphrodite, which frees her from being polluted by menstruation, intercourse, or childbirth. This solution, which does violence to the myth of Pattiṇi, is generally rejected in favor of its alternate, the impotence of Palanga (Obeyesekere 1980, pp. 935–36). For the two solutions are equivalent: the consort of a female androgyne is impotent or castrated.

The combination of anger and lust is at the heart of the myth of Śiva and the mare. It is a combination that underlies many other myths of this corpus, as well; Reṇukā, for example, is beheaded as a result of the combination of her lust with the anger of her husband, Jamadagni, and Śiva is castrated as a result of the combination of the lust of the wives of the sages in the Pine Forest and their husband's anger. The parallels between these two particular myths are instructive: both take place in the uneasy limbo of the forest dweller's attempt to control his sexuality through compromise (O'Flaherty 1973, pp. 79–82); both result in new cults, either of an ambivalent goddess or of the *liṅga* in the *yoni* (itself a multiform of the mare under water); and both satirize the sage's attempts to control his own sexuality by controlling his wife (Brubaker 1977). Moreover, the South Indian version of the Reṇukā myth, where she is given the body of an Untouchable woman, presents a split image like that of the fire with the head of a mare; unable to accept the possibility that a "chaste" woman could have sexual impulses, the Hindus split her into a chaste mind and a literally polluted body. This ambivalence is attributed to the male as well in a Sanskrit version of the myth of the transposed heads (the analogue of the tale of Reṇukā) in which the woman confuses the heads of her husband and her brother (adding the problem of incest to the dilemma of adultery) and prays for guidance to the goddess "who has taken half of her husband's body [in the form of the androgyne] even though he is the enemy of Kāma [the god of lust]" (*KSS* 80. 38).

The link between the doomsday mare and the suppressed woman is made explicit both in texts describing the mare (as like the woman) and in those describing the woman (as like the mare). For example, Viṣṇu/Kalki plays the role of the mare/woman:

> Viṣṇu becomes the sun and dries up the ocean with his scorching rays. . . . He goes down to Hell and drinks the water there, and then he sucks out the urine, blood, and other moisture in the bodies of living creatures. . . . He is the mare's head in the ocean of milk, the whirlpool fire that drinks the oblation made of water (*Matsya P* 166. 1–4; 167. 58–59).

This process of sucking out the fluids of the body is attributed not only to the seductive female but to the Tantric Ḍākinīs, female ghosts whose favorite food is (ritual) menstrual blood and "the seed of bodily conception." These harpies eat both the stuff of birth and the stuff of death; when someone dies, "the Ḍākinīs attach themselves to the body and . . . suck up the person's breath, drink his blood, and steal away his life."[4]

The Indo-European mare was dangerous in her erotic powers precisely because they were untamed; as raw forces of a Goddess, they were overpowering. For this very reason, however, the mare was also able to bless and make fruitful, not merely because she was both mother and whore, both cow and mare, but because her powers flowed freely down to her mortal consort. The underwater mare, by contrast, is a symbol of angry, thwarted sexuality, of power blocked by authority. In the Hindu view, a woman's suppressed or repulsed eroticism is as volatile and explosive as nitroglycerine. We say that Hell hath no fury to match this, and the Hindus say that this *is* the Fury that breaks forth out of Hell at doomsday.

8 Sacred Cows and Profane Mares

Two animals stand out from all the rest as sacred Indian images: the horse and the cow. The degree of their power and its positive or negative force have varied both in different periods of Indian history and with regard to the male and female of the species. The persistence of cow and horse symbolism and its compelling emotional power make it possible to use the images it produces as lenses for bringing into focus the evolution of certain basic Indian ideas about men and women and gods and goddesses.

A. The Vedic Stallion

The most charismatic animal in the Ṛg Veda is the stallion. The sun is depicted as a bright bay stallion galloping across the sky; a stallion is sacrificed to ensure fertility and royal prosperity; the image of sacrificial success is the victorious horse winning the race. The popularity of the Vedic stallion can easily be explained in the context of history: the Indo-Aryans were a nation of warriors whose conquest of much of Europe and Asia was made possible by the fact that they alone had tamed the warhorse and harnessed him to the chariot. Men rather than women are the creators of Vedic life—aggressive, sexually potent men, symbolized by the stallion.

The Vedic horse was linked with fire through the rituals of the sun stallion and the sacrificial fire; the stallion symbolized controlled aggression, the taming of violent powers that are "curbed" as an unruly horse is checked by a strong bridle with a curb chain. The Upaniṣads and Plato liken the senses to horses, which must either be controlled or remain vicious and wild (*KU* 3. 4–6); and a monk said to the Buddha, "The senses of others are restless like horses, but yours have been tamed.

Other beings are passionate, but your passions have ceased" (*Buddhacarita* 15. 1–7, 13).[1] A striking example of the early association of the horse not only with the taming of wildness but with fire and water as well may be seen in a passage of the *Gopatha Brājmaṇa* in which the four Vedas compete over the taming of a wild horse. The horse, produced from "terrible, destructive water," is referred to as "she," but no word for "mare" is used; the horse is also identified with Agni Vaiśvānara (the fire that dwells within the human body in the form of the digestive fire) and is said to have fire smoldering within it. The verb used to represent the taming of the horse (*śam*) is the same as the term for the extinguishing of a fire or a passion (hence *śanti*, "spiritual peace"). Finally, the Atharvan, the tamer, prepares the waters of tranquillity and sprinkles them over the horse; the *rasa*, or fluid essence, of the horse enters the ocean and burns it, and flames shoot forth from every limb of the animal, who is henceforth perfectly tame (*GB* 1. 2. 21). Like the submarine mare, the stallion is controlled under water; but the text adds ominously that, because the horse was tamed, it is the hungriest of beasts.

The sinister aspect of taming is, as we have seen, an important part of the mythology of the suppressed mare; it appears in this text both in the enduring hunger of the tamed horse and in the inconsistent reference to the animal as female. When applied to the stallion, however (and, later, to the yogi), the taming is generally regarded as auspicious. Thus the horse in the *Gopatha Brāhmaṇa*, finally referred to with the unmarked masculine form, is said to be "perfectly tame" and is at least no longer actively destructive. This concept of the possibility and, indeed, the necessity of safely taming the dangerous male horse persists in the tradition that the ancient winged horses were too strong and too proud of their strength until Indra had their wings cut off (a variant of the mutilation/castration of the horse) to make them useful to gods and men (*MBh* 1. 16. 34–36; *Aśvaśāstra, pakṣacchedakathā*).

The connection between the horse and the ocean is an ancient Indo-European one. We have seen the close mythic tie between horses and Poseidon, god of the ocean; in ritual, too, the Greeks sacrificed horses to Poseidon (Penzer 1924, 4:14–16). Celtic mythology describes aquatic monsters known as Goborchinn ("horseheads," which in English is another name for moonfish), as well as horse eels and water horses (the forerunners of the equine Loch Ness monster). In the Avesta, the star horse, Tir or Tiśtrya, fights against a black horse named Apasśa in the cosmic ocean; here one sees both a splitting of colors and moral qualities and an association with the ocean that remain typical of the mare in later mythology.

In the Vedas, the horse is sacred to Varuṇa, god of the waters (*ŚB*

5. 3. 1. 5; 6. 2. 1. 5); the horse is born in the ocean or comes from beyond the sea (*RV* 1. 163. 1–2). The ocean is the womb of the horse (*TS* 7. 5. 25. 2; *ŚB* 5. 1. 1. 5; 10. 6. 4. 1); it is also the womb of the family of the horse (*VS* 13. 42). The naturalistic basis of this association is straightforward; as Hopkins remarked on the birth of Uccaiḥśravas from the ocean, "The divine ever-youthful horse, produced at the churning of the ocean and famous only as the white roaring charger of the sea. What can that be save the roaring breakers?" (Hopkins 1915, p. 125). And the British, good Indo-Europeans, speak of the foaming crests of the waves as "white horses."

The ruins of Pompeii contain images of sea centaurs, evidence of the possible Indo-European basis not only of the link between horses and the sea but between semiequine deities (like the Aśvins or the Hindu mare's head) and the sea. Another Hindu image, the androgyne, is combined with the oceanic horse in a peculiar survival (both in Indo-European culture and in nature): the creature that we call the seahorse is a male who carries the fertilized eggs in his body and gives birth to the young; a recent article on this strange animal calls him "the pregnant stallion of the sea" (Odum 1978). He is an example not only of an androgyne (the male equivalent of the phallic mare) but of the yogi who keeps his seed within his own body—the human figure symbolized by the stallion tamed under water in Vedic texts.

B. The Vedic Cow and Bull

The cow was already a powerful symbolic figure during the heyday of the mare (and the stallion); the Hindu cult of the cow represents a reemphasis and revalidation of existing sacred models rather than the usurpation of an old model by a new one. Cattle are of great value in the Ṛg Veda, as in all ancient Indo-European cultures. The magic wishing-cow is found in Norse, Iranian, and Irish traditions (Koppers 1936, pp. 320–27); in India, too, this myth has wide currency. The magic wishing-cow is the earth milked of good and evil substances by gods and demons. She is churned out of the ocean of milk; and the ocean of milk, from which all else is churned forth, in turn flows from the udder of the wishing-cow (*MBh* 1. 23. 50; *R* 7. 23. 21). In almost all parts of Ireland the Milky Way is called "the path of the white cow"; in Southwest Ireland, however, the atavistically horsey Irish also call it the white mare's tail (a term we apply to certain clouds).[2] Thus in Ireland, where the myth of the White Goddess has greatest staying power, the mare is still able to play the role of a cow.

The bull is also sacred throughout the Indo-European world. Using

Germanic, Roman, and Indo-Iranian texts, Bruce Lincoln (1975) has reconstructed a complex proto-Indo-European creation myth in which "twin" victims are sacrificed. In one variant, the pastoralist or Indo-Iranian variant, a man and an ox (or bull) were sacrificed; in another variant, the European agriculturalist variant, a man and a cow were sacrificed. Lincoln suggests socioeconomic reasons for the use of the bull in one set of myths and the cow in the other: the pastoralist values the whole animal—leather, bone, dung, and even urine—while the agriculturalist treasures his animals only for their milk. Therefore the pastoralists sacrificed the bull, who was sacred to them because of the ways in which all of his parts were used, and the agriculturalists sacrificed the cow, who was sacred to them because of her milk.

This logic, though not entirely convincing in itself, becomes more compelling when we take into account factors that Lincoln has underplayed, primarily the variation in the gender of the animal. Though Lincoln places no importance on this variation, he does point out that Roman national pride led them to refashion the myth of Romulus and Remus by replacing "the passive cow with the ferocious figure of the she-wolf as a means of emphasizing the military strength of Rome." This transition in the attitude to the passive cow may be seen as another manifestation of the contrast between the pastoralist with his bull (the "ferocious" animal of the pair, and appropriate for land-conquering nomads searching for pasture) and the agriculturalist with his cow (the "passive" animal of the pair, appropriate for settled farmers).

We will note a similar contrast, specifically in the form of a historical transition (such as that implied by Lincoln in the transition from cow to she-wolf in Rome) rather than in the form of an atemporal contrast (such as that implied by Lincoln as obtaining between pastoralists and agriculturalists), in the shift from the stallion in the myths produced by the pastoral Vedic culture to the cow in the myths of Hindu culture, which was agricultural. Moreover, the transition in the Roman attitude to the "passive cow" may be seen as the inverse of another hypothetical transition that we will explore in this chapter, one in which an earlier attitude of respect for the "ferocious" mare (the nurturing but ferocious she-wolf) is replaced by respect for the passive cow. Finally, several theological and ethical variations in the myths discussed by Lincoln—the fact that the dismemberment of the bull or cow is performed by gods in some accounts, by demons in others; that the act is treated sometimes as a sacrifice, sometimes as a murder—take on greater significance in the context of shifting sacred traditions surrounding the mare and the stallion as well as the cow and the bull.

In Iranian myth and ritual, the bull functions much as the horse does in India: he is sacrificed to create the world (Koppers 1936, p. 322). In both cases, the male animal is used; yet both Ireland and India have the image of the magic wishing-cow as well, and this triad (bull, horse, and cow) also appears in Norse materials: the magic cow named Authumla in the *Snorre Edda* is associated with brother-sister incest, and bulls and stallions are also prominent (ibid., p. 320). The bull appears in complementary distribution with the stallion (Puhvel 1977); a cult of the bull may have been replaced by a cult of the horse (Koppers 1936, p. 391). Man, too, appears as a victim in this pattern; the "macho trio" of stallion, bull, and ram (as well as king) replace one another in Indo-European sacrifices (Puhvel 1977). It may be argued that the primary sacrificial beast (and fertility symbol) of the Indo-Europeans was the bull and that the sacrifice of the primeval Puruṣa involved the dismemberment of a man who was a bull (Puruṣa, from *pu* + *vṛsa*) (Lincoln 1977a); or, on the other hand, the horse may be given pride of place (Puhvel 1977). But it is evident that cattle as a whole (cows and bulls) were highly prized, whereas, of equines, only the stallion was ritually valued.

In later Indian mythology, the bull functions as the "inappropriate" member of his species even as the mare is "wrong" in hers. But the Ṛg Veda is as rich in bull-and-cow mythology as it is in horse mythology, if not richer. The protean god Indra in the Ṛg Veda is said to be a bull and to ride on a bull; but he is also said to be, and to ride on, a horse, and in later texts he seldom rides a bull. A common epithet for Indian kings is "bull among men," never "stallion among men," but royal epithets often end in "-horse" (-aśva). In Greek mythology, too (though probably under Cretan influence), bulls play roles similar to that of horses: we have seen how Dionysus is replaced by a bull when he dances with the equine maenads and how Poseidon sends a bull from the sea to drive Hippolytus's horses mad.

In the Vedas, as throughout Indo-European civilizations, cattle (cows and bulls) are the measure of wealth and the symbol of all that one wants to possess. The species as a whole plays a passive role. In contrast with the horse (who is often depicted as a seeker, though he is also one who flees and is sought, as in the myth of Saraṇyū), cattle are not only sought but are often stolen (for the Indo-Aryans were the first great rustlers), rescued, possessed. They are also slaughtered, eaten, and offered to guests and gods.

Thus in the Ṛg Veda both horses and cattle are sacred, though stallions are far more sacred than mares, and cows are more sacred than bulls. All are sacred; all are killed and eaten. Horses are, as a species, revered for masculine, aggressive qualities, and this in part accounts for the preference for stallions over mares. Cattle, on the other hand, are passive and play a receptive, creative role; hence the preference for cows over bulls.

Though the bull is revered as a potent, seed-giving animal, it is the stallion's seed that has great ritual value, not only in the *aśvamedha* sacrifice but in Upaniṣadic cosmic imagery. The stallion's seed is the counterpart of the cow's milk; his phallus is the counterpart of her udder (see above, chap. 2, sec. A). The creative fluids that flow from both are androgynously, unilaterally capable of giving life. Thus, when the ocean of milk is churned, the two sacred animals that emerge are the magic wishing-cow and Uccaiḥśravas, the sun stallion.

The Ṛg Veda thus presents three positive theriomorphic images—cow, stallion, and bull—and faintly adumbrates the fourth image, the mare, who, descended as she is from the ambivalent Indo-European mare, is potentially negative. But several elements in the cluster of Vedic symbolic and ritual patterns become greatly altered within a thousand years. In the Hindu period, cows are even more preeminent over bulls, and cattle have become preeminent over equines; mares are now regarded as dangerous and demonic. Most important, the sanctity of cows has made them animals *not* to be eaten instead of the *pièce de résistance* at the feasts of Vedic gods, sacrificers, and guests. To explain this transition, it is tempting to turn to other parts of the Indian subcontinent.

C. The Turnabout and the Indus Civilization

Ludwig Alsdorf has discussed at some length the complicated historical development of the bovine turnabout; he points out that the idea of vegetarianism (i.e., of not eating or killing any animals) is complementary to but by no means synonymous with or dependent on the peculiar veneration of the cow (Alsdorf 1962, p. 610).[3] Where do these non-Vedic ideas originate?

Alsdorf's answer will come as no surprise to students of Indology: the new ideas originate in some "pre-Aryan" civilization, probably that of the Indus Valley. The Indus Valley Civilization has, for Indologists, the supreme virtue of being largely unknown, since we have not succeeded in deciphering its script; anything, therefore, that is not found in the Vedas but appears in later Hinduism is blamed on the Indus Valley, a most convenient catchall and a dignified academic way of saying "I don't know." Non-Vedic religious and social phenomena are said to "come from the Indus Valley," much as werewolves or visitors from outer space appear from Hungary or Mexico in English and American films, respectively. But every idea has to be "new" at some moment in time; *someone* has to think of it first. Why does it seem more likely that a new idea came into India from another culture than that it developed in the head of some Indian raised within the Vedic tradition? More specifically, what is the basis for the hypothesis that the cow (as opposed to the bull) or cattle (as opposed to horses) were venerated in the Indus Valley?

The second half of the second question is easily answered: there is no evidence that there were any horses at all in the Indus Valley Civilization, and there is much evidence of cattle. No horses are depicted on the steatite seals, and there is only one, much disputed, possibility of a horse's skeleton. Many seals show a unicorn standing under a sacred fig tree (the *pīpal*, later called the *aśvattha*—the tree "under which horses stand"), but this is hardly evidence of a cult of the horse, particularly since the "unicorn" is almost certainly a one-horned bull. Indeed, bulls abound in every form: on the seals, as terra-cotta toys for children (roly-poly bulls with wobbly heads), and in skeletal remains.

But the first half of the question—cows vs. bulls—must be answered in the negative. Cows do *not* appear on the Indus seals. The Indologist in search of symbols is thus in a bit of a quandary: cattle, the genus we have designated as relatively "feminine" in its symbolic associations—as the animal of settled, passive, unaggressive, domesticated civilizations, like that of the Indus Valley, in contrast with the culture-creating Aryan horse—is present in abundance, but only in its male form. Scholars intent on preserving the hypothetical pattern at any cost, and reluctant to let go of the Indus loophole, might support the "cow-oriented" hypothesis by reference to other "feminine" aspects of the Indus Civilization: the presence of crude cult figures identified as mother goddesses (and hence regarded as the source of Hindu cults of the mother), ring stones, which prefigure the icons of the *yoni*, and so forth.

Indus seals depicting women jumping over the horns of a bull have been connected with seals from Crete showing the same thing (Fabri 1934–35, pp. 93–101); the image is certainly suggestive of Freudian interpretations, but it hardly clarifies the symbolic confusion, unless we regard the women as cows (jumping over the horned moon?). The Indus Valley bull is indubitably male, as is evident from the most superficial glance at his formidable anatomy on the seals. The sum total of data from the Indus Valley is, therefore, primarily negative: the culture is *not* horse-oriented, nor is it cow-oriented. The Indus people were almost certainly bull-worshipers and perhaps were worshipers of mother goddesses; however, these two strains do not develop in tandem in later Hinduism.

A far more likely candidate for the source of the cow-woman concept in later Hinduism is the literature of early Tamil, which may possibly be linked with the Indus Valley Civilization (it has been suggested that the Indus script, like Tamil, represents a Dravidian language). It has been convincingly argued that the exaggerated emphasis on female chastity in Sanskrit literature is borrowed from early Tamil sources, having originated with the indigenous peoples of India, probably with the megalithic Dravidian civilization of the first millennium B.C. In many Tamil poems the sacred power of the chaste woman resides in her breasts, which contain milk dangerous to her husband (Hart 1975, pp. 98–99). Clearly, the sacred Tamil woman is procreative rather than erotic. Yet the Tamil cannot provide the source of the animal symbolism, for the concept of reverence for the cow is almost entirely absent from the early Tamil texts. Together, the Indus Valley Civilization and the Tamil texts provide us with a bull (whom we already had in the Ṛg Veda) and a woman whose chastity is her power. For the development of the cow imagery, we must turn to later Hinduism.

D. The Hindu Stallion and Mare

The failure of the Indus Valley Civilization to supply the missing link leaves us, nevertheless, with a clearly defined Hindu model (to contrast with the Vedic model): good stallion and bad mare; good cow—and the bull, an animal who stubbornly refused to become a cow in the Indus Valley and balks at fitting the hypothetical Hindu pattern as well. The first three animals of the group present few problems and may be dealt with first, while we hold the bull restlessly in reserve.

In Hinduism, especially on the royal level, the stallion remains a sacred animal; it is primarily a sacrificial animal, for horse sacrifices continued to be performed, albeit rarely, long after the general rule of noninjury to animals put an end to most Hindu animal sacrifices. The stallion also retains its connotations of fertility. The mare, by contrast, has taken on new, negative dimensions: she is erotic but not fertile—a significant distinction in the Hindu context (O'Flaherty 1973, pp. 262–66), and not only is she not part of the sacrifice to the Vedic gods but, on the contrary, she is associated with demons and demonic destruction. The reasons for this may be seen in the change in the attitude toward women from the Vedic to the Hindu period: the Vedic poet made no distinction between erotic and fertile women, though women were in general relegated to the background of Vedic life. In sub-Vedic (i.e., village) and pre-Vedic (i.e., Indus Valley) India, too, there is no evidence of a separation between the roles of woman as erotic object and woman as mother; the cheerful Yakṣiṇīs and callipygian Indus figurines are well equipped to be both. These cultures present non-Indo-European parallels to the Indo-European mare goddess in terms of integration, though not in their theriomorphic symbolism; for there are no mares at Mohenjo-Daro or in village shrines.

But from the period of the Upaniṣads and Buddhism (ca. 700 B.C.), the cult of asceticism reared its ugly head; lust came to be regarded as the work of the devil, and woman was seen as the servant of the devil and the most dangerous enemy of the ascetic. Even in the Ṛg Veda, as we have seen, one encounters the myth of the dangerous woman who sucks the man dry (*RV* 1. 179. 4). By the late Vedic period, the Indo-European cult in which the king drained and swallowed the fluid powers of the mare had been replaced by the model in which his vital fluids flowed into her as the seed flowed into her mouth (see above, chap. 6, sec. C). Where the king in the ancient ritual had devoured the mare, now the mare devoured the man. The Vedic image of the fertile cow that gives milk is retained and is now contrasted with the image of the erotic mare who steals the equivalent of milk—the stallion's seed. The cow feeds her child; the mare eats her child (and her husband). The cow that symbolizes the breast from which all good things flow is contrasted with the bad cow, the breast that feeds itself, the mare that drinks the fluids.

Ironically, this basic female image (the self-nourishing breast) is applied in India more often to the male (the yogi) than to the female (the bad mother), and the associated moral values are polarized: it is good for a man to hold in his fluids but bad for a woman to do so. The Ṛg Vedic stallion who sprinkles his seed upon the earth to fertilize it has now been changed into the stallion whose powers are bottled up inside him, curbed and bitted to generate power like a Ferrari revving up its motor in neutral. In this context, it is instructive to look back on the strangely involuted horse sacrifice, recorded several hundred years *after* the Ṛg Veda, in which the stallion is *fed seed* and thus combines the functions of the ancient Vedic stallion or Indo-European mare (to give seed) and the Vedic or Hindu mare (eat seed). The stallion of the horse sacrifice behaves like a yogi: he contains his seed within himself and is, like a yogi, under a firm vow of chastity, even (or, rather, especially) in the presence of the mares at the sacrifice.

The yogi resembles the stallion and the mare/cow goddess in his ambivalent relationship to eroticism and fertility. In the Ṛg Veda the stallion is primarily fertile, sprinkling his seed freely upon the earth; at that time, woman is beginning to be split into erotic or fertile personae, as in the myth of Saraṇyū and the Shadow. In the Upaniṣads and Brāhmaṇas the stallion becomes the symbol of the control and harnessing of powers, the recycling of the semen; and woman is now split into more clearly opposed roles, the erotic whore and the fertile mother. The yogi, who comes on the scene in the late Vedic period, is also split into roles corresponding to the two roles of stallion and woman: he can be either erotic and nonfertile or fertile and nonerotic. The first role is played by the yogi who draws up his seed in Vedāntic renunciation or Tantric ritual; to avoid involvement in Vedic commitments to progeny, he holds in his seed but is a highly erotic figure in myth as well as ritual (O'Flaherty 1973, pp. 55–57), like the stallion in the horse sacrifice or like the Hindu mare/whore. The second role, in which he is fertile but nonerotic, is played by the yogi who bestows Vedic fertility by virtue of his total conquest of the senses, the yogi whose seed is *amogharetas* ("never shed in vain," i.e., always productive of a child); he corresponds to the Hindu cow-mother or the Ṛg Vedic stallion.

Both roles are acceptable in a yogi, and they often overlap or clash in a single myth. Thus the sage Ṛṣyaśṛṅga, never having seen a woman, has great powers of chastity, which are *said* to be able to bring rain; on this level he is the nonerotic, fertile sage, and therefore the king of a country suffering from drought sends his daughter (the fertile woman) to bring him to the city. This is the explicit level—what people think they think—and it expresses Vedāntic values: chastity is good. But the action of the myth reveals that Ṛṣyaśṛṅga's chastity has *caused* the drought in the first place; he is the nonfertile, erotic sage, and the drought ends when his seed falls after he has been seduced by a prostitute (the erotic woman). This is the implicit level—what people do think—and it expresses certain Vedic values: chastity is bad (ibid., pp. 42–54).

The persistent separation of eroticism and fertility in Hindu myth is reflected in actual behavior patterns that in turn resonate in the myths. The separation of mother (wife, cow) from whore (mare) dries up the erotic side of marriage, and the following psychological cycle of avoidance is produced: the wife has no outlet for erotic impulses in her marriage and therefore displaces them onto her son (see above, chap. 4, sec. C). His inability to see her in an erotic role, a natural impulse that is also strongly reinforced by the culture, adds further fuel to the flames of attraction/repulsion in his perception of the mother's sexual aggression. These exacerbated schisms then feed back into the mythology of mares and cows and attribute to the mare a dangerous, nonfertile eroticism.

The mare mythology developed further by absorbing and often reversing elements of the mythology of the stallion. The Vedic symbolism of the fiery stallion tamed under water—a positive image, reinforced by the Upaniṣadic concept of the harnessing of the senses (which are likened to wild horses) and the fiery seed—was given demonic overtones and a change of sex. The result was the myth of the mare-fire beneath the sea, lurking there until the time of its release at doomsday, smoldering, in hair-trigger balance with the floods of the ocean, constantly straining at the bit to burst forth and destroy us all.

Thus erotic, nonfertile female energy—mare power—came to be contrasted with nonerotic, fertile energy—cow power; although the yogi could in fact produce either one, he was more usually associated with the latter, if only because he usually played a positive role, like the stallion. The mare represents chastity under unwilling compulsion, in contrast with yogic chastity, which is knowingly and carefully undertaken.

The mare is thus evil, lascivious, and destructive, while the stallion and cow are sacred, fertile, and creative. The horse as a genus is fierce and male, and so the stallion (or horse-headed male god, like Viṣṇu as Hayagrīva) is good, while the mare (or the horse-headed woman) is evil. The fact that only the male horse is ritually acceptable is evident from a traditional belief that horses used to have breasts until Śiva cut them off (simultaneously cleaving the hooves of bulls but not castrating them), just as Indra cut off their wings (*MBh* 8. 24, app. 1. 4. 15–19; *Matsya P* 138. 40–42). Horses should not have breasts; cows should have breasts.

E. The Hindu Cow

The clear moral contrast between stallion and mare is somewhat blurred in the bull and cow, though it may still be found if we persist in looking not for the blanket categories of "good" and "bad" but for the relevant Hindu clusters: nonsacred, lascivious, and destructive in contrast with sacred, fertile, and creative. The first category applies to the mare and bull, the second to the stallion and cow.

The qualities feared in the mare are the mirror image of the qualities revered in the cow. The mare is transformed from a deity who is eaten (the eucharistic Goddess) into the demon who eats; the cow is transformed from the sacrificial animal who is eaten into an animal who is *not* eaten. In the pattern of the mare, the alternative to being eaten is eating—which is what demons do; in the pattern of the cow, the alternative to being eaten is a combination of feeding without being eaten (by giving milk) and *not* being eaten. This option is not available to the mare, and one can only speculate why. Apparently the ancient Indians did not drink mare's milk, as so many other Indo-Europeans did. Perhaps the fact that the mare came to be defined as nonmaternal precluded the use of her milk; perhaps she could never be regarded as the source of any fluid other than her own seed, the equivalent of the seed of the stallion, who replaced her so early in the Vedic rite. As to the reasons for the cow's transition from an animal sacred and therefore to be eaten to an animal sacred and therefore *not* to be eaten, many factors, social, economic, and historical, are clearly at play (Alsdorf 1962), but among them must surely be a revulsion against the once devoured and now devouring mare, a corresponding sanctification of the nurturing cow mother, and a mythology of milk expanding to eclipse the mythology of blood and seed.

The cow's goodness, basic though it is in Hindu mythology, appears to be challenged in some episodes. However, the negative aspect of the cow is a result of her failure to fulfill her role rather than a negative quality inherent in that role. Even in the Vedas, the earth cow is both black and white; she yields good milk as well as bad (*ŚB* 5. 3. 5. 4–7; *AV* 8. 10. 22–29; *JUB* 2. 13. 1–5; cf. above, chap. 2, secs A–B). The shadow aspect of milk emerges in the Ṛg Vedic episode in which Saramā, sent to fetch some cows from the demons, is deluded by the demonic milk they feed her; the cows are finally obtained when Indra causes Saramā to vomit forth the demonic milk and goes himself, driving horses and accompanied by the Soma-drinking sages to confront the demons (*RV* 10. 108. 1–11; O'Flaherty 1975, pp. 71–74). The cows are demonic here, the horses divine; the milk is poisonous, the Soma revivifying.

In later Hindu mythology, too, the earth cow on one occasion holds back her nourishment until she is physically attacked and made to yield her food; she must be forced to change from the evil mother (holding back her fluids) to the good cow from whom all things flow in the form of milk, which she explicitly calls her seed (*Viṣṇu P* 1. 13. 80). The magic wishing-cow is the image of the mother full of milk, a primary psychological symbol of goodness and love. When the ogress Pūtanā offers the infant Kṛṣṇa her breast, smeared with poison instead of milk, Kṛṣṇa kills her, but she goes to heaven; for by offering him her breast—even in a spirit of hatred—she has performed the supreme act of maternal devotion (*Bh P* 10. 6. 1–44). Thus even bad mothers are good in Hinduism; the only bad women are nonmothers. Similarly, even bad cows (and there are some) are good: a cow whose calf had been beaten by a Brahmin vowed to avenge him and assuage her own sorrow; she kicked the Brahmin's son to death and immediately turned from white to black, but she regained her white color (and her purity) after bathing in a sacred river (another Hindu symbol of the milky goddess) (*ŚP* 4. 6. 1–65). The cow cannot remain evil; she is immediately purified, for she *is* purity: she is nonerotic fertility.

Another instance of a destructive cow who is not truly destructive appears in a Tamil tale illustrative of the fact "that in Indian culture semen and milk are regarded as closely kindred substances" (Egnor 1978, p. 69):

> A wishing-cow poured milk onto a Śiva-*liṅga* from her udder. A king tried to shoot her; she killed him, but in doing so she squashed the *liṅga* with her hoof. The *liṅga* was not angry, as her touch was as sweet as a child's kiss, but it was pressed out of shape and remains so to this day in the temple, "its shape that of a melted candle, its color milk-white" (ibid., p. 70).

The mother becomes aggressive only when she is attacked or when her son is in danger, and when she mutilates the phallus, she does so in a way that is acceptable; for her touch must, by definition, be gentle and harmless. In many myths of the cow who kicks the *liṅga*, the *liṅga* is identified with a serpent and the wishing-cow with the goddess herself, whom Śiva embraces in one version. This erotic aspect of the myth becomes even more explicit in another text, in which Śiva appears from the *liṅga* and says, "I receive the scars of horn and hoof with joy akin to that I felt when Umā scarred me with her breasts and bracelets," a reference to a time when Umā embraced a sand *liṅga* to protect it from a flood, leaving the imprint of her nipples and bracelets upon it forever (Shulman 1978, pp. 107–9).[4] The injury is forgiven and even desired; the sentiment here is closely related to that of the love battle and Liebestod.

The good and evil cow is, like the mare, assimilated to the figure of the good and evil woman, though the contrast between the animals remains good cow/evil mare. Cows are often attacked by witches in Indo-European mythology; finding blood in the milk is a sign of the witch's presence, as in the myth of Pūtanā. Blood flows from the *liṅga* in many of the myths of cows attacked/attacking *liṅgas*, and through the identification of the udder with the phallus the cow acts as the counterpart, if not the alter ego, of the mutilated *liṅga*. If this identification is taken literally, it leads to an analysis that identifies the cow herself with the phallic witch in European mythology, though this pattern does not seem relevant to the Indian myths; moreover, it has been suggested that the Indian taboo against aggression toward cows has resulted from the latent significance of the udder as "phallic nipple." This notion seems not only convoluted and far-fetched but superfluous, given the quite convincing socioeconomic and theological reasons for this taboo; to identify the cow solely with the enemy of the witch/mare seems not only simpler but more heuristic than to identify her with the witch as well. The udder of the cow is the acceptable counterpart of the phallus of the stallion, a fertile female equivalent; the phallic behavior of the mare (and witch), on the other hand, is a threatening and unacceptable challenge.

F. The Hindu Bull

Myths of apparently evil cows appear in several texts composed in South India, but these texts often present bulls in an atypical role as well, so that the two clusters of symbolic qualities remain intact, albeit attached to the "wrong" gender of the species. In one such myth a group of wicked Jainas create a demonic cow who attacks Nandi, the bull of Śiva; when Nandi displays his beauty, the cow is overcome by desire, dies, and is transformed into a mountain (*Tiruviḷaiyāṭaṟ Purāṇam* 29. 1–23; cf. Dessigane et al. 1960, pp. 45–46). The cow in this myth is erotic (susceptible to desire), demonic, and dangerous—as the mare usually is; and so she must die. Nandi, on the other hand, is here passive, nondestructive, and divine; indeed, since his horn is described as "milk white," it is he who functions as a cow, his horn (a phallic symbol) replacing the udder.

The udder is usually, however, the counterpart not of the bull's horn but of the stallion's phallus, from which fertilizing seed or Soma flows as milk flows from the breast. The early Aryans (in Iran as well as India) may have drunk bulls' urine as well as that of cows (Alsdorf 1962, p. 64); and it has been suggested that the hallucinogenic properties of the Soma remained potent in the urine of the priest who had drunk the juice and that it thus became the practice to drink the urine of one who had drunk the Soma (Wasson 1968, pp. 25–34, 71–77). In the epic, Indra—the great Vedic stallion and bull—urinates Soma for a sage to drink (*MBh* 14. 54. 12–35), though this Hindu sage of course rejects it (ostensibly because Indra takes the form of an Untouchable hunter in order to present the Soma in as unsavory a form as possible). This rejection reflects the fact that post-Vedic Hindus ceased to drink the urine of the male animal (the bull's urine or the horse's Soma urine) and drank instead the "five products of the cow"—which included milk and urine. Thus, with the decline of the Soma cult and the rise of the cult of the cow, milk replaces Soma/urine/semen and the cow replaces the bull.

This simple formulation is somewhat complicated, however, by the equally simple and unavoidable fact that the bull neither withdraws from the religious world nor, like the mare, assumes negative connotations, as the procrustean model-maker would wish (so that the bull would correspond to the mare as the cow corresponds to the stallion). The bull remains sacred in at least one very important way: he is the vehicle of Śiva, the phallic god who comes to replace Indra. Even in the Ṛg Veda,

Indra complicates matters by being associated not only with the stallion but with the elephant and the bull as well. In one myth of conflict between the old Indra and the *arriviste* Śiva, Indra's elephant fights against Śiva's bull and loses the battle (and his head); to compensate for the lost elephant Śiva gives Indra a bull to be his mount and also promises that Indra will get another elephant when they churn the ocean; however, he does *not* promise Indra the horse, Uccaiḥśravas, who emerges from the ocean at the same time, the animal who is Indra's true original mount (*BDP* 2. 60. 1–108). This story not only reverses the normal Hindu vehicles (Śiva taking the elephant, Indra the bull), but it reverses the actual historical sequence; for Indra bequeathed his mount (the bull) to Śiva, along with other aspects of fertility and phallicism.

Yet the bull of Śiva is never an active part of the ritual; he is passive, the servant of Śiva, the worshiper of Śiva. Though he is sometimes depicted by himself, as at Ellora and Khajuraho, he is also frequently shown in a posture of obsequious adoration.[5] Śiva is the truly sexual, phallic member of this partnership; Nandi (in his semihuman, bull-headed aspect) is stationed at the door of the bedroom to guard against interruptions when Śiva makes love to his wife (*Sk P* 5. 2. 20. 1–25; 6. 70–71; *PP* 6. 282. 20–36; *R* 7. 16. 1–10). Nandi himself has few procreative sexual encounters, for a bull (O'Flaherty 1973, pp. 265, 305–10). The sublimation of the bull in his relationship to Śiva has been well expressed by Alain Daniélou (1964, p. 219): "The bull which wanders about, anxious to find a mate, is taken as the embodiment of the sex impulse. Most living creatures are governed by their instincts; they are ridden over by the bull. . . . But Śiva . . . rides on the bull."

The bull thus comes, like the mare and the post-Vedic stallion, to represent controlled sexuality. Carstairs interprets this fact in terms of the Hindu family situation:

> An interesting aspect of the deification of the cow (which represents the wholly gratifying mother of one's earliest recollection) is the way in which the role of her consort, the bull, is minimised. He is a benevolent nonentity, as is the child's father during his first year of life; and yet as Nandi, the divine bull, this mild and passive figure is always associated with Lord Shiva, the essence of maleness (Carstairs 1958, pp. 162–63).

The clue to the apparent paradox lies in the fact that the association of Nandi with Śiva is one of contrast rather than identity; Nandi is the symbol of virility held in check—either by the ascetic, who controls the sexual impulse (Śiva), or by the mother, who overwhelms and blocks it (the cow). As the meek devotee, Nandi is the consort of Śiva.

Chart 3. Variations in the Myths of Mares and Cows

	Eats	Eaten	Feeds	Kills	Killed	Gives Life	Seduces	Seduced	Chaste	Mortal	Immortal
Irish ritual											
mare		X	(X)		X	(X)		X			X
king	X			X			X			X	
Vedic ritual											
mare									(X)		
king	(X)								X	(X)	
stallion	X	(X)			X	X		X			X
queen			X	(X)			X			X	
Vedic myth											
mare	X					X		X			X
king (Vivasvant)					X					X	(Vedic)
stallion		X					X				X
queen (Saraṇyū)				X						X	(Purāṇic)
Hindu myth and ritual											
mare	X			X			X				X
cow		Not to be eaten	X		Not to be killed	X			X	X	
Tantric ritual											
mare	(X)	X	(X)			X	X				X
cow	X			X					X	X	

G. Sun Stallions and Moon Mares

In the Indo-European cycle of the mare, several sets of parallel models are at work, as we have seen—models in which significant roles are played by stallions, mares, and bulls but not by cows. In Hinduism, too, the cow is often omitted from the foursome in myths and rituals of erotic behaviour, in which the remaining three form a triad (with the bull in a sometimes ambivalent role). Here, too, several models interact, some derived from Indo-European patterns and some appearing in reaction to those patterns (see chart 3).

In one Hindu model, the stallion, symbolic of the sun and the day, is contrasted with the mare, symbolic of the moon and the night; both are associated with the loss and restoration of power. In another model, the stallion, symbolic of the sun, is contrasted with the bull, symbolic of the moon (often expressed through the imagery of the "horned" moon); thus Śiva, who rides on Nandi, wears the moon in his hair, while Viṣṇu, the solar god, appears as Hayagrīva, the horse-headed, and as Kalki, the centaur. The stallion is the pivot: as a male equine he is contrasted with an equine female or a bovine male.

A similar contrast may be seen in the cult of the god Khaṇḍobā in Mahārāṣṭra; his worship culminates on the day when sun and moon meet in a union that is by implication sexual (Stanley 1977, pp. 36, 42). (In classical Hinduism the moon and the sun are both masculine. This is an exception to the prevalent Indo-European habit of making the moon feminine.[6] In Maharaṣṭra, the moon is feminine in the usual Indo-European manner.)

The sun and moon as symbols of constant male and inconstant female occur in esoteric Indian symbolism: in the Upaniṣads, the path to the sun is release, while the path to the moon is rebirth (*BAU* 6. 2. 15–16; cf. *Praśna U* 1. 5). In Tantrism, both models appear: the interior androgynization of the yogi is expressed in terms of the union of male sun and female moon (Piṅgala and Iḷā) (Eliade 1958, pp. 236–39),[7] but it is also said that the moon in the head is the cool semen, while the devouring fire in the stomach is the red female sun (menstrual blood); the thunderbolt phallus (*vajra*) is white, while the vagina is a red lotus (S. B. Dasgupta 1946). This symbolism is made explicit in one Tantric text:

> The clever Yogi first of all, with great care, kindles the fire of the penis, after that, introduces it into the female organ of generation and then, according to the rules, draws out the female flux and absorbs it into his own body. . . . The male semen represents the moon, the female flux represents the sun, therefore the Yogi with

> great care must combine the sun and moon in his own body (Roy 1910, pp. 63–64, citing the *Śiva Saṃhitā*).

The Vedic and Purāṇic pattern (male fire in female water) outweighs the Vedāntic pattern (female fire and male water, heated blood and cool semen) in the first part of the text, and so the penis is a fire; but in the second half of the text, the second model prevails, and the semen is the moon, Soma, as in most post-Vedic texts.

In present-day South India, where women are thought to have a kind of white seed of their own, the sun is masculine and the moon feminine:

> T. regards coolness as a female quality, and heat as a male quality. The two are united in the linga and the yoni. The linga rises up (*ōnkum*) like a flame; the yoni that encircles it spreads out (*parakkum*) like water. The sun, *katiravan*, is male; the moon, *nilavu*, whose rays are cool, is female. So cool rain is like milk (Egnor 1978, p. 39).

As a result of a similar chain of associations, rain was likened to male semen in the Ṛg Veda (see above, chap. 2, sec. A); here rain is likened to female milk.

The fact that in some situations the sun is personified as male and the moon is female, while at other times the reverse is true—the sun is female, the moon male—is yet another example of the simultaneous existence of contrasting metaphoric models. In the Brāhmaṇas, it is said that Soma is a male, Sūryā is a female, and together they form a couple (*RB* 1. 3. 3. 2). However, Indra (who is both bull and stallion) is identified with the sun; the moon, identified with the demon Vṛtra, is devoured by the sun (*ŚB* 1. 6. 4. 12–13). The god devours the demon, and both participants in the drama are male. However, in a late commentary on the Ṛg Vedic myth of Dadhyañc (see above, chap. 7, sec. C), the sun, though still explicitly identified with Indra, is said to be a cow (Sāyaṇa on *RV* 1. 84. 15; see also O'Flaherty 1975, pp. 56–60). In the *Mahābhārata*, both moon and sun are masculine, but they appear in a context that has implications of sexuality: they are in conjunction at the time of Skanda's birth (*MBh* 3. 213–16). This text also invokes the double model of fire and water as, respectively, male and female and then as female and male. Finally, in this text the sun is, like the moon, devoured.

In the cult of Khaṇḍobā, where the male sun and female moon unite, another interesting shift takes place: "[Khaṇḍobā's] vehicle, the horse, is regarded as an *avatār* of Śiva's bull Nandi" (Stanley 1977, p. 32). When the bull is the god's vehicle and is closely identified with the god in a role with strong sexual overtones, he reverts to his more fertile counterpart; the cult of the stallion is brought back out of the past. Moreover, because Khaṇḍobā represents both sun and moon (who unite in an interior androgynization within him), his mount is both stallion and bull.

H. Stallions, Mares, and Bulls

The triad of stallion, mare, and bull is used in the *Kāmasūtra* (2. 1) to symbolize men and women with various sexual dimensions (see chart 4). In fact, five different animals are used to express three levels in each of the sexes: in ascending order of size, men are hares, bulls, and stallions,

Chart 4. Sexual Symbolism of Animals in the *Kāmasūtra*

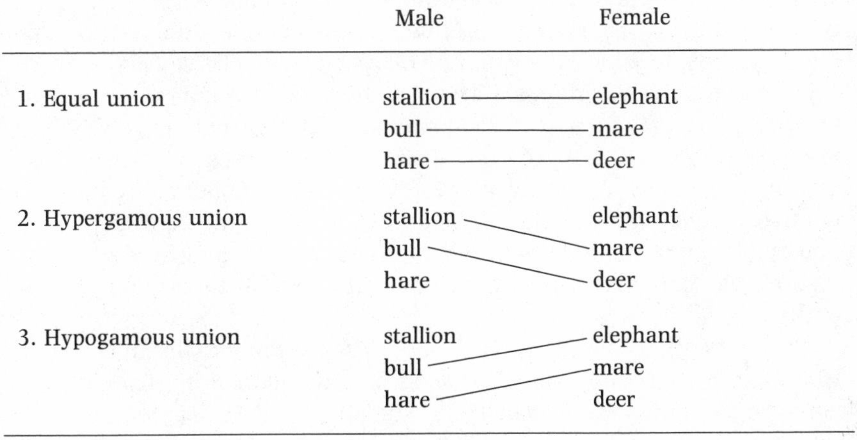
Male
Female
1. Equal union
stallion
elephant
bull
mare
hare
deer
2. Hypergamous union
stallion
elephant
bull
mare
hare
deer
3. Hypogamous union
stallion
elephant
bull
mare
hare
deer

while women are deer, mares, and elephants. It is certainly significant that the horse is the only animal to appear in both lists and that stallion and mare are not regarded as a balanced pair; that is, a man who is of the "horse" type is the equal of a woman who is of the "elephant" type, while a woman who is a mare is the equal of a man who is a bull. This last pair is highly relevant to our inquiry, for it supports the argument that mare and bull are paired in Hindu thought and that the bull has ceased to be a virile animal in comparison with the stallion. Moreover, it should be noted that in both of the other "equal" pairs the man is in fact ludicrously smaller than the woman: a male hare is paired with a female deer, a stallion with a female elephant. (This disparity occurs in related animal images used to express the dangerous imbalance of power between a man and a woman and the necessity to control that imbalance. The Tamils say that a man must force a woman to use her *śakti* as he commands, like a mahout controlling a strong elephant; a woman has so much more *śakti* than a man that she is like an elephant compared with an ant [S. Daniel 1978, pp. 5–6]. In both metaphors, the woman is the elephant cow, the largest female.) In the *Kāmasūtra*, in the middle pair alone (mare and bull) the actual sizes are reversed, male being larger than female, and one might speculate that this is because the mare is felt to be far larger in her sexual dimensions than the bull is in his. Moreover, it is significant that this *is* the middle pair—the average, the model for most human pairings.

Finally, the *Kāmasūtra* regards "equal" unions (male hare and female deer, or doe; bull and mare; stallion and elephant cow) to be the best, and it regards "high" unions, in which the male is larger than the woman by one degree (stallion and mare, bull and doe)—i.e., hypergamous unions, preferred in intercaste marriages—to be better than "low" unions, in which the woman is larger by one degree (elephant cow and bull, mare and male hare)—i.e., hypogamous unions, forbidden in most intercaste marriages. The preference for high unions may be interpreted to mean that men and women are more "equal" when the man comes from a higher category, a belief that is supported by the relative equality in *actual* size of the animals in these theoretically "unequal" pairs (stallion and mare, bull and doe), as compared with the theoretically equal but actually unequal pairs used as the defining terms of the model.

Of the six animals in the group, only three are of sexual significance in Hindu mythology: the bull, the stallion, and the mare. The elephant plays no straightforward sexual role. Though the mythology of Gaṇeśa has sexual overtones, some of which we have encountered, these are highly ambivalent, and Gaṇeśa is usually said to be chaste, in contrast with his phallic father (Leach 1962, pp. 81–102). The Tantric sect of Ucchiṣṭa Gāṇapatyas is accused of worshiping an image of Gaṇeśa in which the tip of his trunk nuzzles the vagina of his consort (*Saṅkaradigvijaya*, chap. 17), and this equation of the trunk with a phallus merely makes explicit what is implicit in other aspects of the mythology; but the passage in question owes more of its sexuality to the Tantras' preoccupations than to the character of Gaṇeśa or the symbolism of the elephant.

The elephant, particularly the white elephant (in contrast with Gaṇeśa, whose elephant head is red), serves as a symbol of royalty, as a symbol of the Buddha, and as an animal churned from the ocean, together with the white horse and white cow. It is never sacrificed, though it is a symbol of fertility (it pours water on the head of Lakṣmī in a cloud symbolism like that of bulls and horses in the Ṛg Veda), and in this the elephant resembles the bull: it is fertile (for women touch the statue of Nandi when they want to have male children) but not erotic. The female deer is a common metaphor for a beautiful woman and hence has certain erotic connotations, but these are poetic rather than mythological; and the rabbit does not (as in Western civilization) symbolize sexuality or fecundity but rather cleverness and fragility. These three animals, therefore—elephant, hare, and female deer—are of very little sexual significance in contrast with the bull, stallion, and mare.

I. The Return of the Mare Goddess and the Demise of the Mare

The *Kāmasūtra* triad—bull, stallion, and mare—together with their natural complement, the cow, form a quartet of animals that are charismatic symbols of power, divine power as well as erotic and fertile power. In the course of changes in the cultural context, Indian civilization called up different theriomorphic images from this iconographic storehouse to express changing concepts of sexual and ritual attitudes to women; in the process, certain recombinations and inversions took place. Eventually the mare ceased to be worshiped, though she remained a powerful religious symbol. The cow, by contrast, became enshrined as the quintessential sacred animal, the fertile mother who feeds husband and children. Though Indian cows (in myth and reality) are hardly the docile Elsies that we associate with the word "cow," they are indeed docile in comparison with mares (particularly mares in heat, who are unpredictable and treacherous creatures). The cow is beneficent and sacred, honored and protected.

The rise in the cult of the cow can hardly be blamed for the demise of the mare (for the mare also becomes a negative figure in other Indo-European cultures, where cows are not so highly regarded), but it must have hastened the process and exacerbated it; and the cow, in her turn, must have benefited from the surplus of female divinity, now going to waste. Nevertheless, the cow is not divine; she is not a goddess in Hindu India. Quite the contrary: she is the image of the mortal woman with the immortal man, for she is the very model of the Hindu wife who regards her husband as a god, as the Hindu lawbooks remind us *ad nauseam*. Thus Manu says, "Though he may have no good qualities or virtue, and seek pleasure (elsewhere), yet a husband must be constantly worshiped as a god by a faithful wife" (Manu 5. 154). The immortal male must be accepted despite his all-too-human failings, including his rejection of her; so too, as we shall see, the immortal goddess must ultimately be accepted in this way. But the primary image of the cow is that of the mortal woman to whom her husband is a god.

That Indians "worship" cows and "worship" their mothers has become a cliché, but the statement is true only in the most debased and fatuous sense of the word "worship." Most Indians do not actually dedicate temples to cows or (heaven forfend) sacrifice goats to cows. They do, however, worship and offer blood sacrifice to a mother—but she is hardly the cow mother. She is the mare mother.

The actual image of the mare plays only a vestigial role in contemporary Hinduism, and it is not hard to see why this should be so. Theriomorphic symbols may lose their valence when the animals themselves lose their charisma. If there is a continuity in the cult, the symbol may survive, albeit in a distorted form; but if there is a discontinuity, as there is in the case of the mare, who enjoyed a period of general worship followed by a long period of disgrace and disrepute, the new cult may well find no use for a symbol emptied of its cultural and practical essence. When the animal actually becomes extinct, the symbol may survive; lions continued to be powerful symbols in Greece after they were extinct, and dragons and unicorns were *always* extinct. But dragons are mythical snakes, and unicorns are mythical horses/deer/goats; composite animals are thus never purely mythical. Moreover, the image of an extinct animal may survive in a weakened form; thus the Indian goddess who rides on a lion is nowadays, when lions are virtually extinct in India, generally depicted on a tiger or on a big pussycat, obviously drawn by someone who has never seen a lion.

In any case, the myth seems to survive better in the complete *absence* of the animal than in the presence of a mere shadow of the beast. Horses do not thrive in India; the humid heat does not suit them, their hooves soften and break, and there is no decent pasturage. As a result, to maintain the supply, horses had to be imported at an astronomical rate throughout Indian history, from Parthia and Bactria at first, later from Persia and Arabia (Leshnik 1978). But Indians are notoriously poor horse-masters, often from the highest of religious motives.[8] The king's stallions were fed enormous quantities of melted butter, symbolically the perfect food for a horse—redolent of semen and power and Vedic oblations and the sun—but hardly designed for his delicate digestion. The myth has thus led to the downfall of the animal and hence to the demise of the model for the theriomorphic symbol of the myth. The pathetic creatures that one encounters today, pulling carts, could not inspire worship; vanished are the sinuous power and fiery brilliance that suggest the presence of god. The secular symbolism of the animal has survived, however, in a negative way, on the two subdivine levels, royal and domestic. The positive royal associations of the ancient mare are meaningless or even pejorative for the Tantric and village devotees who form the backbone of the contemporary cult of the Goddess; and these negative royal connotations could only have been reinforced by the activities of the British cavalry in India for two centuries. Moreover, to the extent that the mare retained her symbolic power on the domestic level, it was a negative power, with connotations of voracious sexuality and destruction, which could only serve to preclude the use of the symbol in the now respectable cult of the Goddess.

There are some exceptions, some instances of the positive symbolism of the horse in contemporary India. In Rajasthan (where the royal equestrian image has native meaning and power as a symbol of the courageous Rajputs), horses made of brass or clay or elaborately embroidered cloth adorn many Indian homes, but these are secular symbols. The tribal Bhils use clay representations of horses as votive objects and place clay images of horse and rider under village trees; this may be a survival of Central Asian customs or an imitation of Rajputs. In South India, clay horses are the mounts of the divinity Aiyanar (Leshnik, 1978). Viṣṇu's mount at the Alagarkoil temple near Madurai is a cult figure,[9] as is the mount of Khaṇḍobā. Various horse cults have been attested in western India: clay horses are worshiped on the sixth day after a child is born, horses are sprinkled with the blood of sacrificed sheep, and a stone horse is worshiped at the opening of the rainy season (Crooke 1861, 2:204–8). Cautionary tales enforcing the taboo against consuming horseflesh are also known: a king's horse died, and the sweepers who were meant to bury it prepared to eat it, cutting off one leg to give to the king's priest; when their deception was discovered, the patron saint of the sweepers revived the dead horse, but he stood on only three legs; the priest was executed, and the horse then died too (ibid., p. 206). The mutilation of the horse's leg and his revival are classical elements reflected in this local tale, as is the ancient contrast between the low-caste executioner and the high priest.

These are all cults centering on male horses, however; sacred mares are extremely rare in all of Indian folklore. Indeed, one exceptional tale of this sort is striking in its atavistic resonances, as Crooke (who told the story) himself noted:

> Gūga had no children, and lamenting this to his guardian deity, he received from him two barley-corns, one of which he gave to his wife and the other to his famous mare, which gave birth to his charger, hence called Javādiyā or "barley-born." We find this wonderful mare through the whole range of folk-lore, but the best

> parallel to her is the famous mare of Gwri of the golden hair, and Setanta in the Celtic tale (ibid., 1:212).

"Gwri of the golden hair" is the name of the son born to Rhiannon and Pwyll, and Setanta is the early form of Cuchúllain born to Deichtíre and Cónchobor. The parallel human and equine maternity, together with the theme of impregnation by mouth, identifies this as a remarkably persistent survival of the Indo-European myth.

In general, however, the ancient cultural predilection for the stallion still prevails in India. Goddesses have the heads of various animals (Narasiṃhī the head of a lion, Kālī the head of a jackal), but not of mares.[10] There may still be a vestige of the sacred mare in the South Indian image of the fiery horse in the water, an image that "has become uncannily one with the powers of Aiyanar and also with the eery, fatal Seven Virgins" (Kramrisch 1968, p. 57). These mysterious goddesses are little understood and of minor importance in comparison with the temple worship of the Goddess in other forms. Here there is a significant discontinuity between "Great" and "Little" traditions of worship.

J. Currents of Power: The Two-Way Tantric Flow

Despite the decline in her worship, the mare is present everywhere, in roadside shrines and great temple cities, holding sway over most of India, among villagers as well as kings. For she has returned in spirit, though not in hippomorphic form. She has returned as the Tantric Goddess, whose presence is invoked by her human male worshipper, whom she invigorates with her substance through ritual intercourse (just as the cow gives her fluid, milk, and the ancient mare gave her own broth) instead of stealing his substance from him. By reversing the flow of the fluids, reinvoking the Vedic image of the flow of seed from woman to man (see above, chap. 2, sec. A, and chap. 6, sec. B), Tantrism reverses the flow of power. The woman is not merely a mortal, however, but a visualization of the Goddess herself, potentially an even greater source of danger. Not so; for the split is reversed even as the fluids are: the erotic goddess is a source of power, the fertile woman a danger expressly shunned by the Tantric philosophy that elevates nonmarital, nonfertile love (*parakīyā*) above conventional married love (*svakīyā*) (Dimock 1966, pp. 202–17). The erotic woman is the immortal whose power flows down to the man, while the fertile woman is the mortal who drains his fluids away. In this world view, mares are safe and cows dangerous, though these ideas are not expressed theriomorphically. Normal life is living death; ritual life, by inverting normal sexual processes, procures immortality (Eliade 1958). The Goddess bestows her immortality upon her mortal consort by uniting with him in the ritual.

This Tantric ritual functions in many ways as a simple inversion of classical Indian ideas about sexuality. For in orthodox Hinduism, as we saw in chapter 3, it is dangerous to have contact with someone more powerful than oneself; there is danger in the contact of a mortal with an immortal. There is also danger for a man in sexual contact with a woman, a theme I sought to demonstrate in chapter 2. To have sexual contact with an immortal woman thus places a man in double jeopardy; the flow of power from the woman to the man is accompanied by a simultaneous flow of life (fluid) from the man to the woman. This is the negative model of the mare goddess and her mortal consort, the degraded symbol of the hierogamy.

There is, however, another way of looking at the flow of power:

> Power is released at the moment of the sexual union of a god and a goddess, and . . . some of the power thus released becomes available to the devotees of the god. . . . When any two things are joined (god and goddess, god and devotee, sun and moon, human and ghost, etc.) by copulation, bathing, eating, or any other penetrating intercourse, some of their substances—and thus some of their powers—are loosened and transferred between them. . . . For the sun and moon, powerful but unmatched beings, to conjoin bodies is ambivalent, resulting in the loosening of both power-giving and polluting power-substance; hence the heightening of accessibility of both power and pollution (Stanley 1977, pp. 41–42).

In the Tantric view, power flows from the woman to the man, *especially* when she is more powerful than he, though pollution (danger) may also be released at the same time. This reversal is expressed through the concept of female semen transferred from the woman to the man, the reverse of the normal draining from man to woman. For the Tantric seeks sexual contact with the Goddess, and in this he revives the stance of the hypothetical proto-Indo-European worshiper of the fully accepted, integrated mare goddess. Clearly the major flow of power will be between the two partners in the sexual ritual, but this ritual (like the ancient Irish rite of the mare and the king) takes place in front of other people, and these onlookers also participate in the flow of powers. The devotees of the Goddess present at this union experience the "heightening of accessibility of both power and pollution" that is characteristic of the holy, of the *mysterium fascinans et tremendum*.

The concept of a transfer of personal substance between god and devotee, resulting in an exchange of both power and pollution, is also at work in the Vedic myth of Indra, who transfers to his worshipers, particularly to his female worshipers (O'Flaherty 1976, pp. 146–59), both pollution (the defilement of the sin of having killed a Brahmin) and power (the same power of rejuvenation and sexual procreation that looms so large in the mare myths). In this model, both power and pollution flow from above, a pattern that characterizes the union of mare goddess with human consort.

Sexual contact with a male god results in the increase of the power of the woman; here there is no conflict. Leda takes on the power of Zeus—an ambivalent power, as Yeats points out ("A shudder in the loins engenders there / The broken wall, the burning roof and tower / And Agamemnon dead"). The queen takes on the fertile powers of the stallion. Power flows from above: thus the worshipers of Kṛṣṇa become women in order to let his power flow into them. This power is also transferred by eating ("or any other penetrating intercourse"): the worshiper eats the *prasāda*, the eucharistic substance of the god, through which the body of the god becomes part of the body of the worshiper.

But sexual intercourse with a goddess invokes both models at once: power from above, danger from the woman. There is no significant conflict when the partners are equal, for then there is very little, if any, flow; perhaps this is one reason why, in the ancient ceremony of the mare, it was essential that her consort be a king, a divine figure in his own right. On the other hand, when the mare's consort is a mere commoner, as he is in much of the Indian and later Indo-European material, problems arise. The contact can still be productive; the ancient myth of the white mare goddess shows that power can indeed flow from a higher female without ill consequences; but it can also be dangerous.

K. Eat or Ye Shall be Eaten

We have seen from the myth of Dionysus and Pentheus, as well as from the post-Vedic and Hindu myth of the mare, that the woman is the eater and the man is eaten; the woman is the mare who devours her consort. In the Indo-European ritual of the sacrifice of the mare, however, it was the reverse: the female is eaten and the male is fed (a pattern that remains in the Vedic ritual, too); the woman is the cow who feeds.

The first pattern may be related to simple physiological processes; for a woman, intercourse involves taking something into the body as one takes food (hence the myth of impregnation by mouth, the swallowing of the seed), whereas for a man it is the reverse (a possible contributing factor to the earth-diver myth of male procreation by defecation) This first pattern is thus the model of the draining of fluids, and hence of power, from male to female.

The second pattern also has a physiological basis: the woman's body provides food in the form of milk from the breast; this is her "good" creation. The two roles are clearly opposed: the woman devours her husband and feeds her son. This is the world of nature. In mythology, the alter ego of the cow/mother is the mare who devours both son and husband (often the same hapless male), and in contemporary images of society under Tantric influence the wife feeds both husband and son.

For when the Goddess is regarded as a positive figure, a source of power, she ceases to devour and begins to feed—but without turning into a mere cow. This pattern is a female version of the positive eucharistic model of the myth of Dionysus: to dismember and eat the mare is to absorb the deity's power and to accept one's sexual nature. This sexuality is not pure license, however; the Tantric rituals were not orgies, nor were the rites of Dionysus. For the power of the Goddess in these myths and rituals rests upon the fact that she is fully integrated; she is both mare and cow. We have seen the mare nature of the maenads; Otto points out that they are also cows:

> There is nothing so foreign to the orgiastic dancers of the god as unrestrained erotic sensuality. . . . The modesty of the women in ecstasy is explicitly emphasized in the face of the malicious stories told about them. . . . True womanliness reveals itself in the slighter importance of sexual desire, which must, of necessity, vanish before the eternal emotion of a mother's care and concern. These women are mothers and nurses. How eloquent the myth is concerning their infants! In the forests they suckle the young animals with their mothers' milk. On vase paintings one sees nymphs and maenads taking care of male children (W. Otto 1965, pp. 177–78).

Otto is perhaps too adamant in denying the mare nature of the maenads, but he is certainly right about their bovinity. The Dionysian accepts all the fluids that flow from the god and goddess; the wine, of course, is the ritual intoxicant (like Soma in India), to which are assimilated the physiological fluids of milk and female seed, female power. In the Tantric ceremony, too, the man takes the woman's seed and accepts the flow of power from the Goddess.

The positive theology of ingesting the deity or having fructifying contact with the deity interacts with the negative theology of being eaten by the deity or being sexually drained by contact with the deity. Either pattern can apply to either male or female divinities, though the transition is most dramatic in the case of the Goddess because of the negative valence placed on the feminine in most Indo-European contexts. At first, the mare is mutilated: Viśpalā loses her leg; the Irish mare is chopped up in the cauldron. The immortal mare dies so that the mortal king may live; the ultimate power transferred from her to him is the power of immortality.

But then, in the Pales festival, a stallion is mutilated, and the Vedic stallion is castrated; the mantle of immortality now passes from a male divinity to a human king. Human sacrifice of a male victim (usually royal) may have formed a bridge between the two animal sacrifices (equine female, human male, equine male) or, more logically but not necessarily more true in history, it may have followed them both (equine female, equine male, human male). Since the male victim, like the stallion, could represent a god, one still has two basic patterns of variation on each of the many levels of the myth: equine/human, immortal/mortal, male/female, killed/killing, being eaten/eating, being accepted/being denied.

L. Rebirth from the Devouring Goddess

The threat of being devoured by the Goddess is tempered, however, by the force of another compelling line of mythology and theology, one that suggests that the way to obtain immortality is not (or not only) by devouring the deity but by allowing oneself to be devoured by the deity. This concept is foreshadowed in the Vedas and Upaniṣads in the concept of a cycle in which the eater is eaten, and in another in which god is both the food of the universe and the eater par excellence. The idea of a cycle of mutual devouring persists in the Āyurvedic scheme of medicine, in which a patient is made to eat the meat of the eaters of meat, thus, by participating in the circulation of body fluids (*rasas*) in the universe, promoting it in the microcosm of his own body. Here it is interesting to note that *rasa* usually denotes a soup or medicinal decoction made by boiling meat to make a broth.[11] Broth is the form in which the mare is eaten in the ancient Irish ritual, and the broth made from a meat-eater (the mare who eats the stallion) is particularly potent in the logic of this scheme.

In the Brāhmaṇas, the mythology of rebirth through being devoured emerges clearly (cf. *ŚB* 2. 6. 1–5; *JB* 2. 156). There it is said that the god Indra obtained Soma, the elixir of immortality, by being devoured by the demon Śuṣṇa, who kept the elixir in his mouth (*KS* 37. 14; Dange 1969, pp. 157–237; O'Flaherty 1975, p. 281). The demon swallows the god and brings him back to life, thus rendering him immortal (as does the elixir). This pattern is replicated in three epic and Purāṇic myths revolving around Śukra, the priest of the demons (O'Flaherty 1976, pp. 118–22).

1. Śukra had the power of reviving the demons who fell in the battle between the gods and the demons. To prevent him from using this power, Śiva swallowed Śukra; but, when praised by Śukra, Śiva released him, after giving him an epiphany of the universe within his belly. Because he emitted Śukra through his penis, Śukra was from then on called Śukra, "semen." When Śukra emerged, Śiva still wished to harm him, but Devī, the Goddess, interceded, pointing out that, since he had come out of Śiva's phallus, Śukra was now not only an immortal but *her son*. Śiva then let Śukra go (*MBh* 12. 278. 1–38).

2. Śukra continued to use his mantra of immortality to revive all the demons who fell during the battle. Śiva, knowing that Śukra could not be killed (perhaps because he, Śiva, had once swallowed him), created a horrible woman with a mouth like a great cavern, with teeth and eyes in her vagina. At Śiva's command, she grabbed Śukra and stripped him and embraced him, and she kept him inside her until the battle was over (*PP* 6. 18. 82–90).

3. The gods sent Kaca, the son of the priest of the gods, to obtain the secret of immortality from Śukra. Śukra swallowed Kaca unknowingly: the other demons had killed Kaca, pulverized him, and mixed him in wine, which they fed to Śukra. When he found out what had happened, Śukra emitted Kaca at the intercession of his daughter, who was in love with Kaca; Śukra first taught Kaca the mantra of immortality and then called him forth from his own stomach; Kaca burst forth, killing Śukra, and immediately revived him again with the mantra. Kaca then refused to marry Śukra's daughter, as she wished, for he argued that, by dwelling in Śukra's belly, he had become the son of Śukra and could hardly marry Śukra's daughter, his own sister (*MBh* 1. 71–72).

In all of these episodes, the act of devouring is performed as an act of aggression, but the person who is devoured becomes immortal. He is reborn as the child of the gods, the son of the terrible mother. These myths may be seen as symbols of initiation and of the rebirth implicit in violent, death-mimicking initiation. Although a god or demon or demoness (it matters little which) is usually the devourer, it is in each case a goddess who intercedes and procures immortality for the initiate. In the second instance, though the swallower is a textbook image of the *vagina dentata*, she nevertheless prevents Śukra from being injured; in effect, she brings him back to life, out of her womb, after the battle. So too, though the daughter of Śukra behaves like a mare, subjecting Kaca to an incestuous sexual assault, she saves his life—and is then denied by him, as the mare so often is. Elsewhere it is said that when Śukra and Śiva were in competition, each invoked the same goddess—but she gave Śukra the secret mantra of immortality (*Sk P* 6. 1. 149). The classical competition between son and father here has a happy ending: the devouring mother blesses her son.

It would appear, therefore, that the Hindus retained a memory of a myth in which being devoured by the mare goddess was a source of religious rebirth. Although in androcentric texts it was a male god—a stallion (for both Śiva and Śukra are powerful yogis)—who was said to do the swallowing, it was still a goddess who made the initiate immortal—a goddess who reappears in one variant of the myth as the actual devourer. Indeed, whereas in the pejorative mare myths the evil goddess simply devours her son, in these texts, perhaps under Tantric, devotional, and Śāktic influence, the devotee *becomes* her son after she devours him—and thus becomes safe from her sexual assaults, as Kaca points out. When a male god swallows the devotee, he imitates the Goddess by becoming pregnant, with the child growing in his belly; he then reverts to male status and emits the "child" through his phallus, like seed. This "seed," however, is swallowed by the god in imitation of the mare; it is thus a feminine rather than a masculine form of procreation.

In this context, the many Hindu myths of male pregnancy may be seen as instances in which a god, in imitation of a goddess, gives rebirth to the initiate by swallowing and disgorging him. Many male gods do in fact swallow their devotees; Tamil devotional poetry speaks of the devotee's desire to drink Kṛṣṇa and bathe in him (as the Irish king drank and bathed in the mare) but speaks also of the desire to be consumed, eaten by god (*Tiruvāymoli* 2. 3. 9 and 10. 7. 3; Yocum 1979, p. 21). This process, which A. K. Ramanujan has called "mutual cannibalism," underlies the most well-known and well-loved cycle of the poems of the Tamil saint Nammāḻvār (9. 6. 1–10), in which the god devours the devotee who simultaneously realizes the god inside him. The same kind of *bhakti* may be seen in the episode in which Kṛṣṇa's mother, after feeding him her milk, sees within his mouth the whole world that he has swallowed, along with her milk, along with her (*Bh P* 10. 8. 21–45).

The link between swallowing semen and swallowing Soma is implicit in the Vedic myths of Indra and becomes explicit in the myths of Śukra, who is actually called "semen" as a result of being swallowed and ejaculated by a male god. This concept reemerges in Tantrism, where the seed is called *amṛta*, the elixir of immortality. Tantric ritual holds interesting implications for the development of new attitudes to the devoured and devouring goddess; for Tantrism retains the ancient yogic concept of the man's need to retain his semen but adds to it the even more ancient concept of his rejuvenation through consuming the woman's seed.

Some Tantric texts apparently allow the man to emit his seed, but only in order to draw it back again into his body. One text even seems to specify that he should emit it into the mouth of the woman, but again it is eventually restored to him: the semen is passed back and forth from the mouth of the woman to the mouth of the man and is then placed in a consecrated vessel, whence finally it is eaten by both (Eliade 1971, p. 101).[12] One Tibetan Tantric text offers several variations on this theme. First the male adept emits from his mouth a stream of sacred syllables; then he visualizes the goddess before him, "the diamond demoness"; he then visualizes himself as the god and visualizes the Mother on his lap. The white *vajra* (phallus) of the Father unites with the red lotus (vagina) of the Mother; then the deities enter into union in the sky and enter the male adept through his mouth or between his eyebrows; they descend, pass through his *vajra*, and fall and mix into the lotus of the Mother. Then the mantra goes "upward from mouth to mouth" (i.e., from the woman's mouth back to the man's). This is regarded as the forward recitation of the mantra; but "if the direction is reversed, upward through the diamond path and into the mouth of the goddess, this is the fierce recitation; & I practice each of these in turn." This reverse direction has the seed-mantra traveling up the spine, out of the mouth of the man into the mouth of the woman, down into her womb and into his *vajra*, up through his spine, and so forth as the cycle continues and is continually reversed (Beyer 1974, pp. 140–53).[13]

Several images from our classical corpus are reflected in this esoteric episode. The fluid that circulates is primarily mantra; hence its primary locus is the mouth. It is also the substance of deity, which enters through either the top of the head, the spot between the eybrows, or the mouth; these are also the loci of semen in yogic tradition. The process of circulation begins with the entrance of the deities into the mouth of the adept; this is the devouring of the goddess (and the god). It ends, if a cycle can be said to end, when the power that has left the body of the adept comes back into him through his mouth, where it entered in the first place; that is, he again devours the seed of the goddess, this time directly from his female partner. Thus he behaves like the *aśvamedha* stallion who swallows his own seed, for the ritual of swallowing seed forms a transitional link between rituals of taking in fluid (the Indo-European mare's or the Tantric deity's) and giving fluids (the Vedic stallion's or, again, the Tantric deity's). The reverse process is called "the fierce recitation." Here the seed-mantra goes directly into the mouth of the woman (the dangerous process of being devoured by the mare). It does not stop here, however, but returns to the man through the Tantric process of sexual reversal: the drawing of the fluid from the woman's vagina into the man's penis. This reversal makes the "fierce" process of being devoured by the woman safe once again; there is no ultimate loss of fluid. Indeed, by positing an endless cycle, the system becomes eternally sealed; there can *be* no loss, only the constant infusion of deity. Thus the fear of sexual death is overcome, as the fear of death in general is overcome through the concept of rebirth. Steady decline and loss is replaced by a self-renewing cycle. In this way the Tantric ritual allows the adept to gain immortality by being devoured by the goddess as well as by devouring her.

Much of the symbolism of the Tantric ritual is designed to replace conventional ideas of rebirth (through progeny) with esoteric concepts of immortality (through the denial of progeny). This is implicit in the statement that the man does not give his seed (as he would to procreate) but draws it back and, with it, takes in the woman's seed (a process that does not impregnate him). This procedure is first documented in the Upaniṣads (*BAU* 6. 4. 4 and 6. 4. 10; see also O'Flaherty 1979, chap. 1), the *locus classicus* for both misogyny and *mokṣa* in ancient India. In the Tantric ceremony, one of the five essential ingredients is *mudrā*, parched grain. In contrast with sprouting rice—which is the root metaphor for the processes of both embryology and karmic rebirth (O'Flaherty 1979, chap. 1), symbolic (as we have seen) of semen, Vedic fertility, and *saṃsāra*—parched grain is symbolic of retained semen, eroticism, Vedāntic/Tantric detachment, and *mokṣa* or immortality.

In many Tantric rituals, the participants eat both male and female seed, or male seed and female menstrual blood, which are regarded as the site of both male and female divinities. We have seen this in Tibetan texts of a highly esoteric nature; yet Carstairs also encountered it in the folk beliefs of the Rajasthani villagers with whom he lived:

> It was believed that the deity to whom their devotions were addressed made itself manifest in the climax of the sexual act [in the ritual], and in the "male and female semen," of which the celebrants jointly partook at the end of the ceremony: this was their prashad (Carstairs 1958, p. 103; cf. above, chap 2, sec. B).

That this is a eucharist is explicit; it is even identified as such by the word used for the same procedure in orthodox temple Hinduism:

prasāda. For *prasāda* itself is a cyclic form of feeding and eating: the worshiper feeds the god something that he has sanctified and that is symbolic of his offering of himself, a part of his coded substance; the god eats this and returns the "rest," now imbued with the god's substance, to the worshiper, who eats it.

A closely related use of the term *prasāda* may be seen in the statement made by a Bengali woman who regarded herself as the Sādhikā (female adept) in a Tantric cult; she spoke of her partner's expectations of what would happen "if his Guru, after making a 'Prasadi' of me (that is, tasting me in a divinised capacity), recommended me to him" (Bhattcherjee 1977, p. 391). In the course of this process (which seems to have amounted to nothing more nor less than *coitus reservatus*), the woman steadied her breathing and that of her partner by reciting a rhythmic Bengali verse about "going and then still not going, eating and then not eating, and not eating despite food being offered" (ibid., p. 392). In this context, apparently, the sexual act itself—explicitly said to avoid the loss of sexual fluids by either partner—is regarded as a kind of *prasāda* in which food is *not* eaten.

The use of the term *prasāda* by both non-Tantric villagers and Tantric adepts to describe a Tantric ritual raises a point similar to the one that we encountered in the context of yogic ideas about fluid retention (see above, chap. 2, sec. B): How esoteric are these esoteric doctrines? Clearly, Tantrism is not *practiced* by any significant proportion of Hindus. Though one field worker claims to have interviewed forty-eight "Sadhikas" or women participants in Tantric sexual rituals (ibid., p. 387), most of the "rituals" described in his report are demonstrations of techniques (and terminologies) straight out of the *Kāmasūtra*; far from being shy about exposing their secret doctrines, most of the women boldly propositioned the interviewer.

In the case of the more extreme rituals, one sometimes gets the impression that Tantric cult is like the Indian rope trick: everyone knows someone who knows someone who has seen it done, but no one has seen it done himself. Some aspects of Tantrism are well documented and visible to this day, such as the behavior of the Aghoris ("to whom nothing is too ghastly"); some aspects survive in a reduced form, as is evident from this recent interview with the disciple of a Tantric guru in Benares:

> He says they have another puja [ritual] called Kumari Puja—Virgin Puja. Avadhut [the adept] lies on his back and girl is standing over him. Then she pours wine over head and it runs down her body and into the mouth of Avadhut. After this he has intercourse with

> her but without orgasm—thus she is still virgin. It is difficult to find girls in India for this puja and now they are only doing it in Assam. He says he has not yet performed this puja but he has special kiss between legs for barren women. He is wanting to give this kiss to a lady at the hotel who is barren, but husband is not allowing it (Newby 1966, p. 232).

Some of the elements of the Tantric ritual are here bowdlerized or misunderstood: the wine flowing from the virgin is the seed of the goddess, which he drinks; he holds back his seed, not to keep her a virgin, but to absorb her fluids himself; the special kiss is another vestige of devouring the goddess. In any case, the ritual is admittedly in desuetude: they are doing it only in Assam (the mythical site of the *yoni* of the Goddess); it is difficult to find girls to do it; most significantly, "husband is not allowing it."

Yet some form of the Tantric ritual is known on some level to almost all Hindus. Moreover, even among those who reject it openly, it may serve an important function:

> In their horrified, and yet fascinated, accounts of these practices of the laja-dharma ["shame religion," i.e., Tantrism] and the Aghoris (as before, of the behaviour of hinjras) my informants were portraying the direct antithesis of their own religious values; and the very vehemence of their condemnation seemed to carry an undertone of relief that someone else should have acted out their most strongly repressed urges. By describing these atrocities in others' behaviour, they seemed to experience a vicarious release of the same impulses in themselves (Carstairs 1958, p. 104).

Thus even the rejected Tantric philosophy plays an essential part in the world view of orthodox Hindus, resolving tensions generated but not resolved within the conventional Hindu world. In some cases, new tensions may be created (or old ones exacerbated) in the same way. Manisha Roy (1975, p. 46) suggests that an erotic version of Tantrism may be a decisive influence in creating romantic longings (unfulfilled and therefore problematic) in Bengali women. Tantrism is more erotic, yoga less erotic, than middle-range Hinduism, and each provides fantasies that establish the boundaries of the real Hindu world. Through these mythologies—for Tantrism may be a ritual for Tantrics, but it functions primarily as a mythology for other Hindus—it is possible to totter on the brink without actually falling into it and then to come back to the realm of the possible—now a world whose bounds have been extended, if only by a little.

M. The Vicious Circle of the Mother and the Son

In the classical myths, being devoured by the mare retains only its superficial, negative valence. In these texts the danger that the mare will mutilate or devour the king is almost a certainty if the Goddess is malevolent, as Devī is toward Mahiṣa and Saraṇyū is toward Vivasvant. But the Goddess is likely to *become* malevolent if she is mistreated. In the worship of South Indian village goddesses, aggressive male sexuality and other forms of mistreatment transform a mortal woman into a wrathful goddess, though these brutalities are in part provoked by fear of her wrath (Brubaker 1978). This pattern appears throughout our corpus: Mácha is murdered when pregnant, Deichtíre is impregnated against her will, Saraṇyū is raped by Vivasvant, Rhiannon is wrongly accused, and Demeter is raped by Poseidon, Leda by Zeus. In each case the Goddess vents her wrath only after she has been mistreated; this is what makes her murderous rather than benevolent.

There is a circular pattern at work in the myths of the mare: the goddess is feared because she is fierce because she is denied worship because she is feared. This pattern is a theological parallel to the one that emerged from the psychoanalytic analysis of the hierogamy myths: the mother is sexually aggressive (to the son) because she is avoided (by her husband) because he fears (or experiences) impotence because he has been subjected to sexual aggressions by his mother (Kakar 1978, p. 95). In this context, we may note the significance of the myths in which the son beheads his mother (lest she behead/castrate him) and she is reborn as a goddess (Reṇukā and Sandhyā/Arundhatī) (see above, chap. 4, sec. C). The hypothesis that aggression and seduction are the two essential components of the Evil Mother is further supported by the myths in which the mare is literally created out of a combination of lust (Śiva's, or a woman's, or a demon's) and anger (Śiva's again, or the anger of a son toward those who have mutilated and killed his father or have accused his mother of excessive sexuality [see above, chap. 7, sec. E]). It is also significant that the mare myths are rife with incestuous relationships that can be expressed precisely because they are masked by animal symbolism (see above, chap. 6, sec. D). *Verbum sapienti satis:* the point need not be belabored.

On several occasions the central pattern of interaction between mother and son is embroidered with secondary conflicts between father and son. Vivasvant is mutilated not only by his mother but also by his father (who sends him to the world of the dead), his father-in-law (who "trims" him), and his brothers (who also trim him). In Greece, too, we have a father-daughter interaction that resonates with aspects of the Saraṇyū myth (where the father—jealously?—cuts down her husband) and the Uṣas cycle, where the father actually commits incest with her. But the central episodes of the Saraṇyū myth reveal the most striking affinity to the hypothetical patterns of the Hindu nuclear family: Vivasvant is attacked by his mother; therefore he avoids his wife (or is impotent with her); therefore she castrates her son (an episode doubly veiled, the castration appearing as the mutilation of a leg and the mother acting through her alter ego).

The mare holds back her fluids (milk) and drinks the fluids of the stallion (seed); the first is an act of aggression (killing her child), the second an act of sexual seduction. She behaves this way as a result of being excessively tamed and controlled, a factor that emerges from the myths of the birth of the mare (see above, chap. 7, sec. F). Thus again we see a circular pattern: the mare is controlled because she is feared because she is sexually aggressive because she is controlled.

This circularity, which invites a rather pessimistic view of sexual and theological interaction, is not, however, entirely inevitable, for the ritual may step in and introduce a reversal that short-circuits the compulsive self-perpetuation of destructive emotion. The ritual produces a special and controlled, highly structured context in which it is relatively safe to have sexual contact with the mare, to drain her fluids or even to be devoured by her. Moreover, it replaces the destructive cycle with a creative cycle of fluids, constantly reinfused with deity, flowing into her mouth and back out of her womb (or the reverse: into her womb and out of her mouth). The devouring mare/whore gives back to the mature male worshiper who confronts her sexually the powers that the cow/mother took from him when he confronted her as a child—or as a nonworshiper. By reintegrating the split goddess, the Tantric ritual transforms the castrating erotic mother, who holds back milk and saps virile fluids, into the invigorating goddess, who gives life by giving and taking fluid and who gives birth not as a cow, with milk, but as a mare, with female seed. The mare in her degraded Hindu form made her consort grow old; the Indo-European mare made the king grow young again, and so does the Tantric goddess.

One important function the Tantric ritual performs is to expose and confront incest in a formal ceremony. This is particularly the case on the popular rather than the esoteric level; for whether or not Tantrics actually do perform sexual acts with women within the range of the incest taboo, non-Tantric Hindus *think* they do. In this regard, then, as in others, the Tantric ceremony serves as a ritual for those who engage in it and as a myth for those who do not. The importance of incest in this "myth" is illustrated by the following typical statement made by one of

Carstairs' informants: "In those mandlis [Tantric ceremonies] they go and lie together with whomsoever they chance to be paired off—mother, sister, it is all one to them." Carstairs also notes (1958, pp. 103–4) the belief that the Tantric adept "must have intercourse with the wife of his guru. Thus, the dreaded incest was realized in a ritual act." Intercourse with the guru's wife is a very serious sin in Hinduism, an act whose meaning is revealed by the most famous commentator on the laws of Manu, who simply points out that the word "guru" in this prohibition refers to the father (Manu 11. 54, 103–4).[14] By allowing the adept to act out the sexual confrontation with his mother, Tantric ritual short-circuits yet another phase of the obsessive cycle between mother and son.

In addition to this "mythic" function of Tantric ritual for non-Tantric Hindu society, the function of the mythology itself, the mythology of the mare, must not be overlooked. For despite the fact that repetition of myths of the destructive goddess contributes to a pattern of sexual avoidance, on another level the telling of the myths is in itself a form of relief and reassurance. The goddess Pattini is regarded as the source of fire in the universe; she is propitiated not only by a cooling ritual (the boiling of milk) but by the *telling of her myths*, which is said to have the power to cool her anger (Obeyesekere 1980, p. 98). The recitation of the myths of the devouring goddess assures the worshiper not only that the goddess will be pleased (cooled) but also that he himself is able to acknowledge and accept the heat that is her nature—and his.

N. The Denial of the Goddess

The mare thus becomes benevolent in the ritual. Outside the ritual, however, she remains a terrible threat. Even if no overt act of aggression or calumniation is directed against her, she may be incited if she is denied. The pattern of denial is manifest on many different levels of the mythology, all of them characterized by the male's refusal to *give* to the female. On the level of physiology, he withholds his seed from her; on the theological level, he withholds his worship. In between is a continuum of encounters between mortal and immortal figures, encounters in which the male's refusal to give is both a cause and an effect of his belief that she will take his life's blood from him. Even in the Ṛg Veda we have encountered numerous women rejected by their husbands—Lopāmudrā and Mudgala's wife, for example—to whom others, such as Apālā (8. 91), Ghoṣā (10. 40), Indrāṇī (10. 86), and the wife of Bṛhaspati (10. 109) may be added if we follow the tradition of later commentaries.[15] Vedic and post-Vedic mythology abound in myths about women who suffer from being "unfortunate," *durbhagā*, a word that soon comes to have two highly significant particular meanings: "ugly" and "rejected by the husband" (in contrast with *subhagā*, "beautiful," hence "loved by the husband," hence "fortunate"). These women are often confounded with widows, and here again the secondary connotation of the word is revealing: "widow" may also designate the wife of an impotent man. Thus the husband rejects his wife willingly (because she is ugly) or helplessly (because he is impotent or dead); the two conditions of helplessness are closely linked in the mythology and may be a direct result of the first cause of rejection: the husband's abhorrence of his threatening wife.

The circle of theological denial, parallel to the circle of fear and avoidance between mother and son, has one escape: ritual worship. If one seeks the Goddess, her presence may be a source of power or a loss of power; she may bless or damn, feed or devour. Yet one *must* seek her, for the alternative is brutally clear: if she is ignored, she will *certainly* wreak havoc.

This pattern is evident in a very early myth in which the Goddess becomes a lioness:

> The Aṅgirases and the Ādityas were contending for the sacrifice. The Ādityas brought Vāc [goddess of speech] as a sacrificial fee, but she was not accepted; then they brought Sūrya [the sun], and he was accepted; and so a white horse is the sacrificial fee. Now Vāc was angry with them: "How is he better than I, so that they accept him and not me?" And, so saying, she became a lioness and began seizing everything from the two contending parties, the gods and the demons. Both called her to them, but she went to the gods when they promised her that she would receive the offering even before it reached Agni; and she promised them blessings if they invoked her. And so the oblation into fire reaches her before Agni, because the fire is Vāc (*ŚB* 3. 5. 1. 18–22).

The sun is a white horse; contrasted with him, Vāc is the mare. She is explicitly identified with the fire that drinks the oblation—the devouring female fire that takes the male seed, the underwater mare; she takes the oblation/seed even before it reaches the mouth of Agni, the oblation-drinker and seed-swallower par excellence. Competition takes place on several levels: between Aṅgirases and Ādityas, gods and demons, Vāc and Sūrya/Agni, and mare and stallion. Vāc is wooed here as she is wooed by "vain" dance when the gods have lost Soma; there she is bribed by a devalued form of eroticism (dance and song); here she is bribed by the oblation. But the point most relevant to the present discussion is the fact that she becomes a fierce deity, a lioness, only when she is rejected; when she is invoked, she promises blessings.

This pattern is maintained in the mythology of the South Indian goddesses as well as in such figures as Sītalā or the Bengali Manashā, who doggedly and ruthlessly torments the foolish merchant who will not worship her (Dimock 1963, pp. 197–294; Dimock 1987; Dimock and Ramanujan 1962 and 1964). We have seen it in the myth of Dionysus and Pentheus, and it is also present in the myth of Śiva and Dakṣa; here the parallels between the Greek and Indian myths may be due to actual contact. Dionysus is said to have traveled to India, and the Greeks who first visited India called Śiva Dionysus (Kirfel 1953; J. B. Long 1971).[16]

Both Śiva and Dionysus are phallic gods who appear in female dress or androgynous form; both handle snakes; and both indulge in "mad" dances with wild, uncontrollable women. Dodds' remarks on the Greek cult are equally applicable to the Hindu:

> The Power of the Dance is a dangerous power. Like other forms of self-surrender, it is easier to begin than to stop. . . . Also the thing is highly infectious. As Pentheus observes at *Bacchae* 778, it spreads like wildfire (Dodds 1951, pp. 271–72).

But in addition to these general correspondences, specific details of the myth occur in both Greek and Sanskrit. When Dakṣa denies Śiva's right to worship, Śiva beheads Dakṣa and castrates Kratu, Dakṣa's alter ego (O'Flaherty 1973, pp. 128–29). Like Dionysus, Śiva employs as the instrument of his wrath an orgiastic woman intimately related to his enemy: Satī is Dakṣa's daughter, as Agave is Pentheus' mother. Even the early, pre-Śākta texts make it absolutely clear that Śiva himself had no desire to make trouble, that Satī drove him to it by insisting that *she* was dishonored when her father dishonored her husband, Śiva. When Satī commits suicide, Śiva has no choice but to destroy Dakṣa. Moreover, immediately after the holocaust of Dakṣa's sacrifice, Satī's body is dismembered (though not eaten), and her sexual organ becomes a shrine. In other words, she becomes a Tantric Goddess, a mare.

The lesson taught by Dionysus to Pentheus is taught to Dakṣa by Śiva: deny the orgiastic deity and the deity will dismember you. The first corollary is also relevant: deny your sexual nature and the deity will kill you. Dakṣa's hatred of Śiva is based in part on his unnatural attachment to his daughter (ibid.); in this he joins the large company of the Greek fathers of mares, fathers who murdered their daughters' suitors. The second corollary—eat the god or the god will eat you—does not pertain to the Dakṣa story but is highly relevant to other aspects of Hindu myths in this corpus.

Carstairs (1958, p. 157) comments on two closely related phenomena.

The first is that Indian men regard women (particularly their wives) as sexually demanding, as more libidinous than men; the second is that "*any* woman whose demands one has refused is liable to be feared as a witch who may exact terrible reprisals," and he gives specific instances of this:

> In most cases the supposed witch was a woman (not necessarily old) who had been refused something she had asked for. . . . In two instances, men described how women had importuned them to make love, and on being rejected, had struck them with witchcraft (ibid., p. 57).

The logical chain is inescapable: women, being more libidinous than men, are going to make demands that cannot be satisfied; therefore, women are going to become witches. But one man's witch is another man's goddess. Carstairs even notes that the "demon-goddess" Mataji, worshiped by everyone, "has the same appearance as a witch" because she drinks the blood of her decapitated male adversary. Witches (or evil goddesses) are mares who have been refused. The fear of repulsed women gains momentum from the great emphasis placed in India on the duty to give to those who beg and the consequent fear of denying anyone anything that he (or *she*) asks for.

The traditional necessity to answer a woman's demands is at the heart of a statement made by the enchantress Mohinī when she is attempting to seduce Brahmā: "A man who refuses to make love to a woman tortured by desire is a eunuch. Whether a man is ascetic or amorous, he must not spurn a woman who approaches him, or he will go to Hell. Come now and make love to me" (*BVP* 4. 31–33). Mohinī's threat is double-pronged: to refuse her is to take refuge in self-castration and also to be condemned to Hell. Brahmā's grounds for refusing her are highly significant: he says to her, "Go away, Mother," in one breath, and in the next he argues that he is too old for her; when he continues to insist that he is like a father to her, Mohinī archly reminds him that he has already committed incest with his own daughter.

Once again we are embroiled in the family drama: the woman who is rejected is incestuously dangerous, either as mother or as daughter. By calling Mohinī "Mother" (as Arjuna addresses the nymph Urvaśī in the same circumstances; see below, chap. 9, sec. B), Brahmā hopes to protect himself from her by retreating into the nonsexual condition of a child. But he doth protest too much, arguing contradictorily that he is like a father to her—a desperate measure, which she immediately exposes for the paltry thing it is. The first excuse is the better of the two; for clearly, the woman who makes demands and is refused is the mother, not the daughter. The mother is the witch, and Carstairs suggests a reason for the persistence of this identification: the child sees the mother periodically secluded during her menstrual period, regarded as dangerous and defiling, since blood is polluting. "The association of seclusion and blood brings to mind accounts of the *dakan*, or witch. She also is said periodically to shut herself in a darkened room and abandon herself to her hostile desires, drinking the blood of some, eating the livers of others of those who have slighted her" (Carstairs 1958, p. 73). The mother is a witch not only because of the blood but because of the projected guilt "of those who have slighted her" and the fear that she will take revenge.

The realization of the power of the goddess, and of the danger of denying her, is the explicit reason given in many myths for the origin of her worship: Forgive us for not recognizing your power; do not continue to injure us, and we will worship you forevermore. Fear is a major factor in the propitiation of the Goddess to this day, but other emotions are equally prominent: ecstasy, joy, affection, reverence, and a need for comfort. That these latter feelings may find a place in the cult of a deity whose threats and depredations have such deep roots in the individual psyche is a striking demonstration of the complexity and power of ritual and of the persistence of the myth.

O. The Acceptance of the Goddess

By the time of the flowering of Śāktism in medieval India, between the tenth and fifteenth centuries A.D., a new Goddess had emerged, one who remains a potent figure in contemporary Hinduism. Among the factors that combined to produce her were the resurgence of non-Aryan (perhaps even pre-Aryan) local cults of the Goddess, the increasing importance of widespread regional cults of ambivalent figures like Sītalā and Manashā, and the pervasive contributions of Tantrism to non-Tantric Hinduism.

This new Goddess was perhaps not so new at all. The Tantric ritual view had roots in the ancient Vedic ceremony of the chaste student and the prostitute (Eliade 1958, p. 257), which had been rejected by the orthodox Vedic tradition but filtered back into non-Tantric Hinduism, where it confronted the image of the dangerous mare and the safe cow. The result was that, in the local and regional cults of the Goddess in India, the ancient ambivalence characteristic of the full Goddess was revalidated, fully integrated—a step that went far beyond the mere one-dimensional inversion of an equally one-dimensional orthodox Hindu model. This full goddess remains the object or worship for many Hindus today.

When the Goddess is worshiped and accepted in her full ambivalence, the worshiper asks her to be present with him always. But if part of her nature is pestilence and mindless destruction, why should one want her near? Why not merely placate her and ask her to go away? The answer to this may lie, in part, in her maternal nature: "The central feature of the 'good mother,' incorporated by every major goddess in the Hindu pantheon and dramatized either in her origins or in her function, is not her capacity to feed but to provide life-giving reassurance through her *pervasive presence*" (Kakar 1978, p. 84). If the essential function of the Goddess is to *be there* for you, you want her there even when she is in her shadow aspect. The only unbearable harm that the Goddess can inflict on the worshiper is to abandon him, as the immortal mare so often does, fleeing from her mortal consort, abandoning her child. This, not the mutilation, is the source of devastating grief, the terrible longing for the vanished divinity, the cruel pangs of *viraha*. The only evil mother is the one who is not there.

Here, perhaps, is the key to the distinction between demonic goddesses and straight demonesses: you worship demons to get them to go away, but you worship gods, even demonic gods, to get them to come to you. One way out of the dilemma of eating the mare or being eaten by her was to refuse to eat the female animal (the cow) so that she would not eat you: "If you kill the cow, who is your mother, then in some future lifetime your mother will kill you."[17] But the one who does not retreat from incestuous cannibalism attains freedom from all normal human constraints.

Thus the worshiper invokes Sītalā even though she will infect him with smallpox if she comes to him; without her, pestilent though she may be, life has no value. To allow the goddess to devour one takes courage; the goddess remains ambivalent, and being devoured is a risky form of worship. Even when she is gracious, to receive her grace is a terrifying and painful form of religious passion. But one has little choice: if that is the way that god is, what can one do? If she is denied, she is certain to be destructive; if she is worshiped, she may or not be destructive, and the worshiper may become immortal. The myth of Pūtanā shows how the worshiper who treats god as a mother treats a son is assured of salvation—even if the worshiper takes the form of an aggressive, destructive mother. But this theology of *bhakti* implies a two-way flow: the deity, too, may become manifest in a destructive way and yet bring blessings, ultimate salvation, and rebirth.

V Androgynes

9 The Comparison of Androgynes

A. An Introduction to the Androgyne

Androgyny is, at least for the moment, a trendy word in Jungian, feminist, and homosexual circles, to mention but a few; people are "into" androgyny. This fact should not, however, obscure the importance of the androgyne as an enduring religious symbol; for when the primal screams and Rolfings and skateboards have taken their place with bloodletting and chastity belts, androgyny will still be with us. As a media term, however, it is often applied to a range of phenomena far broader than the specific symbolism under examination here; and as a serious religious term, on the other hand, it is also capable of wider extensions than are relevant to the androgyne in the strict sense in which it is convenient to define it here: as a creature simultaneously male and female in physical form. Such figures may be divided horizontally (where breasts may replace the vagina as the emblem of the female, on top, with a complete phallus below) or, more often, vertically (one side, usually the left, containing a breast and half of a vagina, the other side containing half of a phallus).

In religious parlance, androgyny is a much more comprehensive and abstract concept than is implied in this visual image of the androgyne; to say that God is androgynous is very different from saying that God is an androgyne (Gross 1977a and 1978b).[1] If we limit ourselves to the narrow image, however, there are still several broad philosophical distinctions that must be kept in mind when classifying these figures. One is the distinction between "good" androgynes and "bad" androgynes in two different senses: morally acceptable and symbolically successful. In the first sense, it must be noted that although androgynes are popularly supposed to stand for a kind of equality and balance between the sexes, since they are technically half male and half female, they more often represent a desirable or undesirable distortion of the male-female relationship or a tension based on unequal distribution of power. Thus in some societies androgynes play positive social roles, affirming culturally acceptable values, while others are despised as symbols of an undesirable blurring of categories. In the second sense, androgynes may be regarded as "good," in the sense of symbolically successful, when the image presents a convincing fusion of the two polarities and as "bad" when the graft fails to "take" visually or philosophically—when it is a mere juxtaposition of opposites rather than a true fusion.

Even when the androgyne is "positive" in the first sense—affirming culturally validated concepts of the relationship between the sexes—he/she (one can hardly avoid nonsexist language here) may be "unsuccessful" in the second sense, i.e., be lopsidedly male or female. For the androgyne may be primarily male—playing male social roles, having overwhelmingly male physical characteristics, manifesting male sexual patterns—and be regarded as highly positive by an androcentric society. On the other hand, the androgyne may be primarily female—playing female roles, having primarily female physical characteristics, manifesting female sexual patterns—and be regarded as highly negative by an androcentric society. In either case, the image is "unsuccessful" in terms of its aesthetic balance, but it is morally positive (if male) or negative (if female). In fact, male androgynes by far outnumber female androgynes and are generally regarded as positive, while female androgynes (like the mythical mare) are generally negative.

The true mythical androgyne is equally male and female at the same time. But the term "androgyne" is often applied to folk figures that might better be termed "pseudo-androgynes"; they have some sort of equivocal or ambiguous sexuality that disqualifies them from inclusion in the ranks of the straightforwardly male or female. These liminal figures include the eunuch, the transvestite (or sexual masquerader), the figure who undergoes a sex change or exchanges his sex with that of a person of the opposite sex, the pregnant male, the alternating androgyne (male for a period of time, female for a period of time), and twins.

One final distinction should be made at the start. In addition to classifying androgynes by physical appearance (horizontal or vertical), balance (male or female), or moral status (positive or negative), it is possible to distinguish between them according to their way of coming into existence. Some are the result of the fusing of a separate male and female; others are born in a fused form and subsequently split into a separate male and female. These distinctions will become clearer in the course of our detailed examination of the typology; for now, they will simply serve as a basis on which to proceed to the preliminary survey of androgynes in world mythology.

B. The Search for the Androgyne

The androgyne is popularly regarded as a universal, archetypal symbol. In fact, though it is widespread, beyond any single culture, many religions, particularly the "primitive" ones, have managed to survive without it (Kluckhohn 1960, p. 52). Its popularity is a result of its utility for Western historians of religion as much as for the cultures they interpret, though this utility is a valid reason for taking it seriously as a religious symbol. In this chapter I will be concerned primarily with South Asian images of the androgyne but will begin with a survey of its occurrence in other cultures in order to establish an idea of the range of the symbolism and to set the stage for a cross-cultural typology. A brief glance at native North American, Australian, African, and popular American materials will demonstrate that here we do not encounter an Indo-European limit, as we do in the case of the mare; rather, we are dealing with a symbol that has meanings—different meanings—for several independent cultures.

North American Androgynes

In Navajo origin myths, both so-called androgynes or hermaphrodites (whom the Navajo call *nadle*, which means "weaver" or "being transformed") and transvestites ("those who pretend to be *nadle*") figure prominently, but neither of these is a true androgyne. *Nadle* are men dressed as women, and the lopsided physical and moral balance of their androgyny is patent: "Among the Crows I saw a warrior who, in consequence of a dream, had put on women's clothing and subjected himself to all the labors and duties of that condition, so humiliating to an Indian" (de Smet 1905, p. 1017). The *nadle*'s role and value in mythology are male-oriented. Barren themselves, the *nadle* are useful as mediators, and, perhaps related to this, they serve as ferrymen. When there was a quarrel between the men and the women and the latter secluded themselves on one side of the river, the *nadle*, by deciding to bring the women back across, enabled the men to overcome the women (Matthews 1897). In doing this, they acted as sexual strike-breakers or scabs, reversing the course of the age-old theme of the strike of one sex against the other.

In Navajo, Zuñi, and Crow society, the *nadle* would take the place of the woman when trouble arose between a husband and a wife (Stevenson 1904, p. 310; Alexander 1964, pp. 308–9); they then had the legal status of women and would supervise women's work (Matthews 1897, n. 30; W. W. Hill 1935, p. 275). But the *nadle* are physiologically and functionally men and return to male roles after taking over leadership of the women. In one tribe, a woman who dreamed she was a man was permitted to hunt like a brave, but this is exceptional (de Smet 1905, p. 1017). His basically male nature and allegiance make the *nadle*'s social function appear to be a betrayal of the female and a method of control rather than any sort of true balance or equality. A more likely candidate for a mythical androgyne, though still primarily male, is the Navajo Mountain Man ("he looks like a woman but is a man" [Khah 1942, p. 40]), who owes more to the concepts of sex change and transvestism than to true androgyny. Another figure, Wound-in-a-Rainbow, was said to be both man and woman, but he behaved like a *nadle*, going with the men and doing the work of women (ibid., pp. 41, 46).

This predominance of "male" androgynes, playing positive, culturally accepted social roles (in this instance, controlling women), is in striking contrast with another type of North American androgyne, who is female and evil. The Navajo say that First Man and First Woman had five sets of twins, of which the last four were each composed of a boy and a girl but the first pair were barren hermaphrodites (C. H. Long 1963, p. 53). The last four sets procreated, but the first set were the first people to die, and "she" (i.e., the female hermaphrodite of the pair) went to the underworld to become associated with the dead and the devils in the lower world (Spencer 1947, p. 98). The male hermaphrodite simply dies; the female androgyne becomes the devil. Both are barren. Among the tribes of the northwest coast, too, mythic hermaphrodite dwarfs are killers, banished not to the underworld but to the moon (Boas 1895, vol. 23, pt. 3, p. 53), a symbol of waning and, often, of the feminine. Among the Zuñi, however, one does find a central and positive androgynous creator, named "He-She" (Awonawilona) (Stevenson 1887, pp. 23, 37), an early precursor of nonsexist language and a powerful mythological figure.

A more complex candidate for androgyny is the notorious North American Trickster. He is primarily a "he," but he not only masquerades as a female but actually gives birth to children. He normally keeps his detached phallus in a box and is thus self-castrating; in order to have sexual intercourse, he removes it from the box and sends it to the woman. What his character represents, however, is a coincidence of opposites far more general than androgyny: it is primeval chaos, in which the basic social, moral, sexual, and even gross physical distinctions are yet unmade (Radin 1972). The Trickster is the embodiment of the infantile consciousness (Jung 1959, pp. 135–52; Róheim 1951, pp. 190–94; Makerius 1973, pp. 663–75). He is thus androgynously creative and psychologically "full," but the bitter humor with which he is depicted and the tragedy that follows upon his creative enterprises produce a sardonic vision of theological "wholeness" and a satire on human sexual integration. This aspect of his nature has led many scholars to identify him as a devil rather than a god, but this is not a useful distinction in dealing with a character who is morally so protean as the androgyne.

African and Australian Androgynes

In Africa, among the Dogon, there is a complex androgyne:

> The source of all disorder was the loneliness of the jackal, God's first-born. Unquestionably the jackal was bad, because his loneliness drove him to his mother. Because of this, in order to avoid loneliness, the Nummo at each child-birth prays to God for the birth of twins. But the Nummo's prayers are not always answered, and that is why he has given two souls to every child at birth. . . .
>
> The Nummo has previously drawn on the ground the outlines of two souls shown in human form. The first outline is female, and the second male. As the new-born child touches the outlines, the two souls take possession of him. His body is one: but the spiritual part of him is two. . . .
>
> In so far as the child retains the prepuce or the clitoris—characteristics of the sex opposite to its own apparent sex—its masculinity and femininity are equally potent. It is not right, therefore, to compare an uncircumcised boy to a woman: he is, like an unexcised girl, both male and female. If this uncertainty as to his sex were to continue, he would never have any inclination for procreation.
>
> The clitoris of the girl is in fact a symbolic twin, a male makeshift with which she cannot reproduce herself, and which, on the contrary, will prevent her from mating with a man. Just as God saw the earth's organ rise against him, so a man who tried to mate with an unexcised woman would be frustrated by opposition from an organ claiming to be his equal (Griaule 1956, pp. 156–58).

At puberty, therefore, the child undergoes ritual circumcision or clitoridectomy, by which the "other" soul is removed. The androgyne is gelded in punishment for a sexual crime; the mountains, identified with the threatening phallus/clitoris, are cut off, like the wings of the mountains or winged horses in Hindu mythology.

This complex symbolism incorporates a number of themes that we have encountered in Hindu mythology. A recurrence of the primeval incest between mother and son is prevented by creating twins—twins whose function in many mythologies is to procreate incestuously. Thus one form of incest replaces another; but this second type is forestalled by making each twin incapable of sexual activity—by making him or her a barren androgyne. Though this androgyne—the normal human being—is said to have one body (and two souls), its "soul" appears in the "other" sexual organ; thus it is a physical as well as a psychological androgyne. The only unilateral sexuality it has lies in its social role, given to it at birth when the mother places a spindle in the hand of a girl and an arrow in the hand of the boy. The female androgyne is not only barren but dangerous: she is a woman with a phallus, the erotic mare in the "wrong" species, who threatens the seducing man with opposition. (Theoretically, the same danger ought to threaten a woman who tried to mate with an uncircumcised male, but nothing is said of this in the text.) Finally, the unexcised woman's natural tendency to oppose the man is likened to the action of the earth (whose mountains were a phallic obstacle to her mate, the God in the sky); the phallic woman is the mortal consort of the immortal male, who must subdue her by castrating her. This primeval act is inverted in the puberty ritual, in which the symbolic umbilical cord tying the mortal to his mother earth is cut and she is repaid in his blood. Sudanese and Dogon art depicts horizontal androgynes, with breasts as well as penises (Leiris and Delange 1968, pls. 247–48, 307; Campbell 1956, pl. x). These figures may represent the primeval state of androgyny—man the way God made him, before the intervention of society made possible the perpetuation of the human race, reducing the dangerous full creature to a more manageable and useful half. The Dogon androgyne is a true divine androgyne, a creative figure containing both male and female physical and psychical elements; but it must be transformed into a human androgyne *manqué*—a figure whose complete nature has been defaced physically and psychically. God may be an androgyne; but man must not.

In Australian puberty rites, the male undergoes both circumsion and, a year later, subincision, to open a "penis womb," a symbolical male vagina (Spencer and Gillen 1899, p. 263; Eliade 1973, pp. 91–92; Eliade 1965, p. 112). Géza Róheim even suggests that by means of this ritual "a 'vaginal father' replaces the 'phallic mother' of the infantile situation" (Róheim 1945a, pp. 164–65). (This interpretation, it must be cautioned, has been open to challenge; some have suggested that the subincision wound is intended to simulate the pocket of a kangaroo.) The subincision *restores* the primeval androgyny of the male, where the Dogon ritual, and the first Australian ritual, removed it. When the subincision wound is broken open again on ceremonial occasions, the blood that flows is said to symbolize "at once the menstrual blood of the vagina and the semen of the male, as well as urine, water, and male milk" (ibid., pp. 94, 218–19), the last item a telltale sign of the pregnant male (see above, chap. 2, sec. A).

Star Trek Androgynes

A final set of androgynes, closer to home, may be seen in that supreme example of contemporary American mythology, *Star Trek*. At least three different types of androgynes have appeared in *Star Trek*. One of these consists in the visual image of a creature split in half vertically, one half black and the other white, used to express not sexual but racial and political polarization; in another a woman's mind is transplanted into a man's body and vice versa: finally, the consciousness of a man and that of a woman (Spock and the Nurse) are shared in a single body (the Nurse's). These episodes and images are utilized to express political, literary, and psychological truths somewhat remote from the theology of our "traditional" myths, but the imagery is strictly classical: the first androgyne is a variant of the moral split described in R. L. Stevenson's "The Strange Story of Dr. Jekyll and Mr. Hyde," expressed in terms of the vertical color bisection of the medieval court jester—a Trickster; the second is a reworking of the old plot recently employed in Thorne Smith's novel and film *Turnabout*, in which a man's mind is transferred to his wife's body and her mind to his body; and the third is, like the Dogon description of the prepubescent (divine) androgyne, two minds in one body (the inverse of the type with two bodies and one mind).

This is hardly an exhaustive cross-cultural survey of androgynes, but it may at least serve to demonstrate that such a survey is theoretically possible and that it is hedged with pitfalls. For even in this brief foray it has become evident that there are many different kinds of androgynes and that apparently identical forms in two different cultures may be loaded with symbolic meanings specific to each culture. Some androgynes are more "universal" than others; the androgyne who splits apart at the beginning of creation occurs widely—in Oceania, for instance, as well as in the Greek sources; but the androgyne as an image of total merging is rare outside of India (and even there it is found primarily in visual icons), where this type may be regarded as a special case of the truly universal image of the divine couple, the hierogamy.

C. Types of Androgynes

Western androgynes are more often "failed" than "fused."[2] Jung, Eliade, and, after them, Joseph Campbell have documented many visual images of medieval androgynes that express complicated alchemical and occult concepts but generally offend the eye. Writing on the way the French and English decadents used the theme of the androgyne, Eliade remarks, "As in all the great spiritual crises of Europe, here once again we meet *the degradation of the symbol.* When the mind is no longer capable of perceiving the metaphysical significance of a symbol, it is understood at levels which become increasingly coarse" (Eliade 1965, p. 100). The coarseness of many visual images of the androgyne is immediately apparent. Maurice Henry has produced a brilliant and hilarious series of cartoon androgynes who, ludicrously unable to fuse at all, are at last driven to saw themselves apart so that they may come together (see plate 8). Here, as so often, there are male androgynes and female androgynes. Indian androgynes are usually, though not always, more subtly fused.

The success or failure of the depiction (which may or may not be related to the soundness of the underlying philosophical concept) is to some degree determined by the features that are selected to be portrayed. Social features, such as clothing (trousers on one side and a skirt on the other), ornaments (the single earring of Śiva), and hair styles, do not usually jar the eye, for they are never "unnatural." So, too, iconographical conventions may be used to distinguish the god from the goddess without inspiring a feeling of serious incongruity: the male half holds a trident, the female half a lotus. But when the physical body itself is androgynously split, one is forced to confront the statement of androgyny in its inescapably naked form, and a deep artistic sympathy may be needed to persuade the eye that a single breast or half an erect phallus presents a profound human truth and not a grotesque miscarriage of nature.

Androgynes in the Human World

Physical Androgynes

Androgynes or hermaphrodites do occur as natural freaks, but it would be misleading to regard them as the source of androgynous symbolism (occurrence in nature is usually a risky basis for the analysis of *any* myth or symbol). In the first place, physical hermaphrodites could not have been so frequent or well known in ancient and primitive societies as to inspire and support such an important symbolic image, nor would they be necessary: one did not have to see winged people to imagine angels. Moreover, when such anomalies did occur, they were hardly regarded as sacred; in ancient Greece, androgyny was accepted only as a ritual reality; children born with actual marks of hermaphroditism were immediately killed by their parents. The physical androgyne does occur in decadent literature, but not as a religious symbol. As Eliade remarks, "The androgyne is understood by decadent writers simply as a hermaphrodite in whom both sexes exist anatomically and physiologically. They are concerned not with a wholeness resulting from the fusion of the sexes but with a superabundance of erotic possibilities" (Eliade 1965, p. 100). But even here, as we shall see, the image of the androgyne is misconstrued, for true androgynes usually have *no* erotic possibilities.

Nowadays, when medical anomalies are the darling of the media, hermaphrodites are still rare in the headlines, in part because they remain statistically uncommon and in part because the taboo that surrounds this particular physical peculiarity is still strong enough to prevent its victims from making journalistic capital out of it. Studies of physical hermaphroditism do not shed much light on the spiritual role of the androgyne (H. H. Young, 1937). Androgynes occur frequently in nature in other species; one example that we have encountered is the seahorse, the "pregnant stallion of the sea." Occasionally, human androgynes do make the headlines: in California, recently, a man who underwent a sex-change operation was able to become pregnant and then took hormone injections so that he could breast-feed the baby. More frequently, athletes who have undergone sexual surgery have been disqualified for being of the "wrong" sex. These operations, designed to turn the androgyne into an unambiguous sexual entity, closely resemble the operation performed by the Dogon and the Australian tribes at puberty.

Although physiological androgyny is quite rare (between 2 and 3 percent), it is the basis of several different mythologies or classificatory reactions to natural phenomena. Clifford Geertz (1975), citing Robert Edgerton, discusses the various ways in which physiological androgynes are treated by different cultures: Americans react by forcing the ambiguous child to change or disguise itself in order to go through life as one sex or the other; the Navajo respect and give social leadership to the "intersexuals"; and the East African Pokot, who regard them as useless, as unfortunate errors committed by god, sometimes casually kill them or, just as casually, allow them to live lonely, neglected lives (ibid.). Even without the existence of people with "markedly intersexual" physical characteristics, however, there is a basis for the concept of androgyny within the mythologically conceived body of a normal woman, and that is the clitoris. We have seen the equation between clitoris and penis made explicit in several puberty rituals; we have seen it, too, in the mythology of the *vagina dentata*. For the woman whose vagina contains a tooth, or a poisonous snake, or a penis, or a devouring mouth is always the erotic woman—the woman who experiences pleasure in sex. By denying this to her, by a blatant clitoridectomy or by sexual rejection or by the double standard that regards chastity as a natural female virtue ("Close your eyes and think of England"), the male myth-maker identifies evil women with physical androgynes.

Psychological Androgynes

Sex-change operations are performed not only in cases of physical anomaly (a double set of organs) but in cases of psychological incongruity, when a person feels that his or her body is physically unambiguous but is inhabited by an equally unambiguous mind or soul of the opposite sex. The psychological androgyne, far more common in folklore than the physical androgyne, may be regarded in either of two basic ways:

1. *Splitting*. The splitting androgyne begins as a combination of male and female but must split before it can become physically creative. This is the type that in its extreme form finds it impossible to remain in the physical/psychological ambivalence that it perceives as a masquerade (another widespread folk motif). He/she therefore undergoes some sort of operation to resolve the ambiguity: a physical operation in extreme cases (the Dogon model), psychological in others (psychoanalysis), or social (transvestism). This androgyne has been discussed by the followers of Freud and, more recently, by those of Piaget, who posit a stage in early infancy in which none of the opposites—not merely male and female, but opposites as basic as "self" and "other" and as subtle as "good" and "bad"—has meaning, the mind inhabiting an undifferentiated chaos. This chaos, the world of the Trickster, can have no moral quality, for it is a purely natural phenomenon; but it is necessary for the individual to progress out of it, to mature beyond it, in order to become truly human and creative. One must learn to be one thing or another, to fish or cut bait sexually.

2. *Fusing*. In sharp contrast is the view that the androgyne begins as a creature who is destined to become truly bisexual but appears to be

either male or female; this person must merge with the submerged side of the personality (the other sex) in order to become psychologically whole. This is the theory held by the followers of Jung and adopted in certain branches of the gay-liberation movement (to which classical Freudianism is unsympathetic). To realize one's full maturity, to become fully "integrated," requires no physical operation but may require training or analysis. Here, as in the splitting type, the individual often feels that he is living a masquerade; but this time the androgyne is masquerading (before society and before his own consciousness) as merely male or merely female. The transformation therefore entails no removal of the physical or social trappings of the "wrong" sex (though the Australian subincision ceremony performs a comparable function) but a removal of the psychological trappings of any particular sex, a realization of one's wholeness. This is not unlike the process of mystical realization of nonduality described in many religions, and it is therefore not surprising that a form of religious realization is often found compatible with this kind of androgynous transformation. In either case, some sort of "conversion" takes place, but for the splitting androgyne this is merely a conversion to Freudian doctrine (a religion unto itself), whereas the fusing androgyne is usually more sympathetic to other religious forms, particularly to mysticism.

3. *The Two-in-One.* A third psychological androgyne, less closely tied to any particular doctrine, is found not in a single individual but in two: the man and woman who join in perfect love, Shakespeare's beast with two backs. This is the image of ecstatic union, another metaphor for the mystic realization of union with godhead. This is the romantic ideal of complete merging, one with the other, so that each experiences the other's joy, not knowing whose is the hand that caresses or whose the skin that is caressed. In this state, the man and woman in Tantric ritual experience each other's joy and pain.[3] This is the divine hierogamy, and, in its various manifestations—as yab-yum, yin and yang, animus and anima—it is certainly the most widespread of androgynous concepts.

Mythological Androgynes

Chaos

The myths of androgynes correspond to these psychological concepts of androgyny, at least in their broad outline. For example, in creation myths, as in hypotheses about infantile consciousness, we encounter the chaos that precedes all differentiation, the chaos in which there is neither being nor nonbeing, neither dark nor light, and neither male nor female (though the sexual component is usually of comparatively minor significance in these myths). Moreover, creation myths describe different kinds of chaos, and the distinctions made are roughly parallel to the distinctions among the psychological types of androgynes.

1. *Negative Chaos (Splitting).* In orthodox mythology, chaos is something that must be transcended before life can begin (O'Flaherty 1975, introd.); it can therefore be termed "negative" chaos. Distinctions must be made—male distinguished from female, one social class from another. This is the philosophy underlying the Dogon puberty rituals. It also corresponds to the Freudian belief that the desire to return to undifferentiated chaos, to return to the womb, is a wish for death, for Thanatos (though Eliade [1965, p. 119] has demonstrated that this is a facile and incorrect interpretation of the wish to return to chaos).

2. *Positive Chaos (Fusing).* In the mythology of mysticism, however, the desire to merge back into chaos is the goal of human existence, the supreme integration toward which one strives. In ritual, too, androgyny is "a symbolic restoration of 'Chaos,' of the undifferentiated unity that preceded the Creation, and this return to the homogeneous takes the form of a supreme regeneration, a prodigious increase of power" (ibid., pp. 114, 119, 122). This power is not unlike the force that is released during the ritual hierogamy, a ceremony that calls upon the symbolism of the androgyne. The mystic striving toward positive chaos is a clear parallel to the Jungian integration of the individual, for it celebrates the merging of two apparently separate entities (the self and God) that are in fact one.

Anthropomorphic Androgynes

When we come to androgynes actually embodied in a human form (anthropomorphic in a rough sense) we again find them divisible into categories roughly analogous to those of the psychological and the chaotic androgynes. The two forms of creation, out of chaos or into chaos, have parallels in two forms of creative sacrifice: the dismemberment of a primeval god into disparate parts—the distinct parts of the universe (as in the Vedic sacrifice of Puruṣa [*RV* 10. 129])—and the reverse, the creation of a destructive divinity from all the parts of the universe (as in the creation of Śiva's chariot to destroy the cities of the demons, or in the creation of the goddess herself [*MBh* 8. 24; *MP* 82; *Sk P* 3. 1. 6. 8–42; O'Flaherty 1975, pp. 126-27, 239–41]). So codified are the parts in each case that the latter episode appears almost like a home movie of the first run backwards, with people leaping out of lakes onto docks. It is perhaps significant that the one who is dismembered is male, while the one who is reassembled is female; since the androgyne (particularly in India) is primarily male, the male creator is complete and can create from within himself, whereas the female creator must be made up out of parts of male gods in order to become androgynously powerful. So close are the analogies between the splitting of the androgyne and the dismemberment and sacrifice of the primeval deity that at least one scholar has advanced the suggestion that the basic Indo-European myth of creation was in fact a combination of these two themes: the sacrifice and dismemberment of an androgyne (this hypothesis is not, however, generally accepted).[4]

In the conventional images, androgynes may be "coming" or "going," fusing or splitting:

1. *Splitting*. The splitting anthropomorphic androgyne is originally created as a male and female in combination and must subsequently separate in order to create. Our term "hermaphrodite" comes from this theological image in classical Greek writings, where Hermaphroditus is the child of Hermes and Aphrodite (Ovid *Met.* 4. 288). Plato depicts Aristophanes as the author of a complex myth of the primeval androgyne:

> In the ancient times there were three kinds of beings, each with four legs and four arms: male, female, and androgynous. They grew too powerful and conspired against the gods, and so Zeus sliced them in two. The parts derived from the whole males are the ancestors of those men who tend to homosexuality and pederasty; the parts derived from the whole females are the ancestors of women who incline to be lesbians. The androgynes, who are nowadays regarded with scorn, gave rise to men who are woman-lovers and adulterers, and to women who are man-lovers and adulteresses (*Symposium* 189E–191E).

The androgyne is explicitly denigrated in this myth, not only in the statement of reproach for its present-day physical manifestations but in the implication that creatures derived from it are excessively lustful; the splitting of the androgyne (as a punishment for mortals who challenge the gods or draw too close to them, the danger underlying the hierogamy of a mortal with an immortal) is responsible for the fact that we expend so much time and trouble trying to get back together again. In the Bible, this effect is attributed to the origin of Eve from Adam (Gen. 2:24).

2. *Fusing*. The fusing type of anthropomorphic androgyne is originally created as a male and female in isolation and must fuse in order to create. The separate components are barren; only the androgyne is creative. This may appear as an internalized hierogamy, as in the mythology of Tantrism, in which the individual (male), by activating the

female principle within himself—the dormant goddess Kuṇḍalinī—to rise and unite with the male godhead, experiences the full bliss of the merging within himself. The yogi becomes an androgyne. In the Sāhajiyā school of Tantrism it is sometimes said that all human beings are female on the left and male on the right and that one must unite them in order to become whole (Bose 1927, p. 22). The female in this model is associated with lust (*kāma*), the male with love (*prema*); thus, even here there is a clear hierarchy within the androgyne, for the Sāhajiyā believes that lust is merely the raw material from which love must be developed, as semen is transmuted into Soma.

3. *The Two-in-One*. The Two-in-One is another name for the hierogamy, or sacred marriage, and is represented by the androgynous image of the god and the goddess, Śiva and Pārvatī, united as the Ardhanārīśvara. In broader theological terms, it is the merging of complementary opposites —the *coniunctio oppositorum*—two opposites that must have something in common in order to be opposed and united (Eliade 1965, pp. 103–25).

4. *Twins*. In some myths the splitting anthropomorphic androgyne is the original divine being, who subsequently turns part of himself into a female and mates with her. That incest between father and daughter is implied in this situation is evident from the Indian materials, as we shall see. Even when there is no explicit androgyne, a primeval male being often creates a daughter in order to procreate; the inverse, mother with son, also occurs but is less common (since the androgyne is usually male).

When the splitting androgyne is not himself the original divine being, however, but is created by that divinity (this situation also occurs in the Indian materials), there is no father-daughter incest. Instead, there is the incest of brother and sister, as told in the myth of the primeval twins. We have seen how closely androgynes and twins are associated in the Dogon myths, and many of the twins we have encountered in the Indo-European cycle of the mare may be androgynes *manqués*. As Eliade remarks, "In certain traditions the mythical androgynous ancestor has been replaced by a pair of twins; in India, for example, by Yama and his sister Yami, and in Persia by Yima and Yimagh" (Eliade 1965, p. 111). And in Hindu myths and medical texts that discuss the formation of the embryo, twins may replace androgynes or eunuchs in ambiguous situations where neither a boy nor a girl will be born (see above, chap. 2, sec. B).

Pseudo-Androgynes in Folklore

When there is a smaller theological component, the material shades off from mythology into folklore. Still, androgynes in folklore often interact with or replace divine androgynes, and they are therefore essential to our typology.

The Eunuch

Like the anthropomorphic androgyne who must split, the eunuch is barren—but he remains barren. The eunuch is often confounded with the androgyne, since both are technically neither male nor female; the eunuch appears in the same theological metaphors of mediation in which the androgyne is found (see O'Flaherty 1973, pp. 256–59) but with an important difference: where the androgyne is both one and the other, the eunuch is neither one nor the other; he is empty where the androgyne is full. Both are primarily male (*pace* Germaine Greer): the androgyne is man plus woman, the eunuch man minus man. In India the eunuch is often confused not only with the androgyne but with the transvestite and the male homosexual; the notorious Hinjras (or Hijras) of northern India are all three at once. Their sexual ambivalence in the eyes of other Hindus was apparent from the reactions given to the word "Hinjra" on a word-association test administered by Carstairs:

> Most Banias responded with an abusive rejection of the hinjra, but Bhurmal's response was unusual. He said: "Female penis." Later he explained: "You have male penis, and female penis and eunuchy. These hinjras often cut their penis short, it's a part of their code. Only those who cut it off are really of that caste" (Carstairs 1958, pp. 323–24).

In this view, the Hinjra's sexual activity—the fact that it takes place with men rather than with women—and his transvestism distinguish him from the classical eunuchs of the harem, who are inactive, associated with women, and dressed as men. The Hinjra is therefore able to mediate between the eunuch (who has "no penis," in the Hindu view) and the normal man. His "female penis" is a kind of male clitoris. That Hinjras are subjected to tremendous abuse (in contrast with eunuchs) is not surprising, for they are anomalies and are regarded as female androgynes —always negative figures.

Masquerade and Transvestism

Often a man will pretend to be a woman (or, less often, a woman will pretend to be a man). In rituals this behavior usually simulates androgyny—the reintegration of opposites and the return to chaos (Eliade 1965, pp. 112–13). It is also a common feature in shamanism. As a folk motif it occurs in the tales of the Trickster in North America and in the Tibetan figure of Uncle Tompa, who often pretends to be a woman in order to have access to women (Dorje 1975, pp. 17–27).[5] The motifs of masquerade and eunuch may be combined:

> The nymph Urvaśī fell in love with Arjuna, but he clapped his hands over his ears when she propositioned him, for he said she was like a mother to him. Furious, the spurned nymph gave him a curse to be a dancer among women, devoid of honor, regarded as a non-man, a eunuch. But Indra, the father of Arjuna, softened the curse and promised Arjuna that he would spend only a year in dancer's guise and then would be a man again. Years later, when it was time for Arjuna and his brothers to hide in disguise, Arjuna put on woman's clothing (though he failed to disguise his hairy, brawny arms) and told his brothers, "I will be a eunuch." He offered his services as a dancing master to the women in the harem of a king. The king was suspicious at first, remarking that Arjuna certainly did not *look* like a eunuch, but he then ascertained that "her" lack of manhood was indeed firm (*sic*) and so let "her" teach his daughters to dance (*MBh* 3, app. 1. 6. 36–162; see also 4. 2. 20 and 4. 10).

Here Urvaśī (the immortal lover of the mortal king Purūravas) appears as the familiar figure of the destructive dancer—more specifically, as the castrating dancer (see above, chap. 5, sec. B). She also plays the roles of the spurned, vengeful goddess and the incestuous mother who punishes her unwilling son. Arjuna's response to these threats is to disguise his manhood twice over: he pretends to be a eunuch pretending to be a woman; that is, he castrates himself symbolically in order to avoid being actually castrated by the mother (see above, chap. 4, sec. C). This myth has been interpreted as a "collective male fantasy of the child's encounter with the sexual mother [and of] anxiety about his inadequacy to fulfil her sexual needs. The conflict is resolved through a self-castration which appeases the mother" (Kakar 1978, pp. 96–98). Here, as in other instances that we will encounter, androgyny is a denial of sexuality, an antierotic state.

Another instance of transvestism overlapping with a different variant of androgyny appears in the hagiographies of Caitanya. Caitanya was regarded by some as an avatar of Kṛṣṇa but by others (including himself) as an avatar of Rādhā. Thus it is said that Kṛṣṇa became Rādhā in the form of Caitanya in order to experience what it was like to be Rādhā (and to make love with Kṛṣṇa), and he became Kṛṣṇa in Caitanya's body in order to make love to Rādhā (Dimock 1976, pp. 146–52). Caitanya dressed like a woman and retired each month during menstruation, but he was not merely a woman; he was an androgyne, "Rādhā and Kṛṣṇa in a single body, thus tasting in as intimate a way as possible the sweetness that is the highest characteristic of the divine pair" (Dimock 1966b, p. 43). In this way, Caitanya was a fusing androgyne (creating a female within himself to merge with) as well as a two-in-one androgyne (the locus of a hierogamy—internalized); he is also the body in which a god undergoes a change of sex, while he appears as a transvestite. When the scene of Arjuna as eunuch/transvestite is enacted by troops of players in South Indian village theaters nowadays, the actor playing the part of Arjuna wears a sari and paints his face one color on the left and another on the right;[6] that is, in his face he takes on the conventionalized form of the vertical androgyne (as it appears in Indian paintings) while masquerading below the neck as a horizontal androgyne (two breasts and a complete phallus). In this way the costume expresses the sexual ambivalence of the man/woman/eunuch/transvestite.

Sex Change, Exchange of Sexes, and Male Pregnancy

The androgyne may carry profound and positive theological meanings; but when taken literally, it was the object of fear and mockery in ancient India. A character in a Sanskrit play is a prostitute named Sukumārikā ("Good Little Girl") who is referred to as the "third sex" and is an inauspicious thing to see. She is accused of having a heart insatiable by any amount of sex, but she has certain advantages in her profession: she has no breasts to get in the way of a tight embrace, no monthly period to interrupt the enjoyment of passion, and no pregnancy to marr her beauty (Vararuci's *Ubhayābhisārikā*). The last "advantage" is a strange one; apparently only mythical androgynes are capable of becoming pregnant. Or, perhaps it is because Sukumārikā is a female androgyne that she happily avoids pregnancy. This, together with her insatiability, brings Sukumārikā into line with the mainstream of evil erotic goddesses.

Male pregnancy is not without its dangers; we have seen that Agni was mocked for his pregnancy, Yuvanāśva was unable to feed his child, Dadhīca died "giving birth" to the gods' weapons, and Śukra was killed in giving birth to Kaca. One Sanskrit story expands upon these themes and relates them to the selfishness of the woman:

> During a festival of Śiva on Mount Kailāsa, the mountain-dwelling Vidyādharas were assembling when one female Vidyādharī, who was pregnant, felt unable to go. She asked her husband to take the

> embryo so that she could attend, and, because of his great affection for her, he consented, having assumed the necessary shape. With her beautiful figure restored, the female Vidyādharī went to the festival. After several days, enjoying the pleasures of the flesh with another young Vidyādhara who took her fancy, and recalling the pains of childbirth, she decided not to return. Her husband suffered for the full nine months as the embryo grew, and finally, unable to find a passage for the delivery, he died in agony (*Tantropākhyāna* 10).

The Vidyādharī abandons fertility for eroticism; her foolish husband, deluded by the power of his affection for his wife (*prema*, "love," rather than *kāma*, "lust"), uses his magic powers to assume the "necessary shape" to become pregnant; his magic does not, however, seem to have the power to allow the episode to come to its usual mythical end; abruptly the real world intervenes, and the Vidyādhara dies. His wife, by changing from mother to whore, has killed him. This cautionary tale (one of a series pointing cynical morals) seems to satirize the husband's foolishness as much as the wife's cruelty. It follows the pattern of exchange of sex roles, though here the roles are physically enacted. The man's female role is obvious, but her maleness is implicit: her erotic freedom, and freedom from childbirth, makes her a phallic woman—and a killer.

It is evident that the themes of androgyny, male pregnancy, change of sex, exchange of sexes, and eunuchhood overlap in many ways. Male pregnancy may be viewed as the positive aspect of a syndrome whose negative facet is manifest in self-castration; but male pregnancy is also hedged with dangers, as the story of the Vidyādhara makes clear. Michael Flanders' "Sea-Horse Lullaby"[7] views with humor the male pregnancy/androgyny of the seahorse:

> On the morning after her bridal night
> The lady sea-horse bolts,
> Leaving her sea-horse groom to hatch
> Sea-fillies and sea-colts. . . .

The father is the good parent, albeit under compulsion ("The sea-horse never leaves his young; he would not if he could," says Flanders), while the mother seahorse abandons her children (Flanders calls her "mare-faced," which is, of course, the term [*vaḍavā-mukhā*] applied to the underwater fire).

Yet another subvariant of the motif of sex change, and one still more closely linked to androgyny, is what might be termed unconscious change of sex: a person of one sex is mistaken by someone else as belonging to the other sex. A famous example of this is the tale of Isisinga (the Pali name; in Sanskrit he is known as Ṛṣyaśṛṅga):

> The sage Isisinga had been raised by his father alone in the wilderness; he had never seen a woman. The sage performed such great asceticism that Indra determined to break down his virtue, and so he sent no rain for three years, advising the king, "Send your daughter Naḷinikā to break the virtue of Isisinga and it will rain, for his fierce asceticism has caused the rain to stop." She went to him and enticed him, and he thought her to be a marvellous ascetic; when he noticed the difference between her naked body and his, she explained to him that a bear had wounded her between the legs, and begged him to help her assuage the pain of the wound. This he did gladly, and thus his virtue was broken. She ran away from him, and Indra sent rain that day. When Isisinga continued to pine for the "ascetic," his father asked him to describe the boy; Isisinga praised the ascetic's beautiful rosaries (garlands), matted locks (long hair perfumed and bound with gold), the lovely berries (drugs) and fruit juice (wine) "he" had given Isisinga, and the charming games "he" had taught him to play. His father told him that this had been a Yakṣinī, a female demon, and the terrified boy returned to his asceticism (*Naliṇikā Jātaka* 526. Cf. *MBh* 3. 110–113; O'Flaherty 1973, pp. 42–52).

The tale of the bear's wound is an evocation of castration fear, reinforced by the later identification of the woman as a Yakṣinī. She does in fact take from Isisinga not his sexuality but his power to keep back both his own sexual fluids (semen) and those of the cosmos (rain). By mistaking her for a man, Isisinga expresses the epitome of his own renunciation of sexuality; the satirical possibilities of the episode have made it a favorite with both Buddhists and Hindus.

Both the North American Trickster and Uncle Tompa are capable not only of masquerade but of actual transformation: they become women, have intercourse with men, and give birth. The shaman, too, often takes a husband (Eliade 1965, pp. 116–17; Eliade 1964, pp. 257–58). The obvious comic opportunities of this genre have made it very popular in world folklore; in myth, too, gods and demons often undergo sex changes. We have seen the demon Āḍi turn into a woman to attack Śiva and will see Viṣṇu change into the enchantress Mohinī in order to dupe the demons.

In a more serious vein, sex change often replaces androgyny in cosmogonic myths. Plato in the *Symposium* quotes Aristophanes' attribution of erotic urge to the splitting of the primeval androgyne, but in the *Timaeus* he attributes it to the gods' having pierced a spinal passage from the head to the sexual organs. This idea is introduced in a striking statement: "Of the men that are born, such as are cowards and have lived a life of injustice were, according to a probable account, transformed into women in the second generation. And at that time for this reason the gods devised the love of copulation" (*Tim.* 90E, trans. Grene 1965, p. 198). Here the androgyne is replaced by a primeval group of men, some of whom, by being turned into women, make sexual reproduction possible. And, here again, it is explicit that women are failed men.

Competitive Androgynes

1. *Unilateral Pregnancy.* The fecundity of the Trickster androgynes and Plato's scorn for the primeval females reflect yet another aspect of androgyny in folklore, the implication of aggression and competition, often ignored by those who wish to assume that the androgyne represents a harmonious merging of the sexes. This aggression is particularly apparent in the motif of the pregnant male; for, even as many androgynes are primarily male, so the unilateral pregnancy is more often accomplished by a male. Adam gave birth to Eve in this way; the midrash on Genesis 1:27 explicitly states that when God created the first man, he created him androgynous. Man being made in the image of God, this would make the creator himself an androgyne, though there is nothing explicit about this in the text of Genesis itself.

2. *Exchange of Sex Roles.* Competition similarly underlies the common folk motif of the man who exchanges roles with a woman for a while and then resumes his original role. This is a variant of the motif of masquerade, distinguished from it by the fact that an exchange between two individuals takes place and that there is an element of competition. For implicit in this story is the question: Who is better, the man or the woman? This motif, typified by the Grimms' tale in which the wife is as clumsy at working in the fields as her husband is at running the house, is further linked to the motif of women on strike: Who can get along better without the other? These much-loved stories, rich in obvious slapstick possibilities, serve a serious social function by justifying the status quo, affirming that it is good for a man to be a man and not a woman. In effect, they deny the value of androgyny.

3. *Exchange of Sexes.* A frequent corollary of this tale is the episode in which an actual exchange of sexes takes place (as in Thorne Smith's *Turnabout*). This is a development of the sex-change motif, again distinguished by the element of reciprocity, and it often poses the

question: Who has more pleasure in the sexual act? (The usual androcentric answer: the woman.) It may also be a wish-fulfillment device expressing the male's desire to experience what the woman experiences in intercourse.

4. *The Alternating Androgyne.* The motifs of sex change and exchange of sexes may be combined in the tale of the alternating androgyne, queen for a day and king for a day. A good example of this is the Indian tale of King Īḷa:

> Īḷā, the eldest daughter of Manu, became a man named Sudyumna, by the grace of Mitra and Varuṇa. But he became a woman again by the command of Śiva, in order to increase the dynasty of the moon, when he entered the Forest of Reeds. Then, by means of a horse sacrifice, she became a Kiṃpuruṣa, and in this state was called both Īḷā and Sudyumna, as he was a man for one month and a woman for one month. In the form of Īḷā she lived in the palace of Budha, the son of the moon, and bore him a son, when he had found his opportunity [during her female state] to urge her to have intercourse with him. As Sudyumna, he had three other sons, who were at first given the land to rule when Sudyumna's female condition kept him from ruling. But at the insistence of Vasiṣṭha, Sudyumna was installed as king, and he passed the rule on to Purūravas, the son of Budha and Īḷā (*LP* 1. 65. 19–30; cf. *MBh* 1. 75. 18–19).

A series of changes take place here, from female, to male, to female, and finally to an ambiguous condition. The change to female is said to be for the sake of the dynasty of the moon, to increase it (through procreation) and establish it as "lunar"; hence the monthly vacillation of king/queen. Although there are political objections to the gender of the "father" of the ruler, it is the son of the female rather than the male who inherits the throne. The second change, in the Forest of Reeds (the place where Skanda, the son of Śiva and Pārvatī was born), is further expanded in another set of variants, which also expand the equine motif, here represented by the horse sacrifice and by the Kiṃpuruṣa (a creature often depicted as half equine and half human):

> Īḷa's parents had wanted a boy; but the priest had made a mistake, and so a girl was born instead, named Īḷā. The priest then rectified his error, and she became a man, Īḷa. One day he went through a special forest that Śiva had enchanted: Pārvatī, provoked by having her love play with Śiva interrupted by sages dropping in on them all the time, had persuaded Śiva to cast a spell upon the place, so

> that any male creature who entered it would become female. When Īḷa reached this spot, he became a woman; his stallion became a mare, and all the men in his entourage became women. Īḷā, as she had become again, married and gave birth to King Purūravas. Eventually, she begged Śiva to help her change back, and was allowed to be a woman for one month and a man for one month (*Bh P* 9. 1. 18–42; O'Flaherty 1973, pp. 304–5; cf. *KP* 20. 4; *PP* 5. 8. 75; *H* 1. 10. 3; *MP* 111. 6; *VP* 4. 1. 8).

The core of the story, in which Īḷa becomes Īḷā, is here justified by the addition of a prologue showing that he was originally, by mistake, a girl; that is, he was a boy who seemed to be a girl, a motif we have encountered before. Pārvatī, in the role of the castrating mother (attempting in vain to prevent a recurrence of the primal scene), is responsible for his change of sex; the transformation of stallion into mare is also surely significant in this context.

Both elements, the role of Pārvatī and the symbolism of the horse, are further developed in another variant of the myth:

> One day Īḷa came to the place where Śiva was making love with Pārvatī. Śiva had taken the form of a woman to please Pārvatī, and everything in the forest had become female; when Īḷa came there, he was turned into a woman. When she approached Śiva to seek relief from her misery, Śiva laughed and said, "Ask for any boon except masculinity." Īḷā pleaded with Pārvatī, who granted half of her boon and made her a man for one month, a woman for the next. She also granted that when he was a man he would forget his existence as a woman, and the reverse. Later, Īḷa performed a horse sacrifice for Śiva, who permanently restored his masculinity (*R* 7. 87. 10–29; 7. 90. 15–20).

In this version, Śiva (in his own androgynous form, or one closely related to it) is responsible for the initial transformation, and Pārvatī, acting as the consort mediating between the worshiper and the awesome god, is responsible for its modification and ultimate removal. One may see a kind of historical irony in the fact that the stallion whose sacrifice restores Īḷā to manhood was originally (in terms of cultural history) a mare. The horse is even more closely associated with the myth in the first variant, which states that as a result of the horse sacrifice Īḷa became a Kiṃpuruṣa—a creature with the head of a man and the body of a horse, a centaur (see above, chap. 7, sec. B). In this way he becomes a horizontal androgyne (the inverse of the submarine mare) as well as an alternating one. The element of competition is present in the

Īḷa myth in an argument about inheritance (here slightly different from that of the first version): because he had been a female, Īḷa was disinherited, but the son (Purūravas) whom he had begotten when he was a woman inherited land directly from Īḷa's father, while the three sons he had begotten as a man did not (*Matsya P* 11. 40).

This same conflict appears in the tale of Bhaṅgāśvana, who is, like Īḷa, transformed into a woman, together with his horse:

> Bhaṅgāśvana had one hundred sons. Indra hated him because he had performed as many horse sacrifices as Indra had, and so one day, when Bhaṅgāśvana had led his horse to drink at a lake and had plunged into the lake himself, Indra changed him into a woman. As he came out of the lake, he was a woman; she mounted her horse with some difficulty and rode away. Eventually she married an ascetic and had one hundred more sons. The two hundred shared the kingdom until Indra incited them to war against each other, citing the battle of gods and demons as a good example to justify this fratricidal enterprise. All the sons were killed, but later Indra was placated, revived all the sons, and asked Bhaṅgāśvana to choose which sex he would like to remain for good. Bhaṅgāśvana preferred to remain a woman, saying that as a woman he had greater pleasure in sex (*MBh* 13. 12. 1–49).

Unlike Īḷā, who wants to become male again (as the vast majority of sex-changed Hindus do; see Brown 1927, pp. 202–4), Bhaṅgāśvana is quite content to remain female. Indeed, the whole story is told in order to answer the question posed by the interlocutor: "Who has more pleasure in sex, the woman or the man?" Bhaṅgāśvana's metamorphosis is thus a happy accident; though it results from a conflict with the jealous Indra, the castrating father (who behaves with similar malevolence when Pṛthu performs too many horse sacrifices [*Bh P* 4. 19–20; *PP* 2. 134; O'Flaherty 1976, pp. 347–48]), the god is appeased in the end and revives everyone.

But even here there are insidious implications. The statement that Bhaṅgāśvana had more pleasure as a woman is part of a syllogism that pervades the mythology: a woman should not take pleasure in sex (i.e., be erotic, a mare); a woman who does enjoy sex is a phallic woman and thereby deprives the male of his own virility (Róheim 1945b, p. 197). The statement that all women do experience greater pleasure than men (a conclusion that Teiresias also reached, under similar circumstances) is therefore a grave accusation in support of the Hindu contention that all women are destructively, voraciously appetitive. Seen in this light,

Bhaṅgāśvana's transformation is yet another instance of androgyny as a sign of conflict between the sexes.

A closely related tale of serial androgyny makes use of the motif of exchange of sexes in a manner similar to the way it is used in the tale of the pregnant Vidyādhara:

> King Drupada, whose wife had had no sons, asked Śiva for a son, but Śiva said, "You will have a male child who is a woman." In time the queen gave birth to a daughter, but they pretended that it was a son and raised the child as a son, whom they called Śikhaṇḍin. When the child reached maturity, "he" married a princess; but when she found out that her husband was a woman, she was humiliated, and her father waged war on King Drupada.
>
> When Drupada's daughter, Śikhaṇḍinī, saw the grief and danger of her parents, she resolved to kill herself, and she went into the deserted forest. There she met a Yakṣa named Sthūṇa and begged him to use his magic to turn her into a man. The Yakṣa said that he would give her his own sign of manhood (*puṃliṅga*) for a while if she would promise to return to him after that; meanwhile he would wear her sign of womanhood (*strīliṅga*). They made this agreement and exchanged sexual organs. When Drupada learned from Śikhaṇḍin what had happened, he rejoiced and sent word to the attacking king that the bridegroom was in fact a man. The king sent some fine young women to learn whether Śikhaṇḍin was female or male, and they happily reported that he was absolutely male.
>
> Meanwhile, Kubera, the lord of the Yakṣas, found out what had happened and cursed Sthūṇa to remain female forever and Śikhaṇḍin to remain male forever—or rather (upon reconsideration), to remain male until Śikhaṇḍin's death, when Sthūṇa would regain his own form. When Śikhaṇḍin returned to Sthūṇa to keep his part of the bargain, he learned of Kubera's curse and returned to the city, rejoicing (*MBh* 5. 189–93).

As in the story of Īḷa, the transformed male does not wish to remain female, and Śiva is the source of both the original transformation (in the sense that the son that Drupada longs for is transformed into a daughter at birth) and the subsequent transformation (the prediction that the daughter will become a son). The Yakṣa who makes the bargain is unable to regain his original shape, like the Vidyādhara (a closely related species of demigod; both are magicians noted for their ability to change shape, a talent highly relevant to the theme of change of sex), though here it is said several times that Sthūṇa was fated to undergo this tragic translation and so could not help making such a foolish agreement with Śikhaṇḍin(ī). Indeed, Śikhaṇḍin(ī), like his benefactor, meets a violent and appropriately androgynous end: he is pierced between the eyes and cut in two with a sword. This mutilation links him still more closely with Śiva, the androgyne who is split in two and has a third eye in the middle of his forehead.

Śikhaṇḍin's prehistory also involves Śiva and androgyny:

> A princess named Ambā was abducted by Bhīṣma. Though she was eventually returned to her chosen husband, he rejected her, and even Bhīṣma then refused to take her back. Ambā tried to get Paraśurāma to kill Bhīṣma in order to defend her honor, but the river Ganges, mother of Bhīṣma, joined together with Paraśurāma's ancestors to put an end to the duel. Then Ambā became an ascetic in order to amass the power to kill Bhīṣma herself. The Ganges tried at first to dissuade her and then cursed her so that she would become a crooked river, dried up except in monsoon and teeming with crocodiles. Ambā did become a river, but only with one half of her body; the other half remained a woman, continued to propitiate Śiva, and obtained the promise that she would be reborn as a man who would kill Bhīṣma. Ambā then entered the fire and was reborn as Śikhaṇḍin (*MBh* 5. 170–87; 8. 59–60; cf. Hiltebeitel 1967, pp. 249, 325).

Like Sītā, Ambā is abducted, rejected by her husband, and driven to suicide by fire. Ambā's need to take revenge, however, transforms her into the familiar witch or fury (or goddess) who haunts and destroys the man who has sexually assaulted her; she becomes, successively, three forms of the mare goddess. First, she withdraws (like Arundhatī in similar circumstances) into asceticism, designed to destroy a man; she becomes a Yoginī, a dangerous, phallic woman. Second, she is cursed so that she endures an intermediary period of ambivalence, half woman and half "crooked" (perverse) river, lacking in fluids and teeming with toothy crocodiles—the essence of the destructive mother. This aspect of her character is heightened by its contrast with the goddess who inflicts the curse upon her—the milky Ganges, who saves the life of her son, the essential act of the good mother. Third, and finally, Ambā enters her incarnation of seesaw sexuality as Śikhaṇḍin; but even here her previous demonic qualities dog her, for Śikhaṇḍin is said to be the incarnation of a flesh-eating demon, a Rākṣasa.

All of these myths lend themselves to the psychological interpretation that a man transformed into a woman is a man suffering from impotence, a hypothesis given substance by other myths in the corpus of hierogamies of human males with the goddess. The Hindus themselves sometimes make an explicit connection between impotence and serial androgyny. One striking case is that of Āsaṅga, who is the subject of a brief but rich verse in the Ṛg Veda: "His phallus appeared firm in front of him, that had been hanging down like a boneless thigh. Āsaṅga's wife, Śaśvatī, seeing it, said, 'You have there, my lord, a splendid instrument of pleasure'" (*RV* 8. 1. 34). This verse seems plain enough on the face of it, and plainer still in the context of the many Vedic verses alluding to virility lost and restored, to say nothing of the locker-room anatomical boasts made by the wives of Indra and the monkey (*RV* 10. 86. 16–17). But the *Bṛhaddevatā* and Sāyaṇa's commentary change the impotence into womanhood and tell the story in significantly different versions. According to the *Bṛhaddevatā*, by far the earlier text, Āsaṅga was a king's son who had been a woman; a sage turned him into a man, for which Āsaṅga praised and rewarded the sage, and Āsaṅga's wife praised him (*Bṛhaddevatā* 6. 40–41). Sāyaṇa tells the story twice; first he explains that Āsaṅga had originally been a man but had been turned into a woman by a curse of the gods (thus adding a previous change of sex to the one narrated in the *Bṛhaddevatā*); here too, it was the power of the sage's asceticism that brought about the second, restorative change. The second time he tells the story, however, Sāyaṇa says that by the gods' curse Āsaṅga had become a non-man (*napuṃsaka*), a term that may designate a eunuch, an androgyne, or an impotent man; in this case, Sāyaṇa goes on to say, his wife, "disgusted with her husband's lack of manhood, performed great asceticism, and by means of that he obtained manhood. When she discovered that he had obtained the mark of a man that night, she praised him" (Sāyaṇa on *RV* 8. 1. 1 and 8. 1. 34). Though the gods are responsible for the loss in either case, it is surely significant that Sāyaṇa attributes the transformation from woman to man to the efforts of a sage and the overcoming of impotence to the efforts of the man's wife. The fact that this latter situation is far closer to the spirit of the original Vedic texts suggests that a human problem (impotence) became a myth (androgyny). That these two motifs frequently overlap is further facilitated by the similar psychological orientation that allows one word (*napuṃsaka*) to designate non-men of such different natures as eunuch, impotent man, and androgyne; in English, "unmanned" covers the first two but not the third.

These various confusions serve to emphasize beyond any doubt that the image of the androgyne was frequently associated with fears of loss of power and virility, a fact that is not surprising in the context of the many myths associating male pregnancy with death and attributing the change from male to female to a curse by the gods. Whatever positive theological connotations androgyny may have (and we will encounter many), there is a deep substructure of shadow and terror inherent in the image.

One positive aspect of apparent androgyny is often seen in the syncretistic figures of gods who are masculine at one point in history, or in one culture, and become feminine in another. The sun is such a deity (generally masculine, but feminine in German and in some of the mare myths), as is the moon (generally feminine, but masculine in classical India; see above, chap 8, sec. G). The Bodhisattva is male in India but becomes the goddess Kwan Yin in China. These are cultural variants and do not carry any of the symbolic or psychological power of the spontaneous, simultaneously perceived androgyne (*pace* Campbell 1956, pp. 152–53, 169–71). (A genuine, and typically misogynist, androgynous aspect of the Bodhisattva appears in the Mahāyāna Buddhist belief that in order for a woman to become a Bodhisattva she must first become a man.)

5. *The Horizontal Androgyne*. In some variants of the story of Īḷa, the dilemma is solved by transforming him from an alternating androgyne into a horizontal androgyne (a Kiṃpuruṣa), split at the waist or neck rather than along the vertical axis, as most androgynes are. Horizontal splits of this kind are easily assimilated to the pattern of sexual beheadings, and so it is not surprising that they often reflect sexual tensions; when Reṇukā is beheaded by her son at her husband's command, in punishment for her mental infidelity, she is imperfectly reintegrated, her head being placed on the body of an Untouchable woman, and vice versa (Brubaker 1977). In many cultures, androgynes are represented with both breasts and phallus rather than with half a phallus and half a vagina, a closer approximation to "natural" androgynes than is the traditional vertical figure.

6. *Sexual Strikes*. Another element of the battle of the sexes takes the form of a strike: one or both of the partners refuses sexual favors to the other. This may be seen as a part of the motif of the exchange of sex roles, in which each not only refuses to perform its own role but undertakes that of the other. We have seen an example of this in the Navajo myth of the *nadle*. A more famous instance occurs in Aristophanes' *Lysistrata*, where the women so torment their husbands with sexual deprivation that the men end up "walking around hunched over like men carrying candles in a gale" (trans. Fitts 1959, p. 53); the women eventually win their strike, ending the war of the sexes when the men end the military war against Sparta.

D. The Evolution of the Androgyne in India

Many types of androgynes occur in Indian mythology and iconography, and their variations evolve in the context of a changing set of ideas about ideal and real relationships between male and female.

Textual Development

The Vedic period has left us no visual images, but the texts are rich in relevant imagery. We have already encountered both the Vedic androgyne and the Vedic pregnant male, symbols of tension and competition rather than fusion and integration. Indra is an alternating androgyne, a man among men and a woman among women (*KS* 8. 5; cf. *AV* 7. 38. 2); he is also a simultaneous androgyne when, as the result of a curse, he is marked with a thousand *yonis* (*BVP* 4. 47. 31–32; *KSS* 17. 137–48; Penzer 1924, 2:46; *MBh* 12. 329. 14. 1; 13. 41. 12–23); and in punishment for the same crime (adultery with Ahalyā), he is sometimes said to be castrated, made into a eunuch (*R* 1. 47–48; *PP* 1. 56. 15–33; *ŚB* 12. 7. 1. 10–12; 5. 2. 3. 8; O'Flaherty 1973, pp. 85–86). Since Indra is in so many ways the antecedent of Śiva (O'Flaherty 1973, pp. 84–89), who is the supreme Indian androgyne, these scattered references provide a Vedic basis for the later iconography, a link between Vedic and Purāṇic androgyny.

Prajāpati and Śiva as Splitting Androgynes

The earliest of all Indian androgynes, Sky-Earth (Dyāvā-Pṛthivī), is a splitting androgyne: the first cosmogonic act (variously attributed to Viṣṇu, Indra, or Varuṇa) is to separate the two halves. In the Brāhmaṇas, the anthropomorphic overtones of the act become explicit, and the separated parties (here three, in an alternative cosmology that depicts a third basic unit) suffer *viraha*, love in separation:

> These three worlds were united; the gods divided them into three. The worlds grieved that they had been divided in three, and the gods said, "Let us take the three sorrows from these three worlds." Indra removed their sorrow, and the sorrow which the god removed from this earth [fem. noun] entered the whore; the grief which god removed from the atmosphere [neut.] entered the eunuch; the grief from heaven [masc.] entered the sinful man or the rogue (*TB* 7. 10. 1; 8. 1. 9–11; *JB* 1. 145; 3. 72).

The sexual nature of the cosmic divorce is emphasized by the transfer of sorrow to an excessively sexual woman and man and to a nonsexual creature—the eunuch, the counterpart of the androgyne with which the myth begins.

Since the Sky Father and Earth Mother are the primeval parents, both having seed (*RV* 1. 159. 2; 1. 160. 3; 6. 70. 1), their separation on the anthropomorphic level is an instance of the child (the cosmogonic god) interrupting the primal scene. Melanie Klein has suggested that the young child has an image of the "combined parent"—the parental androgyne. On the cosmic level, the separation reflects the need to dispel chaos (here regarded as noncreative) and establish order.

In the Brāhmaṇas, Prajāpati assumes the role of the pregnant male, foreshadowed by Ṛg Vedic figures such as Soma and Parjanya. By the time of the Upaniṣads, Prajāpati becomes a more explicit androgyne:

> In the beginning this world was Soul (*ātman*) alone, in the form of Puruṣa. He had no joy, and desired a second. Now he was as large as a woman and a man in a close embrace, and so he caused his self to fall into two pieces, which became a husband and a wife. Therefore it is said, "Oneself is like a half-fragment." He copulated with her and produced human beings. But then she thought, "How can he copulate with me when he has just produced me from himself? I will hide." She became a cow; he became a bull, copulated with her, and produced cattle. She became a mare; he a stallion. . . . Thus were born all pairs there are, even down to the ants (*BAU* 1. 4. 3–4).

Though Prajāpati is recognizable from his behavior, he is actually called Puruṣa. The splitting of the androgyne is thus directly tied in to the more general, and nonsexual, splitting of the primeval Puruṣa; androgyny is seen as a variant of sacrificial dismemberment. This further emphasizes the fact that the splitting androgyne must separate in order to create, and the incestuous implications become explicit when the female half flees from him, taking the form of a cow and a mare, just as Saraṇyū assumed the form of a mare to flee from Vivasvant. Theriomorphism, which masked other forms of incest in that myth, here masks and justifies it: though in human form the daughter censures her father's attack and avoids it, the myth shows that it is in a sense justified, because it results in the creation of all the species of animals, who are allowed to procreate incestuously. The myth exists in a nonmoral form, as a purely descriptive statement of how things *are*; later texts then bracket the basic myth, as it were, placing positive or negative moral valences about it, framing it with appropriate material to rationalize or undercut the central events.[8] We have seen this process at work in the mythology of the mare; we will see it also in the myths of the androgyne.

In the Purāṇas, Prajāpati's incestuous androgyny is still looked at askance, especially in texts where the daughter does not become an animal:

> Prajāpati became pregnant and created progeny from his right thumb, nipple, and other organs, without the benefit of mothers. But he became dissatisfied with this creation, and so he divided his body in half and made one half a woman. He tried to make love to her, and although she and her brothers were shocked at this incestuous act, he eventually married her and created progeny with her (*Matsya P* 3. 1–12 and 3. 30–47; cf. *Manasāmaṅgal* 1–20, cited by Maity 1966, pp. 199–200).

In the Dogon myth, androgyny is a result of incest; here, and in most mythologies, androgyny is a cause of incest. Since the androgyne is male, as usual, this incest is of the father-daughter type (in contrast with the Dogon myth, mother-son). When the creator produces an androgyne separate from himself and the parts separate and mate, the result is brother-sister incest, the myth of the twins.

In the majority of the earliest Purāṇic texts, however, the androgyne is Prajāpati himself, and there is no implication of incest when his two halves separate and procreate (Manu 1. 31–32; *MP* 50. 9–11; *KP* 1. 8. 1–10). In these texts, the primeval androgyne is often regarded as both parents, and it is sometimes explicitly stated that the androgyne broke apart because of its desire to create. In one set of variants, Brahmā creates a separate androgyne to people the universe, and his invariable command to this creature is "Divide yourself." This secondary model—the creator and a separate androgyne—is used in a modified form in the next stage of androgyny, in which Śiva replaces Brahmā. For Prajāpati is, like Indra, a source of much of the later mythology of Śiva, and Śiva's androgyny develops in tandem with Prajāpati's (O'Flaherty 1973, pp. 111–40). Śiva's androgynous form was well known to early Sangam poetry in South India, was mentioned by a Syrian ambassador in the second century A.D. (Sircar 1971, p. 221), and is first cited in Sanskrit literature in the poetry of Bhāsa (fourth century A.D.; see Adiceam 1968, p. 147). In one cycle of myths, when Śiva remains chaste and refuses to create, Brahmā (the later form of Prajāpati) becomes an androgyne, divides himself into a man and woman who separate and mate, and thus begets the race of mortals (*ŚP* 7. 1. 12, 14, 17).[9] In later cycles, Brahmā creates by himself, but his creatures fail to continue their own propagation because they have no women; at Brahmā's entreaty, Śiva becomes an androgyne, splits the woman away from himself, and mates with her to produce the race of mortals (*ŚP* 3. 3. 1–29; *Viṣṇu P* 1. 7. 1–19; *PP* 5. 3. 155–72; *Vāyu P* 9. 67–93; *MP* 47. 1–17). One text combines both traditions: first Śiva appears as an androgyne to assist Brahmā; then Brahmā himself creates the androgynous pair, from whom creation proceeds (*Viṣṇu P* 1. 7. 13 and 17).

The myth of the androgyny of Prajāpati and/or Śiva is then developed in various ways. In order to distance the two gods from the implication of incest, the androgyny is sometimes transferred to someone else. Kāma, who is present (and sometimes actively responsible) when Brahmā or Śiva becomes lustful toward his female half, is said to be an androgyne (*BVP* 4. 35. 39). Dakṣa, a multiform of Prajāpati, is also an androgyne; he divides his body in two, begets a number of daughters, whom he supplies to the gods for their wives, and then gives away the female part of his form (*H* 3. 22. 1–7). Dakṣa also acts as an intermediary to prevent Śiva from committing incest: Brahmā created Rudra, an androgyne, who divided himself into male and female, as Brahmā told him to do; then Dakṣa took the female half of the androgyne and made her his daughter; and then he gave her to Rudra to be his wife (*Sk P* 7. 2. 9. 5–17). In yet another variant, Śiva uses the form of the androgyne precisely in order to avoid any sexual involvement in creation:

> Brahmā asked Śiva to create when his own creatures, lacking wives, failed to multiply. Śiva meditated upon his wife Satī and mentally created terrifying creatures like himself, the immortal Rudras, who devour the oblations. When Brahmā saw them and asked Śiva to create mortals instead, Śiva withdrew into his chastity and refused to create any more. Later, at Brahmā's renewed entreaties, Śiva reverted to his androgynous form, detached his female half, and instructed her to supply wives for the gods so that creation could proceed (*LP* 1. 70. 300–339; *Vāyu P* 10. 42–59).

Although Śiva has a wife at first, he merely meditates upon her and creates as Brahmā does, mentally. When forced to participate despite his vow of chastity, he delegates the female half of himself to produce females for the other gods (as Dakṣa gives Śiva his wife in other variants), so that he will not have to become involved with his own wife. Another text adds a final step to this process: after Śiva created, from his female half, the Goddess as a separate being, she created a goddess like herself to continue with procreation and then reentered Śiva's body, so that Śiva again became androgynous (*Saura P* 24. 55–67; 25. 5–29). As usual, the androgyne itself is barren; Śiva becomes the androgyne when he does *not* want to procreate sexually, but he produces replicas of his female half to procreate in the normal manner.

Śiva as a Fusing Androgyne

The final episode in the myth cited above describes the reintegration of the androgyne from its separated halves, and this process occurs in many later Śiva texts. For gradually the emphasis shifts from Śiva as the splitting androgyne to Śiva as the fusing androgyne. This second form is not fertile, but it may be erotic—a distinction we have encountered in many aspects of Hindu mythology.

The Purāṇas and folk traditions tell us that this form arose when, out of passion, gratitude, or some other emotion, Śiva embraced Pārvatī so closely that their bodies fused into one. According to one account, Śiva was a beggar, but one day he smoked so much hashish that he could not go out on his usual rounds; Pārvatī begged in his place and when she returned she "fed him with the food she had collected, and Mahadeva [Śiva] was so pleased with her that he embraced her violently and became one with her" (P. Thomas 1958, pp. 104–5; Beswick 1959, pp. 106–7). Pārvatī in this form is Annapūrṇā, the mother full of food; in this context, Śiva's embrace is neither erotic nor productive of erotic possibilities: he is forestalling sexual activity with the mother.

Pārvatī's role as mother is woven in and out of another and far more complex myth of the fusing androgyne, one that combines several other episodes from the classical mythology of Śiva.

> One day, after Śiva and Pārvatī had been married, Śiva was intent upon his worship of Sandhyā ["Twilight"], and Pārvatī became deeply upset, thinking that Śiva was deceiving her with another woman. She determined to leave him and to practice asceticism in order to assure herself of marital happiness—that is, of a husband who loved only her. As she departed, she thought to herself, "The Ganges will raise the two little boys [Gaṇeśa and Skanda], for she is extremely fond of children."
>
> As Pārvatī was engaged in meditation, the demon Mahiṣa saw her and sent a messenger to say, "It is a good thing that you left that clod Śiva, frigid with asceticism. But Mahiṣa is well suited to you; one look at him and you will give up your asceticism." When Pārvatī refused him, Mahiṣa attacked her and she killed him by causing Durgā to emit armies of Yoginīs and Mothers from her body. But when the head of Mahiṣa remained stuck fast to her hand and she discovered that he was a devotee of Śiva, Pārvatī again

> undertook a vow of asceticism, this time to expiate the sin of killing Mahiṣa. Śiva came to her and said, "Why do you torment yourself like this, when you could obtain whatever you want merely by asking me? You are the oblation and I am the fire; I am the sun and you are the moon. Therefore you should not make a separation between us, as if we were distinct people." As he said this, Śiva caused her to enter the side of his own body, as if she were hiding there in embarrassment, and their paired bodies became one, because of their love [*prema*].
>
> Then he said to her, "Let there be an end to your anger, Goddess. You abandoned Skanda when he wished to suckle at your breast, and you went off to perform asceticism, and so you will be called the Goddess Whose Breasts Are Not Sucked [Apītastanī]" (*Sk P* 1. 3. 2. 18–21).

The myth begins with Pārvatī's anger at being rejected by her ascetic husband, a pattern typical of Hindu mythology; she reacts to this by performing asceticism. Here, as elsewhere in the marriage of Śiva and Pārvatī, she suspects him of adulterous behavior, and the ultimate result of her action—the establishing of the androgynous form—is elsewhere cited as a direct result of her wish to curtail his philandering. Her experience of rejection—whether because of her husband's excessive sexuality or because of his inadequacy—leads her to reject not only him but her sons; the text emphasizes this, contrasting her explicitly with the Ganges, the Good Mother, and describing her as a mother who denies her breast to the child—i.e., as the quintessential breast that feeds itself. Thus the pattern of reaction turns Pārvatī into a mare contrasted with a cow.

This pattern is a direct replica of one that we have encountered in another myth, the tale of Gaurī/Kālī and Āḍi (see above, chap. 4, sec. C). There, the immediate result of Pārvatī's rejection by Śiva (who taunted her for her dark skin) was the creation of the goddess Kālī (the destructive, angry Fury) and the death by castration of the amorous demon Āḍi, who died in the embrace of Śiva. In the present myth, Pārvatī's rejection of husband and son in order to perform asceticism results in the creation of a series of furious goddess (first Durgā from her own body, then the dangerous Yoginīs and Mothers from Durgā's body) and in the Liebestod of the amorous demon Mahiṣa (a death described in a significantly sexual form, for the phallus of Śiva appears on Mahiṣa's neck after he is beheaded). The splitting-away of the dangerous part of Pārvatī results in the fusing of Pārvatī with Śiva; so too, in the tale of Āḍi, at least one version states that, as a result of her asceticism, Pārvatī obtained from Brahmā not only the boon of a golden skin but the promise that she would share half of Śiva's body (*Matsya P* 156. 12).

The conflict between Śiva and Pārvatī appears on several levels, beginning with their original fight. Some of this tension is expressed through the parallel behavior and treatment of Mahiṣa and Śiva: both seek to dissuade Pārvatī from her asceticism, and both succeed—at a price: Mahiṣa gives up his head (and life), while Śiva merely gives up half of his body. Though the text states that this fusion took place because of love, it is clear from Śiva's speech to her that his purpose was also to prevent her from becoming angry and leaving him again and to keep her from abandoning her son.

One South Indian series of myths of the fusing of the androgyne suggests a very competitive and entirely nonerotic cause. These myths center on the figure of the skeletal sage Bhṛṅgin:

> The gods and sages came to pay homage to Śiva, and all but the sage Bhṛṅgin circumambulated both Śiva and Pārvatī. But Bhṛṅgin, having vowed to worship only Śiva, circumambulated him alone. In anger, Pārvatī persuaded Śiva to join her to his own body, to thwart Bhṛṅgin. The sage, however, took the form of a beetle, pierced a hole through the composite form of the androgyne, and circumambulated Śiva alone. Then Pārvatī admired him and forgave him (Gopinatha Rao 1968, 2. 1. 322–23).

Since Bhṛṅgin is an adopted son of Śiva and Pārvatī, his persistent wish to separate them has strong Freudian overtones, which are the only erotic element in the myth. A variant of the myth states that, to foil Bhṛṅgin, Pārvatī persuaded Śiva merely to press his body closely against hers; Bhṛṅgin then took the form of a bee and passed between their necks. In both myths, however, Pārvatī is said to have punished Bhṛṅgin by taking from him his flesh and blood—that half of his body that belongs to the female, given by the mother—leaving him a mere skeleton, reduced to bones, given by the father. When Bhṛṅgin is about to fall down, Śiva gives him a third leg to support him. Ostensibly, this teaches Bhṛṅgin that all creatures are truly androgynous, that a male cannot remove or ignore the female half of his god, or of himself, and still be whole; and so he worships Her as well as Him. On a latent level, it teaches him that to try to separate his parents is to cause his mother to mutilate him. Though this mutilation is symbolic of the removal of the female parts of his body, it is also clearly a form of emasculation; this is supported by the way that it is restored here (as in the myths of Vivasvant) by the father, whose gift of the "third leg" requires no particularly ingenious psychoanalytic gloss.

Bhṛṅgin's desire to separate the androgyne in order to be with only one of his parents (the male parent) is inverted in a poem in which Menā, the mother of Pārvatī, wants to embrace only the female half—her child; when she realizes that Pārvatī is half of her (Menā's) son-in-law, she lowers her eyes (*Bālagopālastuti*, v. 63). In both instances, family relationships are thwarted by the androgynous merging of Śiva and Pārvatī.

A third version of the myth of Bhṛṅgin combines the usual account with the story of the asceticism Pārvatī undertook in order to win Śiva's love. We have already encountered an elaborate version of that episode; it appears elsewhere in a simpler form, in which it is said that Pārvatī once playfully covered up Śiva's eyes and plunged the universe into darkness; to expiate this misdeed she went on a great pilgrimage and was rewarded by Śiva's giving her the left half of his body. This episode is then grafted onto the story of Bhṛṅgin in the following way. As a result of Bhṛṅgin's persistent desire to worship Śiva alone, and of Śiva's persistence in aiding Bhṛṅgin against her, Pārvatī performed asceticism until Śiva gave in to her wish to become one with him (Adiceam 1968, pp. 145–46).[10] From these variations it is evident that the myth of Bhṛṅgin can be weighted in several different directions: to show Bhṛṅgin how mistaken he is in believing that Śiva can be separated from Pārvatī, or to show Pārvatī how mistaken she is in believing that they *cannot* be separated, or both. As usual, the androgyne is capable of more than one interpretation.

Despite its occasionally nonerotic or even antierotic rationalizations, the image of the androgyne often serves as a sexual symbol. The myths almost certainly arose as an afterthought to explain an already existing icon (Rawson 1966, pp. 46–47), which is often cited as an apparent example of the perfectly balanced marriage of a god and goddess. But the image still retains the marks of its antecedents in less satisfactorily fused forms. For one thing, Ardhanārīśvara is always regarded as a form of Śiva, not a form of Śiva and Pārvatī; the literal meaning of his name is "The Lord (*īśvara*) who is half (*ardha*) a woman (*nārī*)," a masculine noun for a male androgyne. When Pārvatī fuses with Śiva, she becomes half of *his* body—losing half of her own substance—while he is usually said to become enriched by her (though sometimes, too, he gives her half of his body). Similarly, in Hindu marriage, the woman becomes "half of her husband," but he does not become half of *her*.

Another of Śiva's androgynous forms that is lopsidedly male is the so-called Śiva-*liṅga*. In fact, the phallic *liṅga* is almost always accompanied by the *yoni*, the symbol of the Goddess's sexual organ, and as such is an iconic, though not anthropomorphic, androgyne (cf. Gross 1978a). In this form, the male is surrounded by the female, in representation of sexual union. But the female may be androgynously within the male, as well; the Goddess is sometimes depicted emerging from inside the Śiva-*liṅga* (Jung 1967, pp. 209, 221, and pl. 29). This is an imitation of the epiphany of Śiva himself in the myth of the *liṅgodbhava*, the emergence of the god out of the flame pillar in the middle of the ocean. During the festival of Śiva-rātri ("the night of Śiva") in Benares in 1978, at dawn on the banks of the Ganges I saw a chalk drawing of a Śiva-*liṅga* out of which was emerging the androgynous form of Śiva, neatly split down the middle.

The concept of the androgynous *liṅga* appears in contemporary South India in a modified form:

> The stone *civalinkam* or the phallus is a male form, but the substance within it, which is liquid (semen) or light (the deity), which is its action, is *cakti*, female. . . . The sign of maleness is really the locus of female qualities in a man, the male womb [that yields a] milky, generative substance (Egnor 1978, p. 69).

Tamils are also receptive to more general ideas of androgyny: "M. was fond of saying that all people are born as female and only later differentiate sexually, as the body itself differentiates, left side female, right side male" (ibid., p. 80). Here the primeval androgyne is female rather than male and, like the Dogon androgyne, differentiates only later, under social pressure.

Despite the presence of such strong female symbolism surrounding the *liṅga*, it is traditionally regarded as a form of Śiva alone, and it functions in mythology as a phallus pure and simple (interacting with various female forms and even with women who use it as a dildo [Elwin 1949, p. 473][11] or as an instrument through which Śiva himself becomes manifest in his anthropomorphic form. In the context of Indian ideas about self-contained fluids, the *liṅga* in the *yoni* may be regarded as a male image in yet another way: it may symbolize the fantasy of protecting the phallus by taking it inside the body—the *male's* body—a narcissistic fantasy of self-sufficiency (Kakar 1978, pp. 158–59). This would be an inversion of the myth in which the full body of the god Śiva emerges from inside the *liṅga*.

The Problem of the Androgyne: Getting Together

Thus in its origins and in its iconic forms, the androgyne is not always a symbol of perfect union and balance between Śiva and Pārvatī.

Sanskrit court poetry abounds in gentle satires on the idyllic couple, which (like Maurice Henry's cartoons) pointedly call attention to the fact that Śiva's and Pārvatī's being permanently fused together means that they are in the one form guaranteed to prevent sexual activity. Despite their origins as a "fused" androgyne, they, like the splitting androgynes, must separate in order to get together:

> Let the god's delight have been unsurpassed
> that bearing your slender body joined to his,
> he receives, oh Gaurī, your tight embrace;
> still, Śiva's heart must often grieve
> to think your glance cannot by him be seen,
> sweet, loving, innocent, and motionless with love.
> (*SRK* 82, trans. Ingalls)

As Ingalls remarks, with his customary understatement and gentility, "The androgynous union of Śiva and Gaurī has one disadvantage" (Ingalls 1965, p. 474).

The poem's ironic insight is an inversion of the theme of *viraha*, the longing for the beloved and the implication that only in separation is there true longing (O'Flaherty 1973, pp. 256–58). The Tantric variant of this philosophy of *viraha* stresses not the separation but the union, arguing that only when sensuality is entirely satiated (and, in Tantric tradition, entirely internalized) is lust truly conquered; only when male and female are united is there no desire (cf. Herman 1979, pp. 91–94). As Alan Watts remarks, the Tantric androgyne symbolizes a state "in which the erotic no longer has to be sought or pursued, because it is always present in its totality" (Watts 1963, pp. 204–5). The androgyne in the poem, however, implies that the greatest longing may be felt in complete union, when satiation is so near and yet so far; water, water, everywhere, nor any drop to drink. Thus the androgyne may symbolize satiation without desire (as in Tantra) or desire without satiation (as in the poem).

The logic by which sexual union is characterized as desireless is beautifully expressed by a contemporary Tamil:

> The fulfillment of the desire is cool, and this only is what is sought: . . . "After the two have united, the body becomes cool. . . . When husband and wife stand separately, wanting to unite, because of the feeling the whole body becomes hot. When they unite, feeling spreads, and the heat cools. As that feeling, as the feeling that cools the heat, the lord enters inside." . . . Thus standing separately is hot, uniting is cool (Egnor 1978, p. 103).

The androgyne as a symbol of satiation is a cool image; as a symbol of *viraha*, it is a hot image. It may thus symbolize union without desire or desire without union.

A final disadvantage of the androgynous state lies in the way that it makes each of the partners vulnerable. This is a marriage, one would think, that cannot end in divorce. Not so. In a Tamil version of the myth of Dakṣa's sacrifice, when Dakṣa insults Śiva and Śiva appears to be unwilling to defend himself, "Devī actually stalks out of the androgyne in a fury, leaving Śiva with half of his body aching" (Shulman 1978, p. 113).[12] The longing of one half of the androgyne for the other when they are conjoined is matched only by the longing of one for the other when they have been split apart, a longing here expressed in stark physical terms.

Viṣṇu as a Fusing Androgyne

The image of Śiva and Pārvatī joined androgynously served as a rallying point for other androgynous or pseudo-androgynous mythological figures. Several episodes of sex change became assimilated to the mythology of Śiva during the epic period. In the first, Śukra is born from Śiva (who himself undergoes male pregnancy in order to have this son) and then in turn gives birth to Kaca (who thus becomes Śukra's son) (see above, chap. 8, sec. L). In the second, Agni as a pregnant male gives birth to Skanda (a feat later attributed to Śiva (*MBh* 3. 213–16; O'Flaherty 1973, pp. 90–110); in his own right, Agni is an androgynous figure, a serial androgyne who varies according to the ritual context (see above, chap. 2, sec. B). A third epic androgyne is King Īḷa, whose androgyny is resolved sometimes by Śiva but occasionally by Viṣṇu (*Viṣṇu P* 4. 1. 8).

Viṣṇu himself is closely associated with Śiva's androgyny. At first, Viṣṇu undergoes not androgyny but pseudo-androgyny, a sex change: he transforms himself into the enchantress Mohinī in order to take back the Soma from the demons who have stolen it (*MBh* 1. 15–17; O'Flaherty 1973, p. 277), a typical Trickster sex change. This myth is then tied to Śiva through a cycle in which Śiva becomes inspired by lust at the sight of Mohinī, embraces her, and sheds his seed (which is said to give birth to Skanda, Ayyappan-Aiyanar [also called Hariharaputra, "Son of Viṣṇu-Śiva"], or Hanuman; *Bh P* 8. 12. 12–35; *AP* 3. 17–20; *ŚP* 3. 20. 3–7). Strangely, but significantly, lust is here the motivating factor, though it usually is not in the fusion of Śiva and Pārvatī; for this reason, perhaps, as well as in sheer embarrassment, Pārvatī lowers her head in shame when Śiva embraces Mohinī (*Br P* 4. 10. 41–77). This episode is then used to produce an androgynous form of Viṣṇu and Śiva, by grafting the Mohinī episode onto the episode of the tricking of the demon of ashes, Bhasmāsura:

> When Śiva was threatened by Bhasmāsura, Viṣṇu took the form of Mohinī and tricked the demon into reducing himself to ashes. Then Viṣṇu "found himself a prey to the uncontrollable passion of Śiva. The result of this incestuous connection between" Viṣṇu and Śiva was Aiyanar (Oppert 1893, p. 508; cf. *BhB* 10. 88. 14–36; see also Obeyesekere 1980, p. 416).

A variant of this myth recorded in Sri Lanka early in the present century contains several significant changes:

> Great Vishnu having taken the appearance of a woman whose name was Surānganā ["Celestial Nymph," that is, Mōhinī] was rocking in a swing. At that time Basmasurā [i.e., Bhasmāsura] was a servant of the God Īswara [Śiva]. The Goddess Umayanganā [Pārvatī] was married to Īswara. While Basmasurā was employed under Umayanganā she went alone to the river to bathe, and . . . created a prince, made of grass, to guard her. She then entered the water. A tale-bearer went and falsely told Īswara that Basmasurā had gone to watch the Goddess bathe. Then Īswara being angry mounted his elephant, and taking his sword . . . he cut off the prince's head, which fell into the water. Śiva replaced the head of the prince, who became Gaṇeśa. Pārvatī then created seven more princes out of grass. The God Īswara, saying, "I am going to eat my sons," clasped his arms round them, and all seven were caught, but one escaped beneath his hand and fled. The other six were crushed together, and became the God Kanda-Swāmi [Skanda]. The one who escaped became a demon. Basmasurā tried to kill Śiva in order to marry Pārvatī, but Mohinī enticed him and tricked him into burning himself to ashes.
>
> Then Śiva embraced Mohinī, and Basmasurā, through his love for her, was conceived in her womb. Afterwards Surānganā resumed her male form [as Vishnu]. Ten months being fully accomplished, he split his right hand, and took out the prince, who received the name of Ayiyanār Baṇḍāra (Parker 1909, pp. 157–58).[13]

Bhasmāsura, though falsely accused of lust (as the Goddess herself often is) then becomes truly lustful and is killed, in an episode that duplicates many of the motifs of the myth of Āḍi, with a reversal of the sexes (here, the husband believes that his wife has been accosted during his absence) but with the same injury to the son who protects his mother. This injury is then emphasized by Śiva's blatant statement that he is going to devour his sons, a danger that six of them escape by merging, while the seventh becomes demonic. The first of these two motifs is borrowed (with modifications) from the Sanskrit texts of the birth of Skanda, in which the single-headed child sprouts six heads in order to be nursed by six mothers, or is born as the result of the merging of six sparks of fire that melt into one (O'Flaherty 1973, pp. 98–107, 267–77). The second of the motifs—the escape of the seventh son—recalls the episode in which the first six sons of Aditi become gods, while the seventh becomes the doomed Mārtāṇḍa. Finally, Bhasmāsura himself becomes reborn as the son of the woman he lusts for, a classically oedipal act for which there is much precedence in classical Sanskrit texts (see above, chap. 4, sec. C), and this child, though conceived in an androgyne, is ultimately born through a male pregnancy, breaking out of the right hand of Viṣṇu just as other gods break out of the right thigh of Vena or the thumb of Śiva or Prajāpati.

This tendency to change the parent of Ayiyanār from an androgyne into a pregnant male is further developed in Sri Lanka in a text that substitutes Pārvatī for Śiva as the one who gives Skanda his final form and further distances Śiva from the birth of Ayiyanār as well:

> When Viṣṇu became a woman to trick Bhasmāsura, Śiva also became infatuated and wanted to marry "her." He obtained permission from his wife, Umā, to marry this woman, but, each time he went to bring her home, she was pregnant, and he had to wait for the birth to take place. This occurred six times, and six children were born. When it happened for a seventh time, Śiva "thought that this was a wonder, a miraculous creation and not normal birth". Umā then came with him and saw the woman and six of her children (the eldest was picking flowers elsewhere in the forest). Umā embraced all the children together and the six-headed Skanda was born; the eldest child was Ayiyanayake (Obeyesekere 1980, p. 416; my paraphrase).

Although one might see a direct connection between Śiva's infatuation with Mohinī and Mohinī's subsequent pregnancy, suggesting a glossed-over or bowdlerized sexual encounter, Śiva himself does not take this view; he regards the births as miraculous, though they are certainly far more conventional than the traditional tales of Ayiyanār's birth—from the androgynous union of Śiva and Viṣṇu or, as in the text recorded by Parker, from the male pregnancy of Viṣṇu alone. The abnormal births are in fact superfluous to this second version, for the seventh, who in

Parker's text escapes, necessitating the further impregnation of Viṣṇu, is here simply made into Ayiyanār (Ayiyanayake). The demonic child of the androgyne is made divine, just as the aggressive father is replaced by a loving mother—both roles played by Śiva in Parker's text.

Various reasons are given for the union of Viṣṇu and Śiva; one that we have encountered is the statement that Śiva, after finishing his *tāṇḍava* dance, joined half of himself with half of Viṣṇu to please Pārvatī (see above, chap. 5, sec. G), the reason often given for his fusion with Pārvatī herself. But the union of Viṣṇu and Śiva (often called Hari-Hara, Viṣṇu-Śiva) generally proves a theological rather than a sexual point: when the gods come to visit Viṣṇu, he shows them that he is half Śiva so that they will worship them both (*Vām P* 36. 1–31). Viṣṇu himself is the androgyne in one strange variant of the myth of Brahmā and Śiva:

> When Brahmā's creatures failed to increase, Śiva became the androgyne at Brahmā's request. But Śiva burnt Brahmā up, and then by means of yoga he enjoyed the female half of himself. In her he created Viṣṇu and Brahmā. Then Viṣṇu split his body in two and created all creatures (*LP* 1. 41. 7–12).

The burning of Brahmā by Śiva is an expression of their competition as sexual creators (O'Flaherty 1973, pp. 136–38); when Śiva succeeds in eliminating his rival, however, he behaves chastely, as his androgynous form usually does: spurning sexual intercourse, he engages in yoga. The result of this creation is a new androgyne: Viṣṇu, who splits his body and proceeds with creation—the text does not tell us how. We will encounter both the Viṣṇu-Śiva androgyne and the Viṣṇu-Lakṣmī androgyne in visual images.

The Mockery of the Androgyne

Śiva as the androgyne expresses a number of theological insights in medieval Hinduism, many of them related to the *coincidentia oppositorum* that is Śiva's forte. But he is also satirized with banal literal-mindedness for the very qualities that are praised in the abstract. Thus a hymn of praise says to him, "You are not a god or a demon nor a mortal or an animal; you are not a man or a woman or a eunuch" (*ŚP* 2. 2. 15. 61; *MBh* 13. 17. 56).[14] But almost the same expressions occur in Dakṣa's scornful diatribe against Śiva: "He belongs to none of the four classes and is neither male nor female. And he certainly cannot be a eunuch, because his phallus is an object of worship" (*Sk P* 4. 2. 87. 29–35). Śiva is in a no-win situation; for, just as Dakṣa spurns him as a son-in-law for being not enough of a man (half a man), so is he scorned as an ascetic for being so completely overcome by his wife that he gives his body to her:

> "So now this [Śiva], whose asceticism is known through all the world,
> fearful of absence from his mistress, bears her in his very form.
> And they say that we were overcome by him!"
> Victory to Love, who, with these words,
> presses [Rati's] hand and falls to laughter.
>
> (*SRK* 323, trans. Ingalls)

This sentiment is reversed in a passage in praise of Śiva, where Pārvatī is mocked for regarding Śiva as uxorious (*straiṇam*) because he has shared half of his body with her, even though she saw him burn Kāma to ashes (*Mahimnastava* 23). And Śiva is pitied not only for being half a man but for having only half a wife: an inscription states that a certain king gave Śiva a hundred beautiful women because Śiva had only half a woman (Sivaramamurti 1974, p. 5).[15]

We have seen several examples of androgynes resulting from a child's stumbling upon the primal scene (Īḷa and Bhṛṅgin assuming the role of the child). Sanskrit poetry gives explicit examples of this, expressing humorous empathy with Śiva's child's difficulty in puzzling it all out, making the transition from the infantile perception of the "combined parent" to a mature differentiation of male and female:

> "This is Ma. But no, it can't be Ma;
> she never had a rough red beard on half her face.
> This is Da. But no, it can't be Da;
> I never saw a breast on Father's chest.
> Who is this then? Who this? What is it: man or woman?
> Or can it be still something else?"
> With such doubts [Skanda], having seen the form of [Śiva],
> starts back, and may he so protect you.
>
> (*SRK* 90, trans. Ingalls)

This poem plays on the incongruity of the physiological signs of male and female. A similar satire focuses only on the superficial social and iconic characteristics; Śiva's neck is dark (with the poison he swallowed at the churning of the ocean) and he wears the crescent moon:

> "On the left is the eye with collyrium,
> and on the right is the dark neck.
> Here is a mirror in the (left) hand,
> and there the moon on the headdress.
> That is mother, and this is father."

Thus, after a long time,
Skanda gradually realizes whose lap he is on.
(Sivaramamurti 1974, p. 130)[16]

When Skanda cannot figure it out at all, or when he asks more difficult theological questions about the androgyne, his older brother Gaṇeśa comes to the rescue:

"When father and when mother became a single body,
what happened, elder brother, to the other halves of each?"
Victory to Gaṇeśa, who explains to the young prince,
"The one on earth was born as everyman,
the other as everywoman."
(*SRK* 85, trans. Ingalls)

Gaṇeśa is an established authority on this subject, for he himself indulges in androgyny in a strange imitation of his parents:

May the single-tusked Gaṇeśa guard the universe,
who imitates his parents' custom
in that his bride, it seems, has been allowed to take
that half of him wherein his face is tuskless.
(ibid., v. 94)

Though Gaṇeśa is usually chaste, he is sometimes depicted as married to Success and Intelligence, who appear as goddesses incarnate beside him, sometimes holding his broken tusk. Since this tusk may be the symbol of a castrated phallus (Leach 1962), the poet's fancy may be close to one level of the underlying symbolism: the tuskless cheek is indeed a female cheek, and the woman beside Gaṇeśa may be aggressively implicated in his loss of masculinity. Gaṇeśa takes an explicitly androgynous form in an eleventh-century Sanskrit poem (Sircar 1971, p. 228).[17]

A final satire on the androgyne occurs in a poem which suggests that Pārvatī asked to be incorporated into her husband in order to keep him from his customary philandering:

Perhaps because she could not bear the presence of
the Ganges on his head,
Pārvatī took refuge in half of Śiva's body
and by uniting with him brought her husband
into her own power, to her complete satisfaction.
(Sivaramamurti 1974, p. 93)[18]

As Sivaramamurti comments on this verse, the androgyne "is fancifully conceived to be an expression of Devī's impatience to curb Śiva [and is formed so that she can] have a greater control over him and feels satisfied he cannot now flirt" (ibid.). Here the androgyne is a symbol not of conjugal bliss but of adultery (for Śiva's liaison with the Ganges is a constant thorn in Pārvatī's side [O'Flaherty 1973, pp. 229–33]) and of jealousy and the struggle for sexual control over the consort.

This challenge to the androgynous image of perfect union is expressed on the folk level, as well:

> The husband and wife are thought, on a mythological level, to form one body. The androgynous form of Śiva-Śakti symbolizes this union and the harmony of function that should ideally obtain. But in the villager's perception of marriage, the husband and wife are also distinct people with separate wills that can be pitted against each other (S. Daniel 1978, p. 9).

Even within the myth, the myth is debunked, as we have seen; when the myth is taken as a metaphor for actual human interaction, it quickly falls apart.

The androgyne is frightening as well as funny. In one text, Rudra as the androgyne is said to be "fearsome and dreadful to behold." Brahmā stays only long enough to tell him to split into two parts and then disappears in terror. When the androgyne proceeds to split, each half (male and female) further splits into contrasting pairs: gentle and fierce, beautiful and ugly, light and dark (*KP* 1. 11. 1–47). These negative connotations and abstract extrapolations indicate that the image often lost much of its charismatic power and religious meaning in the medieval Purāṇas and court poetry, a hypothesis supported by the changes that occurred in the visual image during the same period, roughly between 500 and 1500 A.D.

Visual Images

Early examples of Indian androgynes occur in two small images dating from the late Kuṣāṇa period[19] and in a larger image carved on the outer wall of a fifth-century Pallava temple at Mahabalipuram. The first two are naked, the third clothed, and all are visually "fused" rather than sharply split down the middle. Slightly later, but even more beautifully integrated (in part thanks to the "triple bend" pose [*tribaṅga*] that bends the figure so that there is no straight vertical axis), are stone carvings from temples at Pattdakal and Badāmī.[20] Here the presence of clothing over the genitals may serve to soften the image, though there is a single naked breast. The famous androgynes at Ellora and Elephanta are among the masterpieces of Indian art (see Zimmer 1960, p. 256; plate 9, above);

their success may be due to the brilliance of the individual sculptors as much as to a *rapprochement* of the sexes during this period. But some sort of celebration of eroticism and an appreciation of the woman in her erotic role are certainly important at Khajuraho, where Tantrism is so much in evidence (Desai 1975, pp. 112–45) and where several fine androgynes appear, fully clothed (Sivaramamurti 1974, p. 92).[21]

The bronze images from this period are sharper, as a result of the sharper medium, but are still brilliant and convincing in their fusion. There are several examples of Chola Ardhanārīśvaras,[22] including a magnificent dancing androgynous Śiva, now in the Madras Museum. But the stone carvings from the later Pāla period, in Bengal (a very Tantric time and place), are more rigid and perhaps even grotesque (Rawson 1973, pl. 161; Rawson 1968, pl. 6), though this is in part a result of the realistic depiction of half a naked erect phallus, a feature of many Nepalese androgynes as well.[23]

Many of these images are entirely anthropomorphic, and thus they depict each of the partners as having one arm; but some of them give him two arms and her but one, a development that not only makes difficult any satisfactory visual balance but reveals once again that the image is lopsidedly male.[24] Furthermore, it implies that he is a god while she is a mere mortal, an assumption shared by the texts from this period (see above, chap. 4, sec. C). Clearly, the spirit of integration and fusing is now slipping away.

When one turns to two-dimensional illustrations of androgynes, in paintings and manuscripts, the visual fusion is almost entirely gone. A straight line separates the two rigid halves, and although they are fully clothed they are ridiculous; it is as if someone had cut a drawing of Śiva in half and then a drawing of Pārvatī in half and had then stuck the two together. This is true of the crude Kalighat images (Rawson 1971, p. 98, pl. 499) as well as the Early Western paintings (*Mahimnastava* 23), and it is hilariously true of a modern painting by an Indian artist, Laxman Pai (Rawson 1968, pl. 7). One cannot simply blame the medium for distorting the message, however, for folk paintings by women artists in Mithilā present highly stylized but brilliantly integrated androgynous forms of Śiva (cf. Vequaud 1977, p. 55). In one of these (see plate 10, above) the tiger skin worn by the Śiva half has a face that simultaneously represents several significant planes of symbolism: it is a sun face (symbolic of solar power) but it is also a face, symbolic of the source of phallic seed in the head, in which the nose is placed precisely where one would expect the phallus to be and approximates its shape, the eyes actually replace the sexual organ that they so often represent, and the mouth is situated—ambiguously, as befits the androgyne—to express the devouring aspect of sexuality. On an explicit level, the face is that of a tiger, symbolic of the center of Śiva's animal powers as well as sexual powers.

For the most part, the late-medieval and modern depictions represent a sad degeneration from the vision preserved at Ellora and Elephanta. This must reflect, at least in part, the mounting tension between male and female during this period, as evinced by the Purāṇic myths of uneasy hierogamies. In support of this hypothesis is the fact that at Khajuraho, under Tantric influence, "fused" androgynes continue to be carved in the late medieval period. It is perhaps significant that even in the middle period the female imagery was not altogether suppressed, and in this context one might view these decadent androgynes as attempts to preserve some perception of complementarity and symbiosis despite all the tension.[25]

One final development of the visual image might be interpreted as evidence either for the moribundity of the androgyne or of its flexible adaptation to other uses, like a fish suddenly developing lungs or wings when life in the water became impossible—evidence of the vitality of the fish (the image) and the degeneration of the water (the social context). This is the adaptation of the androgyne to express the union of Śiva and Viṣṇu, a process documented in myth.

The transition took place in four stages. First, the Śiva/Pārvatī image was imitated by Vaiṣṇavas, who constructed similar images of Viṣṇu/Lakṣmī (after all, they had a hierogamy too) (Waldschmidt 1970, pl. 20). Then the half-Viṣṇu was joined to the half-Śiva, which required a significant shift of place: in the Śiva/Pārvatī image, she was always on the left and he on the right; so too in the Viṣṇu/Lakṣmī. But when the two right-hand men got together, Śiva's prior claim to the right-hand spot apparently took precedence over his relative "left-handedness," and so he maintained the place that he had held for centuries before anyone ever dreamed of splitting Viṣṇu in half: Śiva on the right, Viṣṇu on the left, in the images of Hari-Hara (Gopinatha Rao 1968, vol. 2, pt. 1, pp. 332–34; Rawson 1971, p. 98; Adiceam 1966). So, too, a Purāṇic text states that when Śiva merged with Viṣṇu at Pārvatī's request, Viṣṇu was on the left (Adiceam 1968, pp. 143, 148). One reason for this was that in the image of Hari-Hara, Viṣṇu was treated like a *śakti* of Śiva; the "terrible" (*raudra*) form of Śiva was on the right, while the "gentle" or "refreshing" (*saumya* or *śītala*) form of Pārvatī or Viṣṇu was on the left.

The third step was the construction of a female version of the image of Hari-Hara: the right half of the woman, Lakṣmī, holds the emblems of Viṣṇu (conch, discus, mace, lotus, and thunderbolt) and rests on the

Garuḍa bird that is Viṣṇu's mount; the left half, Pārvatī, holds the emblems of Śiva (trident, etc.) and rests on the bull Nandi; the right half has a garland of flowers and the left a garland of skulls (Sivaramamurti 1974, p. 371). [26] Here, as in the male counterpart, the Śaiva figure maintains its place, but the sectarian alignment is the opposite: the Śaiva image is on the left, the Vaiṣṇava image on the right. A late text produces still other variations on Vaiṣṇava androgynes:

> At the time of creation, the Goddess was born from the left side of Kṛṣṇa. By the will of the Lord, she suddenly divided into two, both of them equal in beauty and glory: the left side was Mahālakṣmī, and the right side was Rādhā. Rādhā chose the two-armed lord, and then Mahālakṣmī desired the god as her lover. Kṛṣṇa therefore divided himself into two: the right side had two arms and became the lover of Rādhā in the world of cows; the left side had four arms and became the lover of Lakṣmī in Vaikuntha (*BVP* 2. 35. 4–15).

Kṛṣṇa here splits into an androgynous form, with the woman appropriately on the left; this goddess then further splits, and now the left side is the Goddess, the right side the anthropomorphic woman (supreme in this particular text, which exalts Kṛṣṇa and Rādhā as godhead); Lakṣmī stays on the left, as she is when joined to Viṣṇu, rather than on the right, as she is when joined with Pārvatī. Kṛṣṇa then splits into two once more in order to satisfy both women: again the left side is the god, the right side the anthropomorphic form. In terms of visual images, this does not work: the left side of Kṛṣṇa cannot unite with the left side of the goddess, if one takes it literally. But in terms of matching powers, it is entirely appropriate: the two lefts go together, and the two rights go together. Thus Rādhā ends up on the right side here because she is the other of the other, the left of the left, contrasted with Lakṣmī, who is contrasted with Kṛṣṇa in his supernatural form, on the right. Moreover, since Mahālakṣmī is often a form of Durgā,[27] she belongs on the left by virtue of her Tantric and Śaiva associations.

Finally, to combine the two combinations, at least one iconographer had the bright idea of combining Śiva and Lakṣmī; since Śiva is apparently less left-handed in his excesses than Lakṣmī is in her femininity, both of them revert to their original positions: Lakṣmī is on the left, and Śiva is on the right (Mookerjee 1968, p. 35).[28]

There is therefore a clear pattern of variations in the placement of gods and goddesses on right or left (see chart 5). Pārvatī and Śiva are entirely consistent: she is always on the left, sinister in her femininity and in her association with the Dionysian Śiva, and he is always on the

Chart 5. Left-Right Positions within Hindu Androgynous Pairs

Positions of the Androgyne

Left	*Right*
Pārvatī	Śiva
Viṣṇu	Śiva
Lakṣmī	Śiva
Pārvatī	Lakṣmī
Lakṣmī	Viṣṇu
Viṣṇu	Kṛṣṇa
Lakṣmī	Rādhā
Rādhā	Kṛṣṇa

right, because of the primacy of the original image, in which he is on the right. The Vaiṣṇava figures, arriving late on the scene, vacillate. Viṣṇu, when paired with Lakṣmī, is on the right because he is consistently "right" in both ways—he is male and he is Apollonian. But he shifts place when he is paired with Śiva (who has prior claim to the right-hand spot) or with Kṛṣṇa (in a Tantric text in which Kṛṣṇa is supreme over Viṣṇu). Kṛṣṇa, like Śiva, remains consistently on the right, in contrast with Rādhā's (sinister) femininity as well as with Viṣṇu's less numinous and, hence, more sinister character.

The placement of Lakṣmī and Rādhā, who are the most distant from the original image, is the most confused. Lakṣmī is "left" in her femininity and in her lowliness, as compared with the supreme authority of the Tantric Rādhā. But she is "right" either in her association with the Apollonian Viṣṇu, which contrasts with Pārvatī's "left-handed" Śaivism, or in response to Pārvatī's basic claim to the left-hand position, which she had in the original androgyne. Similarly, Rādhā is doctrinally "right" in comparison with Lakṣmī, as Lakṣmī is in comparison with Pārvatī; but Rādhā is "left" by virtue of her femininity when paired with Kṛṣṇa. The placing of these two figures is somewhat arbitrary and perhaps not of great significance. When Lakṣmī is finally paired with Śiva, gender is again found to outweigh questions of orthodoxy and heterodoxy, and Lakṣmī is more "left" than Śiva, who steadfastly maintains his place on the right. Thus the images are conjoined and ranked hierarchically in a way that shows that the androgyne was still regarded as a primarily sexual image; but the visual icon is lifeless.

E. Meanings of the Androgyne

From our horizontal survey of several cultures and our vertical bore into Indian religious history, several meanings of androgyny emerge. That there are several should not surprise us. Eliade notes the complexity of the symbolism when writing about two basic types of androgyne regarded as one (the primeval androgyne, who, though created as an integrated being, like our "splitting" androgyne, is still regarded as a symbol of fusion):

> We have observed on many occasions that by transcending the opposites one does not always attain the same mode of being. There is every possible difference, for instance, between spiritual androgynisation and the "confusion of the sexes" obtained by orgy; between regression to the formless and "spooky" and the recovery of "paradisaical" spontaneity and freedom (Eliade 1965, p. 123 n.).

These, and other meanings, are all present in the Indian myths and symbols of androgyny.

The Hindu myths assume that a man can be a woman; there is no problem about it at all. But this assumption is the source of several corollary problems: (1) A man can be a woman, but a woman cannot be a man. (2) A man can be a woman; but to create in this form is dangerous, since it is often fatal to him. (3) A man can be a woman, but this makes it difficult, if not impossible, for him to be *with* a woman. (4) If God is a man who is a woman, how is the worshiper to be his consort?

The first of these problems emerges from the Indian textual and visual material that demonstrates the nonequality, the primary maleness, of the androgyne. The androgyne seems to express a conflict between one sex's need for and fear of the other—primarily the male's need for and fear of the female. Female genitals are seldom if ever depicted; the breast, not the vagina, is the emblem of the woman that contrasts with the phallus. This may indicate a disinclination to unite the male with the "tooth" goddess rather than the breast goddess (see above, chap. 4, sec. C); it underscores once again the uneasiness evident in so many of these images. The maleness of the androgyne may represent not only the androcentrism of the religious context but a deeper feeling of imbalance, a male's need to correct his own incompleteness by assimilating to himself the form of the female.

The negative connotations of androgyny highlight a danger not unlike the danger inherent in the encounter with the mare goddess. Ritual androgyny is a source of power, but it also opens up the possibility of great loss. As Eliade remarks,

> Every attempt to transcend the opposites carries with it a certain danger. This is why the ideas of a *coincidentia oppositorum* always arouse ambivalent feelings; on the one side, man is haunted by the desire to escape from his particular situation and regain a transpersonal mode of life; on the other, he is paralysed by the fear of losing his "identity" and "forgetting" himself (Eliade 1965, p. 123 n.).

To open the floodgates holding back unknown feminine powers—those from above (the mare) or from within (the androgyne)—is an enterprise that can never be undertaken lightly.

As a theological symbol, the androgyne changes to accommodate the shifting currents of the religious movements that give it life. Androgynes may be "pro-chaos" or "anti-chaos." In India, the anti-chaos element is represented by Vedic and Purāṇic Hinduism, the religion of hierarchy and caste; the pro-chaos element is found in various forms of Indian mysticism, beginning in the Upaniṣads and continuing in early forms of *bhakti*. The Vedic/Purāṇic androgyne must split apart in order to be creative; the mystic must merge with undifferentiated godhead to realize his nature (a process often described in sexual metaphors). The Vedic Puruṣa or Upaniṣadic Puruṣa androgyne dismembers himself; Śiva or Devī is reembodied from the disparate parts.

Vedic/Purāṇic Hinduism, however, also celebrates the hierogamy and the positive value of procreation, while Vedāntic Hinduism avoids a god (let alone a goddess) possessing specific attributes and denies the value of procreation. Vedic/Purāṇic Hinduism is phenomenal and dynamic; Vedāntic mysticism opposes to this dynamism a kind of stasis. This dichotomy is resolved in many ways in the theology of *bhakti*, where the abstract sexual imagery of Vedānta is combined with the specific sexual hierogamy of Purāṇic Hinduism. Tantrism proposes a different but equally valid resolution: sexuality is the instrument of liberation; *mokṣa* is achieved through *bhokṣa* (O'Flaherty 1973, pp. 258–59). Another powerful opposition in Indian religion is that between the religion of orthodox marriage—connected as it is with caste distinctions and with the temple hierogamy—and the religion of unorthodox passion, *viraha*, and the longing for the forbidden god. Here *bhakti* does not resolve the conflict but is itself an element in a new conflict; and here again the androgyne serves to express a possible syncretism. For one kind of androgyne (the merged androgyne) is the mirror image of *viraha*: this androgyne is the symbol of complete satiation and desirelessness. But another kind of androgyne is an expression of *viraha* itself, the epitome of tantalizing but unfulfilled proximity; the two halves, having split, long to reunite. The middle type can be interpreted either way: as a fusion, representing sexual ecstasy and satiation, or as a static juxtaposition, representing barrenness and fruitless desire.

Hindus have for many centuries wrestled with the problem of *bhedābheda*, "distinction/nondistinction," or *viśiṣṭādvaita*, "qualified nondualism," which is, at heart, the problem of how, if at all, one may *unite* with god when one *is* god. In contrast with the reams of involuted philosophical texts devoted to this enduring paradox, the image of the androgyne expresses with stark simplicity the problem of how one may be *separated* from god when one is united with god, separation (*viraha*) being an essential component of love. As a theological image, therefore, the androgyne may represent either the bliss of union with god or the ironic agony of eternal longing for a deity with whom one is in fact consubstantial.

Caitanya was thought to symbolize the first of these two possibilities: "He was the earthly representation of the principle of *acintya bhedābheda*, the theory that postulated simultaneous and incomprehensible difference and non-difference between human and divine" (Dimock 1966b, 43; see above, chap. 4, sec. C). For Śiva and Pārvatī, however, fusion raised new problems of identity and differentiation and even served as a means of satirizing the entire Advaita concept of God; for the mockery of the androgyne also mocks the striving for union with a deity who cannot be differentiated from oneself.

The psychology of the androgyne emerges clearly from episodes in which a child tries to separate his parents, but this psychology, too, is implicit in the image itself. The Freudian view, which denies the creativity of chaos, views the androgyne as something that must be split in order for life to proceed. But when the androgyne is taken not as a symbol of combined mother and father but rather as a single androgynous parent, different implications emerge. When the androgyne is primarily male, there are problems within him; he is weakened, or mocked, or unable to give birth, or threatened with death when he tries to give birth (as is explicit in the myth of Śukra and the tale of the pregnant Vidyādhara). But when the androgyne is primarily female, the physical dangers are replaced by moral dangers.

For the female androgyne evokes the syndrome of the mare: she is a phallic threat to the male. Just as the androgyne can symbolize union or separation, so the female androgyne in particular comes to symbolize *bad* union in contrast with the *good* union symbolized by the male androgyne. The male androgyne is an example of the positive theology of the *coincidentia oppositorum*, though the negative aspects of this symbolism are occasionally expressed; the female androgyne is, however, generally regarded as a negative instance of *coincidentia oppositorum*, the freak that violates taxonomy, dirt symbolizing matter out of place. When the Goddess is worshiped as a positive instance of deity, the paradox is accepted; when she is feared as a demon, the paradox is unacceptable.

The negativity of the female androgyne is strikingly illustrated by a Śākta text composed in Bengal, perhaps under the influence of the myth of the incarnation of Kṛṣṇa and Rādhā in the androgynous form of Caitanya:

> The gods begged Kālī to rid the earth of demonic kings, and she agreed to become incarnate as Kṛṣṇa. Śiva prayed to Kālī and was given permission to become incarnate as Rādhā, in order to enjoy intercourse in reverse. "Kṛṣṇa" resumed the form of Kālī temporarily in order to kill Pūtanā. At Śiva's wish, Rādhā's husband became impotent immediately after marriage.[29]

Śiva and Pārvatī change both sex and sect simultaneously; to these psychological and theological reversals are added the sociological, the implication that Kālī would have to become a male (Kṛṣṇa) to be on top (the "reversed" position). "Kṛṣṇa" reverts to his true role as the dangerous erotic woman (Kālī) in order to overcome Pūtanā, the stereotype of that female in Kṛṣṇa mythology. In paintings of the killing of Pūtanā, Kṛṣṇa is often depicted as a small male child on top of a supine Pūtanā, whose gaping mouth reveals sharp teeth and a protruding, phallic tongue.[30] Most significantly, the husband of the other half of the female androgyne (the woman who is really a man, Śiva impersonating Rādhā) is impotent. Here, that impotence makes it possible for the apparently mortal wife to commit adultery with the god who is her true husband, the immortal male who, in this text, is said to be an incarnation of the Goddess, the ancient immortal female.

The androgyne thus serves to express simultaneously love in union and love in separation, merging with god and splitting away from god. It expresses the awe and fear of the deity in whom all oppositions merge. Dangling before us the sweet promise of equality and balance, symbiosis and mutuality, the androgyne, under closer analysis, often furnishes bitter testimony to conflict and aggression, tension and disequilibrium, between female and male and between the human and the divine. And yet the vision of wholeness remains, the ideal mold into which we would pour our own experience, tempered in the crucible of human reality.

Notes

Chapter 1

1 Carroll 1872, chap. 5, "Wool and Water."
2 I am grateful to John P. Reeder, Jr., for this clarification.
3 Thanks go to Joan Erdman for this anecdote.
4 Translating Nāgārjuna's *Madhyamakaśāstra*, chap. xxv, v. 17.
5 A. K. Ramanujan taught me this story; it is in the Pali canon.
6 I am indebted to Daniel Gold for his ideas on the problem of "scientific" study of religion.
7 This is one of Zwi Werblowsky's maxims.
8 This aphorism was given to me by Stephan Beyer, who cannot recall where he got it but thinks it did not originate with him.
9 Many people have lately encouraged me to come out of the (anti)methodological closet, among others McKim Marriott, Paul Friedrich, A. K. Ramanujan, John Reeder, and William K. Mahony; but I was finally persuaded to do so by Alf Hiltebeitel, who read the penultimate draft of this book with great care and offered me many astute and sympathetic comments on both method and detail.
10 From a speech by Mircea Eliade at the University of Chicago, April 25, 1979.

Chapter 2

1 *RV* 1. 134. 6; 1. 164. 7; 1. 164. 27; 2. 34. 10; 3. 53. 14; 4. 23. 10; 4. 41. 5; 4. 57. 2; 5. 69. 2; 8. 9. 19; 8. 14. 38; etc.
2 I am indebted to John Stratton Hawley for this reference.
3 Citing *Bai.dur.sngon.po.*, fol. 109. Cf. *Saṃvarodaya Tantra* 2. 34 and Carstairs 1958, p. 225.
4 Personal communication from Edward C. Dimock.
5 Personal communication from Charles Pain, based on field work in Maharashtra; personal communication from Jeff Reinhard, based on field work in North India.

6 David Grene has brought to my attention a passage in Plato's *Timaeus* (90E–91D) that contains striking similarities to the Hindu concept: "The gods devised the love of copulation. . . . They pierced an opening communicating with the compact marrow which runs from the head down to the neck and along the spine and has indeed in our earlier discussion been called seed." When this marrow seeks a downward outlet, "in men the sexual member is disobedient and stubborn like a creature that will not listen to reason and through its frenzied appetite would master everything." The frustrated animal within women becomes discontented and angry, wandering through the body and driving them mad, "until at last the desire of the one and the Eros of the other" brings men and women together. (Translations by David Grene, in *Greek Political Theory* [Chicago, 1965], pp. 198–99). The seed, in man and woman, has life and behaves like an animal, furious when restrained; it is this animal that causes "hysteria" in women, the madness of the mare.

7 See the excellent discussion of this cognitive dissonance in R. Gombrich 1971 and in the film *Kataragama: A God for All Seasons*, made under the supervision of Gananath Obeyesekere for Granada Television. See also O'Flaherty 1980, introduction, and O'Flaherty 1976, introduction.

8 Variants too numerous to cite, including *MBh* 1. 57. 35–52; 3. 110. 13–15; *Bṛhaddevatā* 6. 162–63, 7. 1–6; *MP* 103–5; *BVP* 1. 20. 12–45; *Vām P* 28. 50; 46. 16.

9 Citing the *Guhyasamāja Tantra*, p. 128.

10 *Time Magazine*, October 24, 1977, reprinted from the British *Spectator*; also Charles McCabe in the *San Francisco Chronicle*, October 30, 1977, p. 39.

11 Citing Lakṣmīdhara's commentary on verse 75 of the *Saundaryalaharī*.

12 I am grateful to Gananath Obeyesekere for this insight.

13 For the dangers of sexuality, see O'Flaherty 1973, pp. 155–93, and O'Flaherty 1976, pp. 368–69.

Chapter 3

1 From a paper presented by Edward C. Dimock at the March 30, 1978 meeting in Chicago of the Association of Asian Studies. See also Dimock 1978.

2 I am grateful to Brian K. Smith for these references.

3 From a paper presented by Peter Claus at the same panel at the 1978 AAS.

4 Śiva does, however, sometimes appear as a child. See below, chapter 4, section C.

5 Remarks by Edward C. Dimock, same paper at the same panel at the 1978 AAS.

6 I am indebted to Stephan Beyer for this point.

7 Personal communication from Aditi Nath Sarkar.

8 Another Bengali story from Aditi Nath Sarkar.

9 Personal communication from Jan Heesterman.

10 Citing the *Śaṅkaradigvijaya* of Mādhava, 1. 28–43.

11 Citing *Maṇimañjarī* 5–8. Cf. also Grierson, "Madhvas," in Hastings 1911.

12 Citing *Basava Purāṇa* 2. 32.

Chapter 4

1 I am indebted to David M. Knipe for this source.
2 Alf Hiltebeitel gave me this reference.
3 Rawson 1971, pl. 216; Rawson 1973a, pls. 86 and 104; Rawson 1973b, pls. 17 and 22.
4 Richard L. Brubaker pointed out the aptness of my "angler-fish" metaphor for the corpselike Śiva.
5 Also discussed in Rūpagosvāmin's *Bhaktirasāmṛtasindhu* 2. 27. I am indebted to David Haberman for bringing these sources to my attention.
6 The phenomenon is well documented. McKim Marriott informs me of the widespread practice in Maharashtra of transvestites worshiping the goddess.
7 This useful terminology is A. K. Ramanujan's.
8 From remarks made by Norvin Hein at the Harvard conference on Rāḍhā.
9 These insights came from David Shulman.
10 This Tamil poem from the third decade of the poems of Nammāḻvār, the Vaiṣṇava saint and singer, was found and translated for me by K. Kailasapathy.
11 I am grateful to Elinor Gadon for text and illustrations of the *Bālagopālastuti*, v. 19.
12 Citing Tirukkutanti Arul Miku Cārṅkapāni Cuvāmi Ālaya, *Thalavaralāru* (Kumpakonam, 1973), pp. 31, 33.
13 P. S. Jaini told me this story, which he got from a Jaina Purāṇa, though he cannot locate the precise source. See also Jaini 1980, n. 27.
14 For the motif of regarding all women as one's mother, see O'Flaherty 1973, motif 27a, the inverse of the motif of incest (27e).
15 Citing *Bai.dur.sngon.po.*, folios 153–55, and *Caṇḍamahāroṣaṇa Tantra*, folios 409–10.
16 From comments by Richard L. Brubaker at the Harvard conference on Rādhā.
17 From remarks made by A. K. Ramanujan at the Harvard conference on Rādhā. See also L. Dumont 1970, pp. 74, 167–68, 213–14.
18 Barbara Stoler Miller pointed out the aptness of the epithet, at the Harvard conference on Rādhā.
19 Winternitz 1959, vol. 3, fasc. 1, pp. 40–41, cites elaborate arguments on this subject, including those by Ānandavardhana (*Dhvanyāloka* 2. 6. 137) and Mammaṭa (*Kāvyaprakāśa* 7, remarking on the gods' love play being like that of parents).
20 R. Pañcantam Piḷḷai, *Tiruviḻākaliṉ Uṇmaiviḷaikkam* (Madurai, 1962), p. 10; found and translated for me by William P. Harman.
21 From remarks by Cheever Mackenzie Brown at the Harvard conference on Rādhā.
22 An insight from David Shulman.

Chapter 5

1 I am indebted to Ari Darom, an exponent of Bharat Natyam, for the realization of the intimate connection between dance and yoga.

2 The demon Jalandhara receives a similar treatment. See O'Flaherty 1973, pp. 184–86.
3 Citing Nīlakaṇṭha Dīkṣita's *Ānandasāgarastava* 56.
4 Many other examples appear in Thompson and Spencer 1923. Kinsley 1978 cites passages in the *Adbhūta Rāmāyaṇa* from Kashmir, Sāralā Dāsa's Oriyā *Rāmāyaṇa*, and the Bengali *Jaiminibhārata*, in which even the meek Sītā dances out of control until Śiva intervenes.
5 Citing *Tirupputtūrppurāṇam*, 115th *carukkam*, *Tiruvālaṅkāṭṭupurāṇam*, and *Tirukkūvappurāṇam*. See also Kinsley 1975, p. 105.
6 Citing *Tiruvālaṅkāṭṭuppurāṇam* 10. 177, 11. 1–32, 12. 1–61, 13. 1–35. I am indebted to David Shulman not only for bringing this myth to my attention but for helping me to understand the relationship between the Sanskrit and Tamil myths of the dance.
7 Personal communication from Glenn E. Yocum.
8 Citing the copperplate inscription of Dharmapāla of Prāgjyotisha, *Epigraphica Indica*, 30:205. See also Sivaramamurti 1974, pp. 11, 119, and 145.

Chapter 6

1 Schröder first noted the striking parallels between Indian and Irish horse sacrifices in 1927, basing his hypothesis on Pokorny's (1927) description and interpretation of Giraldus' record of the Irish consecration ritual. Paul Emile Dumont's massive study of the Indian horse sacrifice, also published in 1927, is unaware of the Irish connection but notes close parallels with Greek horse sacrifices. Long before any of this, in 1893 Bloomfield had pointed out parallels between the myths of Demeter and Saraṇyū. When I was first put on the track of this legend, I found that several French scholars had been trampling over the ground and muddying the scent ahead of me. In 1925, H. Hubert had identified the Gallo-Roman goddess Epona with the Welsh goddess Rhiannon; in 1954, Gricourt further identified this pair with the Irish Mácha and several Greek figures; he also connected the myth of Deichtíre/Mácha with Giraldus' ritual. Dumézil (1954) pointed out parallels between the Irish chariot race of Mácha and the Vedic chariot race of Mudgala's wife, and Le Roux (1955 and 1963) brought to light further material on the Irish cult of the horse, while Sjoestedt-Jonval (1940) first related the myth of Cuchúlainn to the cult of Epona. Puhvel (1970) finally gave detailed evidence of a Celtic tradition in which a king sacrificed and mated with a mare, as well as a ritual myth of the mating of a "transfunctional goddess" with "a probably hippomorphous second-function representative"; he also connected this with the Vedic myth of the birth of the Aśvins. It remained for me merely to put all the materials together and to look for the patterns emerging from this rich treasury of myth.
2 A second-century B.C. Greek text cited by Le Roux 1963, p. 133. Also cited by Zwicker 1934–36, 1:64, and Reinach 1895, p. 317.
3 Pages 460–501 of the Kashikar edition, cited by Marglin 1978b, p. 21.
4 See also two texts cited by Gricourt 1954, pp. 75–86: the *Lebor na-h-Uidre*

and Ms. Egerton 1782 in the British Museum. See also Le Roux 1952 and 1953.

5 Citing Arbois de Jubainville 1906, p. 72, in arguing against Sjoestedt-Jonval's emphasis on the importance of incest as a motive in the creation of a hero (1940, p. 84).

6 Personal communication from Jaan Puhvel, letter of September 9, 1977.

7 From a Gaelic text translated by Professor O'Curry in the *Atlantis*, nos. 7 and 8.

8 I am grateful to Jane Stimpert for telling me about this work and lending it to me.

9 It was Paul Friedrich who pointed out to me the strong parallel between raped mare and devoured child/lover.

10 Cf. Bellerophon, and the discussion of rituals that may have been associated with kingship and horse-taming, in Graves 1955, 1:255.

11 Told by the scholiast on Aeschines *In Timarchon* 182 (p. 38 of Dindorf edition, Oxford 1852) and by Photius (s.v. Hippomenes, par *hippon*) and Diodorus Siculus (8. 22. 1). I am indebted to Professor Jock Anderson of Berkeley for these references.

12 Part 7 of Antonius Liberalis, who took the story from Boeus's *Generation of Birds*, book 1. The stories come from Greek folk religion and may go back to the sixth century B.C. The unpublished translation is by E. N. O'Neil; I am grateful to him for permission to use it here, to Hans Dieter Betz for bringing it to my attention, and to David Grene for the translation of *korus*.

13 The relevance of this parallel was pointed out to me by David Grene. See also his discussion of the problem of incest in the *Hippolytus*, in the introduction to his translation of the play (Chicago, 1958).

14 The gloss on the iconography of St. George and the dragon was given me by Jill Raitt.

15 A reference from Alf Hiltebeitel.

16 Citing Biezais 1966, pp. 22, 127.

17 Personal communication from Bruce Lincoln.

18 Personal communication from Phyllis Zerger.

Chapter 7

1 A strikingly similar saying appears in Proverbs 30:15–16, all the more striking for the fact that the variant versions (in the Hebrew text and the Septuagint) indicate a significant ambivalence as to whether the woman experiences or inspires insatiability. The Greek texts list four things that are insatiable, that never say, "Enough": Hades, lust for a woman (or of a woman), and Tartarus, and the earth that is not satisfied with water, and water and fire that will not say, 'It is enough.'" Despite the duplications and ambiguities, it is clear that fire, water, death, and women are the four insatiable quantities. The Hebrew list is more straightforward, though evidently corrupt: the grave (or the world of the dead, Sheol), the closed womb (or "restraint from love"), the earth, ever thirsty for water, and fire, which never says "Enough." Death, fire, and water are the elements common to both texts, all natural phenomena. The human phenomenon to which they

are parallel concerns women and lust, but in many different ways: man's lust for woman or woman's lust, or, on the contrary, the insatiety that results from female barrenness or chastity. The variation in texts may be the result of a Greek confusion of *erōs*, "lust," with *herkos*, "enclosure," a likely translation from the Hebrew; but the parallelism remains significant in either case. I am grateful to Hans Dieter Betz for helping me sort out these variant texts and to Jill Raitt for bringing the Proverbs text to my attention.

2 Dr. J. C. Harle of the Ashmolean Museum, Oxford, has brought to my attention similar reliefs on temples 7 and 9 at Aihole.

3 Citing *Tiruvŏṟṟiyūr Purāṇam* 5; cf. *Kāñcippurāṇam* 55. 3–9.

4 Japanese Tachikawa skull ritual; translation by James Sanford.

Chapter 8

1 From Tibetan translations, cited by Conze 1959, p. 53.

2 Personal communication from John Leavitt.

3 But cf. Jan Heesterman's review of this work (1966), and see also Crooke 1912, pp. 275–306, Jacobi 1911, 4:224–26, and W. N. Brown (1957).

4 From the Sthala Purāṇa of the Marundisuran temple in Tiruvanmiyur. This myth may be read in the context of an entire corpus of South Indian myths about cows and *liṅgas*; in all of them, the *liṅga*, injured after the cow has poured her milk onto it (often with an accompanying mutilation of a human worshiper of the *liṅga*), is eventually established as a sacred icon. See O'Flaherty 1976, p. 345; H. Whitehead 1921, p. 125; Gopinatha Rao 1968, vol. 2, pt. 1, pp. 205–9; *Periya Purāṇam* 20. 54.

5 See the Nandi at the feet of a Śiva image, Kandarīya Temple, west hall, Khajuraho; reproduced by Kramrisch 1946, vol. 2, pl. 25.

6 One atypical Indo-European example of the "female fire/sun, male water/moon" pattern (as it appears in Upaniṣadic imagery) occurs in the Baltic variant of the swan-maiden(-god) myth, in which there is a female solar figure and a male aquatic one. See Friedrich 1979, p. 46. Another example occurs in Norse mythology, where a girl drives the chariot of the sun while a boy drives the chariot of the moon.

7 The Īḷa is further identified by Eliade with the semen, and the Piṅgalā (usually masculine, but here feminine, in a reversal typical of Tantric embryology) with the ovum, as well as with the blood and *rajas* of women.

8 For a "scientific" text on ancient Indian horsemanship heavily laced with religious beliefs, see the *Aśvaśāstra*.

9 I am indebted to Alf Hiltebeitel for this information.

10 Again a contribution from Alf Hiltebeitel.

11 Paper presented by Frances Zimmerman, University of Chicago, April 12, 1979.

12 Abhinavagupta's *Tantrāloka*, pp. 88–89, 91; chapter 29, stanzas 127–28. Cited by Masson and Patwardhan 1969, p. 42; by Tucci 1968, p. 292; and by Eliade 1971, p. 101. For a similar contemporary ritual, see above, chap. 2, sec. B. A contrasting (and perhaps historically related) ritual occurs among the

Gnostic Phibionites, whose ritual intercourse involved the swallowing of male semen and female menstrual blood in an explicit Eucharist (Eliade 1971, pp. 109–11). This ritual is directly linked to a myth in which a (good) goddess reclaims her power from the (evil) Archons by seducing them and taking their sperm, thus regaining her own power while performing a salvific function—purifying creation. The taking of the sperm is clearly destructive of those from whom she takes it, but in the ritual this process is given new meaning for the worshiper whom she saves.

13 *Pad-ma dkar-po*, folios 1–19.

14 See also Kullūka's commentary on Manu 11. 54, and cf. Goldman 1978.

15 Sāyaṇa on *RV* 10. 109, 10. 40. 8, and 10. 86. 16–17.

16 Cf. Megasthenes' *Indica* and Nonnus's *Dionysiaca*.

17 Śrīla Prabhupāda, *Back to Godhead* 14 no. 9 (1979): 4.

Chapter 9

1 I am also indebted to Ms. Gross for personal communications on the concept of androgyny.

2 See, for example, a bizarre depiction of an androgynous form of fire (masc.) and water (fem.) in Jung 1966, p. 147. A detailed bibliography of works on Western androgynes appears in Eliade 1965, p. 103.

3 *Ānandabhairava* of Premadāsa, verse 151.

4 Hermann Güntert, *Der arische Weltkönig und Heiland* (1923), pp. 315–70, cited by Lincoln (1975).

5 Chapter 2, "Uncle Tompa Becomes a Nun," and chapter 3, "Uncle Tompa Becomes the Bride of a Rich Man."

6 I am indebted to Alf Hiltebeitel for a photograph of such an actor.

7 Michael Flanders, "The Sea-Horse Lullaby," from *The Bestiary of Flanders and Swann*, Angel Records 35797.

8 This is William Harman's useful insight.

9 Cf. the discussion of the Sthāṇu myths in O'Flaherty 1973, p. 139, and O'Flaherty 1976, pp. 224–28.

10 Citing *TiruccenkōṭumāNmiyam* (1924), pp. 28–42, and *Ciraparākkiramam* (1898), chap. 22, p. 70.

11 Cf. the image at Konarak, reproduced in Lal 1967, pl. 73, and the prohibition against this act in *Arthaśāstra* 4. 13. 41.

12 Citing *Takkayākapparaṇi* of Ŏṭṭakkūttar (1945), pp. 323–34.

13 I am indebted to Paul Courtright for showing me this obscure text.

14 See also Nīlakaṇṭha's commentary on *MBh* 13. 17. 58.

15 Citing the Deopara inscription of Vijayasena.

16 Citing Śaṅkara's *Ardhanārīśvarastotra* 2. My translation.

17 Citing the *Halāyudhastotra*.

18 Citing *Epigraphica Indica* 1:234; the translation is my own.

19 One is in the Victoria and Albert Museum (for which reference my thanks to John Irwin and Robert Skelton), the other in the Avery Brundage collection in San Francisco.

20 My thanks to George Michell and Jeffery Gorbeck for numerous photographs of androgynes at Pattadakal. For Badāmī, see Zimmer 1960, p. 139. and Frédéric 1973, p. 192.

21 Sivaramamurti reproduces a sculpture at Khajuraho and also describes other dancing androgynes from Mathurā, fourth century A.D. (p. 165, fig. 10), eastern Ganga, seventh century A.D. (p. 292, fig. 161), Gurjara Pratīhāra, ninth century A.D. (p. 308, fig. 187), and Nepal (p. 91, pl. 3, and p. 369, fig. 35).

22 A beautiful Chola bronze androgyne from the eleventh or twelfth century A.D. appears as the frontispiece in C. Sivaramamurti's *South Indian Bronzes* (1963). See also Gopinatha Rao 1968, vol. 2, pt. 1, pp. 321–32.

23 Rawson refers here to a dancing androgynous Śiva with half of an erect phallus, in the Dacca Museum.

24 Rita Gross pointed out the inequality in the arms of the androgyne.

25 Another insight from Rita Gross.

26 Describing an image from Rāṇī Pokhara in Kathmaṇḍu.

27 Alf Hiltebeitel pointed this out to me.

28 There is also an androgynous image of Śiva and Lakṣmī from Trichinopoly, now in the Victoria and Albert Museum. I am indebted to Robert Skelton, who found it for me.

29 *MBP* 49–58, cited by Rajendra Chandra Hazra, *Studies in the Upapurāṇas*, vol. 2: *Śākta and Non-Sectarian Upapurāṇas* (Calcutta, 1963), pp. 272–73.

30 A fine example of this motif is an illustration of a *Bhāgavata Purāṇa* manuscript, reproduced as plate 25 of Pratapaditya Pal's *The Classical Tradition in Rajput Painting* (New York: Pierpont Morgan Library, 1978). Pūtanā herself is split into two in this drawing: scenes across the top depict her alternately as a beautiful woman and a hideous ogress.

ABBREVIATIONS OF PERIODICALS AND SERIES

ASS	Ānandāśrama Sanskrit Series
ERE	Encyclopedia of Religion and Ethics
HOS	Harvard Oriental Series
HR	History of Religions
IIJ	Indo-Iranian Journal
JAAR	Journal of the American Academy of Religion
JAOS	Journal of the American Oriental Society
JAS	Journal of Asian Studies
JOIB	Journal of the Oriental Institute of Baroda
JRAS	Journal of the Royal Asiatic Society
SBE	Sacred Books of the East
WZKM	Wiener Zeitschrift zur Kunde des Morgenlandes
WZKS&O	Wiener Zeitschrift zur Kunde des Süd- und Ostasiens
ZDMG	Zeitschrift der Deutschen Morgenländischen Gesellschaft

Bibliography

A. Texts in Indian Languages

Abhidharmakośa of Vasubandhu. Varanasi, 1970–73.
Abhijñānaśākuntala of Kālidāsa. Bombay, 1958.
Agni Purāṇa. ASS no. 41. Poona, 1957.
Aitareya Brāhmaṇa, with the commentary of Sāyaṇa. Bibliotheca Indica. Calcutta, 1896.
Āpastamba Śrauta Sūtra. Edited by Richard Garbe. Calcutta: Asiatic Society of Bengal, 1882–1902.
Aśvaśāstra, attributed to Nakula. Edited by S. Gopalan. Tanjore Saraswati Mahal Series no. 56. Tanjore, 1952.
Atharva Veda, with the commentary of Sāyaṇa. Bombay, 1895.
Baudhāyana Śrauta Sūtra. Vaidika Samśodhana Mandala. Poona, 1958.
Bhāgavata Purāṇa, with the commentary of Śrīdhara. Bombay, 1832.
Bharadvāja Sūtras. Critically edited and translated by C. G. Kashikar. Vaidika Samśodhana Mandala. Poona, 1968.
Bhaviṣya Purāṇa. Bombay, 1959.
Brahma Purāṇa. Calcutta, 1954.
Brahmāṇḍa Purāṇa. Delhi, 1973.
Brahmavaivarta Puraṇa. ASS no. 102. 4 vols. Poona, 1935.
Bṛhaddevatā of Śaunaka. HOS no. 5. Cambridge, Mass., 1904.
Bṛhaddharma Purāṇa. Bibliotheca Indica. Calcutta, 1888–97.
Carakasaṃhitā. 2 vols. Delhi, 1963.
Caturvargacintāmaṇi of Hemādri. Bibliotheca Indica. Calcutta, 1873.
Devī Purāṇa. Calcutta, 1896.
Devībhāgavata Purāṇa. Benares, 1960.
Drāhyāyana Śrauta Sūtra. London, 1904.
Garuḍa Purāṇa. Benares, 1969.

Gītagovinda of Jayadeva. Edited and translated by Barbara Stoler Miller [*Love Song of the Dark Lord*]. New York, 1977.
Gopatha Brāhmaṇa. Leiden, 1919.
Harivaṃśa. Poona, 1969.
Jaiminīya Brāhmaṇa (Talavakara). Sarasvatī-vihara Series no. 31. Nagpur, 1954.
Jaiminiya Upaniṣad Brāhmaṇa. Edited by Hanns Oertel. *JAOS* 16 (1894): 79–259.
Kālikā Purāṇa. Bombay, 1891.
Kalki Purāṇa. Calcutta, 1873.
Kāmasūtra of Vātsyāyana. Bombay, 1856.
Kāñcippurāṇam of Civañāṉayokikaḷ and Kacciyappamuṉivar. Madras, 1937. See also Dessigane 1964.
Kāṭhaka Saṃhitā. Leipzig, 1900.
Kathāsaritsāgara of Somadeva. Bombay, 1930. See also Penzer.
Kātyāyana Śrauta Sūtra of *Śuklayajuḥprātiśākhyam*. Benares, 1883–88.
Kumārasambhava of Kālidāsa. Bombay, 1955.
Kūrma Purāṇa. Benares, 1972.
Liṅga Purāṇa. Calcutta, 1812.
Mahābhāgavata Purāṇa. Bombay, 1913.
Mahābhārata, critically edited. Poona, 1933–69.
Mahābhārata, with the commentary of Nīlakantha. Bombay, 1862.
Mahimnastava. Edited and translated by W. Norman Brown. Poona, 1965.
Maitrāyaṇī Saṃhitā. Edited by L. von Schroeder, 1881. Wiesbaden, 1970.
Mālatīmādhava of Bhavabhūti. Trivandrum Sanskrit Series no. 170. Trivandrum, 1953.
Manasāmaṅgal of Jagajjīban. Edited by S. C. Battacharya and A. Das. Calcutta, 1960.
Mānavadharmaśāstra, with the commentary of Medhātithi. Bibliotheca Indica. Calcutta, 1932.
Maṇimañjarī of Nārāyaṇa Paṇḍita. Bombay, 1934.
Mārkaṇḍeya Purāṇa. Bibliotheca Indica no. 29. Calcutta, 1862. Reprinted, with commentary, Bombay, 1890.
Matsya Purāṇa. ASS no. 54. Poona, 1907.
Meghadūta of Kālidāsa. Text and translation by Franklin and Eleanor Edgerton. Ann Arbor, 1964.
Mudgala Purāṇa. Bombay, 1976.
Nāgānanda of Harṣa [*Sri Harsha's Plays*]. Delhi, 1964.
Nirukta of Yāska. Edited by Lakshman Sarup. Oxford, 1921.
Padma Purāṇa. ASS no. 131. Poona, 1893.
Padma Purāṇa, Svarga Khaṇḍa. Edited by Asoke Chatterjee Śāstrī. Benares, 1972.

Pañcatantra of Pūrṇabhadra. Edited by Johannes Hertel. HOS, no. 11. Cambridge, Mass., 1908.
Prabodhacandrodaya of Kṛṣṇamiśra. Edited by Vāsudeva Śarman. Bombay, 1898.
Rāmacaritamānasa of Tulsī Dās. See W. D. P. Hill, 1935.
Rāmāyaṇa of Vālmīki. Baroda, 1960–75.
Rāvaṇa Vaha or *Setubandha*, with commentary. Kāvyamālā Series no. 47. Bombay, 1895.
Ṛg Veda, with the commentary of Sāyana. 6 vols. London, 1890–92.
Sāmba Purāṇa. Bombay, 1942.
Saṃvarodaya Tantra: Selected Chapters. Text and translation by Shinichi Tsuda. Tokyo, 1974.
Śaṅkaradigvijaya of Mādhava. Poona, 1915.
Śaṅkaravijaya of Ānandagiri. Bibliotheca Indica. Calcutta, 1868.
Śarvadarśanasaṃgraha of Mādhava. Bibliotheca Indica. Calcutta, 1958.
Śatapatha Brāhmaṇa. Chowkhamba Sanskrit Series no. 96. Benares, 1964.
Saura Purāṇa. ASS no. 18. Poona, 1923.
Śiva Purāṇa. Benares, 1964.
Śiva Purāṇa, Dharma Saṃhitā. Bombay, 1884.
Skanda Purāṇa. Bombay, 1867.
Subhāṣitaratnakoṣa of Vidyākara. Edited by D. D. Kosambi and V. V. Gokhale. HOS no. 44. Cambridge, Mass., 1957. See also Ingalls 1965. (All citations are of Ingalls' translation.)
Suśrutasaṃhitā. Delhi, 1968.
Taittirīya Saṃhitā, with the commentary of Mādhava. Bibliotheca Indica. Calcutta, 1960.
Tāṇḍya Mahābrāhmaṇa [*Pañcaviṃśa*], with the commentary of Sāyaṇa. Bibliotheca Indica. Calcutta, 1869–74.
Tantrāvarttika of Bhaṭṭa Kumārila. Commentary on Śabarasvāmin's *Jaiminīya Mīmāṃsā Sūtra* commentary. Benares Sanskrit Series. Benares, 1903.
Tantropākhyāna. Ten tales from the *Tantropākhyāna*. Edited and translated by George T. Artola. Madras, 1965.
Tiruvālankaṭṭuppurāṇam. Madras, 1864.
Tiruviḷaiyāṭaṟpurāṇam of Parañcotimuṉivar. Madras, 1965. See also Dessigane 1960.
Tiruvŏṟṟiyūrpurāṇam of Tiruvŏṟṟiyūr Ñāṉappirakācar. Madras, 1869.
Upaniṣads [*One Hundred and Eight Upanishads*]. Bombay, 1913. Reprinted, with the commentary of Śaṅkara, Poona, 1927.
Vājasaneyī Saṃhitā. Berlin, 1952.
Vāmana Purāṇa. Benares, 1968.
Varāha Purāṇa. Bibliotheca Indica no. 110. Calcutta, 1893.

Vaśiṣṭhadharmaśāstra. Bombay Sanskrit Series no. 23. Bombay, 1883.
Vāyu Purāṇa. Bombay, 1897.
Viṣṇu Purāṇa, with the commentary of Śrīdhara. Calcutta, 1972.
Viṣṇudharmottara Purāṇa. Bombay, n.d.

B. Texts in European Languages

Aarne, Antii. 1961. *The Types of Folktale: A Classification and Bibliography*. Folklore Fellows Communications no. 3. Translated and enlarged by Stith Thompson. Folklore Fellows Communications no. 23. Helsinki.
Adiceam, Marguerite E. 1966, 1968. Les Images de Śiva dans l'Inde du Sud. V: Harihara; VI: Ardhanārīśvara. *Arts Asiatiques* 13:83–98; 17:143–64.
Alexander, Hartley Burr. 1964. *North American Mythology*. Vol. 10 in *The Mythology of All Races*. New York. (First published, 1916.)
Alsdorf, Ludwig. 1962. *Beiträge zur Geschichte von Vegetarismus und Rinderverehrung in Indien*. Abhandlungen der Geistes und Sozialwissenschaftlichen Klasse, Akademie der Wissenschaften und der Literatur, no. 6. Wiesbaden.
Apollodorus of Athens. *The Library*. See Frazer 1921.
Babb, Lawrence A. 1970. Marriage and Malevolence: The Uses of Sexual Opposition in a Hindu Pantheon. *Ethnology* 9:137–48.
Baldaeus, Philippus. 1672. *Naauwkeurige beschryvinge van Malabar en Choromandel*. Amsterdam.
Beck, Brenda E. F. 1969. The Vacillating Goddess: Sexual Control and Social Rank in the Indian Pantheon. Paper delivered at the 1969 meeting of the Association for Asian Studies.
Benoit, Fernand. 1954. Archétypes plastiques en Ibérie de l' "Epona" Gallo-Romaine. *Ogam* 6:105–12.
Bergaigne, Abel. 1883. Etudes sur le lexique du Rig-Veda. *Journal Asiatique*, October-November-December, pp. 468–74.
Berlin, Sir Isaiah. 1953. *The Hedgehog and the Fox: An Essay on Tolstoy's View of History*. London.
Beswick, Ethel. 1959. *Tales of Hindu Gods and Heroes*. Delhi.
Beyer, Stephan. 1974. *The Buddhist Experience: Sources and Interpretations*. Encino, Cal.
Bhattacherjee, Bholanath. 1977. Some Aspects of the Esoteric Cults of Consort Worship in Bengal: A Field Survey Report. *Folklore*, pp. 385–97.
Biardeau, Madeleine. 1975. Review of O'Flaherty 1973. *L'Homme* 15:119–21.
Biezais, Haralds. 1976. *Lichtgott der alter Letten*. Stockholm.

Blau, A. 1908. Purāṇische Streifen. I. Der Itihāsa von Saraṇyū in seiner Fortbildung durch die Purāṇa. *ZDMG* 62:337–57.

Bloomfield, Maurice. 1893a. Contributions to the Interpretation of the Veda. *JAOS* 15:143–71.

———. 1893b. The Marriage of Saraṇyū, Tvaṣṭar's Daughter. Ibid., pp. 172–88.

Boas, F. 1895. Indianische Sagen von der Nord-Pacifischen Küste. *Zeitschrift für Ethnologie*, vols. 23–26.

Bolle, Kees W. 1968. *The Freedom of Man in Myth*. Nashville.

Bosch, F. D. K. 1961. The God with the Horse's Head. In F. D. K. Bosch, ed., *Selected Studies in Indonesian Archeology*, pp. 144–55. The Hague.

Bose, Manindra Mohan. 1927. An Introduction to the Study of the Post-Caitanya Sahajiya Cult. *Journal of the Department of Letters* 16:20–43. University of Calcutta.

Brewer, J. S., ed. 1861–91. *Topographia Hibernica*, vol. 5 of Giraldus Cambrensis, *Opera*. London.

Brown, Cheever Mackenzie. 1974. *God as Mother: A Feminine Theology in India, An Historical and Theological Study of the Brahmavaivarta Purāṇa*. Hartford, Vt.

Brown, W. Norman. 1927. Change of Sex as a Hindu Story Motif. *JAOS* 47:3–24. (Reprinted in Brown 1979, pp. 201–15.)

———. 1942. The Creation Myth of the Ṛg Veda. *JAOS* 62:83–98. (Reprinted in Brown 1979, pp. 20–34.)

———. 1950. Indra's Infancy according to Ṛg Veda 4. 18. In *Siddha-Bharati: A Rosary of Indology, Dr. Siddheshwar Varma Presentation Volume*, pp. 131–37. Hoshiapur. (Reprinted in Brown 1979, pp. 37–40.)

———. 1957. The Sanctity of the Cow in Hinduism. *Journal of the Madras University*, sec. A, Humanities, 28:29–49. (Reprinted in Brown 1979, pp. 90–101.)

———. 1979. *India and Indology, Selected Articles*. Edited by Rosane Rocher. Delhi.

Brubaker, Richard Lee. 1977. Lustful Woman, Chaste Wife, Ambivalent Goddess: A South Indian Myth. *Anima* 3:59–62.

———. 1978. *The Ambivalent Mistress: A Study of South Indian Village Goddesses and Their Religious Meaning*. Ph.D. diss., University of Chicago.

Burton, Robert. 1976. *The Mating Game*. New York.

Campbell, Joseph. 1956. *The Hero with a Thousand Faces*. New York.

Carroll, Lewis. 1865. *Alice's Adventures in Wonderland*. London.

———. 1872. *Through the Looking Glass, and What Alice Found There*. London.

Carstairs, G. Morris. 1958. *The Twice-Born*. London.

Conze, Edward. 1959. *Buddhist Scriptures*. Harmondsworth, Eng.

Coomaraswamy, Ananda K. 1935. *The Darker Side of Dawn*. Smithsonian Miscellaneous Collections, vol. 94, no. 1. Washington, D.C.

———. 1936. A Note on the Aśvamedha. *Archiv Orientalni* 8:306–17.

———. 1971. *The Dance of Shiva*. Rev. ed. New Delhi.

Crooke, W. 1896. *The Popular Religion and Folk-Lore of Northern India*. 2 vols. London.

———. 1912. The Veneration of the Cow in India. *Folklore* 23:275–306.

Cross, T. P., and Slover, C. H. 1936. *Ancient Irish Tales*. New York.

Daly, C. D. 1927. *Hindu-Mythologie und Kastrationskomplex, eine psychoanalytische Studie*. Vienna. (Reprinted from *Imago*, vol. 13.)

Dange, Sadashiv A. 1969. *Legends in the Mahābhārata*. Delhi.

Daniel, E. Valentine. 1979. *From Compatability to Equipoise: The Nature of Substance in Tamil Culture*. Ph.D. diss., University of Chicago.

Daniel, Sheryl. 1977. The Tool-Box Approach of the Tamil to the Issues of Karma, Moral Responsibility, and Human Destiny. Paper presented at the SSRC-ACLS Joint Committee on South Asia Seminar held at the University of Chicago, June 9.

———. 1978. Power and Paradox: Marital Roles in a Tamil Village. Paper presented at the panel on Conceptions of Women and Power in Tamil Culture, annual meeting of the Association of Asian Studies, Chicago, March 31.

Danielou, Alain. 1964. *Hindu Polytheism*. London.

Das, R. K. 1964. *Temples of Tamilnad*. Bombay.

Das, Veena. 1978. Review of O'Flaherty 1976. *JAS* 37:575–77.

Dasgupta, Shashibhusan. 1946. *Obscure Religious Cults as a Background to Bengali Literature*. Calcutta.

Dasgupta, Surendranath. 1955. *History of Indian Philosophy*. 5 vols. Cambridge, Eng.

de Jubainville, H. Arbois. 1906. *Les Druides et les dieux celtiques à forme d'animal*. Paris.

Dent, A. A., and Goodall, Daphne Machin. 1965. *The Foals of Epona*. London.

Desai, Devangana. 1975. *Erotic Sculpture of India: A Socio-Cultural Study*. New Delhi.

de Smet, Pierre-Jean, S.J. 1905. *Life, Letters, and Travels of Father Pierre-Jean de Smet*. 4 vols. New York.

Dessigane, R.; Pattabiramin, P. Z.; and Filliozat, Jean. 1960. *La Légende des jeux de Çiva à Madurai*. Publications de l'Institut Français d'Indologie no. 19. Pondichery.

———. 1964. *Les Légendes Çivaites de Kāñcipuram*. Publications de l'Institut Français d'Indologie no. 27. Pondichery.

———. 1967. *La Légende de Skanda selon le Kandapurāṇam tamoul et l'iconographie*. Publications de l'Institut Français d'Indologie no. 31. Pondichery.

Devereux, George. 1951. The Oedipal Situation and Its Consequences in the Epics of India. *Samīkṣā* 5:5–13.

———. 1975. Les Chevaux anthropophages dans les mythes Grecs. *Revue d'études Grecs* 88:203–5.

———. 1976. *Dreams in Greek Tragedy, an Ethno-Psychoanalytic Study*. Berkeley.

Dillon, Myles. 1947. The Archaism of Irish Tradition. *Proceedings of the British Academy*, vol. 32. (Rhys Memorial Lecture, 1947.)

———. 1975. *Celts and Aryans: Survivals of Indo-European Speech and Society*. Simla.

Dimmitt, Cornelia. 1978. Sītā: Mother Goddess and Śakti. Paper presented at the Conference on Rādhā and the Divine Consort, Harvard University, June.

Dimock, Edward Cameron, Jr. 1963. *The Thief of Love: Bengali Tales from Court and Village*. Chicago.

———. 1966a. *The Place of the Hidden Moon: Erotic Mysticism in the Vaiṣṇava Sāhajiyā Cult of Bengal*. Chicago.

———. 1966b. Doctrine and Practice among the Vaiṣṇavas of Bengal. In Milton Singer, ed., *Krishna: Myths, Rites, and Attitudes*. Honolulu.

———. 1976. Religious Biography in India: The 'Nectar of the Acts' of Caitanya. In Frank E. Reynolds and Donald Capps, eds., *The Biographical Process: Studies in the History and Psychology of Religion*, pp. 109–17. The Hague.

———. 1978. A Theology of the Repulsive: Some Reflections on the Sītalā and other Maṅgals. Paper presented at the Conference on Rādhā and the Divine Consort, Harvard University, June. (Publication forthcoming in the South Asia Series, The Asian Studies Center, Michigan State University.)

———, and Ramanujan, A. K. 1962, 1964. Manashā: Goddess of Snakes. *HR* 1:307–21; 3:49–70.

Dodds, E. R. 1951. *The Greeks and the Irrational*. Berkeley.

——, ed. 1960. Euripides' *Bacchae*. 2d ed. Oxford.

Dorje, Rinjing. 1975. *Tales of Uncle Tompa*. San Rafael.

Douglas, Mary. 1966. *Purity and Danger: An Analysis of Concepts of Pollution and Taboo*. London.

Dumézil, Georges. 1953. Le iuges auspicium et les incongruités du taureau attelé de Mudgala. *La nouvelle Clio* 5:249–66.

———. 1954. Le Trio des Macha. *Revue de l'histoire des religions* 146:5–17.

——. 1973. *The Destiny of a King*. Translated by Alf Hiltebeitel. Chicago.
Dumont, Louis. 1960. World Renunciation in Indian Religion. *Contributions to Indian Sociology* 4:33–62.
——. 1970. *Homo Hierarchicus*. London and Chicago.
Dumont, Paul Emile. 1927. *L'Aśvamedha, description du sacrifice solennel du cheval dans le culte védique d'après les textes du Yajurveda blanc*. Paris.
Dundes, Alan. 1962. Earth-Diver: Creation of the Mythopoeic Male. *American Anthropologist* 64:1032–1105. (Reprinted in Dundes 1975, pp. 130–45, and in Lessa and Vogt 1958, pp. 278–88.)
——, ed. 1965. *The Study of Folklore*. Englewood Cliffs, N.J.
——. 1977. *The Hero Pattern and the Life of Jesus*. Protocol of the 25th Colloquy (12 December 1976) of the Center for Hermeneutical Studies, Graduate Theological Union and University of California, Berkeley.
——. 1975. *Analytical Essays in Folklore*. The Hague.
Eck, Diana Louise. 1976. *Banāras, City of Light: The Sacred Places and Praises of Kāśī*. Ph.D. diss., Harvard University.
Egnor, Margaret Trawick. 1978. *The Sacred Spell and Other Conceptions of Life in Tamil Culture*. Ph.D. diss., University of Chicago.
Eliade, Mircea. 1958. *Yoga: Immortality and Freedom*. New York.
——. 1959. *Birth and Rebirth*. New York.
——. 1965. *Mephistoles and the Androgyne*. New York.
——. 1973. *Australian Religions: An Introduction*. Ithaca.
——. 1976. "Spirit, Light, and Seed." Pp. 93–119 in Eliade, *Occultism, Witchcraft, and Cultural Fashions: Essays in Comparative Religions*. Chicago.
Elliot, Sir Walter. *The Aboriginal Caste Book*. 3 volumes of manuscript in the India Office Library, n.d. [1821–60.] Cited by Hiltebeitel 1978 and Brubaker 1978.
Elwin, Verrier. 1942. *The Agaria*. Oxford.
——. 1949. *Myths of Middle India*. Oxford.
Fabri, C. L. 1934–35. The Cretan Bull-grappling Sports and the Bull-Sacrifice in the Indus Valley Civilisation. *Annual Report of the Archaeological Survey of India*, pp. 93–101.
Filliozat, Jean. 1949. *La Doctrine classique de la médecine indienne, ses origines et ses parallèles grecs*. Paris.
Fitts, Dudley. 1959. *Aristophanes: Four Comedies*. New York.
Ford, Patrick K. 1977. *The Mabinogi and Other Medieval Welsh Tales*. Berkeley.
Forster, E. M. 1924. *A Passage to India*. New York.
Foucher, Alfred. 1950–51. *L'Art gréco-bouddhique du Gandhāra*. Paris.
Frazer, Sir James George. 1921. Text and translation of Apollodorus of Athens, *The Library*. New York.

———. 1963. *The Golden Bough: A Study in Magic and Religion.* 8 parts. 3d ed. London.
Frédéric, Louis. 1973. *The Art of India: Temples and Sculpture.* New York.
Freud, Sigmund. 1928. *The Future of an Illusion.* London.
Friedrich, Paul. 1978. *The Meaning of Aphrodite.* Chicago.
Geertz, Clifford. 1975. Common Sense as a Cultural System. *Antioch Review* 33:5–26.
Geldner, Karl Friedrich. 1951. *Der Rig-Veda aus dem Sanskrit ins Deutsche Übersetzt.* 4 vols. HOS nos. 33–36.
Getty, Alice. 1936. *Gaṇeśa: A Monograph on the Elephant-faced God.* Oxford.
Gimbutas. Marija. 1974. *The Gods and Goddesses of Old Europe, 7000–3500 B.C.: Myths, Legends, and Cult Images.* Berkeley.
Giraldus Cambrensis. *Topographia Hibernica.* See Brewer 1861–91.
Goldman, Robert P. 1969. Mortal Man and Immortal Woman: An Interpretation of Three Ākhyāna Hymns of the Ṛg Veda. *JOIB* 18:273–303.
———. 1977. Rāmaḥ Sahalakṣmaṇaḥ: Psychological and Literary Aspects of the Composite Hero in Vālmīki's *Rāmāyaṇa.* Paper presented at the Conference on the *Rāmāyaṇa,* Berkeley.
———. 1978. Fathers, Sons, and Gurus: Oedipal Conflict in the Sanskrit Epics. *Journal of Indian Philosophy* 6:325–92.
Gombrich, Ernst H. 1973. Illusion and Art. In R. L. Gregory and E. H. Gombrich, eds., *Illusion in Nature and Art,* pp. 193–244. New York.
Gombrich, Richard F. 1971. *Precept and Practice: Traditional Buddhism in The Rural Highlands of Ceylon.* Oxford.
Gonda, Jan. 1966. *Ancient Indian Kingship from the Religious Point of View.* Leiden.
———. 1963. *The Vision of the Vedic Poets.* The Hague.
Gopinatha Rao, T. 1968. *Elements of Hindu Iconography.* 4 vols. Delhi. (First published, Madras, 1916.)
Grassmann, Hermann. 1955. *Wörterbuch zum Rigveda.* 3d ed. Wiesbaden.
Graves, Robert. 1955. *The Greek Myths.* 2 vols. Harmondsworth.
———. 1959. *The White Goddess: A Historical Grammar of Poetic Myth.* New York.
Griaule, Marcel. 1956. *Conversations with Ogotemmêli: An Introduction to Dogon Religious Ideas.* Oxford.
Gricourt, Jean. 1954. Epona-Rhiannon-Macha. *Ogam* 6:25–40, 75–86, 137–38, 165–88.
Grierson, G. A. 1911. Mādhvas. In Hastings 1911, 8:235.
Gross, Rita M. 1977a. Menstruation and Childbirth as Ritual and Religious Experience in the Religion of the Australian Aborigines. *JAAR* 45:4.

———. 1977b. Androcentrism and Androgyny in the Methodology of History of Religions. In *Beyond Androcentrism: New Essays on Women and Religion*, edited by Rita M. Gross. Missoula, Montana.

———. 1978a. Hindu Female Deities as a Resource for the Contemporary Rediscovery of the Goddess. *JAAR* 46:269–92.

———. 1978b. Is Androgyny Good for Feminists? Paper presented at the annual meeting of the American Academy of Religion, New Orleans, November 19.

Hart, George Luzerne, III. 1975. *The Poems of Ancient Tamil: Their Milieu and Their Sanskrit Counterparts*. Berkeley.

Hartland, Edwin Sidney. 1909. *Primitive Paternity: The Myth of Supernatural Birth in Relation to the History of the Family*. 2 vols. London.

Hastings, James, ed. 1911. *Encyclopaedia of Religion and Ethics*. 12 vols. Edinburgh.

Hawley, John Stratton. 1977. *The Butter Thief*. Ph.D. diss., Harvard University.

Hayley, Audrey. 1976. Aspects of Hindu Asceticism. In *Symbols and Sentiments*, edited by Ian Lewis. ASA Monographs. London.

Heesterman, Jan. 1962. Vrātya and Sacrifice. *IIJ* 6:1–37.

———. 1966. Review of Alsdorf 1962. *IIJ* 9:148.

———. 1967. The Case of the Severed Head. *WZKSO* 11:22–43.

———. 1978. Veda and Dharma. In O'Flaherty 1978, pp. 80–95.

Henry, Maurice. 1963. *The Thirty-Two Positions of the Androgyne*. New York.

Herman, Arthur L. 1970. A Solution to the Paradox of Desire in Buddhism. *Philosophy East and West* 29:91–94.

Hill, W. D. P. 1952. The Holy Lake of the Acts of Rāma. Translation of Tulsī Dās's *Rāmacaritamānasa*. London.

Hill, W. W. 1935. The Status of the Hermaphrodite and Transvestite in Navajo Culture. *North American Anthropologist* 36:2.

Hillebrandt, Alfred. 1891–1902. *Vedische Mythologie*. 3 vols. Breslau.

Hiltebeitel, Alf. 1976. *The Ritual of Battle: Krishna in the Mahābhārata*. Cornell.

———. 1978. Sexuality and Sacrifice: Convergent Subcurrents in the Fire-walking Cult of Draupadī. Paper presented at the Symposium on Sexuality and Religion, sponsored by the Conference on Religion in South India, at Wilson College, Chambersburg, Pennsylvania, May 12–14.

———. 1979. Review of O'Flaherty 1976. *HR* 18:269–75.

———. 1980. Rāma and Gilgamesh: The Sacrifices of the Water Buffalo and the Bull of Heaven. Typescript.

Hoare, Sir Richard Colt, trans. 1905. *The Historical Works of Giraldus Cambrensis, Containing the Topography of Ireland. . . .* London.
Hooykaas, C. 1964. *Āgama-Tīrtha: Five Studies in Hindu-Balinese religion.* Verhandelingen der Koninklijke Akademis der Wetenschappen no. 60. Amsterdam.
Hopkins, Edward Washburn. 1915. *Epic Mythology*. Strassbourg.
Howard, Gene R. 1977. Socio-Economic Factors Affecting Hospital Utilization. Unpublished paper. Forthcoming in the *Journal of Tropical Medicine.*
Hubert, H. 1925. Le Mythe d'Epona. In *Mélanges linguistiques offerts à M. J. Vendryes*. Paris.
Inden, Ronald B. 1976. *Marriage and Rank in Bengali Culture*. Berkeley.
———, and Nicholas, Ralph W. 1977. *Kinship in Belgali Culture.* Chicago.
Ingalls, Daniel H. H. 1965. *An Anthology of Sanskrit Court Poetry, Vidyākara's "Subhāṣitaratnakosa."* HOS no. 44. Cambridge, Mass.
Jacobi, H. 1893. *Das Rāmāyaṇa.* 2 vols. Bonn.
———. 1911. Cow (Hindu). In Hastings 1911.
Jaini, Padmanabh S. 1980. Karma and the Problem of Rebirth in Jainism. In O'Flaherty 1980.
James, William. 1943. *Essays on Faith and Morals.* Edited by Ralph Barton Perry. New York.
Johannson, K. F. 1917–19. Über die altindische Gottin Dhísana und Verwandtes. *Skrifter Utgifne af Kuninjlik Humanistike Vetenskaps-Samfundet i Uppsala* 20:1–170.
Jones, Ernest. 1971. *On the Nightmare.* New York.
Jones, W. H. S. 1918–35. Translation of Pausanias, *Description of Greece.* London.
Joyce, P. W. 1962. *Old Celtic Romances.* New York.
Jung, C. G. 1954. *Answer to Job.* London.
———. 1966. *Psychology and Alchemy.* New York.
———. 1967. *Symbols of Transformation.* New York.
———. 1972. On the Psychology of the Trickster-Figure. In *Four Archetypes.* New York. (Originally published in English in Paul Radin's *The Trickster: A Study in American Indian Mythology.* [New York, 1956.])
———, and Kerényi, Karl. 1949. *Essays on a Science of Mythology.* New York.
Kakar, Sudhir. 1978. *The Inner World: A Psychoanalytic Study of Childhood and Society in India.* Delhi.
Kennedy, Colonel Vans. 1831. *Researches into the Nature and Affinity of Ancient and Hindu Mythology.* London.
Kinsella, Thomas, trans. 1970. *The Tain, Translated from the Irish Epic "Tain Bo Cuailnge."* Oxford.

Kinsley, David R. 1975. *The Sword and the Flute, Kālī and Kṛṣṇa.* Berkeley.
——. 1978. Blood and Death out of Place: Reflections on the Goddess Kālī. Paper presented at the conference on Rādhā and the Divine Consort, Harvard University.
Kirfel, Willibald. 1953. Śiva und Dionysos. *Zeitschrift für Ethnologie* 78:83–90.
Kirk, G. S. 1974. *The Nature of Greek Myths.* Harmondsworth.
Klah, Hasteen. 1942. *Navajo Creation Myth.* Santa Fe.
Klein, Melanie. 1948. *Contributions to Psychoanalysis 1921–1945.* London.
Kluckhohn, Clyde. 1960. Recurrent Themes in Myths and Mythmaking. In Henry A. Murray, ed., *Myth and Mythmaking,* pp. 44–60. New York. (Reprinted in Dundes 1965, pp. 158–68.)
Knipe, David M. 1977. *Sapiṇḍīkaraṇa*: The Hindu Rite of Entry into Heaven. In Frank E. Reynolds and Earle H. Waugh, eds., *Religious Encounters with Death: Insights from the History and Anthropology of Religions.* University Park, Pennsylvania.
Koppers, Wilhelm. 1936. Pferdeopfer und Pferdekult der Indogermanen. *Wiener Beiträge zur Kulturgeschichte und Linguistik* 4:279–411.
Kramrisch, Stella. 1946. *The Hindu Temple.* Calcutta.
——. 1955. *The Art of India.* London.
——. 1968. *Unknown India: Ritual Art in Tribe and Village.* Philadelphia.
Kuhn, Adelbert. 1886. *Mythologische Studien: I. Die Herabkunft des Feuers und des Göttertrankes.* Gütersloh.
Kuhn, Thomas. 1970. *The Structure of Scientific Revolutions.* Chicago.
Kulke, Hermann. 1970. *Cidambaramāhātmya.* Wiesbaden.
la Barre, Weston. 1972. *The Ghost Dance: Origins of Religion.* London.
Lal, Kanwar. 1967. *The Cult of Desire: An Interpretation of the Erotic Sculpture of India.* 2d ed. London.
Leach, Edmund R. 1962. Pulleyar and the Lord Buddha: An Example of Syncretism. *Psychoanalysis and the Psychoanalytic Review,* pp. 81–102.
——. 1970. *Lévi-Strauss.* London.
Leiris, Michel, and Delange, Jaqueline. 1968. *African Art* London.
Leites, Nathan. 1951. *The Operational Code of the Politburo.* New York.
LeRoux, Françoise. 1953. La Conception de Cuchulainn. *Ogam* 4:273–85, 5:313–14.
——. 1955. Le Cheval divin et le zoomorphisme chez les Celtes. *Ogam* 7:101–22.
——. 1963. Recherches sur les éléments rituels de l'élection royale irlandaise et celtique. *Ogam* 15:123–37.
Leshnik, Lawrence. 1978. The Horse in India. In Franklin C. Southworth,

ed., *The Ecology of Man and Animal in South Asia*, pp. 56–57. Philadelphia.

Lessa, William A., and Vogt, Evon Z. 1958. *A Reader in Comparative Religion: An Anthropological Approach*. New York.

Lévi-Strauss, Claude. 1958. The Structural Study of Myth. In Thomas A. Sebeok, ed., *Myth: A Symposium*, pp. 50–66. Bloomington, Ind.

———. 1966. *The Savage Mind*. London.

Lincoln, Bruce. 1975. The Indo-European Myth of Creation. *HR* 15:121–45.

———. 1976. The Indo-European Cattle-raiding Myth. *HR* 16:42–65.

———. 1977a. Socio-Economics and Religious World-View: Cattle in Indo-European Religions. Paper presented at the annual meeting of the American Academy of Religion, San Francisco, December 31.

———. 1977b. Death and Resurrection in Indo-European Thought. *Journal of Indo-European Studies* 5:247–64.

Lommel, Herman. 1949. Vedische Einzelstudien. *ZDMG* 99:225–57. (See, esp., Saraṇyū-Saṃjñā, pp. 243–57.)

Long, Charles H. 1963. *Alpha: The Myths of Creation*. Vol. 1 of Alan Watts, ed., *Patterns of Myth*. New York.

Long, J. Bruce. 1971. Śiva and Dionysos, Visions of Terror and Bliss. *Numen* 18:180–209.

Lüders, Heinrich. 1951, 1959. *Varuṇa*. 2 vols. Göttingen.

MacCana, Proinsias. 1955, 1958. Aspects of the Theme of King and Goddess in Irish Literature. *Etudes Celtiques* 7:76–114, 8:59–65.

Macculloch, John Arnott. 1918. *Celtic Mythology*. Part 1 of volume 3 of *The Mythology of All Races*, edited by L. H. Gray. New York.

McKnight, J. Michael, Jr. 1977. Kingship and Religion in India's Gupta Age: An Analysis of the Role of Vaiṣṇavism in the Lives and Ideology of the Gupta Kings. *JAAR*, vol. 45, supplement, p. 686.

Magnen, R., and Thevnot, E. 1953. *Epona: Déesse gauloise*. Paris.

Mahalingam, T. V. 1965. Hayagrīva—The Concept and the Cult. *Adyar Library Bulletin* 29:188–89.

Maity, Pradyot Kumar. 1966. *Historical Studies in the Cult of the Goddess Manasā*. Calcutta.

Makarius, Laura. 1973. The Crime of Manabozo. *American Anthropologist* 75:663–75.

Mann, Thomas. 1941. *The Transposed Heads: A Legend of India*. Translated by H. T. Lowe-Porter. New York.

Marglin, Frédérique. 1978a. Devadāsīs as Specialists in "Auspiciousness." Paper presented at the symposium on Sexuality and Religion sponsored by the Conference on Religion in South India, Wilson College, Chambersburg, Pennsylvania, May 12–14.

——. 1978b. Types of Sexual Union and Their Implicit Meanings. Paper presented at the conference on Rādhā and the Divine Consort, Harvard University, June 17.

Marriott, McKim. 1976. Hindu Transactions: Diversity without Dualism. In Bruce Kapferer, ed., *Transaction and Meaning*, pp. 109–42. Philadelphia.

Masson, J. L. (a.k.a. Moussaieff Masson). 1974. The Childhood of Kṛṣṇa: Some Psychoanalytic Observations. *JAOS* 94:454–59.

——. 1975. Fratricide and the Monkeys: Psychoanalytic Observations on an Episode in the Vālmīkirāmāyaṇam. *JAOS* 95:672–78.

——. 1976. The Psychology of the Ascetic. *JAS* 25:611–25.

——, and Patwardhan, M. V. 1969. *Śantarasa and Abhinavagupta's Philosophy of Aesthetics*. Poona.

Matthews, Washington. 1897. *Navajo Legends*. Memoirs of the American Folklore Society. New York.

Meyer, Johann Jakob. 1930. *Sexual Life in Ancient India*. New York.

Mookerjee, Ajit. 1968. *Tantra Āsana: A Way to Self-Realization*. Basel and Delhi.

Newby, Eric. 1964. *Slowly down the Ganges*. New York.

Nicholas, Ralph W., and Sarker, Aditi Nath. 1975. The Fever Demon and the Census Commissioner: Sītala Mythology in Eighteenth and Nineteenth Century Bengal. In Marvin Davis, ed., *Bengal: Studies in Literature, Society, and History*, pp. 3–62. Michigan State University South Asia Series. East Lansing.

Obeyesekere, Gananath. 1968. Theodicy, Sin, and Salvation in a Sociology of Buddhism. In Edmund R. Leach, ed., *Dialectic in Practical Religion*. Cambridge, Eng.

——. 1975. Social Change and the Deities: Rise of the Kataragama Cult in Modern Sri Lanka. *Man* n.s. 12:377–96.

——. 1976. The Impact of Āyurvedic Ideas on the Culture and the Individual in Sri Lanka. In Charles Leslie, ed., *Asian Medical Systems*, pp. 201–26. Berkeley.

——. 1978. Hair: Psychological Symbolism in the Tonsorial Styles of Six Female Ascetics. Paper presented at the symposium on Sexuality and Religion sponsored by the Conference on Religion in South India, Wilson College, Chambersburg, Pennsylvania, May 12–14.

——. 1980. *The Goddess Pattini*. Typescript.

Odum, Anker. 1978. Pregnant Stallion of the Sea. *International Wildlife*, November–December, 1978, pp. 44–45.

O'Flaherty, Wendy Doniger. 1969. The Symbolism of the Third Eye of Śiva in the Purāṇas. *Purāṇa* 11:273–84.

——. 1971. The Origin of Heresy in Hindu Mythology. *HR* 10:271–333.

———. 1973. *Asceticism and Eroticism in the Mythology of Śiva*. Oxford.
———. 1975. *Hindu Myths*. Harmondsworth.
———. 1976. *The Origins of Evil in Hindu Mythology*. Berkeley.
———. 1978a. Contributions to an Equine Lexicology, with Special Reference to Frogs. *JAOS* 98:474–78.
———, ed. 1978b. *The Concept of Duty in South Asia*. London, Delhi, Columbia.
———, ed. 1980. *Karma and Rebirth in Classical Indian Traditions*. Berkeley.
Oldenberg, Herman. 1901. Ṛigveda VI. 1. 1–20. *ZDMG* 55:316–21.
Oppert, Gustav. 1893. *On the Original Inhabitants of Bharatavarsha or India*. London.
Otto, Rudolf. 1958. *The Idea of the Holy*. Translated by John W. Harvey. New York.
Otto, Walter. 1965. *Dionysos: Myth and Cult*. Translated by R. B. Palmer. Bloomington, Ind.
Parker, H. 1909. *Ancient Ceylon: An Account of the Aborigines and of Part of the Early Civilization*. London.
Pausanias. *Description of Greece*. See W. H. S. Jones.
Penzer, N. M., ed. 1924. *The Ocean of Story*. Translated by C. W. Tawney. 10 vols. London.
Piggott, Stuart. 1950. *Prehistoric India to 1000 B.C.* Harmondsworth.
Pokorny, J. 1927. Das nicht-Indo-germanische Substrat im Irischen. *Zeitschrift für Celtische Philologie* 16:95–144.
Potter, Karl, ed. 1978. *Indian Metaphysics and Epistemology: The Tradition of Nyāya-Vaiśeṣika up to Gaṅgeśa*. Princeton.
Potter, Stephen. n.d. *The Theory and Practice of Gamesmanship, or, The Art of Winning Games without Actually Cheating*. New York.
Puhvel, Jaan. 1955. Vedic *aśvamedha-* and Gaulish IIPOMIIDVOS. *Language* 31:353–54.
———. 1970a. Mythological Reflections of Indo-European Medicine. In George Cardona et al., eds., *Indo-European and Indo-Europeans*, pp. 369–82. Philadelphia.
———. 1970b. Aspects of Equine Functionality. In Jaan Puhvel, ed., *Myth and Law among the Indo-Europeans*, pp. 159–72. Berkeley.
———. 1975. Remus et Frater. *HR* 15:146–75.
———. 1977. Ritual and Sacrificial Hierarchies in the Indo-European Bestiary. Paper presented at the annual meeting of the American Academy of Religion, San Francisco, December 31.
Radin, Paul. 1972. *The Trickster: A Study in American Indian Mythology*. With commentaries by Karl Kerényi and C. G. Jung. New York.
Ramanujan, A. K. 1972. The Indian Oedipus. In Arabinda Podder, ed., *Indian Literature, Proceedings of a Seminar*, pp. 127–37. Simla.

———. 1973. *Speaking of Śiva*. Harmondsworth.
———. 1978. Women Saints and Saints as Women. Paper presented at the ACLS-SSRC seminar on the Person, Chicago, October 24.
Rangaswamy, M. A. Dorai. 1958. *The Religion and Philosophy of Tēvāram*. 2 vols. Madras.
Rawson, Philip. 1966. *Indian Sculpture*. New York.
———. 1968. *Erotic Art of the East*. New York.
———. 1971. *Tantra*. London.
———. 1973a. *The Art of Tantra*. London.
———. 1973b. *Tantra: The Indian Cult of Ecstasy*. London.
Reichard, Gladys A. 1974. *Navaho Religion: A Study of Symbolism*. 2d ed. Princeton.
Reinach, Salomon. 1895. Epona. *Revue archéologique*. 26:163–95, 307–36.
Róheim, Géza. 1943. Culture Hero and Trickster in North American Mythology. In Sol Tax, ed., *Indian Tribes of Aboriginal America: Selected Papers of the 29th Congress of Americanists*, vol. 3, pp. 190–94.
———. 1945. *Eternal Ones of the Dream*. New York.
———. 1972. Aphrodite, or the Woman with a Penis. In *The Panic of the Gods and Other Essays*. New York. (Reprinted from *Psychoanalytic Quarterly* 14 [1945]: 350–90.)
Rose, H. J. 1959. *A Handbook of Greek Mythology*. New York.
Roy, Manisha. 1975. *Bengali Women*. Chicago and London.
Roy, U. N. 1910. *Śiva-Saṃhitā*. Calcutta.
Sauvé, James L. 1970. The Divine Victim: Aspects of Human Sacrifice in Viking Scandinavia and Vedic India. In Puhvel 1970b, pp. 173–92.
Sāyaṇa. See Ṛg Veda.
Schröder, Franz Rolf. 1927. Ein altirischer Krönungsritus und das indogermanische Rossopfer. *Zeitschrift für celtische Philologie* 16:310–12.
Schwab, J. 1886. *Das altindische Tieropfer*. Erlangen.
Shulman, David. 1976a. *The Mythology of the Tamil Śaiva Talapurāṇam*. Doctoral diss., University of London. (Now in press with Princeton University Press.)
———. 1976b. The Murderous Bride: Tamil Versions of the Myth of Dēvi and the Buffalo Demon. *HR* 16:120–47.
———. 1978. The Serpent and the Sacrifice: An Anthill Myth from Tiruvārūr. *HR* 18:107–38.
Sinha, Surajit. 1961. A Note on the Concept of Sexual Union for Spiritual Quest among the Vaiṣṇava Preachers in the Bhumij Belt of Purulia and Singbhum. *Eastern Anthropologist* 14:194–96.
Sircar, D. C. 1971. Ardhanārī-Nārāyana. In *Studies in the Religious Life of Ancient and Medieval India*, pp. 221–28. Delhi.

Sivaramamurti, C. 1963. *South Indian Bronzes*. New Delhi.

———. 1974. *Nataraja in Art, Thought, and Literature*. New Delhi.

Sjoestedt-Jonval, Marie Louise. 1940. *Dieux et héros des Celtes*. Paris. English translation by Myles Dillon, *Gods and Heroes of the Celts*. London, 1949.

Slater, Philip E. 1968. *The Glory of Hera: Greek Mythology and the Greek Family*. Boston.

Snellgrove, David N. 1959. *The Hevajra Tantra*. Oxford.

Spencer, B., and Gillen, F. J. 1899. *Native Tribes of Central Australia*. London.

Spencer, Katherine. 1947. *Reflection of Social Life in the Navaho Creation Myth*. Albuquerque.

Spratt, Philip. 1966. *Hindu Culture and Personality: A Psychoanalytic Study*. Bombay.

Stablein, William. 1890. The Medical Soteriology of Karma in the Buddhist Tantric Tradition. In O'Flaherty 1980.

Stanley, John M. Special Time, Special Power: The Fluidity of Power in a Popular Hindu Festival. *JAS* 37:27–43.

Stevenson, Matilda Coxe. 1887. The Religious Life of the Zuñi Child. *Annual Report of the Bureau of American Ethnology* no. 5.

———. 1904. The Zuñi Indians. *Annual Report of the Bureau of American Ethnology* no. 23.

Taddei, Marrizio. 1970. *The Ancient Civilization of India*. London.

The Tain. See Kinsella.

Thomas, P. 1958. *Epics, Myths, and Legends of India*. 5th ed. Bombay.

Thompson, Edward J., and Spencer, Arthur Marshman. 1923. *Bengali Religious Lyrics, Śākta*. Calcutta and Oxford.

Thompson, Stith. 1919. *European Tales among the North American Indians*. Colorado River College Publications no. 34.

———. 1955–58. *Motif-Index of Folk Literature*. Rev. ed. 6 vols. Bloomington, Ind.

———. 1955. Myth and Folktale. In T. Sebeok, ed., *Myth: A Symposium*, pp. 104–10. Bloomington, Ind.

Thurston, E. 1909. *Castes and Tribes of Southern India*. Madras.

Tucci, Giuseppe. 1968. Oriental Notes. 3: A Peculiar Image from Gandhāra. *East and West* 18:289–92.

———. 1969. *Rati-Lila: An Interpretation of the Tantric Imagery of the Temples of Nepal*. Geneva.

Tulsī Dās. See Hill, W. D. P.

Van Gulik, R. H. 1935. *Hayagrīva*. Utrecht.

Vendryes, Joseph. 1918. Les correspondances de vocabulaire entre l'Indo-Iranien et l'Italo-Celtique. *Mémoires de la Société Linguiste de Paris* 20:265–85.

Vequaud, Yves. 1977. *The Women Painters of Mithila*. London.
von Fürer-Haimendorf, Christoph. 1948. *The Aboriginal Tribes of Hyderabad*. Vol. 3: *The Raj Gonds of Adilabad. I: Myth and Ritual*. London.
Waghorne, Joanne Punzo. 1978. Her Lord and Master: Kingship and Sexual Symbolism in South India. Paper presented at the symposium on Sexuality and Religion, sponsored by the Conference on Religion in South India, Wilson College, Chambersburg, Pennsylvania, May 12–14.
Waldschmidt, Ernst, and Leonare, Rose. 1970. *Nepal: Art Treasures from the Himalayas*. New York.
Walton, Evangeline. 1974, 1971, 1972. *The Mabinogion*. Vol. 1, *Prince of Annwn*, 1974. Vol. 2, *The Children of Llyr*, 1971. Vol. 3, *The Song of Rhiannon*, 1972. New York.
Ward, Donald. 1968. *The Divine Twins, an Indo-European Myth in Germanic Tradition*. Folklore Studies no. 19. Berkeley.
———. 1970. The Separate Functions of the Indo-European Divine Twins. In Puhvel 1970b, pp. 193–202.
Wasson, R. Gordon, and O'Flaherty, W. D. 1968. *Soma: Divine Mushroom of Immortality*. New York.
Watts, Alan W., ed. 1963. *Patterns of Myth*. Vol. 3, *The Two Hands of God: The Myths of Polarity*. New York.
Weber, Albrecht, ed. 1850–98. *Indische Studien*. 18 vols. Berlin.
Whitehead, Alfred North. 1929. *The Function of Reason*. Princeton.
Whitehead, Henry. 1921. *Village Gods of South India*. Oxford.
Winternitz, Moriz. 1959. *A History of Indian Literature*, Vol. 3, fasc. 1, *Ornate Poetry*. Translated by H. Kohn Calcutta.
Yalman, Nur. 1963. On the Purity of Women in the Castes of Ceylon and Malabar. *Journal of the Royal Anthropological Institute of Great Britain and Ireland* 93:25–58.
———. 1967. *Under the Bo Tree*. Berkeley.
Yocum, Glenn E. 1977. The Goddess in a Tamil Śaiva Devotional Text, Māṇikkavācakar's *Tiruvācakam*. *JAAR* 45:K372.
Young, Hugh Hampton. 1937. *Genital Abnormalities, Hermaphroditism, and Related Adrenal Diseases*. Baltimore.
Young, Jean, trans. 1954. *Snorri Sturlson: The Prose Edda*. Berkeley.
Zimmer, Heinrich [Henry R.] 1948. *Hindu Medicine*. Baltimore.
———. 1955, 1960. *The Art of Indian Asia*. Bollingen Series. New York.
Zwicker, Johann. 1934–36. *Fontes Historiae Religionis Celticae*. 3 vols. Berlin.

Index and Glossary

Plate 1. Chinnamastā. Gouache on paper, 12″ × 8″. Kangra, eighteenth century. Photograph supplied and reproduction rights granted by Thames & Hudson for reproduction from Philip Rawson's *Tantra: The Indian Cult of Ecstasy* (1973), plate 22.

Plate 2. Kālī straddling the erect lingam of the corpse of Śiva. Folk painting, gouache on cloth, 15″ × 13″. Orissa, nineteenth century. Photograph supplied and reproduction rights granted by Thames & Hudson for reproduction from Philip Rawson's *The Art of Tantra* (1973), plate 88.

Plate 3. The Birth of the Aśvins. Page from a manuscript of the *Harivaṃśa*, colored ink on paper, by a Mughal artist, ca. 1590–95 A.D. $11\frac{3}{4}'' \times 6\frac{7}{8}''$. From the Nasli and Alice Heeramaneck Collection of the Los Angeles County Museum of Art. Reproduction by kind permission of the Los Angeles County Museum of Art.

Plate 4. Nāyikā in intercourse with a stallion. Miniature album painting, Deccan, eighteenth century. Reproduced from Philip Rawson's *The Erotic Art of the East*, plate 121 (New York: G. P. Putnam's Sons, 1968; London: Weidenfeld & Nicolson, 1968), by kind permission of the publishers and of Mr. Rawson.

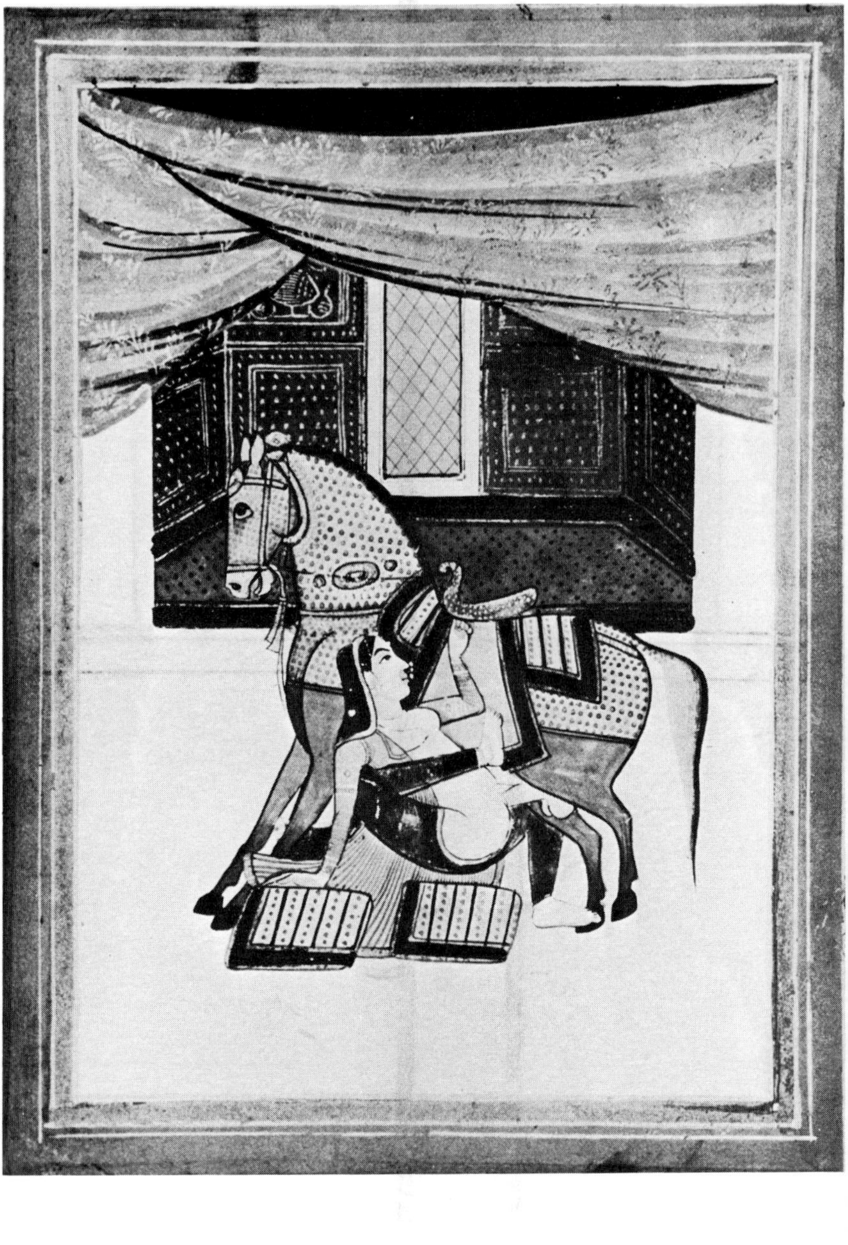

Plate 5. Mare in intercourse with human male. Stone relief on the plinth of the Lakṣmaṇa temple, Khajuraho, c. 1000 A.D. Photograph by the author.

Plate 6. Horse-faced Yakṣī carrying a human figure. Roundel on post of railing of Stupa 2, the Stupa of the Saints. Sanchi, second half of second century B.C. Photograph and permission to reproduce given by Stella Kramrisch and by Phaidon Press, publishers of *The Art of India through the Ages*, 2d ed. (London, 1955).

Plate 7. Centaur (Kiṃpuruṣa) and female rider. Roundel on railing of berm, Great Stupa, Sanchi, middle of second century B.C. Photograph and permission to reproduce given by Stella Kramrisch.

Plate 8. Two androgynes unable to fuse. Reproduced from Maurice Henry's *The 32 Positions of the Androgyne* (New York: G. P. Putnam's Sons, 1963), by kind permission of Société Nouvelle des Editions Jean-Jacques Pauvert, Paris.

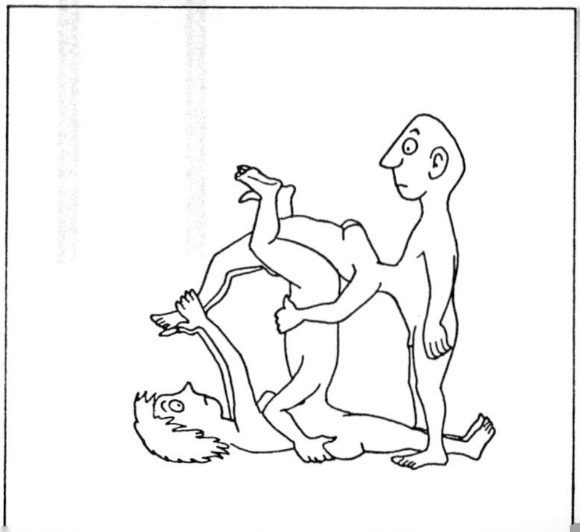

Plate 9. Śiva and Pārvatī as Ardhanārīśvara. Elephanta, eighth century A.D. Photograph by Carmel Berkson.

Plate 10. Śiva and Pārvatī in their androgynous form. Tempera painting (30″ × 22″) by Baua Devi, a woman folk-artist from the village of Jitwarpur in Mithilā. From the collection of the author. See also Vequaud 1977.